# THE ETHNIC CANON

# THE ETHNIC CANON

## Histories, Institutions, and Interventions

DAVID PALUMBO-LIU, EDITOR

UNIVERSITY OF MINNESOTA PRESS

Minneapolis / London

"'Border' Studies: The Intersection of Gender and Color," by Paula Gunn Allen, was previously published in Joseph Gibaldi, ed., *Introduction to Scholarship in Modern Languages and Literatures* (New York: Modern Language Association of America, 1992), 303-19. Reprinted by permission of the Modern Language Association of America.
Excerpts from "The Mexico Texan," "Four Freedoms," "A mi barrio, El Cuatro Veintiuno," "La Libertad," "Alma Pocha," "Ahí nomás," "Mi Pueblo," "Buitarreros," and "Esquinita de mi Pueblo" in "The Borders of Modernity: Américo Paredes's *Between Two Worlds* and the Chicano National Subject," by Ramón Saldívar, are reprinted with permission of the publisher of *Between Two Worlds* (Houston: Arte Público Press/University of Houston, 1991).
Quotations from *Days of Obligation*, by Richard Rodriguez, in "Calculated Musings: Richard Rodriguez's Metaphysics of Difference," by Rosaura Sánchez, copyright © 1992 by Richard Rodriguez. Used by permission of Viking Penguin, a division of Penguin Books USA Inc.
Excerpts from *M. Butterfly*, by David Henry Hwang, in "*M. Butterfly* and the Rhetoric of Antiessentialism: Minority Discourse in an International Frame," by Colleen Lye, copyright © 1986, 1987, 1988 by David Henry Hwang. Used by permission of Dutton Signet, a division of Penguin Books USA Inc.

Published by the University of Minnesota Press
111 Third Avenue South, Suite 290, Minneapolis, MN 55401-2520
Printed in the United States of America on acid-free paper

Library of Congress Cataloging-in-Publication Data
The ethnic canon: histories, institutions, and interventions /
David Palumbo-Liu.
p. cm.
Includes bibliographical references (p. ) and index.
ISBN 0-8166-2556-5 (acid-free paper). —ISBN 0-8166-2557-3 (pbk. : acid-free paper)
1. Literature, Modern—20th century—History and criticism. 2. American literature—Minority authors—History and criticism. 3. Ethnic groups in literature. 4. Ethnicity in literature. 5. Minorities in literature. 6. Canon (Literature). 7. America—Literatures. I. Palumbo-Liu, David.
PN771.E78      1995
810.9'920693—dc20      94-37017

# Contents

v

## PART THREE
## The Ethnic, the Nation, and the Canon

~

# Acknowledgments

I would like to thank the Department of Comparative Literature at Stanford University for providing the ideal environment for this project. In particular, Hans Ulrich Gumbrecht has been as supportive and stimulating a chair and colleague as one could hope for. I also want to thank members of the Cultural Studies Group for stimulating my thoughts on cultural politics and offering a resistant and formidable sounding board for a number of concerns. The Office of the Dean of Humanities and Sciences provided material support that allowed me to enjoy the editorial and "data" services of Barbara Fuchs; I thank her for her many hours of "managing" the manuscript. At the University of Minnesota Press I wish to thank Elizabeth Stomberg for her editorial assistance, Janaki Bahkle for initially contacting me about the project, and Biodun Iginla for his support and for ensuring all that was needed to see this large anthology into print. Finally, and, most importantly, I want to thank the contributors for their diligence, intelligence, patience, and, above all, commitment to the project.

Paula Gunn Allen's essay is excerpted from a piece that first appeared in Joseph Gibaldi, ed., *Introduction to Scholarship in Modern Languages and Literatures* (New York: Modern Language Association of America, 1992), 303–19. I am grateful to that press for granting permission to reprint a portion of her essay.

# Introduction

DAVID PALUMBO-LIU

It is at the moment of infiltration or insertion, sufficiently under threat by the custodians of a fantasmatic high Western culture, that the greatest caution must be exercised. The price of success must not compromise the enterprise irreparably. In that spirit of caution, it might not be inappropriate to notice that, as teachers, we are now involved in the construction of a new object of investigation—"the third world"; "the marginal"—for institutional validation and certification. One has only to analyze carefully the proliferating but exclusivist "Third World-ist" job descriptions to see the packaging at work. It is as if, in a certain way, we are becoming complicitous in the perpetuation of a "new orientalism."[1]

One appreciates the awfulness of this condition (which marks out the historic failure of the Left) by recognizing that the only available ideology which has taken diversity seriously is the social-democratic discourse of 'multi-culturalism' which enjoys little credibility among both racists and anti-racists, Left and Right alike. But in so far as the British Left evacuates and abandons the terrain, it is colonized by the Right and monocultural essentialism is mobilized in the defence of 'our way of life' to deny the very existence of diversity and difference.[2]

The battles for the inclusion of ethnic literature in the curriculum of American literary studies have been fought, and in many cases, won. Not only have works by ethnic peoples been integrated into the course offerings and syllabi of many departments of literature in the U.S. academy, but multiculturalism as a general program of representing the cultures and histories of diverse minorities also has been widely inscribed within college and university curricula, while "diversity" has become a keyword in the marketing of higher education in the United States.[3]

But an understanding of multiculturalism as a synonym of pluralism (which seems the predominant understanding of the term within administrative circles) stands in sharp contrast to the practice of a *critical* multiculturalism. Instead of presenting the occasion for a critique of the ideological apparatuses that distribute power and resources unevenly among the different constituencies of a multicultural society, the insertion of ethnicity into the curriculum can be articulated through pedagogical discourses that ultimately defer to monocultural presumptions of "aesthetic value," "expressive force," "character formation," and the ethnic text reduced to a pretext for the pluralistic argument that all cultures share certain expressive values. Although this may or may not be true, my concern is that as these discourses incorporate minority discourses into the general paradigm of liberal humanistic understanding, they erase the complex material specificities of these texts and vacate the term "multicultural" of its progressive intellectual, pedagogical, and social goals.[4] Indeed, one might argue that it is precisely the omnipresence of "multiculturalism" that betrays the prevalence of this particular mode of inscribing minority cultures in the academy.

The formation of an ethnic literary canon has begun as a central part of this institutionalization of multiculturalism that parallels the modes of inserting ethnicity into the general curriculum—certain "texts" deemed worthy of representing the "ethnic experience" are set forth, yet the critical and pedagogical discourses that convey these texts into the classroom and present them to students and readers in general may very well mimic and reproduce the ideological underpinnings of the dominant canon, adding "material" to it after a necessary hermeneutic operation elides contradiction and smooths over the rough grain of history and politics, that is, those very things that have constructed the "ethnic" in the United States. *The Ethnic Canon* re-views these newly canonized texts to intervene in such neutralizing operations and to offer a set of counterreadings; each in its own way seeks to recover the marks of historical and ideological contradiction and to map out possible spaces of resistance. Furthermore, the authors question those modes of discourse that have made particular critical appraisals of the inaugural texts in an emerging canon of ethnic literary *criticism*.

This project is driven in large part by a recognition of the double bind of progressive academics articulated in the epigraphs that lead off this essay:

on the one hand, a cautionary note regarding the possibilities of containing and co-opting the cultural objects of heretofore marginalized peoples; on the other, the necessity to carry on even in the face of such possibilities. In this introductory essay, I will both detail the particular modes of and rationales for appropriating ethnic literatures to serve specific purposes that ultimately undermine or neutralize the counterhegemonic potentials of those texts, and set forth a mode of critical multicultural practice that might resist such moves. The essays that follow comment, each in its own way, upon this problematic and manifest different modes of critically commenting upon ethnic literature and its canonization. One thing that links all of the essays is the belief that while multiculturalism cum "pluralism" may well be co-opted and contained, there is a pressing need to not abandon the terrain of multicultural studies simply because it may be appropriated by the hegemonic. Rather, the authors agree that it is crucial to acknowledge that a critical multiculturalism may be able to draw forth the potential for resistance and change within the academy and society at large.[5]

## The Point of Insertion

The formation of literary canons is an ongoing process whose fluctuations and inconsistencies, contradictions and tensions, may be elided by institutional resistance. Such resistance is often selectively blind to or dismissive of real changes in social dynamics and cultural expression and opposed to the attempts of progressive educators to revise the way literature is envisioned and theorized in the academy. Nevertheless, canons may be and often are brought to a state of crisis. In his broad overview of modern American cultural history, Hollinger argues that one such moment occurred in the late 1940s and the 1950s, when an academy heretofore dominated by a white Anglo-Saxon Protestant professorate was broken into by Jewish scholars. A crisis in the Western world paralleled a reconfiguration of the American intellectual imagination. This reorientation included a sustained argument for a cosmopolitan vision of culture as the cultural parochialism of the United States was seen to ill serve its adjustment to the modern age:

> The modern canon was an ideal literary agenda for the new, ethnically diverse, secular intelligentsia formed primarily by children of East-European Jewish immigrants and descendants of native American, "WASP" families. Intellectuals from both these backgrounds discovered each other while in the midst of revolts against each's own provincial inheritance, and shared the promise of a new, more cosmopolitan culture.[6]

Within this frame, modern literature was regarded as a reflection of the impasse of modern life; its value lay in both its representation of modern alienation and fragmentation and its articulation of the possible recovery of a lost humanity. Both functions took place within the realm of critical discourse sequestered from the political and social:

> The texts were presumed to be capable of filling cultural space once occupied by philosophy, theology, and political theory *without losing their distinctive aesthetic quality*, and becoming, in themselves, subject to the rules of argument appropriate for philosophy, theology, and political theory. . . . one could militantly and iconoclastically identify oneself with the insights into "society" found in Gide, Mann, or Pound, yet one did so at such an aesthetic distance that one's ostensibly intimate identification with the great moderns carried few programmatic implications for social life.[7] (Emphasis in the original)

It is crucial to note here that this move away from the political was in large part carried out by liberal critics whose leftist inclinations were set back by a disillusionment with communism and socialism after Stalin.[8] This limitation of modernist criticism was confronted by the politicized criticism of the 1960s.

Cornel West has updated the relationship of canon formation and cultural crisis, noting that the current state of "multiculturalizing" the canon forms a correlate movement to that which informed the construction of the modern canon. As the modernist canon reconfigured classical culture with an interest in modern cosmopolitan culture, so the current "culture wars" are founded on a confrontation between one cultural formation and its antecedents:

> During the late '50s, '60s, and early '70s in the USA . . . decolonized sensibilities fanned and fueled the Civil Rights and Black Power movements, as well as the student anti-war, feminist, gray, brown, gay, and lesbian movements. In this period we witnessed the shattering of the male WASP cultural homogeneity and the collapse of the short-lived liberal consensus. The inclusion of African Americans, Latino/a Americans, Asian Americans, Native Americans, and American women into the culture of critical discourse yielded intense intellectual polemics and inescapable ideological polarization that focused principally on the exclusions, silences, and blindnesses of male WASP cultural homogeneity and its concomitant Arnoldian notions of the canon.[9]

While acknowledging the ways that the formation of the modernist canon is similar to that of the multicultural one, it is crucial to recognize that the former's broadening of "culture" under the imperative of cosmopolitanism is significantly rewritten in the activities of a critical multiculturalism. A critical multiculturalism explores the fissures, tensions, and sometimes contradictory demands of multiple cultures, rather than (only) celebrating the plurality of cultures by passing through them appreciatively.[10] It instead maps out the terrain of common interest while being attentive to the different angles of entry into this terrain.

The liberal articulation of pluralism is perhaps best found in the writings of Horace Kallen. Kallen argued for a "federal republic" within the United States wherein each different national group "would have for its emotional and involuntary life its own particular dialect or speech, its own individual and inevitable esthetic and intellectual forms."[11] Yet as Milton Gordon and others have pointed out, Kallen's work lacks precisely an account of the relation of culture to socioeconomic institutions and discourses, and thus his optimistic proposal for a cultural federation cannot anticipate the materialist resistances to such a vision.[12] As well-intentioned as it may appear, "pluralism" is perhaps best regarded as a point of departure for a critical multiculturalism that would be likened in spirit to the antimonoculturalist trajectory of pluralism, but be unwilling to bypass an engagement with the historical and material effects of monocultural discourse, which has argued for a single normative culture to which all may subscribe voluntarily while in fact forcing a sense of consensus from those on the margins.

The cultural politics and the political economies of contemporary multiculturalism are intimately tied to significant changes in material life in the post-Fordist age, an age characterized by the supersession of techniques of mass production with flexible "just-in-time" techniques; the dramatic increase in the centrality of the financial sector to the overall functioning of national, regional, and global capitalist economies and the dramatic expansion of speculative activity; the growing commodification of everyday life, including the packaging of corporations themselves as benevolent and "people-oriented" and the increasing importance of advertising and marketing to the economy.[13] Within this revision of corporate capitalism as transnational, cultural "difference" is an important element to "domesticate" and make not only unobstructive, but attractive. This attraction is in part derived from its translatability, that is, commodification.[14]

The marketplaces of First World countries include a sequestered but nonetheless impressive stock of homogenized "difference" that far exceeds the romanticization of the Harlem Renaissance and the European fascination with negritude in its *transnational* material effects—effects that reinscribe relations of class, gender, race, and ethnicity both within the nation and in its international relations.[15] Upon observing the way diversity recently has become a keyword in political, economic, social, pedagogical, and cultural discourses, it becomes increasingly obvious that to understand the current "multicultural phenomenon" one must address the question, why now?[16] As Foucault notes, "If 'marginality' is being constituted as an area of investigation, this is only because relations of power have established it as a possible object; and, conversely, if power is able to take it as a target, this is because techniques of knowledge [disciplinary regulations] were capable of switching it on."[17]

One way to understand the recent interest in diversity is to see it as a mode of managing a crisis of race, ethnicity, gender, and labor in the First World and its relations with the Third as late capitalism has fostered the uneven flow of capital, products, materials, and labor across more porous borders. As much as it may be an effect of a positive liberalization in social attitudes, the current popularity of diversity may also be a symptom of a larger phenomenon: the contradictions of democratic capitalism as it regards minority populations in the First World in an age that has made such populations at times indispensable to, and at others a strain on, the state—contradictions that can be muted but not eradicated by certain accommodations (e.g., antiracist programs within the public school system) or repressions (unfair labor practices and the writing of more severe and restrictive immigration laws).

In the United States, a prevalent mode of explaining the insertion of multicultural studies into the academy has seen it as an effect of the racial unrest of the 1960s: institutions wished to accommodate and thereby neutralize and manage the "race question." Cameron McCarthy argues that "multicultural education, specifically, must be understood as part of a curricular truce, the fallout of a political project to deluge and neutralize Black rejection of the conformist and assimilationist curriculum models solidly in place in the 1960s."[18] Critics have pointed out that a necessary element of this accommodation is the silencing of debate over structural and material inequities, inequities that must be finessed in order that a harmonious blending of social space may be effected and subjectivities stripped of conflict. These subjectivities in turn reproduce a vision of the world that conforms to that territorialized zone of perfect equality.[19] In such instances, the basic operation of educational apparatuses is evident: to manage and neutralize conflict, channeling it into more "productive" (i.e., nonthreatening) subject formations.[20]

Nevertheless, although the argument that multiculturalism was engendered as a reaction to and an accommodation of social activism in the 1960s and 1970s makes a certain amount of sense, it cannot entirely explain the accelerated and much more widely spread development and institutionalization of multiculturalism in the late 1980s and early 1990s.[21] These phenomena must be looked at as being overdetermined by (at least) the following factors: the continued momentum of the curricular and social changes of the 1960s that has taken place against (and is perhaps fueled by) the resistance posed to them by the Reagan-Bush agenda (this momentum may be attributable to the persistent activity of both older activist academics and newer progressive members of the profession, as well as politicized students); the marked shift in the demographics of the college-age population, which brought about wholesale "recruiting" of particularly defined "diverse" undergraduates by universities (here the market economy of the university makes diversity not necessarily a desirable goal in itself, but rather a necessary economic consideration); and the recognition of the need for a newly skilled workforce that has to draw upon what educators call "nontraditional" students—that is, those from the margins.[22] In other words, the current prevalence of "diversity" in today's social discourse may be traced to the convergence of a number of heterogeneous interests, some of which remain entirely ambivalent to the assumptions of the others.

In 1989, then Secretary of Labor Elizabeth Dole made a series of public statements on the "new" American workforce. Within her argument for an educational system that would acknowledge both the need for a more highly skilled labor force and the fact that its demographics would weigh overwhelmingly toward minorities and women, there was a tacit and entirely persuasive assumption: the Social Security checks of today's middle-aged citizens will be dependent on the productivity of these new workers. Most important, Dole argued that it was essential to recognize the "nontraditional" qualities of these prospective workers, and hence the importance of addressing their particular needs: "As baby boomers move toward retirement and the birth rate stays low, employers are drawing a larger proportion of entry-level workers from populations where the human resource investment has been historically inadequate—women, minorities, and immigrants . . . obviously, the United States faces a serious human resource development challenge."[23] Harold Hodgkinson has compiled huge amounts of data documenting the relationship between demographic change and the need to have educational institutions give "nontraditional" students the skills required for the "workforce of the future":

If these groups continue to be clustered at the low end of the service economy, the country will be the poorer. However, as white fertility levels continue to decline, it is imperative that we educate minorities, immigrants,
and women well enough so that many of them can take the well-paying jobs
in high and midtechnology. . . . We are also entering a truly international
era in economic development. American companies like Ford have become
very sophisticated about international manufacturing and marketing, and
America's skills in pluralism should stand us in good stead during the next
century, both as a manufacturing giant and as the choice of two-thirds of
the world's immigrants. We can make pluralism work.[24]

Although many of the programs looked to for providing such education are
laudable and progressive (literacy, skills training, etc.), it is also clear that
the call for "diversity" was implicated within the program for creating an efficient workforce by way of creating a positive climate for workers. The
gains made in these areas—affirmative action, Head Start programs, and so
on—can be put to work in a number of ways. On one hand, "diversity" can
lead to a better understanding of historical processes affecting diverse populations; on the other hand, it can be used to elide precisely those questions,
as every "participant" is promised a share in the profit of his or her labor,
but without an account of its proportion, actual cost, or long-term effects.
One of the tasks for a critical multiculturalism is to use the positive gains in
educational systems (however produced) to the advantage of the former
and to forestall the latter.

Soon after many of those in the business community discovered that diversity had to be recognized as a fact, it began to be evoked as a positive asset. As Samuel Betances, a professor of sociology, observes:

Diversity must be a feature of excellence in the modern corporation. Demographics require it. A commitment to it reflects justice as well. But most important to corporations, diversity in the workplace contributes to the bottom
line. Managed skillfully, diversity in the workplace has proven to be profit-
able and a contributor to growth. . . . White male-dominated corporate
USA must take on the challenge of responding to these changes. White
males must not view with fear or trepidation the rise of women in the workforce or the growth of Latinos, or the persistence of African Americans,
Asians and indigenous groups, all wanting to make a larger contribution.
   We all must realize that our collective welfare is now at stake. Without
the talents of females and multicultural groups, there will not be a profit-
able future for anyone. In essence, the workplace must be diverse, productive, egalitarian, and sensitive to change.[25] (Emphasis added)

Stephen Joel Trachtenberg puts it more bluntly: "*Like it or not,* our ability to
reach those Americans and to help them become skilled and productive

contributors to the economy will determine our success or failure in the international marketplace"[26] (emphasis added).

These quotes remind one of nothing so much as the reasoning of Hawaiian plantation owners over improving the lives of their workers in one of the first great "multicultural" labor environments:

> Shortly before the massive 1920 strike, the Social Welfare Committee of the Hawaiian Sugar Planters' Association warned that the sugar industry of Hawaii would be "fortunate" if it "escaped" from the "world-wide unrest of labor," and urged planters to expand their recreational and welfare programs. Calling for the employment of more social welfare workers and the provision of more amusements, the committee declared: "Social welfare work should be considered good business and not philanthropy."[27]

We may thus view the recent expansion of the discourse of diversity in both the workplace and the schools as a particular manifestation of a more general phenomenon and generated by a set of quite different and sometimes antithetical interests.[28]

For example, despite sometimes profound differences in terms of the policies advocated by both conservative and liberal-progressive policymakers in *both* the areas of education and labor, all agreed on the need to construct a viable workforce out of heretofore marginalized groups. The interest in "diversity" in the late 1980s and early 1990s thus links together a series of specific operations of subject formation: from drawing in and servicing an increasingly "diverse" student population (as demographics predicated the importance of such groups to the economic viability of colleges) to producing social subjectivities that in turn underwrite the logic of a racialized "conflict management" and liberal accommodation, carrying that logic into the workplace and the marketplace. Yet once again, the challenge to critical multiculturalism is to take advantage of this diversity (which is a product as well of hard-won changes in policies of admissions and financial aid) so as to effect a more democratic educational system.

The next two sections of this essay describe these two projects: first, I want to critique the containment of conflict performed in a conservative/moderate multiculturalism; then I will argue for the act of critical revision as one mode of promoting a polyvocal democratic culture.

## Canons, Managing Diversity, and the Production of Subjectivities

Scholars of critical pedagogy have noted how the issue of diversity has been managed by subsuming conflict and difference under a higher imperative, which Giroux has labeled "normative pluralism": "Liberals consign the struggle of subordinate groups to master narratives that suggest that the oppressed need to be remade in the image of a dominant white culture in order to be integrated into the heavenly city of Enlightenment rationality."[29] In the realm of cultural politics, diversity has served as a springboard for the reaffirmation of traditional assumptions about social negotiations of conflict, a reaffirmation that ironically has the effect of closing down particular sites of difference: "Whether the appeal is to an imaginary unity allegedly free of ideological interests or to a commodity designed to promote pleasure and consumption, difference is delegitimated as a terrain of political struggle and contestation."[30]

Perhaps the most succinct pronouncement pointing up the assumptions and elisions of the liberal argument for multiculturalism is Diane Ravitch's: "It is a matter of more than parochial importance that we closely examine and try to understand that part of our national history in which different groups competed, fought, suffered, but ultimately learned to live together in peace and even achieved a sense of common nationhood."[31] Here "peace" is stated simply as a fait accompli and "conflict" reduced to a historical artifact that only serves to further solidify and mystify the supposed consensus that suppressed it. Once established, this conclusion thus not only diminishes but erases the untidy debates over how such a stability has been arrived at; that is, actual differences in the goals, identities, material existences and political representations of constituent groups are relegated to a transcended past, evacuated from the present. The result is so incontestable that its achievement can now justify the short-circuiting of democratic debate, as no one would want to revisit that contentious past.

To put it plainly, the sentiment that "no one likes to argue" has effectively been validated by a particular revision of history and deployed to silence contestatory voices in the present, whose continued protest is then regarded as "uncooperative complaining," "special interest lobbying," or "manipulative identity politics."[32] Yet it is always interesting to try to ascertain the ratio of concession and advantage, and its real effects in any conflict management formula. Mohanty notes the rise of

> a pedagogy in which we all occupy separate, different, and equally valuable places and where experience is defined not in terms of individual *qua* individual, but in terms of an individual as representative of a cultural group. This results in a depoliticalization and dehistoricization of the idea of culture and makes possible the implicit management of race in the name of cooperation and harmony. . . . While [antiracism workshops] can indeed be

useful in addressing deep-seated psychological attitudes and thus creating a context for change, the danger resides in remaining at the level of personal support and evaluation, and thus often undermining the necessity for broad-based political organization and action around these issues.[33]

Although, as Mary Louise Pratt and others have argued, there is little (if any) evidence that such modes of individualized therapy preclude collective politics (indeed, some would argue that such "recovery" may be a necessary preamble to social action), it is important to leave the question open, and to attend not to the individual phenomena but to the cultural politics that underwrite the production of particular subject positions.[34]

The argument we have been examining may seem to have taken us far afield from literary texts and canons. But this analysis is crucial to an understanding of how multicultural literary studies must be explained in relation to contemporary social formations. In this light we should note with Gayatri Chakravorty Spivak that there can be no general theory of canons; rather, canons must be thought of within specific institutional practices inscribed within particular historical moments and as securing specific positions of authority.[35] Within the specific domain of current uses of multiculturalism within the academy, the reading of ethnic literature may be taken as an occasion for the negotiation of difference, the fusion of horizons, and the "recovery" of equilibrium that creates social subjectivities now "educated" as to the proper negotiations of race, ethnicity, gender, and class.[36] More precisely, the reading of ethnic literature can be seen to set a stage for the performance of difference—race relations are made manageable and students are able to "relate" to diverse and highly differentiated experiences by reducing difference to individual encounters via ethnic "texts"; that is, complex differences crosshatched by gender, class, race, ethnicity, sexual orientation, and so on, are subordinated to the general category of experience of the unfamiliar. The point of such readings of ethnic literature is therefore to "understand" difference as a general phenomenon and subsume it under other categories that do not radically obstruct the smooth functioning of social apparatuses.

One of the more dramatic and fully elaborated proposals to use the reading of ethnic literature to cure the psychic ills of the country is found in an essay by Margaret Bedrosian, who proposes a correlation between such sense-making operations and psychotherapy:

> As students listen to ethnic writers describing the life patterns of their group and becoming more aware of their *own* misperceptions, they will see how easily the actual ethos of each group gets buried in falsehoods. . . .

referring to the model of psychosynthesis, they begin to detect the uniquely creative essence at the core of each national subpersonality.

For students, a growing awareness that ethnic groups have developed distinct and viable patterns of life in this country is pivotal, for it focuses attention to what these groups can teach us, not only about survival, but about the role of diversity in maintaining national health. . . .

Because they have been part of an inclusive dialogue, there is less chance that they will overidentify with their own group; they are much more capable of surveying ethnic groups, writers, individuals from a more detached perspective.[37]

These models of using ethnic literary texts assume their status as authentic, unmediated representations of ethnicity. Thus, under these types of pedagogical arrangements, students are able to partake of that "experience" through the careful guidance of the professor—obstacles to understanding are cleared away, tensions explained, and the resulting "fusion of horizons" stands as an emblematic moment of social harmonizing.

Such uses of ethnic literature conform explicitly to the socializing function of the study of culture: literary texts are read to solicit particular responses that manage conflict and tension at the same time as they reinforce hegemonic "structures of feeling."[38] Such readings produce a mystified "understanding" of difference that restabilizes the individual momentarily disoriented by this encounter with the Other. This process may seem not to differ significantly from previous "experiences of reading" (e.g., the astonishment before the Sublime in the late eighteenth century; appreciation of "paradox" and verbal complexity in New Critical readings of the modern canon), which all relocate the reader in a state of heightened awareness or sensitivity to his or her humanity, but in this case the intersubjective and political consequences of this catechism are all the more clear, for the manifestation of this learned experience informs the individual's assumptions about people of whom he or she now presumes to have a particular, albeit limited, understanding. Most important, in such scenarios, material history is reduced to being an "influence" on the individual writer's art, an influence that, once understood, can be subsumed in the production of understanding, not sustained in a critique of historical, political process.

While this sort of advocacy of multicultural literature at least acknowledges the social dimension of difference in these texts, this acknowledgment seems only to serve as a pretext for the ultimate gathering together of individuals rather than a force to be traced to powerful differences in material histories. As Hazel Carby notes, "Even teachers who would normally eschew the use of filmic, televisual or fictional literary texts to solve 'real-life' problems can find themselves arguing that the use of texts which represent blacks positively somehow reflects the needs of ethnic minorities and would allow teachers to combat racism in the classroom."[39] Although the use of such materials in itself is not necessarily counterproductive, nor are these necessarily the *only* outcomes of such programs and pedagogical attitudes, what demands attention are the pedagogical and political *assumptions* of such decontextualized representations: what kind of effect does reading ethnic literature produce, specifically with regard to the relationships between diverse groups of people?

The deployment of ethnic texts as proxies for ethnic peoples can be related to the general function of "diversity" in contemporary U.S. society. What is particularly striking in the justification of reading ethnic literature is the way it mobilizes the same discourses of "community," evoked as an overriding imperative, as do labor management statements on the value of diversity in the workplace.[40] In the United States, the "championing" of diversity takes on specific modes of management. John Wilcox in particular stresses the fact that "workforce diversity programs are designed to protect the company's return on investment by bringing to the surface the subtle discomforts, fears, and biases most people experience when the [sic] find themselves working with people who are different from themselves."[41] Techniques include precisely the "theatrical" one advocated by Cortland Auser (see note 37). Wilcox notes: "[Digital's "Valuing Differences" diversity program] blends cultural awareness exercises and concrete skills development in an extended business simulation in which participants create a multicultural organization and work together to achieve a group goal. Each participant is given a new name and a new cultural identity. Everyone stays 'in culture' throughout the simulation. Unexpected events are programmed into the simulation to test participants' ability to adapt in unfamiliar cultural settings" (33). As is clear from this description, the "value" of diversity is quickly eclipsed by its management and the channeling of energies into a "productive" community.

Although the value of community is certainly not an objectionable one, what is problematic in the application of multicultural "techniques" is the *way* "community" is arrived at and the purposes such a community serves—one must be attentive to the relative positionings of its constituents and the extent to which such communities are democratic and open to modification rather than managed and represented from above. (For example, while Betances remarks that new "minority" groups "want to make a contribution," it may be more accurate to say that they want a well-paying job!) It is to the advantage of capitalists to create the illusion of participatory democracy, and diversity and multiculturalism are part of today's management techniques. The penetration of both simultaneously into both the academy and the business place evinces their discursive force, as well as the way their function in both may be used to achieve similar effects of creating a normative, "productive," and well-contained pluralism.

If ethnic literary texts are now a critical part of what constitutes the American literary canon, legitimizing liberal education's general claim to diversity and openness, then the positioning of the study of ethnic literature becomes a crucial question not only for literary studies but for the reading of race and ethnicity in the United States. To give up the project of multicultural education in despair over its "contamination" is both shortsighted and politically counterproductive, however, as it would only foster the further appropriation of progressive discourse by conservatives. As much as there is a very real potential for multiculturalism to be co-opted, there is as well the potential for resistance to such appropriation, and for a critical multiculturalism to aid in the production of a counterhegemonic practice.

## For Intervention

Critics of multicultural studies have found it convenient to represent it in a form that takes on the characteristics of the conservative paradigm that progressive critics have attacked: hermetic, one-dimensional, uncritical, self-legitimating.[42] However, there is a key difference in the way *critical* multiculturalism can be constituted; while the traditional canon is based on a presumed set of accepted texts, each of which can be reconciled to similar aesthetic values (even as those values are modified in time yet anchored by the evocation of the same terminologies), an ethnic canon should be always in revision and contestation, its critics conscious of both its historical and ideological constructedness and their own pedagogical goals. In short, any formulation of an "ethnic canon" should be constantly attentive to the complex and often contradictory status of its texts as marginal to and yet inserted within the academy by particular and nonhomogeneous interests. The reduction of such texts within the economics of pedagogy (i.e., within a fixed term of study, serving particular departmental and institutional requirements and having to be read in conjunction with other texts to the exclusion of others) should not be covered up but exposed, queried, and rethought. Such a burden might appear debilitating, yet one must wonder, what's the hurry? Can not this uncertainty and self-critique be interpreted as a healthy sign that the questions that minority discourse poses are now being perceived as important enough to not rush to capitalize upon its idealization, but rather ponder its phenomenal status? While admitting the necessary finitude of lists, a progressive pedagogy would maintain a constant mode of revision and reevaluation, qualitatively different from the conservative tradition's kind of "inclusion" that comes only in an act of submission and "assimilation" to the (given) strictures of the dominant canon. The fact that the essays gathered here do not represent any one critical approach (indeed, I doubt that any of the contributors would agree with the perspectives represented in every essay) should be taken as a sign of such an interest in avoiding the rush to instantiate a restrictive mode of ethnic literary criticism and theory.

Critical multiculturalism has drawn negative reaction from both the right and the left. Although critics from the right have attacked multiculturalism as a radical attempt to destroy the foundations of Western civilization, a more realistic interpretation of their dismay can be located rather in a sense that things in general are slipping badly to the side of diversity— more and more marginalized peoples (gays and lesbians, people of color, members of the working class, and women) are demanding a greater role in the ostensibly democratic institutions of the United States. At the same time, critics from the left have accused multiculturalism as being merely a panacea, or worse, a strategy for the containment of such demands. The authors of this anthology clearly are sympathetic to this latter position, yet it remains the task of critical multiculturalism to be alert both to the ways that multicultural criticism can fall in line with hegemonic assumptions and, indeed, serve to reinforce them, *and* to ways that a truly critical multicultural criticism might theorize points of opposition and resistance.

In the United States, because the far right *may* have been embarrassed by the remarks of Patrick Buchanan and others (perhaps more over form than content) at the Republican convention of 1992 where a vehement defense of the American "way of life" was articulated, monocultural antagonism is now being *rearticulated* in the more benign form of a homogenizing multiculturalism that nonetheless demands that diverse cultural texts conform to a single norm.[43] In the case of minority literatures, this consensus is formulated around a normative aesthetic.

Recent debates over Paul Lauter et al.'s *Heath Anthology* exemplify the resistance to ideological readings of ethnic literature unsubordinated to aesthetic imperatives.[44] What is most striking is the assumption that "politics" and "aesthetics" occupy separate realms, and are, indeed, antithetical to each other. For example, although he reminds his readers of the progressive contributions of Americanists in "opening up the canon" during the 1950s and particularly of their recognition of the political elements in American literary texts, Richard Ruhland forecloses the possibility that anything other than an *already consensually assumed* aesthetic can link up diverse literary objects. He asserts that ideology cannot but interfere with the project to maintain literature as a field of agreement and appreciation:

> We rarely see the word *art* these days, and Americanists discussing what literature is and what it is about are becoming equally rare. The Heath anthology shows little concern for what can be called "literariness," nor does it say much about how students are to recognize it when they see it. What *is* literature, and why do we teach it? To understand society so that it can be changed? Or to see ourselves and our world as a way of understanding human life and the society it deserves? Why read a slave narrative in a survey of the nation's literature? To instruct ourselves on the inequities and suffering imposed on our fellows by slavery? To recognize that African Americans too can organize their experience and commit it to paper? Or is it for the sake of the narrative itself, to appreciate it in the context of human narrative generally, to expand our grasp of what we can suffer and create?[45]

While this is the moderate mode of putting ethnic literature's presence in the canon under surveillance, there is another, subtler way that it may be excluded. The hegemonic hold of the canonical texts may be reestablished by appropriating the critique of ideology and arguing that we can get all we need from the canonical texts themselves in terms of issues of race, ethnicity, class, and so on. Elizabeth Fox-Genovese argues:

> We can, in the spirit of contemporary theory, view teaching as an exercise in hermeneutics: We reread our texts from the perspective of contemporary concerns. In addition, we can transform the entire focus of conventional courses by the themes we select. If one rejects all the pieties about the rise and triumph of the individual as the manifestation of progress and civilization, one can, for example, look closely at the tension between freedom and authority for society at large; one can focus on the shift from particularism to universalism; in short, one can present the individual as the problem rather than the solution.[46]

This argument can easily be truncated and made to serve the purpose of further solidifying the traditional canon.[47]

Although Fox-Genovese rightly points out that recognizing the political dimension of ethnic literature can have the adverse effect of presuming that "nonethnic" literature is apolitical, her argument can be used to reinscribe the dominant canon as all-encompassing and self-sufficient—we do not need to read minority literatures because even our "white male writers" talk about "these things," and in more aesthetically interesting ways (and if they do not explicitly write about them, we can perform a hermeneutic operation to recover the repressed articulation of such concerns). Lauter's critique of the "New Americanists'" retention of canonical texts as their objects of inquiry points up how particularly delimited such revisionist projects may be.[48] Put simply, it is important to recognize that revisionist practices may suffer from remaining contained within hegemonic social and pedagogical practices. In the instance of *The Ethnic Canon,* the goal is to resist the essentializing and stratifying modes of reading ethnic literature that make it ripe for canonization and co-option.[49]

One major problem in this effort is recognizing that minority discourse, *once visible* as a represented and representative object, can indeed be stabilized and forced into a particular relationship with the hegemonic. To use a linguistic analogy, one might describe minority discourse as having the status of an idiom—that is, a linguistic code that circulates in a relatively private space, constructed via an appropriation and reconfiguration of the grammatically "proper" common language. As such, idioms have the weakness of being incomprehensible or only partially understandable outside their particular community of speakers. Nevertheless, this is also their strength, for they operate with relative autonomy from the ideological formations of the dominant linguistic code, and can thus comment upon the hegemonic—they are located in its proximity but not engulfed by it. Yet the dominant code is eminently adept at appropriating and synthesizing diverse linguistic objects. Thus, minority discourse both gains and loses when its idiomatic code is "recognized"—it gains currency within the dominant, and yet may be contained within the particular understandings that the dominant grants it. Upon being brought in from the margins, it loses its latitude as a counterdiscourse and its ability to designate a shifting open space outside the hegemonic.[50]

Furthermore, this objectification through nominalization takes place within the operations of minority discourse criticism itself. Barbara Christian, Renato Rosaldo, and others have noted how the critical operations of contemporary literary discourse have had the effect of objectifying diverse ethnic cultural texts *as* minority discourse in ways that collapse particular modes of articulating resistance within singular theoretical frameworks. This stabilization has the effect of locking ethnic texts into restricted modes of articulation and both creating and maintaining an elite of ethnic critics that reinforce particularized discursive modes.[51]

A critical multiculturalism would focus on the way multiple social positions are generated, stabilized, and displaced, and how culture must be read as a *complex* sign:

> The social specificity of each of these productions of meaning . . . circulates *as a sign* within specific contextual locations and social systems of value. The transnational dimension of cultural transformation—migration, diaspora, displacement, relocations—turns the specifying or localizing process of cultural translation into a complex process of signification.[52]

Critical multiculturalists might see their work as taking place within specific institutional locations and as serving various institutional needs that exceed the "humanities" and the "cloister" of the academy. *The Ethnic Canon* is an attempt to resist the gravitational pull toward "mainstreaming" at the price of complex material historical difference and the particular understandings of ethnicity that are erased in the rush to "incorporate" multicultural literatures.[53]

But within a critical multiculturalism that remains attentive to the problematics of difference and its appropriation, it is crucial to map out common ground. S. P. Mohanty traces this dual purpose in a way worth quoting at length:

> We have just been learning to speak of feminisms, instead of the singular form that implicitly hid the varied experiences of women's struggles along different racial and class vectors under the hegemonic self-image of the heterosexual white middle-class movement; we have learned to write "marxism" without capitalizing the "m," thereby pointing to the need to reconceive the relationship to some originary source; we have, in effect, taught ourselves that if history was available to us, it was always as a *text*, i.e., to be read and reread dialogically, and to be rewritten in a form other than that of a monologue, no matter how consoling or noble the latter's tone or import.
>
> Plurality is thus a political ideal as much as it is a methodological slogan. But the issue of competing rationalities raises a nagging question: how do we negotiate between my history and yours? How would it be possible for us to recover our commonality, not the ambiguous imperial-humanist myth of our shared human attributes . . . but, more significantly, the imbrication of our various pasts and presents, the ineluctable relationships of shared and contested meanings, values, material resources? It is necessary to assert our dense particularities, our lived and imagined differences; but could we afford to leave untheorized the question of how our differences are intertwined and, indeed, hierarchically organized?[54]

It is in this spirit that *The Ethnic Canon* both disarticulates what has come to be recognized as the canonical "ethnic text" and does so with a common purpose—to reinstate the cultural politics of reading and interpreting ethnic literatures. As Kobena Mercer points out, "Solidarity does not mean that everyone thinks the same way, it begins when people have the confidence to disagree over issues of fundamental importance precisely because they 'care' about constructing common ground."[55]

## The Ethnic Canon

In addressing the issue of critical multiculturalism with regard to the canonization of ethnic literatures, three topics are of the utmost importance. First, it is crucial to obtain a sense of the *history* of forming a "canon" of minority literatures and how the convergence of certain cultural political claims (i.e., race and gender) had to be negotiated. It is also necessary to consider how the texts of a particular "group" may occupy *specific* institutional positions. Second, turning to specific texts, one needs to critique how ethnic "voices" are constituted within the interstices of dominant aesthetics and ideologies and minority discourses. How are minority discourses generated differently within the dialectic of dominant and ethnic discourses? And how are tribal and ethnic communities "represented" in these discourses? Finally, moving beyond U.S. borders, how do ethnic texts become canonized and reconfigured as they move across national cultural spaces? And how do race, class, ethnicity, and gender intersect in the aggregation of an ethnic canon?

The first two essays of this anthology speak specifically to the issue of the cultural politics involved in the construction of a set of texts deemed "representative" of a particular constituency and the relation of that body of texts to those of the traditional literary canon. Paula Gunn Allen discusses how the cultural and institutional politics that surrounded the establishment of a canon of ethnic women's writing took place at the "border" of gender and color. Allen's essay provides an essential historical perspective, and shows how the institutionalization of this literature had to negotiate particular interests and antagonisms. Lisa Lowe's essay takes on the specific questions of appropriation that arrive upon the instance of institutionalization, specifically with regard to Asian American literary texts, which she describes as inherently contestatory. It is in recognizing the historical complexities of inserting ethnic literature into the curriculum and probing the conditions of its contestation of dominant readings of literary narrative that we begin to productively engage multiculturalism.

Next comes a cluster of six essays that address specific literary texts and examine the uses to which they are put within both American academics and popular American culture. In particular, each focuses upon the relation between the emergence of the "author function" of ethnic writers, the assumptions of readership, and their ideological underpinnings. Ramón Saldívar's essay on Américo Paredes interrogates the cultural politics that place Paredes within a "modernist" canon, and argues for a more profound reading of Paredes within both the sociohistorical context of New Deal visions of a new world order and the response to that vision by Chicano writers, especially as it constructs a national subjectivity against the presumptions of modernism. Similarly, Jana Sequoya-Magdaleno questions the critical construction of ethnic identity with regard to modernist aesthetics. She takes the "Prologue" to Leslie Marmon Silko's *Ceremony* and its interpretation by critics of Native American literature as a key moment in the inscription and deployment of American Indian identity and critiques the complex subject position of Silko's voice. She points out the investments behind seeing Silko's voice as a particularly powerful amalgam of Indian "orality" and modernist narrative technique. Both these essays point up the tendency to read ethnic literature within the modernist aesthetic, and argue for readings that resist that mode of insertion into the canon, favoring instead a more complex understanding of historical contingency, cultural politics, and ethnic identifications.

Elliott Butler-Evans's essay investigates these issues in African American literature, illustrating the usefulness in Bakhtin's notion of dialogism and the carnivalesque in teasing out the various strands of discourse in Ralph Ellison's *Invisible Man* and Toni Morrison's *Song of Solomon*. Through a critique of minority discourse, he argues that these concepts help us understand these authors' differing senses of the constitution of a Black community within a particular discursive relationship to both African American and the dominant culture. Butler-Evans's essay points out the need to view ethnic literary discourse as engaged in a complex dialogic relationship with multiple discourses, rather than as a thing unto itself. This engagement is further discussed in the two essays on Richard Rodríguez. In the field of contemporary Latino writing in the United States, Rodríguez is perhaps the author most cited in debates on assimilation and cultural identity, and whose writings are most presented within the canon of assimilative American literature. Norma Alarcón and Rosaura Sánchez provide different analyses of his writings, yet each focuses on the complex intersections of ideology, aesthetics, class, sexuality, and ethnicity found in Rodríguez's work. Like the essays that preceded them, these two essays separate out the complex registers of rhetoric that go into the production of ethnic literary discourse and their ideological implications and functions. Alarcón's essay centers on the trope of the "museum," which locates and exhibits Rodríguez both inside and outside the collection of Latino/a "culture" and that of the United States, following his vacillations and recuperations of subjecthood. Sánchez disarticulates the eloquent surfaces of Rodríguez's self-reflections and marks out the contradictions inherent in his program for self-liberation and selective forgetting within the specific historical context of Chicano/a cultural politics.

Sau-ling Wong continues this discussion of the interrelationship of the politics of ethnic representation, its construction via a particularly conceived literary discourse, and its relation to a specific readership. Wong performs a meticulous and historically sensitive account of Asian American women's narratives and their reception in the United States in an attempt to account for the particular success of Amy Tan. She then proceeds to tease out the various elements of Tan's prose style and her modes of representing the intersection of "China" and the United States. Thus Wong opens the topic of transnational cultural politics and draws attention to the specific ways such politics inscribes multicultural texts, fusing them within a particular formation of cultural and historical subjectivity.

The three essays that close this anthology continue this discussion of transnational cultural politics and multiculturalism. E. San Juan Jr. and Barbara Christian address the particular problematic of the use of ethnic literary texts as "representations" of specifically designated groups and the transnational effects and assumptions of such efforts to define ethnic cultures, as evinced in the construction of, respectively, a Filipino American canon and a canon of Caribbean women's literature. Each raises the question of the politics of inclusion—how do each of these formations reveal the process of construction, the defining moments of minority "culture," and the political economies of representation? In particular, issues of the intersections of ethnicity and class (San Juan) and ethnicity and gender (Christian) are foregrounded to account for the more specific modes of canonization. Finally, Colleen Lye draws together issues of gender and ethnicity to analyze a specific text's transmutations within transnational critical discourse. She draws our attention to the way David Henry Hwang's *M. Butterfly* may be appropriated as a text that *necessarily* dismantles hegemonic structures, but only at the cost of writing out the problematics of transnational cultural politics in favor of a decontextualized and extremely localized reading of gender. A crucial element of Lye's critique is her observation of the way particular readings of the play are problematized when it is promoted and performed in different national situations. In such a critique, the underlying universalist assumptions behind the interpretation of ethnic texts are revealed.

*The Ethnic Canon* therefore follows a particular trajectory—from a discussion of the history and political elements of ethnic literature's insertion into the curriculum, to a series of analyses of the cultural politics of minority discourse and criticism, to an opening up of readings of ethnic literature that attempt to account for diverse and often contradictory modes of interpretation and critique within the specificities of history, national cultural politics, and transnational movements of cultural objects. In each instance, the authors argue against the insertion of ethnic literature into the canon via a simple reading of common themes and issues, and for a mode of critically understanding multicultural texts within a complex set of relations that help us recognize larger issues of the formations of contemporary culture and its ideological functions.

# Notes

I want to thank Mary Louise Pratt and the anonymous readers for the Press for their criticisms of a draft of this essay.

1. Gayatri Chakravorty Spivak, "Poststructuralism, Marginality, Postcoloniality and Value," in Peter Collier and Helga Geyler-Ryan, eds., *Literary Theory Today* (Ithaca, N.Y.: Cornell University Press, 1990), 222. For a further discussion of the pedagogical politics of containment and liberation, see Henry A. Giroux, *Theory and Resistance in Education: A Pedagogy for the Opposition* (South Hadley, Mass.: Berghin and Garvey, 1983). For instance, Giroux elaborates a critique of the insertion of oppositional practices within the academy from the argument that "human agency and structures come together most visibly at the point where oppositional practices and meanings contribute to the very nature of the hegemonic process. Such resistance not only reveals the active side of hegemony, it also provides the basis for a radical pedagogy that would make it the object of a critical deciphering and analysis" (165). See also Teresa de Lauretis, "Feminist Studies/Critical Studies: Issues, Terms, and Contexts," in de Lauretis, ed., *Feminist Studies: Critical Studies*, especially pp. 3 and 8.

2. Kobena Mercer, "Welcome to the Jungle: Identity and Diversity in Postmodern Politics," in Jonathan Rutherford, ed., *Identity: Community, Culture, Difference* (London: Lawrence and Wishart, 1990), 66.

3. In this essay I am using "ethnic" to designate those ethnic minorities in the United States who continue to be marginalized within the dominant cultural "tradition."

4. It is of course a question whether "ethnic literature" per se constitutes "minority discourse"—that has as its key elements resistance to and subversion of dominant discourses. It is with the understanding that the overlap I assume between the two, which allows me to speak of ethnic literature as minority discourse, can be provisionally accepted as the process of critique is carried forward; that is, my notion of ethnic literature and its criticism within a critical multicultural framework calls for a sustained probing of the text's various positionings via hegemonic ideologies, positionings that might be recovered or mapped out via an interrogation of the discourses that embody both the literary text and the critical one that seeks to present that text to understanding. This double move seeks not so much to "decide" the text's sta-

tus as minority discourse (either/or) as to theorize the (often tenuous) *nature* of its relation to dominant discourses.

5. In this regard, Giroux's *Theory and Resistance in Education* is a critically important intervention in "reproductive" theories of education. In it, Giroux insists on keeping open the potential for resistance within the *incomplete* reproduction of hegemonic ideologies.

6. David A. Hollinger, *In the American Province: Studies in the History and Historiography of Ideas* (Bloomington: Indiana University Press, 1985), 88. See especially his fifth chapter, "The Canon and Its Keepers: Modernism and Mid-Twentieth-Century American Intellectuals."

7. Ibid., 85 f.

8. See Stanley Aronowitz, *Roll Over Beethoven: The Return of Cultural Strife* (Hanover, N.H.: Wesleyan University Press, 1992). My review of this book appears in the *Review of Education/Pedagogy/Cultural Studies* 16:2 (1994).

9. Cornel West, "The New Cultural Politics of Difference," in Russell Ferguson, Martha Gever, Trinh T. Minh-ha, and Cornel West, eds., *Out There: Marginalization and Contemporary Cultures* (Cambridge, Mass.: MIT Press, 1990), 24–26. See also Cornel West, "Minority Discourse and the Pitfalls of Canon Formation," *Yale Journal of Criticism* 1:1 (1987): 193–201.

10. The foundations of comparative literature are precisely within such a cosmopolitan spirit. For example, Erich Schmidt declares in his inaugural lecture at the University of Vienna in 1880: "The history of literature should be part of the history of a people's spiritual and intellectual development, with comparative glances thrown at other national literatures" (quoted in Ulrich Weinstein, *Comparative Literature and Literary Theory* [Bloomington: Indiana University Press, 1968], 186). In another essay, "Terms of Indifference: Cosmopolitanism, Cultural Politics, and Literary Studies" (forthcoming in *Cadernos do Mestrado Literatura* [Universidade do Estado do Rio de Janeiro]), I offer a critique of comparative literature's historical trajectory and the current multiculturalism.

11. Horace Kallen, *Culture and Democracy in the United States* (New York: Boni and Liveright, 1924), 124; cited in Mario Barrera, *Beyond Aztlan: Ethnic Autonomy in Comparative Perspective* (Notre Dame: University of Notre Dame Press, 1990), 159.

12. See Milton Gordon, *Assimilation in American Life* (New York: Oxford University Press, 1964).

13. For these characteristics and more, see "Post-Fordism: Flexible Politics in the Age of Just-in-Time Production," *Socialist Review* 21:1 (January 1991): 53–55 (editors' introduction to a special issue on post-Fordism).

14. Within this historical context, Henry A. Giroux has also noted in contemporary advertising a phenomenon that suggests that while the exotic has become an indispensable part of First World capitalist imaginations and transnational marketing and production, "difference" has become flattened out and contained within a particular brand of pluralism that advances an image of progressive politics—a politics that is reduced to an attitude of social "concern" but not of commitment, or a vaguely defined yet altogether "current" worldview that would criticize dominant political economies benignly from within. It is especially important to notice how such "democratization of images" forges a psychic link between a glamorized "Other" and a community of youthful, liberal-thinking consumers. See Giroux, "Consuming Social Change: Benetton's 'World Without Borders,'" *Cultural Critique* 26 (winter 1993–94): 5–32.

15. Homi Bhabha remarks that "in fact the sign of the 'cultured' or the 'civilized' attitude is the ability to appreciate cultures in a kind of *musée imaginaire*; . . . Western connoisseurship has the capacity to understand and locate cultures in a universal time-frame that acknowledges their various historical and social contexts only eventually to transcend them and render them transparent. . . . There are two problems with [multiculturalism in Britain]: one is the very obvious one, that although there is always an entertainment and encouragement of cultural diversity, there is always also a corresponding containment of it. A transparent norm is constituted, a norm given by the host society or dominant culture, which says that 'these other

cultures are fine, but we must be able to locate them within our own grid.' . . . The other problem is . . . that in societies where multiculturalism is encouraged racism is still rampant in various forms. This is because the universalism that paradoxically permits diversity masks ethnocentric norms, values, and interests" ("The Third Space: Interview with Homi Bhabha," in Rutherford, ed. *Identity*, 207 f.). Mohanty likewise comments that "in the study of modern literatures, the most crucial political question that arises concerns a history 'we' all share, a history whose very terms and definitions are used to support the proliferation of various minority canons and discourses, the question of historical imbrication, indeed the question of this unequal history itself, is obscured by a narrowly pragmatic logic" (S. P. Mohanty, "'Us and Them': On the Philosophical Bases of Political Criticism," *Yale Journal of Criticism* 2:2 [1989]: 25).

On the popularity of "difference" in Britain, Rutherford remarks: "Capital has fallen in love with difference: advertising thrives on selling us things that will enhance our uniqueness and individuality. It's no longer about keeping up with the Joneses, it's about being different from them. From World Music to exotic holidays in Third-World locations, ethnic tv dinners to Peruvian knitted hats, cultural difference *sells*. This is the 'difference' of commodity relations, the particular experience of time and space produced by transnational capital" (Jonathan Rutherford, "A Place Called Home: Identity and the Cultural Politics of Difference," in Rutherford, ed., *Identity*, 11. See also Martin P. Davidson, *The Consumerist Manifesto* (London: Routledge, 1992).

16. Although it is true that as early as 1962 John F. Kennedy introduced the word "diversity" into the modern political lexicon ("we must make the world safe for diversity"), that articulation was specifically addressed to cold war strategy. Yet, one could argue, that term (and the crisis in Cuba) had an epiphenomenal effect on the presentation and negotiation of civil rights issues that Kennedy addressed only very late (and some say reluctantly) in his presidency.

17. Michel Foucault, *The History of Sexuality*, vol. 1, trans. Robert Hurley (New York: Vintage Books, 1980), 98–99, cited with modification in Spivak, "Poststructuralism, Marginality, Postcoloniality and Value," 224. This scenario, this marginality must be understood in terms of a positionality. Spivak argues, "I am not suggesting that there is a positive space of 'marginality' to be recovered on the other side of the incessant coding. 'Marginality,' as it is becoming part of the disciplinary-cultural parlance, is in fact the name of a certain constantly changing set of representations that is the condition and effect of it" (227).

18. Cameron McCarthy, "Rethinking Liberal and Radical Perspectives on Racial Inequality in Schooling: Making the Case for Nonsynchrony," *Harvard Education Review* 58:3 (1988): 267 f. For similar arguments, see Rosaura Sánchez, "Ethnicity, Ideology, and Academia," *Americas Review* 15:1 (1987): 80–88, and West, "Minority Discourse and the Pitfalls of Canon Formation."

19. Chandra Talpade Mohanty writes: "The effect of the proliferation of ideologies of pluralism in the 1960s and 1970s, in the context of the (limited) implementation of affirmative action in institutions of higher education, has been to create what might be called the Race Industry, an industry that is responsible for the management, commodification, and domestication of race on American campuses" ("On Race and Voice: Challenges for Liberal Education in the 1990s," *Cultural Critique* [winter 1989–90]: 186). See also McCarthy, "Rethinking Liberal and Radical Perspectives," 269, and Hazel Carby, "Multi-Culture," *Screen Education* 34 (1980): 62–70.

20. Henry Giroux notes that in this operation, the "problem" of race and ethnicity is largely identified within the racialized Other, and the "white" is largely erased. See his *Border Crossings* (New York and London: Routledge, 1992), especially the essay "Redefining the Boundaries of Race and Ethnicity: Beyond the Politics of Pluralism" (111–46).

21. It is still too early to predict the direction of multiculturalism in the academy. Already one reads in campus publications that multiculturalism has "outlived its usefulness." Modes of containment and dismantling that have been toyed with recently include redefining multiculturalism as (only) international studies.

22. McCarthy makes a similar, albeit more narrow, argument with particular focus on Black studies and labor.

23. Elizabeth Dole, "America's Competitive Advantage: A Skilled Labor Force," *Adult Learning* 1:1 (1989): 12; cf. similar articulations in her "Preparing the Workforce of the Future," *Vocational Education Journal* 64:7 (October 1989), and in her "State of the Workforce Address," October 26, 1989, published by the Department of Labor.

24. Harold Hodgkinson, "The Same Client: Demographics of Education and Service Delivery Systems" (Washington, D.C.: Institute for Educational Leadership, 1989), 20. See also his "Look Who's Coming to Work" (Columbus: Ohio State University, National Center for Research in Vocational Education, 1986).

25. Samuel Betances, "Diversity," *Vocational Education Journal* November/December 1991): 22.

26. Stephen Joel Trachtenberg, "Multiculturalism Can Be Taught Only by Multicultural People," *Phi Delta Kappan* (April 1990): 611.

27. In Ronald Takaki, *Pau Hana: Plantation Life and Labor in Hawaii* (Honolulu: University of Hawaii Press, 1983), 105.

28. Giroux points out that "schools have emerged historically as social sites that have integrated the traditionally separate tasks of reproducing work skills and producing attitudes that legitimize the social relations in which these skills are located. . . . Schooling represents a major social site for the construction of subjectivities and dispositions, a place where students from different social classes learn the necessary skills to occupy class-specific locations in the occupational division of labor" (*Theory and Resistance in Education*, 78).

29. The term "normative pluralism" is coined in Henry A. Giroux, *Teachers as Intellectuals* (Granby, Mass.: Bergin and Garvey, 1988), 95. See also Michael W. Apple, *Ideology and Curriculum* (London: Routledge and Kegan Paul, 1979), especially 84.

30. Henry A. Giroux, "Rewriting the Politics of Identity and Difference," *Review of Education* 14 (1992): 310. See also Arturo Madrid, "Diversity and Its Discontents," *Academe* (November 1990): 15–19.

31. Diane Ravitch, "Diversity and Democracy," *American Educator* (spring 1990): 18.

32. For example, at a recent conference in Berkeley, this author was accused of creating a "theology of oppression."

33. Chandra Talpade Mohanty, "On Race and Voice," 195.

34. Mary Pratt's comments came in the form of a personal communication; see the recent work of bell hooks on this issue. In my essay "Model Minority Discourse and the Course of Healing" (forthcoming in *Minority Discourse: Ideological Containment and Utopian/Heterotopian Potential*, edited by Adbul JanMohamed), I also try to deal with this topic.

35. "There can be no general theory of canons. Canons are the condition of institutions and the effect of institutions. Canons secure institutions as institutions secure canons" (Gayatri Chakravorty Spivak, "The Making of Americans, the Teaching of English, and the Future of Cultural Studies," *New Literary History* 21 [1990]: 784).

36. Ian Hunter has argued that the establishment of English studies in Great Britain took place within the context of radical social change, specifically within the development of the English public school system. "Culture" in this instance was a powerfully expansive discourse that guided the cultivation and development of social subjectivities. Correspondingly, aesthetics became a sounding board for ethical responses to the outer world, and literature became a representation of the outer world that elicited such responses from a properly schooled indi-

vidual. Hunter notes the emergence of the idea that "English provides a unique vehicle for personal expression and growth; that it imposes no 'special aptitude' and hence no 'special limitation' on the mind; that this completeness of development is achieved through its closeness to the whole range of 'lived experience'; and that it depends on a special relation to the English teacher whose supervision is not coercive but is, apparently, 'drawn from the pupil' himself. In short, we find all the attributes which—whether they are taken as 'signs' of 'man's' complete or distorted ethical completion—supposedly took shape as English when the 'idea of culture as art' was actualized in 'society'" (*Culture and Government: The Emergence of Modern Literary Education* [Houndmills: Macmillan Press, 1988], 16).

37. Margaret Bedrosian, "Teaching Multi-Ethnic Literature: Some Psychological Considerations," *MELUS* 16:2 (summer 1989–90): 10–13. In that same issue, see as well Cortland Auser, "'The Mask is the Face': *Personae* in Teaching Multi-Ethnic American Literature" (69–76), which argues that by taking on different roles in ethnic literary texts, students can transcend their individual identities and gain a sense of what it means to be Other.

38. See Raymond Williams's discussion of "structures of feeling" in his *Marxism and Literature* (Oxford: Oxford University Press, 1977).

39. Carby, "Multi-Culture," 66.

40. Bhikhu Parekh observes that "the assimilationist thrust is inherent in capitalism. It cannot tolerate diversity beyond a certain point, it insists on uniformity, it insists on only those differences that it can regulate." See "Identities on Parade" (conversation between Bhikhu Parekh and Homi Bhabha), *Marxism Today* (June 1989): 28.

41. John Wilcox, "The Corporate View: A Multicultural Workforce Can Be a Competitive Advantage." *Vocational Educational Journal* 66:8 (November–December 1991): 32–33, 76.

42. Marjorie Perloff has remarked upon the abiding institutional practices of canonization that enclose multicultural studies. See Perloff, "An Intellectual Impasse," *Salmagundi* 72 (fall 1986): 125–30. This issue of the journal is devoted to the topic of literary canons, and represents a number of moderate to liberal viewpoints.

43. For a discussion of rearticulations of racism, see Michael Omi and Howard Winant, *Racial Formation in the United States from the 1960s to the 1980s* (London: Routledge, 1986). The resurgence of conservatism that took place as this anthology went to press—the victories of the far right in the November 1994 elections—forces one to recognize even more the political significance of the terrain of "cultures," and the project of critical multiculturalism.

44. The *Heath Anthology of American Literature* (general editor, Paul Lauter; Lexington, Mass.: D. C. Heath, 1990) is distinct from earlier anthologies of American literature in its explicit attempt to include texts by writers (largely ethnic writers and nonethnic women writers) previously unrepresented in such anthologies. An ambitious project in revisionist literary history, it drew both praise and criticism, and remains a frequently referenced work.

45. Richard Ruhland, "Art and a Better America," *American Literary History* 3:2 (1991): 354. The dichotomization of art/politics is further elaborated in Robert Alter, *The Pleasures of Reading* (New York: Simon and Shuster, 1989), and Alvin Kernan, *The Death of Literature* (New Haven: Yale University Press, 1990). See also Frederick Crews, "The New Americanists," *New York Review of Books* 39:15 (24 September 1992): 32–34.

46. Elizabeth Fox-Genovese, "The Claims of a Common Culture: Gender, Race, Class and the Canon," *Salmagundi* 72 (1986): 141.

47. This resembles the diffusion of feminist studies into gender studies, a move that begins with the legitimate assertion that "feminist studies" should not assume a territorialization that effectively contains gender within a marginalized space, and yet when institutionalized can include situations wherein those unsympathetic to the progressive, radical aims of feminist theory can dehistoricize and defuse the acuity of such critiques in a universalizing strategy of containment.

48. See Paul Lauter, *Canons and Contexts* (New York and Oxford: Oxford University Press, 1991), especially 162 ff.

49. For a discussion of the issue of the promise and failure of canonical reform, see John Guillory, "Canonical and Non-canonical: A Critique of the Current Debate," *English Literary History* 54 (1987): 483–527.

50. See Terry Eagleton's description of this dilemma in "Nationalism: Irony and Commitment," in Terry Eagleton, Fredric Jameson, and Edward W. Said, *Nationalism, Colonialism, and Literature* (Minneapolis: University of Minnesota Press, 1990), especially 30.

51. See, in the same issue of *Cultural Critique* (no. 6, spring 1987), Barbara Christian, "The Race for Theory," and Renato Rosaldo, "Politics, Patriarchs, and Laughter." See also Cornel West, "Some Pitfalls," especially 198.

52. Homi Bhabha, "Freedom's Basis in the Indeterminate," *October* 61 (1992): 47.

53. For further discussion of this issue, see Jean Ferguson Carr, "Cultural Studies and Curricular Change," *Academe* (November–December 1990): 25–28.

54. S. P. Mohanty, "'Us and Them,'" 13.

55. Mercer, "Welcome to the Jungle," 68. See also West, "The New Cultural Politics of Difference," especially 29ff. and his "Minority Discourse and the Pitfalls of Canon Formation," 200f; also R. Radhakrishnan, "Culture as Common Ground: Ethnicity and Beyond," *MELUS* 14:2 (summer 1987).

## PART ONE

# Instituting Minor Literatures

∼

# "Border" Studies

## The Intersection of Gender and Color

PAULA GUNN ALLEN

In his exhaustive opus Irenaeus [Bishop of Lyons] catalogued all deviations
from the coalescing orthodoxy and vehemently condemned them. Deplor-
ing diversity, he maintained there could be only one valid Church, outside
which there could be no salvation. Whoever challenged this assertion,
Irenaeus declared to be a heretic—to be expelled and, if possible, destroyed.
. . . . In opposition to personal experience and *gnosis*, Irenaeus recognized
the need for a definitive canon—a fixed list of authoritative writings. . . .
—Michael Baigent, Richard Leigh, and Henry Lincoln, *Holy Blood, Holy Grail*

Not only has littled changed since I entered the profession in the 1970s,
nothing much has changed since Irenaeus, nearly two thousand years ago.
They're still pontificating, excluding, and power-tripping, while we're still
resisting, dissenting, deconstructing, and subverting. Heresies spring up all
around only to die, only to recur persistently like wildflowers, like crab-
grass. We still match personal experience and gnosis with canonicity, and
those who tenaciously cling to the rotting pillars of Rome dismiss us—or
order us purged. It seems that as long as we remain locked into oppositional
structures, nothing but "same ol', same ol' " can occur. As long as we avoid
the creative, we are condemned to reaction.

The profession when I entered it was much the same as it is today, "Still
crazy after all these years," as the song goes. Though I had marched, pam-
phleted, and taught for peace and social justice, for civil, women's, and les-

bian and gay rights, and briefly served as faculty advisor for the Young Socialist Alliance; though I had been writing and publishing for several years; though the poets I published with and read with in coffeehouses and bars, on the streets, and at rallies were fairly frequently not white and on occasion not white men—as far as the academy was, and is, concerned, there was, and is, no literature other than that produced by a Eurocentric formalist elite.

Nearly twenty weary years later, the cops beating African American men is a media sound bite, and the merciless destruction of Native people is largely ignored by all factions in the brawling American polity. Many are glad that "the war has ended," but I am compelled to object: it has not ended; it goes on and on. In the academy we hold rallies, sign resolutions, declare moratoriums, and demand divesture and withdrawal of American involvement in foreign lands, while the mutilation of people of color at home evokes barely a sigh.

I came of age in the 1960s and by the 1970s was seriously burned out. By 1972 I understood several things: If an issue concerned Native people or women, men, and queers of color, neither the academy nor the intelligentsia at large would have a word to say. We are *las disappearadas* (and *desperadas*). We are for the most part invisible, labeled "marginal," the "poor," the "victims," or we are seen as exotica. Our "allies" adamantly cast us in the role of helpless, hopeless, inadequate, incompetent, much in need of white champions and saviors, dependent upon an uncaring state for every shred of personal and community dignity we might hope to enjoy. Right, left, and center see us as their shadows, the part they disown, reject, repress, or romanticize.

Even our few solid backers in academe perceive us as extensions of the great white way; they fail to perceive us as artists, writers, and human beings-in-*communitas* in our own right. And while some of the despised are recognized, most are not seen as other than a pitiable, amorphous blob. Our capacities as creative, self-directing, self-comprehending human beings are lost in the shuffle of ideology and taxonomy; the contributions of our peoples to the literatures, philosophies, sciences, and religions of the world are ignored. Our proper place in the view of the defining others is that of servant; they have consigned us to their margins, and there we must stay.

In the mid-1960s when I was in graduate school, I was not assigned the work of one woman poet or writer. And although assigned reading included the work of a number of homosexuals, their sexuality was, and largely still is, hidden to the eyes of the self-avowed heterosexual professoriat. In the late 1980s, I envied graduate students in the Ethnic Studies Department at the University of California in Berkeley, where I then taught, who enjoyed the privilege of studying women's literature from every period, every nation, including that of the U.S. of Color, and I sometimes cast envious glances at young colleagues who enjoy a growing body of scholarship and works by lesbians and gay men. It is not true that nothing has changed; there have been some shifts in academic offerings, though for the most part these offerings are not in traditional departments or are included only at the patronizing, cynical sufferance of the academic elite.

Despite the good intentions and hard work of individuals, the establishment itself, particularly in literary fields, is unrepentantly proud of its constricted intelligence. Even worse is the willful institutional starvation of our students, accomplished by a narrowness of intellect and an insatiable desire for status and prestige. As academics, perhaps we all should concern ourselves with the consequences of institutional mind abuse.

I spent about ten years on the front of a civil war that has raged for centuries and an additional ten years reconnoitering. During that time I came to understand that the position of power for a true Warrior is the Void. It is from the Void that all arises and into that Void that all returns. The most profoundly creative literature of the twentieth century, the most profoundly *literary* literature, is, as it always has been, the literature of the desperadoes (and, in this case, desperadas). It is we who are creating the shape of the new world from the strokes of our pens, typewriter keys, and computer keyboards.

This body of work, literature that rides the borders of a variety of literary, cultural, and ideological realms, has not been adequately addressed by either mainstream feminist scholarship or the preponderance of "ethnic" or "minority" scholarship. However, in the past decade a new field of study has emerged that resists definition by other critics, that seems determined to define itself. This new field raises questions that mainstream feminist and "ethnic" or "minority" approaches fail to address and simultaneously begins to open before us new possibilities for inquiry.

The process of living on the border, of crossing and recrossing boundaries of consciousness, is most clearly delineated in work by writers who are citizens of more than one community, whose experiences and languages require that they live within worlds that are as markedly different from one another as Chinatown, Los Angeles, and Malibu; El Paso and Manhattan's arts and intellectuals' districts; Laguna Pueblo in New Mexico and literary London's Hamstead Heath. It is not merely biculturality that forms the foundation of our lives and work in their multiplicity, aesthetic largeness, and wide-ranging potential; rather, it is multiculturality, multilinguality, and dizzying class-crossing from the fields to the salons, from the factories to the academy, or from galleries and the groves of academe to the neighborhoods and reservations. The new field of study moves beyond the critical boundary set in Western academic circles and demands that the canonical massive walls be thinned and studded with openings so that criticism, like literary production itself, reflects the great variety of writerly lives and thought, particularly those in the American community. For it is not that writers themselves, of whatever color, class, gender, or sexual orientation, have been bound by ideological barriers a mile thick and two miles high but that academics have found the doctrine of exclusion and Eurocentric elitism a necessary tool in the furtherance of Western cultural goals and their own careers.

The work of women of color arises out of the creative void in a multitude of voices, a complex of modes, and most of these women are quite aware of their connection to the dark grandmother of human wisdom. Thus in *The Salt Eaters* the African American writer Toni Cade Bambara draws Velma back from the edge of daylight and heals her through the shadowy presences of Sophia, the dark spirit of wisdom, and the loas, the spirits. Toni Morrison produces a body of work that draws us ever more enticingly toward the great mysteriousness from which human life and significance always arise and to which they inevitably return. Similarly, in *Love Medicine, The Beet Queen,* and *Tracks,* the American Indian writer Louise Erdrich seduces us into the forest of Ojibway women's magic, winding us ever more deeply into the shadows of ancient trees. She leaves not so much as a crumb to draw us back into the light of patriarchal day. Leslie Marmon Silko reaches into unexplored realms, the gloom of what is long forgotten but that continues to nourish our love and our terror, while Maxine Hong Kingston moves into the deeps of Han myth and memory, who is myth's beloved sister and supernal twin. The Chicana writer Gloria Anzaldúa tells it plainly: The woman in the shadows is drawn again into the world of womankind, and her name is innocence, exuberance, discovery, and passion; her name is our invisible bond.

Women return from the spirit lands to the crossroads over and over; we question, we circle around the center of the fire where the darkest, hottest coals lie. We know it is there—the nothing that bears all signifying, all tropes, all love medicine, all stories, all constructions and deconstructions.

We know this: in the void reside the keepers of wisdom. Women of color are willing and well equipped to approach the still, dark center of the heart of the gynocosmos where nothing at all exists and whence, paradoxically, all must emerge. Other writers, strangers to the source of meaning, have talked about that mysterious, foreboding place, the dark heart of creation, but it is we—perhaps because we are nothing ourselves—who stalk the void and dance the dervish of significance that is born through our parted lips and legs. Other writers have entered the shadow, but they have named it evil, negation, woman. They have fled, running pell-mell away from her living bounty. They call us woman, other, mother, hooker, maid and believe themselves securely superior, safe from the mournful meaninglessness of our lot. Ah, but our lot is passion, grief, rage, and delight. Our lot is life, however that comes, in whatever guise it takes. We are alive, the living among the dead. Too bad those who see us as shadow, as void, as negation miss it all; so sad they haven't the wit to grieve their loss.

The dark woman has long been perceived as the dumb, the speechless, mother. And while the angrier among us protest that perception, we who are wise welcome and celebrate it. One of our sisters—albeit white and Calvinist but marginalized, closeted, all but disappeared—commented on the humor of the situation, writing:

> I'm nobody! Who are you?
> . . . . . . . . . . . . . .
> How dreary—to be—Somebody

Only the disappeared can enter the Void and, like Grandmother Spider, emerge with a small but vital pot, a design that signifies the power of meaning and of life, and a glowing ember that gives great light. We who are nobody are the alive—and no one knows we're here. We are the invisible—and no one cares. Silly them. They are all at the public banquet hobnobbing with the known, the recognized, the acclaimed. And, as in the history of art in our Western world, they missed the god when she passed by, the god that the ignored and dismissed white lesbian crazy lady HD once so accurately described.

The issue I am addressing here is not simply a matter of gender: it is fundamentally a matter of the essential experience of non-Western modes of consciousness. For the most part my sisters of the white persuasion are as culture-bound as their more highly prestiged brothers. In the West it is now held that gender (or sex) is a metaphor, a social construct. Further, it is held that since a metaphor cannot be used to analyze a metaphorical system, meaning is largely a trick of the mind.

But in other systems—systems not so bound in a self-referencing, nearly psychotic death dance—meaning is derived and ascribed along different lines. This interpretive mode, non-Western to its core, is explored in *The Signifying Monkey,* by Henry Louis Gates Jr. That work, though Afrocentric in itself, suggests a way out of the Morton Salt box conundrum of Euro-centric patriarchal self-preoccupation. Gates tells us that the meaning of a Black text derives from the system of significance revealed and shaped by Ifa. The critical task is to render the text comprehensible and by that act as-sess its quality, by interpreting it through Ifa. According to Gates, that task belongs to Esu, the trickster, who is male and female, many-tongued, changeable, changing and who contains all the meanings possible within her or his consciousness. Thus a text that is malformed or incomprehen-sible when held up to Ifa as template is a work that has failed. Ifa, Gates writes, "consists of the sacred texts of the Yoruba people, as does the Bible for Christians, but it also contains the commentaries on these fixed texts, as does the Midrash" (10). Esu (or Esu-Elegbara or, in these parts, Papa Legba) is, in Gates's terms, "the dynamic of process," similar to the process of criti-cal interpretation, who "interrelates all the different and multiple parts which compose the system" (38):

> Esu speaks through Ifa, because it is his *ase* that reveals—or conceals—the roadways or pathways through the text to its potential and possible mean-ings. Whereas Ifa is truth, Esu rules understanding of truth, a relationship that yields an individual's meaning. . . . Esu is the process of interpretation. (38–39)

Similarly, by way of the ceremonial tradition as template, a given work by a Native artist can be assessed. In both instances the canon becomes "the sa-cred," the world of the unseen (but not unheard or unknown), and its pri-mary texts are the myths and ceremonies that compress and convey all the meaning systems a particular cultural consciousness holds. This is not to confuse a relationship to the mysteriousness that underlies and sources the phenomenological with essentialism or absolutism. There is little that is one, holy, catholic, and apostolic in the actual world that lies beyond and within the mundane. Indeed, the true world of the mysteries is more mul-tiplex, polyglot, and free-flowing than any churchman, whether of Chris-tian, Jewish, Muslim, Buddhist, or revolutionary persuasion, can imagine. Its very multitudinousness certainly threatens, even terrifies, the apostles of monotony.

Hortense J. Spillers comments that "the literary text *does* point outside itself—in the primary interest of leading the reader back inside the universe of the apparently self-contained artifact" (244). That is, no cultural artifact can be seen as existing outside its particular matrix; no document, however

profoundly aesthetic, can be comprehended outside its frame of reference—a frame that extends all the way into the depths of the consciousness
that marks a culture, differentiating it from another. Because Western societies are fundamentally the same—they all arise from the same essential
cultural base—Eurocentric critics think that culture is a unified field.
French, English, German, Italian, Swiss, Danish, Dutch, Swedish, Russian,
and Spanish worldviews are, at their deepest levels, part of the same cultural
matrix: they all have the same mother, and that they are governed by members of the same extended family is but one mark of this profound sameness. But though these "cultures" are much alike, others are not of the same
configuration, springing in no way from a similar root.

That difference is understood by many who essay to critique literary artifacts, but most assume, wrongly, that the cultural matrix from which all
literature derives its meaning is the one described by French critics and
other Continental intellectuals. But, to paraphrase Alice Duer Miller, other
nations breed other women. Western minds have supposed (wrongly) for
some time that language is culture and that without a separate language a
culture is defunct. Thus some feminist critics search endlessly for women's
language and, failing to discover it, wax wroth. But maybe the idea that language defines ideational identity of a distinct sort is off the mark. Maybe—
as many writers have suggested—the use of a language and its syntax, structure, tropes, and conjunctions defines identity in its communitarian and
individual dimensions. In this rubric, the external system that a given work
points to and articulates and that renders the work significant takes on major importance.

The worlds of experience, knowledge, and understanding, to which the
works of women of color point and from which they derive, can clarify the
meaning of our texts. At this juncture the critic is faced with a difficult task:
the world embodied in Kingston's *Woman Warrior* is hardly the world that
gives rise to Morrison's *Song of Solomon*. It is of little use to study critical
works concerned with Erdrich's *Love Medicine* if one wishes to explore the
significance of Aurora L. Morales and Rosario Morales's *Getting Home
Alive*.

To be sure, it may seem that elements of Western literary practice are discernible in work by women of color. But the similarities are likely to be
more apparent than actual. The novel itself saw its earliest development in
Japan of the eleventh century in *The Tale of Genji* by Lady Murasaki
Shikibu. It did not appear in Europe until a few centuries later. Nor is poetry a genre confined to Western literature, though a certain shape has un-

folded in recent times that marks it as a modern vehicle. But these modern forms, whether in Middle Eastern, Far Eastern, Native American, African and African American, or Latina communities worldwide, can be shown to derive from preexisting poetic forms in those nations that go back hundreds, even thousands, of years.

Western literary thought is a strong feature of much of the academic criticism produced by scholars of color. The critics who address the work of women writers of color are tightly enmeshed in the training they received in Western-biased universities.

Women of color writing in the United States share the experiences of trivialization, invisibility, and supposed incomprehensibility, but these features characterize the treatment of the critic-less more than that of writers blessed with a critical network that addresses their work within an established critical context. Thus the work of African American women is far more likely to receive appropriate critical treatment than the works of Denise Chávez or Kim Ronyoung are. It seems evident that without a critical apparatus that enables a variety of literatures to be explored within their relevant contexts, the works of las disappearadas are doomed to obscurity. Yet, given the prevailing ethnocentric cultural climate, devising such a system and finding it applied by a great number of critics seems a hopeless task. And if we fail to locate a system that is not ethnically skewed toward the bourgeois male European, the use of which does not obviate the insatiable status needs of literary types who fear loss of promotion and recognition by that same ethnic establishment, separatism seems the only solution.

Nor is the issue simply one of reconstructing the canon or throwing out the concept of canon, literary quality, or aesthetic norms. The recent move toward excising the discussion of these fundamental dimensions of criticism, indeed of thought itself, is hardly a useful response to the conundrum, though one is hard put to imagine creative alternatives to the situation when stuck in Western modes of thought. Perhaps the best course is to begin anew, to examine the literary output of American writers of whatever stripe and derive critical principles based on what is actually being rendered by the true experts, the writers themselves. While we're at it, we might take a look at the real America that most of us inhabit—the one seldom approached by denizens of the hallowed (or is it the hollow?) groves of academe—so that we can discover what is being referenced beyond abstractions familiar to establishment types but foreign to those who live in real time. I am suggesting a critical system that is founded on the principle of inclusion rather than on that of exclusion, on actual human society and relationships rather than on textual relations alone, a system that is soundly based on aesthetics that pertain to the literatures we wish to examine.

A text exists in relation to other texts—particularly, as Gates has demonstrated, to mother texts, that is, the sacred stories that energize and shape human consciousness—rather than in splendid autocratic, narcissistic, and motherless isolation; as should be fairly obvious, texts are cultural artifacts and thus necessarily derive from, pertain to, and reveal oft hidden assumptions and values. Given that the experience of women as rendered in literature is a societally shaped and conditioned trope, how are we to accurately interpret or illuminate texts written by women of color? Do we see them as arising out of some sort of universalist "woman's world"? Do we look to the social world the writer and text inhabit to locate significance? Do we identify women writers of color in terms of their racial or cultural groups identified in terms of our Eurocentric ideologies? Because such categorizations tend to define colored writers—including those who are women—as "marginal" writers outside the boundaries of "real" literature and thus whose struggles and wishes are of interest only when they serve the goals and fit the preconceptions of those defining us, such an approach can only serve to oppress, distort, and silence. Should we step outside the boundaries placed on us by alien preconceptions of our lot, we are dismissed as crazy.

This is the problem posed by the work of social critics who subscribe to Karl Marx's dictate that the critical act exists as "the self-clarification of the struggles and wishes of the age" (Fraser, 253). Nancy Fraser comments that Marx's critical theory "frames its research in the light of contemporary social movements with which it has a partisan though not uncritical identification" (253). She fails to notice that such a narrowly prescriptive (and proscriptive) approach in its narrowness virtually excludes the reality of the voice, text, and human meaning in the work of Third World women. Even the very concept of aesthetics, such a social-movement approach insists, is politically taboo because it is hopelessly engaged in furtherance of the white male supremacist paradigm.

This view might well be valid—but the rendering of beauty as human artifact is hardly an activity exclusive to white males, Western patriarchs, or the bourgeois. In Anna Lee Walters's short story "The Warriors," Uncle Ralph, a homeless alcoholic Pawnee warrior of the old school, counsels his nieces: "For beauty is why we live, . . . [but] we die for it too" (12). In Navajoland, the concept of *hojo* ("it beautiful is moving") is central to the ideal of human life, while in the Pueblos we are instructed to "walk in beauty" (it goes this way, *ivani*). So far as I know, no human society is bereft of devotion to aesthetic principles, though Marxist, bureaucratic, and industrial societies come close.

But though our work draws up the moon from the creative void, signifying our cunning crafting, the critical works concerning our work remain stranded on the far shores of patriarchal positivism. In the world of the patriarchs everything is about politics; for much of the rest of the world, politics occupies little of any part of our preoccupations. Native Americans are entirely concerned with relations to and among the physical and nonphysical and various planetary energy-intelligences of numerous sorts. The idea of expending life force in oppression and resistance strikes most Indians, even today, as distinctly weird. Like Indians, Gnostics the world over, valuing multiplicity, personal experience, community, and simultaneous autonomy, avoid the schizoid dictates of canon-anticanon binary oppositional systems or fixed lists of what is "correct" thought, action, and insight, when the fixing is outside the realm of what is personally known.

For the most part, women of color write from a profound state of gnosis and personal experience, though we refine these in the crucible of community and relationship. But many major feminist critics wish our experience to be otherwise. They deterministically compel it into a mold of their own making, dismissing any work or experience that does not tell the tale they want told. Unhappily, far too many women of color fall into the honeyed trap; having been defined by strangers, many of us accept their definitions and write from the position they have marked out for us. All too unaware, we serve their aim and maintain their comfort—a righteous task for the maid.

In "Marginality and Subversion: Julia Kristeva," Toril Moi suggests that materiality is the point, marginality the key, and subversion the function of the invisibles. Moi praises Kristeva for her outlandishness, her willingness to go to the revolutionary heart of the matter, the mutter, but in extolling the rhetorical pose of the progressive Eurocentric intellectual, Moi reveals her Eurocentric and phallocentric bias. As Moi describes Kristeva's early works, Kristeva wanders hopelessly lost in the master's intellectual house of mirrors, asking and answering her own fantastic ghosts. And while the style of her meanderings is fetching, its self-negating entrancement with patriarchal paradigms is dangerous to writers from the deeps. No patriarch can tell us who we are, nor can any describe the worlds, inner and outer, that we inhabit. Freud, Marx, and Nietzsche—the triumvirate at whose altar Moi and the early Kristeva pay homage—can hardly provide models of intellectual competence that describe and illuminate colored women's works. What they can and do provide are the means whereby gynocosmic energies are bound up in patriarchal structures and thus rendered unusable to ourselves. This situation is well suited to the position of servant we thus occupy. From the confines thus established there is no loophole of retreat; indeed, there is no sense that anything should be retreated from or that there is anywhere to go beyond the servants' quarters.

Interestingly, as Kristeva moves toward consciousness based on some kind of connection to the real, as she goes from the absurdist position of comparing one body of words with another body of words with nary a whiff of human-experienced reality between, Moi rejects her, convinced that "the struggle" is all-important. While Moi admits that women's struggle is unique in its various dimensions and is not to be confused with class struggles, she remains wedded to the correct dialectic: we are only to be perceived and authorized when we cast ourselves as marginal, subversive, and dissident, which she characterizes as Kristeva's fundamental theory, though it is more Moi's than Kristeva's. Moi supports a criticism that furthers neopatriarchalism, though as she sees it neopatriarchalism includes feminist struggles carefully interpreted through the lens of the fathers Marx, Nietzsche, and Freud (Moi, 164).

To my Indian eyes it is plain that subversion cannot be the purpose or goal for women of color who write, though it likely is a side effect of our creating, our transforming, our rite. For to subvert, to turn under, is only the first step in the generation of something yet unborn; no, even less: it is the last step in the process of death. A truly beautiful clay pot from Acoma or San Juan Pueblo signifies on the emptiness it surrounds; Moi is accurate in her appreciation of Kristeva's unwillingness to dissect emptiness when the approach to somethingness will more than suffice. But what she fails to recognize is that the principles of self-determination and communitarian or autonomous creativity provide the true loophole of escape. Like Moi, one might very entertainingly mistake the menu for the meal and starve thereby, a mistake that for the most part shapes elite criticism and allied fields.

It is au courant to criticize, to interpret and analyze, as if no living processes occur—well enough for those who do not buy, earn, prepare, and serve the meal but who have servants and wives to deal with the tiresome mundanities of life. But our art is not, alas, privy to such alienation from human processes, and thus it must issue from the position of creativity rather than from that of reactivity. Subversion, dissidence, and acceptance of self as marginal are processes that maim our art and deflect us from our purpose. They are enterprises that support and maintain the master, feeding his household on our energy, our attention, and our strength.

In their introduction to *The Feminist Reader,* Catherine Belsey and Jane Moore characterize feminist readers as agents of change, asserting that "specific ways of reading inevitably militate for or against [that] process," thus situating the presumed problem of women squarely in the midst of the oppositional mode (1). Later, they comment:

> In poststructuralist theory meanings are cultural and learned. . . . They are in consequence a matter for political debate. Culture itself is the limit of our knowledge: there is no available truth outside culture with which we can challenge injustice. (10)

Odd that the concept of adversariness, deeply embedded in patriarchal structures of both the political and the literary kind, requires the aesthetic concerns of literary women to be defined in terms of the culture that oppresses and disappears us. Given that thought, one must say, with Audre Lorde, "The master's tools will never dismantle the master's house."

It is even more peculiar, albeit depressingly common among Western people, that Belsey and Moore cavalierly assume that culture is itself monolithic, worldwide, universal, and impermeable, echoing Irenaeus of eighteen hundred years ago. As a Native woman I am passionately aware that there are a number of available truths outside Eurocentric culture that enable us not only to challenge injustice but to live in a way that enhances the true justice of creating and nurturing life. And as a Native woman I must protest the arrogance of any critical assumption that human society is European in origin and that all power of whatever sort resides within it.

Artists of color can best do something other than engage in adversarial politics, knowing that since we did not cause patriarchy, we can neither control nor cure it. As recovering codependents of the abusive system under which too many have lived for far too long, we need to invest our energies in our vision, our significances, and our ways of signifyin'. We realize that we are something quote other than Anglo-European critics' definitions of us and that it is at our grave peril that we accept their culture-induced attributions rather than make, shape, and live within our own.

To be sure, women have, as actors, creators, and perceivers, been absented from patriarchal literature—but perhaps that is all to the good. Nor are persons of the female persuasion alone in that exclusion; we belong to a truly massive community of "strangers," one that includes virtually all literary artists on the planet for the past several thousand years. Perhaps, rather than bemoaning our "sorry state" as one of marginality, we might take another look at the actual situation; perhaps, in doing so, we will discover that neither "mainstream" nor "center" is where patriarchal sorts have claimed it to be. In all likelihood, we will discover readily enough that our very exclusion from the old boys' club works to our advantage: having never lived in the master's house, we can all the more enthusiastically build a far more suitable dwelling of our own.

When I was growing up I would often go to my mother with some mournful tale of injustice. My plaints were inevitably centered on what the perpetrator had done to me. Sometimes my tale was a wonder of intellectual intricacy. Sometimes it was little more than a virtuoso emotional performance. But my clear-eyed (and intensely aggravating) mother would listen a bit and then pronounce sentence: "Yes, but what were you doing?" Or "You just worry about you." Or "Go do something else, then. If you can't get along with them, go find something else to do."

In this way, she taught me something Native people have long known and American humorists have recently discovered: the way to liberation from oppression and injustice is to focus on one's own interest, creativity, concerns, and community. Perhaps we literary sorts can put the wisdom of the ancients to good use. It is no concern of ours what "they" say, write, think, or do. Our concern is what we are saying, writing, thinking, and doing. In short, we must "get a life!"

In contemporary feminist circles, a debate rages concerning language: whether men own it; whether it is a fixed, immutable force that is reality; or whether it is merely a process that signifies nothing but through which we are all entertained nonetheless. Some feminist critics debate whether we take our meaning and sense of self from language and in that process become phallocentric ourselves, or if there is a use of language that is, or can be, feminine. Some, like myself, think that language is itself neither male nor female; it is creatively expansive enough to be of use to those who have the wit and art to wrest from it their own significances. Even the dread patriarchs have not found a way to "own" language any more than they have found a way to "own" earth (though many seem to believe that both are possible). However, perusing feminist criticism, I re-realize that patriarchs do own *critical* language, and, sadly, far too many feminist critics sling it as though it had meaning beyond the walls of the literary boys' club.

A literary text can be characterized as a "loophole of retreat," the term Valerie Smith uses in her discussion of Harriet Jacobs's trope. "Jacobs' tale is not the classic story of the triumph of the individual will," she writes; "rather it is more a story of the triumphant self-in-relation" (217).

Self-in-relation, rather than the bildungsroman model of self-in-isolate-splendor that drives American civilization, is a primary characteristic of human cultures. I am aware that in the progressive evolution-as-fact paradigm, a main characteristic said to prove elite white male supremacy is precisely the individualistic hero metaphor. But although quite a few enterprises—literary and otherwise—are founded on the concept of individual superiority over relationship, individual heroics characterize but a small portion of literary work and represent an even smaller portion of art in general. As Smith writes:

> The loophole of retreat possesses an ambiguity of meaning that extends to the literal loophole as well. For if a loophole signifies for Jacobs a place of withdrawal, it signifies in common parlance an avenue of escape. Likewise, the garret . . . renders the narrator spiritually independent of her master, and makes possible her ultimate escape to freedom. (212)

In Smith's discussion we see another new critical direction emerging, like Jacobs, from the constriction of belief in ownership. No one can own the sublime and no one can confine the beautiful, the living, or the moving to the tiny regions too many critics reserve for Indians and other "marginalized" peoples. However, we who are seen as borderline writers can erect a criticism that speaks to the kind of spiritual independence Jacobs found in hiding, the kind that must lead to freedom from domination. We can do so by attending to the actual texts being created, their source, their source texts, the texts to which they stand in relation, and the otherness that they both embody and delineate.

The aesthetically profound story for Third World woman writers is necessarily concerned with human relationships: family, community, and that which transcends and underlies human meaning systems. Without benefit of Ifa and Esu, without possession of metatext, without presence of divine interpreter (that tricky familiar of the mysteries), reader and critic are doomed to read the same book over and over, regardless of who wrote it, why they did so, or the circumstances in which the work was embedded and from which it takes its meaning.

The concept in relation or, more "nativistically," the understanding that the individualized—as distinct from individualistic—sense of self accrues only within the context of community, which includes the nonvisible world of ancestors, spirits, and gods, provides a secure grounding for a criticism that can reach beyond the politicized, deterministic confines of progressive approaches, as well as beyond the neurotic diminishment of self-reflexiveness. To read women's texts with accuracy, we need a theory that places the twin concepts of I and thou securely within the interconnected matrix of all and everything, one that uses the presence of absence to define the manifest and that uses the manifest to locate and describe the invisible. When such a criticism is forged, the significance of the passive, the receptive, the absent, the dark, the void, and the power that inheres to it will be seen as central to the process of the construction of meaning and the reading of aesthetic texts. Like many women of color who write, Anzaldúa tells us of the habitation and the power of the unseen and its relation to the reality we inhabit. In so describing, she also suggests the direction a new criticism of inclusion can take:

> Where before there'd only been empty space
> She's always been there
> occupying the same room.
> It was only when I looked
> at the edges of things
> my eyes going wide watering,
> objects blurring.
> Where before there'd only been empty space
> I sensed layers and layers,
> felt the air in the room thicken.
> Behind my eyelids a white flash
> a thin noise.
> That's when I could see her. (148)

## References

Adnan, Etel. *The Indian Never Had a Horse and Other Poems.* Sausalito: Post Apollo, 1985.
———. *Sitt Marie-Rose.* Trans. Georgina Kleege. 2d ed. Sausalito: Post Apollo, 1989.
Allen, Paula Gunn. *The Sacred Hoop: Recovering the Feminine in American Indian Traditions.* Boston: Beacon, 1986.
———, ed. *Spider Woman's Granddaughters: Traditional Tales and Contemporary Writing by Native American Women.* Boston: Beacon, 1989.
———. *The Women Who Owned the Shadows.* San Francisco: Spinsters, 1983.
Anzaldúa, Gloria. *Borderlands/La Frontera: The New Mestiza.* San Francisco: Spinsters-Aunt Lute, 1987.
———. "Interface." In Anzaldúa, *Borderlands,* 148–52.
Baigent, Michael, Richard Leigh, and Henry Lincoln. *Holy Blood, Holy Grail.* New York: Dell, 1982.
Bambara, Toni Cade. *The Salt Eaters.* New York: Random House, 1980.
Belsey, Catherine, and Jane Moore. *The Feminist Reader.* New York: Blackwell, 1989.
Candelaria, Cordelia. *Chicano Poetry: A Critical Introduction.* Westport, Conn.: Greenwood, 1986.
Castillo, Ana. *The Mixquiahuala Letters.* Binghamton, N.Y.: Bilingual Press, 1986.
———. *Women Are Not Roses.* Houston: Arte Público, 1984.

Cha, Theresa. *Dictée*. New York: Tanam, 1982.

Chávez, Denise. *The Last of the Menu Girls*. Houston: Arte Público, 1984.

Cheung, King-Kok. *Articulate Silences: Double-Voiced Discourse in Hisaye Yamamoto, Maxine Hong Kingston, and Joy Kogawa*. Ithaca, N.Y.: Cornell University Press, 1994.

Christian, Barbara. *Black Feminist Criticism: Perspectives on Black Women Writers*. New York: Pergamon, 1985.

———. *Black Women Novelists: The Development of a Tradition, 1892–1976*. Westport, Conn.: Greenwood, 1980.

Cisneros, Sandra. *The House on Mango Street*. Houston: Arte Público, 1983.

Dickinson, Emily. *Complete Poems*. Ed. Thomas H. Johnson. Boston: Little, Brown, 1960.

Erdrich, Louise. *The Beet Queen*. New York: Holt, Rinehart and Winston, 1986.

———. *Love Medicine*. New York: Holt, Rinehart and Winston, 1984.

———. *Tracks*. New York: Holt, Rinehart and Winston, 1988.

Fraser, Nancy. "What's Critical about Critical Theory? The Case of Habermas and Gender." In *Feminist Interpretations and Political Theory*, ed. Mary Lyndon Shanley and Carole Pateman. University Park: Pennsylvania State University Press, 1991. 253–76.

Gates, Henry Louis, Jr., ed. *Reading Black, Reading Feminist: A Critical Anthology*. New York: Meridian, 1990.

———. *The Signifying Monkey: A Theory of African-American Literary Criticism*. New York: Oxford University Press, 1988.

Hagedorn, Jessica. *Dogeaters*. New York: Random House, 1990.

Harper, Frances E. *Iola LeRoy*. 1892. Boston: Beacon, 1987.

Herrera-Sobek, Maria, ed. *Beyond Stereotypes: The Critical Analysis of Chicana Literature*. Binghamton, N.Y.: Bilingual Press, 1985.

Horno-Delgado, Asunción, ed. *Breaking Boundaries: Latina Writings and Critical Readings*. Amherst: University of Massachusetts Press, 1989.

Hurston, Zora Neale. *I Love Myself When I Am Laughing . . . : A Zora Neale Hurston Reader*. Ed. Alice Walker. Old Westbury, N.Y.: Feminist Press, 1979.

———. *Their Eyes Were Watching God*. 1937. Urbana: University of Illinois Press, 1978.

Jones, Gayl. *Corregidora*. 1975. Boston: Beacon, 1986.

Kadohata, Cynthia. *The Floating World*. New York: Viking, 1989.

Kim, Elaine. *Asian American Literature: An Introduction to the Writings and Their Social Contexts*. Philadelphia: Temple University Press, 1982.

Kincaid, Jamaica. *Annie John*. New York: Farrar, Straus & Giroux, 1985.

———. *At the Bottom of the River*. New York: Farrar, Straus & Giroux, 1983.

Kingston, Maxine Hong. *The Woman Warrior: Memoirs of a Girlhood among Ghosts*. New York: Knopf, 1976.

Lauter, Paul, et al., eds. *The Heath Anthology of American Literature*. 2 vols. New York: Heath, 1990.

Law-Yone, Wendy. *The Coffin Tree*. New York: Knopf, 1987.

Lincoln, Kenneth. *Ind'in Humor*. New York: Oxford University Press, 1993.

———. *Native American Renaissance*. 2d ed. Berkeley: University of California Press, 1985.

Lorde, Audre. "The Master's Tools Will Never Dismantle the Master's House." In Moraga and Anzaldúa, 98–101.

Marshall, Paule. *Browngirl, Brownstones*. 1959. Old Westbury: Feminist Press, 1981.

———. *The Chosen Place, the Timeless People*. 1969. New York: Random House, 1984.

Minh-ha, Trinh T. *Woman, Native, Other: Writing Postcoloniality and Feminism*. Bloomington: Indiana University Press, 1989.

Mohr, Nicholasa. *Nilda*. 2d ed. Houston: Arte Público, 1986.

Moi, Toril. "Marginality and Subversion: Julia Kristeva." In *Sexual/Textual Politics*. New York: Routledge, 1985. 159–73.

Moraga, Cherríe, and Gloria Anzaldúa, eds. *This Bridge Called My Back: Writings by Radical Women of Color*. Watertown, Mass.: Persephone, 1981.

Morales, Aurora L., and Rosario Morales. *Getting Home Alive*. Ithaca, N.Y.: Firebrand, 1986.

Morrison, Toni. *Beloved*. New York: Knopf, 1987.

———. *The Bluest Eye*. 1970. New York: Washington Square, 1972.

———. *Song of Solomon*. 1977. New York: Signet, 1988.

———. *Sula*. 1973. New York: NAL, 1987.

Mourning Dove [Christine Quintasket]. *Cogewea, The Half Blood*. Lincoln: University of Nebraska Press, 1981.

Mukherjee, Bharati. *Jasmine*. New York: Grove, 1989.

Naylor, Gloria. *The Women of Brewster Place*. New York: Viking, 1982.

Pineda, Cecile. *Face*. New York: Viking, 1985.

Ronyoung, Kim. *Clay Walls*. Seattle: University of Washington Press, 1987.

Ruoff, A. LaVonne Brown, and Jerry W. Ward Jr., eds. *Redefining American Literary History*. New York: Modern Language Association, 1990.

Sears, Vickie L. *Simple Songs*. Ithaca, N.Y.: Firebrand, 1990.

Silko, Leslie Marmon. *Ceremony*. New York: Viking, 1977.

———. *Storyteller*. New York: Seaver Press, 1981.

Smith, Valerie. "Loopholes of Retreat: Architecture and Ideology in Harriet Jacobs' *Incidents in the Life of a Slave Girl*." In Gates, *Reading Black*, 212–26.

Spillers, Hortense J. "'In Order of Constancy': Notes on Brooks and the Feminine." In Gates, *Reading Black*, 244–71.

Suleri, Sara. *Meatless Days*. Chicago: University of Chicago Press, 1989.

Tan, Amy. *The Joy Luck Club*. New York: Putnam, 1989.

Villanueva, Alma. *Bloodroot*. Austin: Place of Herons, 1977.

Viramontes, Helen Maria. *The Moths and Other Stories*. Houston: Arte Público, 1986.

Walker, Alice. *The Color Purple*. New York: Harcourt Brace Jovanovich, 1982.

———. *Meridian*. 1976. New York: Pocket Books, 1988.

———. *The Temple of My Familiar*. New York: Harcourt Brace Jovanovich, 1989.

Walters, Anna Lee. *Ghost Singer*. Flagstaff, Ariz.: Northland, 1988.

———. *The Sun Is Not Merciful*. Ithaca, N.Y.: Firebrand, 1985.

———. "The Warriors." In Walters, *Sun*, 11–26.

Williams, Sherley Anne. *Dessa Rose*. New York: William Morrow, 1986.

Yamamoto, Hisaye. *Seventeen Syllables and Other Stories*. Latham: Kitchen Table, 1989.

Yamashita, Karen. *Through the Arch of the Rain Forest*. Minneapolis: Coffee House, 1990.

~

# Canon, Institutionalization, Identity

## Contradictions for Asian American Studies

### LISA LOWE

In our headlong rush to educate everybody, we are . . . destroying our ancient edifices to make ready the ground upon which the barbarian nomads
of the future will encamp in their mechanised caravans.
—T. S. Eliot, *Notes towards a Definition of Culture* (1949)

Mrs. Hammerick . . . Boiling Spring Elementary School . . . I was scared of
her like no dark corners could ever scare me. You have to know that all the
while she was teaching us history . . . she was telling all the boys in our class
that I was Pearl and my last name was Harbor. They understood her like she
was speaking French and their names were all Claude and Pierre. I felt it in
the lower half of my stomach, and it throbbed and throbbed. . . .
—Monique Thuy-Dung Truong, "Kelly," *Amerasia Journal* (1991)

Approaching the question of Asian American Studies, I pose T. S. Eliot's
1949 lament that democratized education places the "ancient edifice" of
Western culture at risk from the encroachments of non-Western cultures
and the mass culture of industrialized society ("barbarian nomads in their
mechanised caravans") against the classroom evoked in Monique Thuy-
Dung Truong's 1991 Vietnamese American short story "Kelly" in order to
ground my discussion in two fundamental relationships. First, the juxtapo-
sition of Eliot and Truong renders explicit a relationship between the culturalist narrative that valorizes Western culture as a separate sphere and the
materially, racially, and sexually differentiated society which that notion of

autonomous culture is constructed against, and whose contradictions it works to conceal. Second, I hope it may reinscribe a connection between the developmental narrative that privileges the elite subject of a "prior" Western civilization and the voiceless invisibility imposed upon students of color in the classroom produced by that narrative. My essay explores the question of Asian American literature as an expression of the contradictions implied by these two relationships and considers the importance of Asian American Studies, as one form of interdisciplinary cultural studies, as an oppositional site from which to contest the educational apparatus that reproduces, and continues to be organized by, both the culturalist and the developmental narratives. Elsewhere I have interrogated the production of ethnic identity by dominant institutions and within the discourse of Asian American cultural politics, and suggested that there are important contradictions between a cultural nationalist construction of identity and the different registers of Asian American heterogeneity (particularly class, gender, and national origin differences among Asians in the United States).[1] In this present discussion, I wish to continue this critical engagement with the notion of identity by focusing especially on questions of the literary canon, pedagogy, and the formation of the subject.

We need not look far to find residues of Eliot's distress over Western cultural "disintegration" within contemporary American discourse about education; William Bennett, Lynne Cheney, Allan Bloom, Dinesh D'Souza, and others have all contributed to this concerted lament. Yet it is evident that these attempts to maintain a fixed, autonomous notion of Western culture belie precisely the material strata and social differentiations for which this notion has traditionally functioned as a resolution; as Mas'ud Zavarzadeh and Donald Morton have pointed out, the rise of modern humanities in the eighteenth century and their institutionalization in the nineteenth century were themselves directly related to the rise of the Western bourgeoisie, who won its battle with the old aristocracy by redefining the liberal subject in the context of competition by free agents in the marketplace.[2] In the last half of the twentieth century in the United States, industrialized society's need for a trained yet stratified labor force, the civil rights movement, as well as demographic increases in racial, ethnic, and immigrant populations, have made it all the more difficult for contemporary discourse about education, both liberal and neoconservative, to ignore, as Eliot's nostalgia for "a more articulated society" did, the mandate for the democratization and diversification of the modern educational apparatus. In this sense, the neoconservative educational agenda, as Henry Giroux and Peter McClaren have ob-

served, operates through two platforms: on the one hand, through the advocacy of "cultural unification" demanding a recanonization of Western
classics, and on the other, through an expansion (at the expense of humanities or social science research) of a technicist or vocationalist curriculum
that blames the demise of U.S. economic hegemony on the failure of education to adequately train competitive professional and technical classes.[3]
The liberal discourse on education has challenged this reformulation of
unified Western culture by advocating a diversification of the humanities
curriculum and urging an integration of the university through student
and faculty affirmative action. Yet to the degree that liberal challenges have
remained wedded to a culturalist paradigm (however "multiculturalist")
that tends still to isolate culture from material relations, they have yet to adequately disrupt the neoconservative management of the function of university education. The university continues to be organized by means of a
bifurcated conception that protects Western cultural study as a largely autonomous domain while "democratizing" the institution only to the extent
that it addresses the needs of an increasingly heterogeneous student population through the development of business, engineering, technical, and
other professionalizing programs. The result is a contradiction in which
"culture" remains canonical in the traditional Western European sense
while the educational system (claiming a "multicultural" conscience) serves
to socialize and incorporate students from other backgrounds into the capitalist market economy. In Martin Carnoy's analysis, the contradiction that
brings new social groups into the educational system for vocationalization
while continuing to universalize a closed, autonomous notion of culture
precisely implies "an exploitable political space for those that are willing to
engage in the struggle for change."[4]

In contemporary universities, this contradiction is visibly animated in
the emergence of interdisciplinary fields such as Ethnic Studies, Women's
Studies, Third World Studies, and Cultural Studies. Interdisciplinary studies express contradiction—or, in Carnoy's phrase, "exploitable political
space"—to the degree that they provide the sites from which to reevaluate
disciplinary methods that assume modern Western cultural autonomy and
the universality of the Western subject. Interdisciplinary studies disrupt the
narratives of traditional disciplines that have historically subordinated the
concerns of non-Western, racial and ethnic minority peoples, and women,
to the degree that they hold the potential to transform disciplinary divisions that guarantee the self-evidence of these narratives. In Women's Studies, for example, work by and about women of color—for example, the very

different theoretical work of Norma Alarcón, Kimberle Crenshaw, Trinh T. Minh-ha, or Evelyn Nakano Glenn[5]—illustrates this interdisciplinarity to the degree that this work makes use of a varied constellation of critical apparatuses that refuses univocality, totalization, and scholarly indifference; this work redefines the traditional separations of subject and object; it persistently argues for the inseparability of the nonequivalent determinations of race, class, and gender. However, to the extent that the institution pressures interdisciplinary studies to formalize and legitimate themselves in terms of established criteria, interdisciplinary programs and departments have needed to be vigilant in relation to institutionalization.

In this sense, Ethnic Studies scholars do not reproduce methods of literary or historical studies in order to merely celebrate "ethnic culture" as an object separated from the material conditions of production and reception; they theorize, in a critical, dialectical manner, the relationship between cultural artifacts and the social groupings by which they are produced and which they, in turn, help to produce.[6] At the same time, institutionalizing fields like Ethnic Studies still contains an inevitable paradox: on the one hand, institutionalization provides a material base within the university for a transformative critique of traditional disciplines and their traditional separations; yet, on the other hand, the institutionalization of any field or curriculum that establishes orthodox objects and methods submits in part to the demands of the university and its educative function of socializing subjects into the state. Although instititutionalizing interdisciplinary study risks integrating it into a system that threatens to appropriate what is most critical and oppositional about that study, the logic through which the university incorporates areas of interdisciplinarity simultaneously provides for the possibility that these sites will remain oppositional forums, productively antagonistic to notions of autonomous culture and disciplinary regulation, and to the interpellation of students as univocal subjects. In terms of Asian American Studies, the way in which we approach questions of reading texts, constituting objects of study, and teaching students can determine the extent to which Ethnic Studies serves the traditional function of the university, and the extent to which it provides for a continuing and persistent site from which to educate students to be actively critical of that traditional function.

One manner by which Asian American Studies' interdisciplinarity and self-determination may be incorporated into the university is through a particular deployment of a brand of "multiculturalism," which must be clearly distinguished from panethnic and panracial coalitions of students and faculty that demand further transformations of the university.[7] Exploiting the notion of "multiculturalism," the university can refer to the study of ethnic cultures in its claim to be an institution to which all racial and ethnic minority groups have equal access and in which all are represented, while masking the degree to which the larger institution still fails to address the needs of populations of color. For example, though many universities have begun to reappraise their curricula in the humanities, adding texts by non-Western or female authors to Western civilization courses, there are fewer Black students attending college today than in 1975. A multiculturalist agenda may thematize the pressures that demographic increases of immigrant, racial, and ethnic populations bring to the educational sphere, but these pressures are registered only partially and inadequately when the studies of ethnic traditions are, on an intellectual level, assimilated as analogues of Western European traditions or exoticized as primitive and less "developed," and, on an institutional level, tokenized as examples of the university's commitment to "diversity" while being marginalized through underfunding. Such pluralist multiculturalism may be, for the contemporary period, a central arena for what Gramsci called "hegemony," the process by which a ruling group gains "consent" of its constituents to determine the cultural, ideological, and political character of a state. The terrain of multiculturalism is marked by the incorporative process by which a ruling group elicits the "consent" of racial, ethnic, or class minority groups through the promise of equal participation and representation; but to the extent that multiculturalism—as a discourse designed to recuperate conflict and difference through inclusion—is itself the index of crisis in a specific dominant formation, the terrain of multiculturalism also provides for the activities of racial, class, and sexual minority groups who organize and contest that domination. Within this context, we can appreciate the evident importance of self-determined "subaltern" interventions by groups that both distinguish themselves from liberal multiculturalism and do not exclusively reproduce pluralist arguments of inclusion and rights.[8]

The establishment of a canon of Asian American literature is one part of a project of institutional change within which ethnic Americans as social subjects articulate an educational space within the university and constitute literary objects as expressions of a distinct, self-determining ethnic culture, and through which the notion of the "subject" interpellated by the university is altered and revised in light of the heterogeneous social formations of racial, ethnic, and immigrant minority subjects. Yet, paradoxically, according to the contradiction that I have just outlined, the definition of an ethnic literature, figured by an ethnic canon, may compromise the critical project of institutional change if it is forced to subscribe to criteria defined by the majority canon in order to establish the formal unity of a literary tradition; for it is precisely the standard of a literary canon that the Eurocentric and professionalizing university demands of Asian Americans and other racial and ethnic minority cultures so as to formalize those cultures as "developed" traditions. In drawing a distinction between "major" and "minor" literatures, David Lloyd has argued that the Anglo-European function of canonization is to unify aesthetic culture as a domain in which material stratifications and differences are reconciled. A "major" literary canon traditionally performs that reconciliation by means of a selection of works that uphold a narrative of ethical formation in which the individual relinquishes particular differences through an identification with a universalized form of subjectivity; a "minor" literature may conform to the criteria of the "major" canon, or it may interrupt the function of reconciliation by challenging the concepts of identity and identification and by voicing antagonisms to the universalizing narrative of development.[9]

In response to the demand that Asian American literature function as a supplement or corollary to the "major" tradition of Anglo-American literature, Asian American literary texts often reveal heterogeneity rather than producing regulating ideas of cultural unity or integration. On one level, this heterogeneity is expressed in the unfixed, unclosed field of texts written by authors at different distances and generations from the "original" Asian culture—cultures as different as Chinese, Japanese, Korean, Philippine, Indian, Vietnamese, Lao—or, as in the case of Hawaiian and Pacific Islander cultures, who are not *immigrants* at all, but colonized, dispossessed, deracinated.[10] The Asian American constituency is composed of men and women of exclusively Asian parents and of mixed race, refugee and nonrefugee, English and non-English-speaking, of urban, rural, and different class backgrounds, heterosexual as well as gay and lesbian. For this reason, even when anthologies have selected literary works to represent the tradition (e.g., *Aiiieeeee!: An Anthology of Asian-American Writers* [1975], or the more recent *Forbidden Stitch: An Asian American Women's Anthology* [1989], and *Between Worlds: Contemporary Asian American Plays* [1990], editors have clearly defined their works as products of particular moments of Asian American cultural definition and thematized the possibility of shifts, revisions, and different formations in order to account for the heterogeneous and uneven development of the various groups that make up the Asian

American community.[11] For example, Tsutakawa warns that "no one should think of [*The Forbidden Stitch*] as the single definitive text. . . . this is not a book with a shelf life of forever" (14). On another level, Asian American literature expresses heterogeneity not merely in the constituency it is construed to "represent" but in the manners by which it puts into relief the material conditions of production. Indeed, the study of Asian American literature has been historically an endeavor committed to a consideration of the work in terms of its material contexts of production and reception. For this reason, Elaine Kim's immeasurably important first critical study, *Asian American Literature: An Introduction to the Writings and Their Social Context* (1982), emphasizes "how the literature elucidates the social history of Asians in the United States" rather than exclusively focusing on its "formal literary merit."[12] Kim makes clear that her decision to interrogate Asian American literature as an expression of social context is not because of the literature's lack of stylistic or rhetorical complexity but rather the way in which the literature itself captures a "movement between social history and literature." Asian American literature *resists* the formal abstraction of aestheticization and canonization. If we evaluate Asian American literary expression in canonical terms, it reveals itself as an aesthetic product that cannot repress the material inequalities of its conditions of production; its aesthetic is not defined by sublimation but rather by contradiction, such that discontent, nonequivalence, and irresolution call into question the project of abstracting the aesthetic as a separate domain of unification and reconciliation. It is a literature that, if subjected to a canonical function, dialectically returns a critique of that function.

In this sense, just as the conception of an Asian American canon animates a contradiction between an institutional demand for assimilation to major criteria and the inassimilable alterity of ethnic differences, so too do Asian American works themselves precisely underscore the tension between unifying cultural narratives and heterogeneous, intersecting formations of ethnic immigrant subjects that are antagonistic to those narratives. Considering one of the core works of Asian American literature, for example, Carlos Bulosan's *America Is in the Heart* (1943), we observe that on one level the novel may be read as an Asian-American version of the form of the bildungsroman, or novel of formation, to the degree that it narrates the protagonist's development from the uncertainty, locality, and impotence of "youth" to the definition, mobility, and potency of "maturity." At the same time, to the degree that the narrative captures the complex, unsynthetic constitution of the immigrant subject between an already twice-

colonized Philippine culture on the one hand, and the pressure to conform
to Anglo-American society on the other, it troubles the closure and reconciliation of the bildungsroman form. If the novel is read as either a narrative of immigrant assimilation or even as a narrative of successful self-definition (the hero leaves the poverty and lack of opportunity of the
Philippines to become a laborer in the United States; he achieves a state of
self-consciousness that allows him to become a journalist and to author his
autobiography), both characterizations privilege a telos of development
that closes off the most interesting conflicts and indeterminacies in the
text. In addition, reading the novel as an analogue of the European novel
subordinates Asian American culture in several significant ways: not only
does the form itself structurally imply an integration and submission of individual particularity to a universalized social norm (which, in the case of
the Asian American novel, is racial or ethnic difference coded as anterior to,
less than, Western civilization), but in privileging a nineteenth-century European genre as the model to be approximated, Asian American literature is
cast as imitation, mimicry, the underdeveloped Other. For these reasons, we
attend instead to the ways in which a novel like *America Is in the Heart* does
not comply with the notion of a unified aesthetic form, and how the concepts of development, synthesis, and identity are themselves challenged in
the text. Taught as an ethnic bildungsroman, as a tale of the subject's journey from foreign estrangement to integrated citizenship, the novel responds to the reconciliatory and universalizing functions of canonization;
taught with attention to social and historical, as well as formal and thematic, contradictions, the novel may eloquently thematize how the demand
for canonization simultaneously produces a critique of canonization itself.

Bulosan's novel portrays its hero as highly seduced by the notion of individual freedom through education. The narrative that begins in the Philippines, where the hero's family sacrifices greatly to send its oldest son
Macario to school, figures both English literacy and American education
as paths to freedom and self-development, particularly in the myths of
Robinson Crusoe and Abraham Lincoln. However, once in the United
States, the hero, Carlos, does not have access to formal schooling and is
forced to teach himself; that he creates his own curriculum out of the fragments of books and resources available to him reveals the disjunction between the promise of education and the unequal access of different racial
and economic groups to that education. From the outset, the protagonist's
literary education is a disrupted, partial, and fragmentary one. Moreover,
his "education" is equally informed by his observations of the exploitation,

violence, marginality, and incarcerations suffered by Philippine immigrants to the United States, which further challenge his belief in the promise of American democracy. This is explicitly thematized when the narrator
ponders the paradox of America: "Why was America so kind and yet so
cruel? Was there no way to simplify things in this continent so that suffering would be minimized? Was there no common denominator on which we
could all meet? I was angry and confused and wondered if I would ever understand this paradox."[13] When he suggests that there is a "common denominator on which we could all meet," the narrator poses his questions
within the adopted language of democratic pluralism, a language that pro-
nounces a faith in the promise of equal opportunity and inclusion. However, it is precisely this notion of common denominator that the narrator
comes to understand as contradictory and riddled with exceptions, strata,
and exclusions when he later quotes his brother Macario at length:

> America is a prophecy of a new society of men: of a system that knows no
> sorrow or strife or suffering. . . . America is also the nameless foreigner, the
> homeless refugee, the hungry boy begging for a job and the black body dan-
> gling on a tree. America is the illiterate immigrant who is ashamed that the
> world of books and intellectual opportunties is closed to him. We are all
> that nameless foreigner, that homeless refugee, that hungry boy, that illiter-
> ate immigrant and that lynched black body. All of us, from the first Adams
> to the last Filipino, native born or alien, educated or illiterate—We are
> America! (188–89)

In this later meditation, two starkly different visions of "America" are posed
against one another—the national fiction of democratic nation-state without sorrow or suffering, and a nation in which members of that national
body barely survive owing to exclusion from that nation-state. The "America" that is "in the heart" is a stratified, contradictory figure divided between
the named promise of democracy and the unnamed refugees, immigrants,
and victims of violence who live beneath that promise. In this sense, the
proclamation "We are America!" does not represent an identification of the
immigrant subject with the national fiction of inclusion but rather contests
that identification by inserting a heterogeneous "we"—"that nameless foreigner, that homeless refugee, that hungry boy, that illiterate immigrant and
that lynched black body"—into the concept of polity; this insertion introduces antinomy into the promise of synthesis, displaces unity with antagonism, and renders visible the political differentiation and disenfranchisement prematurely resolved by a fiction of reconciliation. The narrative of
America Is in the Heart is punctuated throughout by the continual migration of Filipino work crews, moving from job to job up and down the west-

ern United States, and the novel closes with a description of the narrator departing again with another crew en route to Portland. From the window of the bus he observes a group of workers in the fields: "I wanted to shout good-by to the Filipino pea pickers. . . . How many times in the past had I done just that?" (326). The novel ends with the repetition of yet another departure and relocation, framed as symptomatic of a continuing inequality between powerful agribusiness capital and immigrant labor, rather than with settlement, permanence, or resolution. It is an uneven, divided notion of America that concludes the novel, rather than a naturalized unification of those unevennesses and divisions. In this sense, *America Is in the Heart* does not "develop" the narrating subject's identification with a uniform American nation; rather, the achievement of narrative voice is precisely the effect of the subject's critical estrangement from, and dissymmetrical relationship to, American culturalist, economic, and nationalist formations.

The manner in which Asian American literature refuses the premature reconciliation of Asian immigrant particularity is also illustrated in a consideration of a variety of novels portraying the internment and relocation of first- and second-generation Japanese in the United States and Canada during World War II. Monica Sone's *Nisei Daughter* (1953), John Okada's *No-No Boy* (1957), and Joy Kogawa's *Obasan* (1982) represent different narrative treatments of the nisei during and following the internment, who were forced either to identify with the Japanese state and be named enemies of the United States and Canada or to assimilate unquestioningly into American or Canadian culture and repudiate any Japanese cultural affiliation. This impossibly binary demand, encountered in different ways by the Japanese North Americans in all three novels, is not dissimilar to the predicament of many racial and ethnic minority peoples who face disenfranchisement unless they abandon their particular cultures to assimilate as citizens of a common culture; yet for Japanese American and Japanese Canadian men and women this process was coercively enforced through physical detention in the camps, and in addition, for nisei men, through the demand that they prove their patriotism by enlisting in the armed services to fight against Japan. In portraying the effects of the internment on the nisei subject, none of the novels delivers an undivided, assimilated subject who comes to identify with the American or Canadian citizenry; all three narratives refuse, in different ways, to develop, reconcile, and resolve.

Of the three novels, Sone's *Nisei Daughter* is formally the most conventional—a semiautobiographical first-person narrative that proceeds linearly from a girlhood in the Seattle Japanese community through and beyond the events of the internment—and ends by pronouncing that "the Japanese and American parts of me were now blended into one."[14] However, owing to *Nisei Daughter*'s depiction of anti-Japanese racism, employment segregations, immigration restrictions, and ultimately the internment, the blending of "Japanese" and "American" is not conceived of except in terms of the larger structure of unequal power within which Japanese Americans are subordinated by the U.S. government. Throughout the novel, many scenes dramatize the nonequivalent force of Japanese and American cultures on the nisei, and this nonequivalence contextualizes the final statement of "blending" as a rhetorical response to the demand that the nisei resolve their identity by assimilating as American citizens; considering the larger narrative, we can read for the "false ring" of the ending, and call its premature resolution into question. Although the nisei child rebels against the normalizing expectations of both Japanese and American socializations, the Japanese customs are encouraged by parents and family friends, whereas the representative agents of American ways are armed policemen who, in one episode, storm into the Itoi home to arrest Kazuko's father on false charges of which he is later cleared. Thus, midway through the novel when the Itoi family is interned, this nonequivalence becomes even more explicit, and the narrative turns into a concerted critique of the suppression of Japanese and Japanese Americans by the U.S. government. After a family friend has been abducted by the FBI, the Itois are warned that they must destroy everything and anything Japanese that may incriminate them, yet Kazuko cannot bring herself to destroy all the Japanese items in their home:

> I gathered together my well-worn Japanese language schoolbooks which I had been saving over a period of ten years with the thought that they might come in handy when I wanted to teach Japanese to my own children. I threw them into the fire and watched them flame and shrivel into black ashes. But when I came face to face with my Japanese doll which Grandmother Nagashima had sent me from Japan, I rebelled. (155)

The destruction of Japanese language books described in this passage emblematizes the ways in which Japanese Americans were forced to internalize the negation of Japanese culture, and to assimilate into Anglo-American majority culture during World War II. Kazuko's refusal to destroy all Japanese items is reiterated at other moments in the novel in which she expresses defiant anger at the treatment of the Japanese—for example, in the rage she feels while looking at the barrel of the soldier's gun pointed toward internees boarding a bus (170). These moments, which underscore the subordination of Japanese Americans to the American state, render the final "blending" of two equal parts a provisional response to both social and canonical demands for resolution. Rather than a final synthesis that denies the damage of the internment, or reconciles the Japanese American subject divided by the "enemy/not enemy" logic of the state, we can read the declaration of Japanese and American "blending" as a manner of naming a continuing project of suspicion and survival as the nisei subject narrates the violence of a system that demands assimilation through internment, obligatory patriotism, and military service.

The suspicion beneath the premature reconciliation of *Nisei Daughter* is thrown even further into relief when Sone's text is considered in conjunction with Okada's *No-No Boy*, a novel of discontent in which the Japanese American protagonist angrily refuses adjustment to his postinternment and postimprisonment circumstances, and Kogawa's *Obasan*, a weave of personal, familial, and historical memory whose formal modernism suggests the recomposition of fragments, rather than a unified development, as the narrative expression of the relocated Japanese Canadian subject.[15] Virtually ignored when it was published in 1957, and rejected for its uncompromisingly unconventional style, Okada's *No-No Boy* was reissued in 1976 after an excerpt from it was featured in the anthology *Aiiieeeee! No-No Boy* may be characterized as a realist narrative to the extent that its action proceeds chronologically; but it is *antidevelopmental* in the sense that its condensed, almost static portrait takes place within a small period of several weeks, and it repeatedly undermines uniperspectivalism by alternating inconsistently between a third-person omniscient narration and despairing, angry, or confused interior monologues. The narrative shifts back and forth between different voices within long, run-on sentences, conveying the confusion and entropy of the protagonist Ichiro upon his return to Seattle after two years of internment and two subsequent years in prison for refusing to serve in the U.S. Army, and documents his bitter confusion, isolation, and shame as he confronts nisei soldiers and veterans, nisei women, white Americans, his parents and other Japanese issei. Ichiro is a deeply divided subject, antagonistic to both the American government that interned and imprisoned Japanese Americans and to Japanese patriots like his mother who feverishly deny Japan's defeat in the war; in effect, the "no-no boy" not only refuses loyalty to either Japan or the United States but he refuses the "enemy/not enemy" logic of the choice itself. Just as Ichiro's "no" dramatizes the Asian American subject's refusal to accept the dividing, subordinating terms of assimilation, so the novel's stasis, fragmentation, and discontent refuse the development, synthesis, and reconciliation required by traditional canonical criteria.

Formally more complex than either *Nisei Daughter* or *No-No Boy,* Kogawa's *Obasan* makes use of different narrative and dramatic techniques to portray the splitting, silencing, and irresolution of the Japanese Canadian subject. The novel's opening places the narrator in 1972, three decades after the internment and relocation of the Japanese Canadians; the text weaves back and forth between different time periods, making use of private memory, dreams, diaries, letters, and documented history in order to dramatize the narrator's project of reconstructing the events that led to the loss of her mother, father, and grandparents, and the fragmented dispersal of other family and community during the relocation and internment years. Yet the task of recomposing history out of silence and fragmentation require the narrator to first recount her childhood sexual abuse by a neighbor, which has become conflated with the confiscation of property and the dislocation of internment, as well as the separation from her mother, who left for Japan the same year. Throughout the course of the novel, she must reach back to confront and bear the deaths of her uncle, father, grandfather, and grandmother, and ultimately to piece together the details of her mother's anguished suffering in the atomic bombing of Nagasaki. The violences to the narrator and her family, figured throughout *Obasan* in metaphors of abuse, silence, darkness, and disease, cannot be lightened or healed; they can only be revealed, narrated, and reconfigured.[16] Out of the subject's fragmentation there emerges not a unified wholeness, but a recomposed fragmentation. In this sense, all three novels are antagonistic to the reconciliation of Asian American particularity within a narrative of development, as much as the formal differences among the three works further signify the discontinuous, heterogeneous range of Asian American representations.

Other Asian American texts disrupt even more dramatically the narrative that incorporates the immigrant subject into a national or cultural uniformity. For example, Theresa Hak Kyung Cha's *Dictée* (1982) is a Korean American text that refuses to provide either a linear, unified development of the writing subject or an aesthetic synthesis or ethical resolution at the text's conclusion.[17] In combining autobiographical and biographical fragments, photographs, historical narrative, calligraphy, and lyric and prose poems in a complex multilingual piece, *Dictée* blurs conventions of genre and narrative authority, troubling the formal categories upon which canonization depends. Furthermore, *Dictée* challenges the notion of a discrete typology of

"Asian American experience," for it evokes a Korean American subject who is not only the product of multiple determinations—gender, language, religion—but who bears the traces of differentiated layers of colonial and imperial dominations as well. The text juxtaposes a series of disparate episodes that alternately depict subjects incompletely formed within specific linguistic and historical circumstances. For example, the first section thematizes the use of dictation and recitation in the conversion of the student into a faithful French Catholic subject; the section "Clio" alludes to the disciplining of the Korean as colonial subject during the period of Japanese occupation (1910–45); in "Melpomene," the narrator describes the incorporation of the individual into South Korean nationalism during the Korean War (1950–53); and in "Calliope," written from the standpoint of a Korean American returning to South Korea, the narrator recalls her naturalization as an immigrant into American citizenship. The series of unfinished subject formations—illustrating the female student's antagonism to the educational and religious apparatuses, the colonized subject's disloyalty to the empire, and the immigrant's incomplete incorporation into the state—suggests not only that subjectivity is multiply determined, but also that each determination is uneven and historically differentiated, with no single one monolithically defining the subject. In this sense, *Dictée* dramatizes that each interpellation organizes the female/colonized/postcolonial/ethnic subject irregularly and incompletely, leaving a variety of residues that remain uncontained by, and antagonistic to, the educational, religious, colonial, and imperial apparatuses of domination and assimilation. If one function of canonization is the resolution of material contradiction through a narrative of formation in which differences—of gender, race, nationality, or sexuality—are subsumed through the individual's identification with a universalized form, *Dictée* is a text that continually disrupts such identifications. While rendering unavoidably explicit the traces of colonial and imperial damage and dislocation on the subject, it articulates a voice in opposition to those dominations that persistently refuses the assimilation of that subject to fictions of identity and development, and writes this subject as a possible site for active cultural and ideological struggle.

Another important manner in which Asian American literature defies canonization is that it is a literature that is still being written—an unclosed, unfixed body of work whose centers and orthodoxies shift as the makeup of the Asian-origin constituency shifts, and within which new voices are continually being articulated. The diversity of contemporary interventions is evident, for example, in a recent collection of writing by younger Asian/

Pacific authors, "Burning Cane," which includes writings by Asian American gays and lesbians, by mixed-race Asian Americans, and by a variety of Southeast Asian-American writers.[18] While "Burning Cane" is unified by a common project of articulating cultural resistance, the heterogeneous selection of pieces suggests that, owing to the increasingly various Asian American constituency, the profile of traits that characterize Asian American "identity" is as much in flux as is the orthodoxy regarding which constituencies comprise and define Asian American "culture." First-generation post-1975 Southeast Asian writing introduces new themes to, and emphasizes different concerns than, the existing body of multigenerational Asian American literature; for example, some of the pieces by newer immigrants in "Burning Cane" focus on deracination and displacement, rather than on struggles against incorporation or assimilation. In T. C. Huo's short fiction "The Song Sent Across the Mekong," the narrator meditates on the image of a man singing to a woman left behind on the riverbank as a paradigmatic figure for leaving, separation from family, and loss of homeland; while the narrator identifies with the man who has left, his mourning consists of different attempts at narrating the woman's position, reconstructing her thoughts and actions, imagining her dead and alive. Huynh-Nhu Le's poem "Hearts & Minds" expresses a similar grief through a simple yet poignant chiasmus in which Vietnam, the poet's birthplace, is alien and unknown while the new land of the United States is overly familiar, yet unwelcoming: "Vietnam: / A land I know not much, / A water I did not swim, / A mountain I did not climb . . . America: / A land I know quite well, / A river I might have drowned, / A mountain I have fallen" (98). Other stories in this collection broaden the spectrum of Asian American writing by depicting Asian American subjects as formed by a multiplicity of intersecting and conflicting determinations—gender, generation, sexuality, national origin, and economic class, as well as race and ethnicity; some explore the tensions and connections between subjects of different racial and ethnic backgrounds. The narrator of Patrick Leong's story "Graveyard Picnics" is a Chinese/Mexican American who, attending the gravesite of his Chinese grandfather, ponders whether he ought to worship the dead in the traditional Chinese ceremony led by his father or pray for them in church according to the Catholic traditions of his maternal family; inheriting aspects of different cultural systems, yet belonging wholly to neither, the narrator finds himself located as a "hinge" between two separate but interlocking ethnic cultures. Wynn Young's "Poor Butterfly!" is narrated by a bitterly ironic young Asian American gay man as he considers the fetishism of white gays who prefer Asian men, and as he worries about being endangered by his partner's uncurbed sexual activity. A collection like "Burning Cane" opens up the definitions of what constitutes Asian American writing—by drawing attention to recent immigrant writing and by featuring pieces that explore the intersecting complex of determinations that characterize the Asian American subject.

By way of conclusion, I wish to return to the story by Monique Thuy-Dung Truong with which this discussion began, and which appears in "Burning Cane." The narrator is a Vietnamese American woman who recalls her elementary school education in a predominantly white town in North Carolina during the 1970s. Let us consider again the initial passage:

> Mrs. Hammerick . . . I was scared of her like no dark corners could ever scare me. You have to know that all the while she was teaching us history . . . she was telling all the boys in our class that I was Pearl and my last name was Harbor. They understood her like she was speaking French and their names were all Claude and Pierre. I felt it in the lower half of my stomach, and it throbbed and throbbed. . . . It would be so many years . . . before I would understand that Pearl Harbor was not just in 1941 but in 1975.[19]

Truong's story portrays the simultaneous indictment and silencing of the young Asian immigrant student within the classroom regulated by an American nationalist projection of the Asian as *enemy;* a binary logic of patriot and enemy invigorates American nationalism during the Vietnam War period, gathering more force through a conflation of the North Vietnamese and the Japanese that naturalizes American neocolonialism in Vietnam through the appeal to a nationalist historical narrative about World War II. The narrator's observation that the teacher's history lesson addresses "all the boys" further instantiates how the American nationalist narrative recognizes, recruits, and incorporates male subjects, while "feminizing," and silencing, the students who do not conform to that notion of patriotic subjectivity. But at the same time, Truong's story is an epistolary fiction addressed to one of the narrator's few friends within that classroom, a white female student named Kelly. Although the classroom is remembered as a site of pain, the retrospective renarration of that pain, not as individually suffered but as a shared topos between writer and addressee, is, in contrast, a source of new pleasure and a differently discovered sense of community. The narrator writes: "I guess it was Mrs. Hammerick's books that brought you and me together. I think you and I would have had to find each other anyway, but I like to tell our story this way, you know, like it was destiny and not necessity. . . . You and I were library kids, do you remember that?" The repetition of "you and me" and "you and I" sutures, on the narrative level, the intersubjective relationality between the narrator and Kelly. As the story proceeds, it delicately portrays relationships that cross boundaries of race, class, and constructions of femininity; girls are thrown into tentative but sympathetic intimacies based on their quite different exclusions—the narrator is ostracized as a Vietnamese immigrant, her friend Kelly because she is overweight, and another girl, Michelle, because of her family's poverty. The girls' friendships are marked by distinct yet overlapping dynamics of power and powerlessness; yet in response they form courageous bridges across distinct lines of opportunity and restriction.

Truong's story yields several points with which I wish to end this discussion of Asian American literature and the university. First, by focusing on the classroom as the place where the narrator's difference is most sharply delineated, the story emphasizes that education is a primary site through which the narratives of national group identity are established and reproduced, and dramatizes that the construction of others—as *enemies*—is fundamental logic in the constitution of national identity. Second, it is suggestive about the process through which the students' conformity to those narratives is demanded and regulated: the historical narrative about victors and enemies elicits an identification of the student with that victorious national body; in that process of identification, the student consents to his incorporation as a subject of the American state. I refer to this subject of ideology in the classroom as a "he," for just as in Truong's story, where the history lesson is addressed to "all the boys," I would argue that the subject position of the American student/citizen is coded and narrated as a masculine position. We might say that the American nationalist narrative of citizenship incorporates the subject as male citizen according to a relationship that is not dissimilar to the family's oedipalization, or socialization, of the son; in terms of the racial or ethnic subject, he becomes a citizen when he identifies with the paternal state, and accepts the terms of this identification by subordinating his racial difference, and denying his identification with the feminized "motherland."

Third, by representing this classroom from the perspective of the immigrant female student, the story underscores how this identification requires the painful suppression of differences. In terms of group formation, it calls attention to how curricula that universalize the values and norms of a "common" national culture are in contradiction with a society that is materially divided and stratified in terms of race, class, gender, sexuality, and national origin; in terms of individual subject formation, it suggests that the interpellation of the individual splits the subject off from itself, suppressing those material, racial, sexual aspects that are in contradiction with, in excess of, that generic subject formation.[20] But this interpellation/oedipalization is not univocal or total; for even though aspects may be conditionally split off, the subject may be insufficiently captured by the nationalist subject formation such that antagonisms arise against that formation out of the contradiction of interpellation itself. In using the term contradiction to conceive of both group and individual identities, I mean to take up the sense in which contradiction describes how a system, in the course of providing for its effective hegemony, produces the conflicts that will bring about its own expiration and undoing. One of the conditions of the contradiction of nationalist identity formation is that it is precisely the demand for national cultural uniformity that inflects differences with oppositional significance in antagonism to the apparatuses whose function it is to dictate that uniformity; in other words, the dominant construction of American nationalist identity logically provides for the critiques of that identity from the standpoints of groups racialized, sexualized, or classed as *other*. Another condition of contradiction is of course that none of these valences of otherness is independently articulated; throughout lived social relations, race is class-inflected, sexuality is racialized, labor is gendered; there is no contradiction that is not articulated with other contradictions, and society is increasingly characterized by intersections in which racial, gendered, and economic contradictions are inseparable and mobilized by means of and through one another.

In this regard, the final point I would like to draw out of Truong's story is that by focusing on the friendships among three differently marginalized female students, the story ultimately allegorizes a network of alliance across lines of race, class, and gender that is not only a means of surviving the classroom, but is also the basis of contesting the historically differentiated but intersecting determinations of racist colonialism, patriarchy, and capitalism, for which that classroom is a primary locus of reproduction. Sites that express overdetermination, or the convergence of a complex of contradictions, may function either in the direction of an inhibition and neutralizing of contradictory possibility or in the direction of a rupture, a mobilization of contradictions within which the coincidence of racial, gender, and class determinations would bring forward a disruption of the multiply articulated structure of domination. The concerted articulation of converged contradiction "fuses" what Althusser calls a "ruptural unity" that makes possible the emergence of different subjects and constituencies in a "grouped assault" on a specific hegemony, or a specific dominant formation.[21] We may recall that Gramsci writes of hegemony as not simply a political rule but as a process within which any specific dominant configuration exists always within the context of contesting pressures from other sites, classes, and groups in different conditions of self-identification and formation.[22] Put otherwise, the overdetermination of class, race, and gender contradictions in the construction of American nationalist identity makes possible the continuation of painful silences and exclusions in the American classroom, but this convergence of contradictions may also precisely constitute the ground from which antiracist, feminist, and class struggles against those nationalist dominations necessarily emerge.

I want to cast the project of teaching U.S. minority, postcolonial, and women's literatures in the contemporary university as something like the network of alliances described in Truong's story, as a collection of linked alternative pedagogies central to contesting how the educational apparatus traditionally functions to incorporate students as subjects of the state, as well as contesting the narratives through which that socialization takes place. Like the affinities in Truong's story, it is a set of links that is not predicated on notions of similarity or identity, but is a project built out of material, historical, and topical differentiation. Allow me to point out, too, that Truong's story is precisely a U.S. minority, a postcolonial, *and* a woman's text; it is an object that dissolves the notion that these three areas can be conceived as discrete or discontinuous. Through concerted pedagogical and curricular changes taking place in different institutional sites, we can locate and displace the powerful ideological narratives that traditionally structure the current university (that is, the two with which we began, the culturalist one that projects Euro-American culture as an autonomous domain, and the developmental narrative that abstracts and privileges the subject of that "prior" Western civilization, and defines that subject against others who are identified with less autonomous, less developed, disintegrated and disintegrating contemporary cultures). The teaching of racial, ethnic, and postcolonial texts decenters the autonomous notion of Western culture by recentering the complexities of racial, ethnic, and postcolonial collectivities, and unmasks the developmental narrative as a fiction designed to justify the histories of colonialism, neocolonialism, and forced labor and to erase the dislocations and hybridities that are the resulting conditions of those histories. Through these pedagogical and curricular shifts, we may also be able to alter the ways in which students are interpellated as subjects by the educational apparatus, opening the possibility that the university will ultimately offer to students more than a single universalized subject formation, more than an incorporation into a uniform national or cultural identity, and more sites and practices than those permitted by one generic subject position.

# Notes

Ideas for this essay were presented variously during 1991–92 at the University of California, Santa Barbara, the University of California, Berkeley, Columbia University, the University of Hawaii at Manoa, the Minority Discourse Project at the University of California Humanities Research Institute, and the Minority Summer Research Seminar at the University of California, San Diego. I am grateful for the discussions in each of these locations.

1. Lisa Lowe, "Heterogeneity, Hybridity, Multiplicity: Marking Asian American Differences," *Diaspora* 1 (spring 1990): 24–44.

2. Mas'ud Zavarzadeh and Donald Morton, eds. and introduction, "Theory Pedagogy Politics: The Crisis of 'The Subject' in the Humanities," *Theory Pedagogy Politics: Texts for Change* (Urbana: University of Illinois Press, 1991), 1.

3. Henry A. Giroux and Peter McClaren, eds., *Critical Pedagogy, the State, and Cultural Struggle* (Albany: State University of New York Press, 1989), "Introduction."

4. Martin Carnoy, "Education, State and Culture in American Society," in ibid., 6.

5. Norma Alarcón, "Chicana Feminism: In the Tracks of 'the' Native Woman," *Cultural Studies* 4:3 (October 1990): 248–56; Kimberle Crenshaw, "Demarginalizing the Intersection of Race and Sex: A Black Feminist Critique of Antidiscrimination Doctrine, Feminist Theory and Antiracist Politics," *University of Chicago Legal Forum* (1989): 139–67; Trinh T. Minh-ha, *Woman, Native, Other: Writing Postcoloniality and Feminism* (Bloomington: Indiana University Press, 1989); Evelyn Nakano Glenn, "The Dialectics of Wage Work: Japanese-American Women and Domestic Service, 1905–1940," *Feminist Studies* 6:3 (fall 1980): 432–71, and "Racial Ethnic Women's Labor: The Intersection of Race, Gender and Class Oppression," *Review of Radical Political Economics* 17:3 (1983): 86–108.

6. I am thinking, for example, of the work of George Lipsitz in *Time Passages: Collective Memory and American Popular Culture* (Minneapolis: University of Minnesota Press, 1990), Sucheng Chan's coproduction of the Mary Paik Lee autobiography *Quiet Odyssey: A Pioneer Korean Woman in America* (Seattle: University of Washington, 1990), or Rosalinda Fregoso's "Born in East L.A. and the Politics of Representation, *Cultural Studies* 4:4 (October 1990).

7. On panethnic bridging organizations and the solidarity among ethnic subgroups, see David Lopez and Yen Espiritu, "Panethnicity in the United States: A Theoretical Framework," *Ethnic and Racial Studies* 13:2 (April 1990): 198–224.

8. I have discussed the contradiction of multiculturalism in popular art and culture in "Imagining Los Angeles in the Production of Multiculturalism," in *Multiculturalism?* Avery Gordon and Christopher Newfield, eds. (forthcoming, University of Minnesota Press).

9. David Lloyd, "Genet's Genealogy: European Minorities and the Ends of Canon," in *The Nature and Context of Minority Discourse* (New York: Oxford University Press, 1990), and *Nationalism and Minor Literature: James Clarence Mangan and the Emergence of Irish Cultural Nationalism* (Berkeley: University of California Press, 1987), chapter 1.

10. On the political situation of Hawaii and Hawaiian writing, see Haunani-Kay Trask, "Politics in the Pacific Islands: Imperialism and Native Self-Determination," *Amerasia* 16:1 (1990); Geraldine E. Kosasa-Terry, "The Politics of 'Local' Identity in Hawai'i," paper presented

at the Association of Asian American Studies conference, 1992; Rob Wilson, "Blue Hawai'i: *Bamboo Ridge* as 'Critical Regionalism,'" in *What Is in a Rim?: Critical Perspectives on the Pacific Region Idea,* Arif Dirlik, ed. (Boulder, Colo.: Westview Press, 1993).

11. Frank Chin, Jeffrey Paul Chan, Lawson Inada, and Shawn Wong, eds., *Aiiieeeee!: An Anthology of Asian-American Writers* (Garden City, N.Y.: Doubleday, 1975); Shirley Geok-lin Lim, Mayumi Tsutakawa, and Margarita Donnelly, eds., *The Forbidden Stitch: An Asian American Women's Anthology* (Corvallis, Ore.: Calyx Books, 1989); Misha Berson, ed., *Between Worlds: Contemporary Asian American Plays* (New York: Theatre Communications Group, 1990).

12. Elaine Kim, *Asian American Literature: An Introduction to the Writings and Their Social Context* (Philadelphia: Temple University Press, 1982), xv.

13. Carlos Bulosan, *America Is in the Heart* (Seattle: University of Washington Press, 1946), 147.

14. Monica Sone, *Nisei Daughter* (Seattle: University of Washington Press, 1953), 238.

15. John Okada, *No-No Boy* (Seattle: University of Washington Press, 1976); Joy Kogawa, *Obasan* (Boston: David Godine, 1981).

16. For a more extensive interrogation of the ideology of healing in Asian American literature, see David Palumbo-Liu, "Model Minority Discourse and the Course of Healing," forthcoming in Abdul JanMohamed, ed., *Minority Discourse: Ideological Containment and Utopian/ Heterotopian Potential.*

17. See Elaine Kim, ed., *Writing Self, Writing Nation: Selected Essays on Theresa Hak Kyung Cha's Dictée* (Berkeley: Third Woman Press, 1993).

18. "Burning Cane," Grace Hong, James Lee, David Maruyama, Jim Soong, and Gary Yee, eds., *Amerasia Journal* 17:2 (1991).

19. Monique Thuy-Dung Truong, "Kelly," *Amerasia Journal* 17:2 (1991), 42.

20. On interpellation, see Louis Althusser, "Ideology and Ideological State Apparatuses," in *Lenin and Philosophy* (New York: Monthly Review Press, 1971).

21. See Althusser, "Contradiction and Overdetermination," in *For Marx* (London: Verso, 1990), 99. For an elaboration of the unevenness of multiple contradictions, see Stuart Hall, "Signification, Representation, Ideology: Althusser and the Post-Structuralist Debates," *Critical Studies in Mass Communication* 2:2 (June 1985), 91–114.

22. Antonio Gramsci, "Notes on Italian History," *Selections from the Prison Notebooks* (New York: International Publishers, 1971).

## PART TWO

# The Construction of the Ethnic

~

# The Borders of Modernity

## Américo Paredes's *Between Two Worlds* and the Chicano National Subject

RAMÓN SALDÍVAR

> Nations, like narratives, lose their origins in the myths of time and only
> fully realize their horizons in the mind's eye.
> —Homi K. Bhabha, *Nation and Narration*

Renowned as an ethnographer, literary critic, and social historian for more than thirty years of magisterial production, Américo Paredes is being hailed at century's end for special accomplishment in the creative arts as well. His artistic endeavors include distinguished work as an arranger, composer, and performer of ballads and popular music, and as a screenwriter, story-teller, and oral historian. Honored in 1989 by the National Endowment for the Humanities as one of the initial recipients of the Charles Frankel Prize, and in 1990 by the Republic of Mexico as one of the first Mexican American inductees to the Orden del Aguila Azteca (Order of the Aztec Eagle), Paredes is one of the most respected of contemporary Chicano intellectuals and the founder and virtually unparalleled practitioner of what has come to be known as Chicano Cultural Studies.[1]

Paredes's fame rests on his foundational work of the 1950s and 1960s on the ballads and everyday folklife of Mexican Americans and on his subse-quent elaboration of that work during the seventies and eighties. His initial scholarly contribution from this early period, *"With His Pistol in His Hand": A Border Ballad and Its Hero* (1958), is a masterful work of intellectual intervention decades ahead of its time. In an epoch when the intellectual modes dictated either an old historicism or a restrictive new critical formalism, *"With His Pistol in His Hand"* went emphatically against the grain of the accepted analytical methods of the day. Combining literary, sociological, ethnographic, and historical analysis of traditional border ballads—*corridos*—it offered, as José David Saldívar has shown, a stinging rebuttal and a devastating "deconstruction of [the] established [white supremacist] authority and hierarchies" that operated as the common wisdom and official histories of the relations between Anglos and Mexicans in Texas and the rest of the West and Southwest (170). "To dramatize his sense of culture as a site of social contestation," Saldívar continues, "[Paredes] located the sources of meaning not in individual subjectivities, but in social relations, communication, and cultural politics" (4).

Richard Bauman notes, in his Introduction to a collection of Paredes's essays, *Folklore and Culture on the Texas Mexican Border* (1993), that Paredes "has carried out extensive field research and published a considerable body of Border folklore and he has produced the most important and influential scholarship of our generation on the folklore of Greater Mexico in general and the Lower Border in particular" (1). Before Paredes, the cultural politics of Texas and the Southwest were the singular product of the Anglo-American imagination, responding exclusively to the hegemony of Anglo-American material interests. But as Michel Foucault reminds us, "Where there is power, there is resistance" (1978, 95). After Paredes, with the publication of his work, the cultural politics of the region began to be cast in the decidedly different mold of biculturalism, reflecting the true, multicultural realities of the American social world. To this immensely influential body of Paredes scholarship, scholars need to add two new works, the collection of essays referred to earlier, *Folklore and Culture on the Texas Mexican Border* (1993), and a comprehensive study of jokes, jests, and oral narrative entitled *Uncle Remus con Chile* (1993).

Paredes's most recently published literary works—a novel and a book of poetry—have added yet another dimension to the imposing array of his contestational work in the historical, ethnographic, and theoretical realms. These literary works also address the predicaments of contemporary Chicano/a cultural politics, identity formation, and social transformation. Given the contemporaneity of their concerns, it is curious to learn, however, that these newly published literary works are not contemporary pieces, nor even products of the fifties and sixties. They are instead works from the thirties and forties, a period decades before that of his mature work.

As products of an era and of literary formations other than those enjoying current vogue, they belie their postmodern, post-Chicano movement thematics and publication dates. The novel *George Washington Gómez* (1990), and the collection of poetry, *Between Two Worlds* (1991), both written during the Depression years along the Texas-Mexican borderlands of deep South Texas, anticipate with imaginative force the sophisticated insight of Paredes's later exemplary transdisciplinary work of social criticism and cultural intervention. They prefigure crucial aspects of the growing body of postmodern Chicano writing and cultural studies from a high modernist, *pre*-movement historical moment. Together with the later scholarly work, the novel and the poetry can now be seen as part of a larger imaginative project to study what Héctor Calderón correctly identifies as "the organization of life that was formed out of the New World landscape" (25). It seeks as well, I think, to invent a figural discourse of national epic proportions appropriate to the construction of a new narrative of "American" social and cultural history at the borders of modernity.

## *Between Two Worlds* as "Border Writing"

Predating the work of all of the better-known of the present generation of Chicano authors, Paredes's literary productions are richly marked by the flavor of their origins in the era of high literary modernism in both its Anglo-European and Latin American varieties. These works are also self-consciously steeped in an unwavering resistance to the residual effects of nineteenth-century American imperialism and its racist aftermath as well as to the continuing effects of twentieth-century capitalist transformations of production in the Southwest. *Between Two Worlds*, especially—border verses composed during the very moment of what could arguably be called the historical divide between the modern and the postmodern—represents the bifurcated, interstitial, indeed one might say differential, quality of the kind of writing that has come to be called "border writing."[2] Looking as it does from its liminal present both to the past and to the future, speaking an oddly dual idiom that simultaneously celebrates a lyrical history and forebodes a prosaic future, *Between Two Worlds* might well emblematize the features of that postmodern border writing were it not for the fact that it predates the notion by more than half a century.

Despite what could be shown to be this work's allegiance to a certain aesthetics of modernism, albeit in the modified form modernism acquired in the interstices between the Northern and Southern American hemispheres,

I wish to show that the crux of Paredes's work in lyric and narrative poetry lies not in whether or not it is a hybrid product of transcultural or multi-cultural modernism. Rather, its importance rests on what it shows about the relationship of modernism to Chicano literature, and indeed to other "minority" American literatures in general, to the extent that traditional English and American studies are defined, as they continue to be, in *national* terms.

From this perspective, the ideological victory represented by the canon-ization of the generation of the post-World War I European and American high modernists as the teleological end point to which their respective na-tional literatures had been aimed represents an absurd terminus to history. It is absurd because that canonization assumed that the end of the era of modernism could be defined with singular temporal certitude and defini-tive theoretical justification outside of any sociopolitical categories.

The end of modernism, more profitably to be seen coincident with the cataclysmic restructuring of the classical imperialist world system with the onset of World War II than with the arbitrary demarcation of a certain literary period, offers an emblematic break that is less an empirically verifi-able matter than a historiographic decision. It is, nonetheless, a decision of great moment in the articulation of the narrative of the Mexican American community's struggle for justice and self-determination in the twentieth century. Paredes's *Between Two Worlds,* as product and symptom of the end of modernism at the peripheries of modernization, suggests how the com-monly held characterizations of modernist ideologies as ahistorical and apolitical are no longer fully persuasive nor entirely adequate to explaining the cultural productions of writers actively engaged in decolonization struggles on the margins of sanctioned history and at the borderlands of high culture. These productions offer a striking anticipation of Adorno's notion that "modernity is a qualitative, not a chronological, category" (*Minima Moralia,* 218).

Today, near century's end, with many nations once thought fully consol-idated now finding themselves challenged and, indeed, sundered by " 'sub'-nationalisms within their borders—nationalisms which, naturally, dream of shedding this sub-ness one happy day," as Benedict Anderson puts it, it is quite clear that the end of the era of nationalism is "not remotely in sight" (13). Even as the epoch of multi-, trans-, and even postnational "isms" bears down upon us, the idea of "nation-ness" remains "the most universally le-gitimate value in the political life of our time" (13). A work such as Paredes's *Between Two Worlds* is crucial to an understanding of modernity precisely

because it demonstrates with astonishing clarity the fundamental link between basic political economy and ideas of culture on one hand and the
joint constructs of modernism and the nation on the other. Far from apolitical and ahistorical, Paredes's modernity is formed by the very historical
and political legacy of the Mexican American communities of the Lower
Border.

To gain a sense of the formative effect of the historical and the political
on Paredes as a modernist poet, we need first to recognize the peculiar constructions of American nationalism and that its national literature can be
seen as "cultural artefacts of a particular kind" (Anderson, 14), constituted
as much by alternatively defining pressures from the outside at the peripheral borders as by those from the inner central heartland. The particular
constellation of ideologies that demarcate the boundaries of that construct
make up, as Homi Bhabha suggests, its imaginative horizon (1).

In his poetry of the 1930s and 1940s, Paredes represents the limits of the
Anglo-American cultural and political horizon, limits that are precisely in-
stantiated at its borders by the emergence of a modern "new Mexican,"
neither Anglo nor Mexican, nor still less the contemporary avatar of
Guillermo Gómez-Peña's "Border Brujo" or "Aztec HiTech." Paredes's
proto-Chicano consciousness cuts, like Occam's razor, more finely and figures itself more elegantly politically as the product of the newly self-imag-
ined difference between two concrete nationalisms.[3] A lyric poet at the end
of the era of high modernism, Paredes sought to create poetic figures to account for what some are today denoting as the postnational Latino subject
in the very midst of that subject's formation. This subject in process, the
displaced and dispossessed object of official narratives of American history,
the Mexican American that Paredes describes, existed in an empty discursive realm: "He no gotta country, he no gotta flag / He no gotta voice, all he
got is the han' / To work like the burro; he no gotta lan'" (*Between Two
Worlds*, 27).

Paredes's work demonstrates with great imaginative force the filling-in
of that empty discursive space. It represents as well the informing presence
of the extraliterary, the political, and the economic within the borders of
modernist discourse itself to counter the work of one brand of organicist
modernism and its concurrent myths of homogeneity. To understand better the dynamics of modernity within the history of the Chicano subject
and the manner of its expression in cultural production, however, we must
first turn to the narrative of history itself and situate our figures in their social context on the border of modernity.

## Modernity and the Chicano Subject

On the afternoon of January 6, 1941, with American entry into the war now less than a year away, Franklin Delano Roosevelt entered the Senate chamber to deliver his annual State of the Union address to Congress and the nation. In the days before the event, Roosevelt had fretted over how best to address in one unified line the lingering effects of spiritual and economic crisis, the need for a revaluation of political standards in moral terms, and the real urgency of preparing for the coming war. At the very brink of war, its shadow practically touching the shores of the American continent, Roosevelt urged the Congress to prepare the ground for this "new order" by understanding that national security certainly involved vigilance and action on the international stage and in foreign policy, with the United States continuing to serve as the "arsenal" of democracy (Roosevelt, 668). But Roosevelt was also still profoundly aware of how national security depended on the internal stage of domestic affairs. Therefore, in 1941 Roosevelt argued that "as men do not live by bread alone, they do not fight by armaments alone. Those who man our defenses, and those behind them who build our defenses, must have the stamina and the courage which come from unshakable belief in the manner of life they are defending" (670).

This was no time, Roosevelt pleaded, to stop thinking about "the social and economic problems which are the root cause of the social revolution which is today a supreme factor in the world" (670). Having linked national security and domestic tranquillity in the alleviation of the national Depression, private individual interests thus having assumed public collective significance (Arendt, 33), Roosevelt looked ahead, even beyond the war that the United States had not yet officially entered, to "the ultimate objectives of American policy" (Greer, 12) to sketch a vision of what the nation might one day be. What emerged from that vision was the momentous formulation of the "Four Freedoms." "In the future days, which we seek to make secure," Roosevelt proclaimed, "we look forward to a world founded upon four essential freedoms":

> The first is freedom of speech and expression—everywhere in the world.
> The second is freedom of every person to worship God in his own way—everywhere in the world.
> The third is freedom from want—which, translated into world terms, means economic understandings which will secure to every nation a healthy peacetime life for its inhabitants—everywhere in the world.
> The fourth is freedom from fear—which, translated into world terms, means a world-wide reduction of armaments to such a point and in such a

thorough fashion that no nation will be in a position to commit an act of physical aggression against any neighbor—anywhere in the world. (Roosevelt, 672)

Cynics scoffed that Roosevelt offered here no more than a utopian vision of a distant millennium (Greer, 12). Roosevelt himself, however, insisted in his message to the nation that his grand idea of the Four Freedoms was "a definite basis for a kind of world attainable in our own time and generation" (Roosevelt, 672). Even more grandly, for Roosevelt the Four Freedoms constituted both a renewal of the American commitment to basic human rights and an extension of those personal rights into the transpersonal arena of world politics.

The Four Freedoms—*of speech and expression, of religion, from want,* and *from fear*—represented the culmination of Roosevelt's lifelong commitment to liberal democratic notions of justice and fundamental human rights.[4] The New Deal agenda for American renewal, to be understood as an ethical revaluation for the elimination of spiritual and economic maladies, was now turned outward upon the world in general. Modern social conditions in 1941, on the eve of the American entry into the latest of the great European imperial world wars, precluded that on the international as on the national scale "the social and economic problems which are the root cause of the social revolution" affecting the world could be ignored. "The world order which we seek is the cooperation of free countries, working together in a friendly, civilized society" (Roosevelt, 672). To this end, then, Roosevelt asked "all Americans to respond to that call" (671), concluding that "our strength is our unity of purpose" (672).

What is at stake in Roosevelt's momentous pronouncement of a "world order" to be built on the groundwork of the Four Freedoms is nothing less than a renewed commitment to an ideal vision of a unified American nation working to effect that brave new "world order" under the pressure of "modern [American] social conditions." In a hegemonic move worthy of the most enlightened of liberals, Roosevelt urged the personal liberties guaranteed in the Bill of Rights as the constitutional ground for the construction of both a modern new American nation and a modern new world order formed in the American image. Emerging from an older Republican disorder built on neurotic fears and shaken by real depression, the nation's, and the world's, unity is here called into being as a Democratic system of cultural signification, "as the representation of social *life* rather than the discipline of social *polity*" (Bhabha, 1–2). The narrative of global and national unity that Roosevelt elegantly unravels displays exactly this conceptual divide between lived experience on the one hand and the institutional-ized structuration of that experience on the other. It also exemplifies per-fectly Benedict Anderson's thesis that "nationalism has to be understood, by aligning it not with self-consciously held political ideologies, but with large cultural systems that preceded it, out of which—as well as against which—it came into being" (12).

That there were profound ambiguities as well as fissures within the ide-ologies of both the political groundwork and the culturally significant grand unified narrative of American history that underwrites Roosevelt's address to the nation is all too well known. As Tom Nairn has argued, and as the economic conditions of late twentieth-century America have proven, the uneven development of capitalism inscribes within the modern nation social progression in alternate cycle with economic depression, imbricating both "progress and regress in the very genetic code of the nation" (345–46). Consequently, the course of national history and national economies can never run smoothly. Certainly, history offers ample instances of how, in moderate doses, nationalism can provide a positive, collective identity; but it shows concurrently that in immoderate or irrational doses, nationalism creates negative, even lethal, chauvinisms. In either case, what is apparent from a glance at the rhetoric of national discourse—for example, in Roosevelt's use of it in reference to the crisis of the Great Depression—is the psychologistic cast of its tropes and metaphors. There is nothing acci-dental in this link between the discourses of nationalism and subjectivity, as nationalism explicitly provides one way of joining the subjective conditions with the material modes of production. It is this subjectivity that under-writes as well the legitimacy of Roosevelt's "four essential freedoms."

What is surely less well known than the ambivalences of American na-tionalist ideology is how the traditional narrative of national destiny that Roosevelt tried to reimagine in liberal bourgeois terminology at the end of one historical era and on the verge of another was received and revised at the margins of the nation, in the borderlands of history, by those other Americans—African Americans, Asian Americans, and Native Americans, for instance—but particularly, by Mexican Americans, the historical sub-jects of the present discussion. Viewing this response not only allows us to fill in historical gaps in our cultural history but also to understand through dialectical counterreflection the very production of that cultural knowl-edge itself. *Between Two Worlds* offers Américo Paredes's striking response to Roosevelt's millennial vision with his own revision of the Four Freedoms in a Spanish-language poem entitled, in English, "The Four Freedoms":[5]

| | |
|---|---|
| Lengua, Cultura, Sangre: | Language, Culture, Blood: |
| es vuestro mi cantar, | my song is of you, |
| sois piedra de los mares | you are rock of oceans |
| y muro de hogar; | and commorant wall; |
| este país de "Cuatro Libertades" | this "Four Freedoms" nation |
| nada nos puede dar. | can offer us nothing. |
| Justicia . . . ¿acaso existe? | Justice . . . scarcely exists? |
| La fuerza es la justicia, | Might is justice, amusing words: |
| palabras humorísticas: Justicia y Libertad. | Justice and Liberty. |
| Nos queda sólo la Raza, | We have but *la Raza,* |
| nos queda sólo la Lengua; | we have but our Tongue; |
| hay que guardarlas siempre | let's preserve them perpetually |
| y mantenerlas vivas | and living maintain them |
| por una eternidad. | for eternity. (58) |

In contrast to Roosevelt's universalizing liberal ethico-political discourse of national unity that seeks to extend that local unity globally, Paredes cites the local communal aspects of national culture, language, and "race" as the real mainstays of freedom. In this context, "la Raza" plays an ambivalent role, for, as will become clear with other poems in the collection, what Paredes implies with this deployment of the term is less a *genetic* consanguinity than a culturally *fashioned* collectivity ("la raza" can be translated colloquially as "the people," "the folk," or "the community"). In another, related poem of 1937, "Mi Pueblo" ("My People"), Paredes had made this localization of culture even more explicit, dedicating the poem "A mi barrio, El Cuatro Veintiuno" ("To my barrio, the Four Twenty-one"):

> Eres cierta incertidumbre entre cielo y podredumbre,
> del abismo y de la cumbre el destino te formó
> citadino y campirano, eres yanqui-mexicano,
> eres méxico-tejano,
> eres pocho, como yo! (48–49)

You are a certain incertitude between the heavens and putrescence,
destiny shaped you from the abyss and the summit
urbanite and country dweller, you're a Yankee-Mexican,
you are a Mexico-Texan,
you are a *pocho* [U.S.-born Mexican], like me!

Like language and culture, and even "race" itself, personal consciousness begins to emerge as a conceptual invention of the community to guarantee "justice" and "liberty" as aspects of lived reality rather than as abstract notions of political economy. It is assuredly not a romantically constructed ideal *Geist* of the *Volk* that provides the subjective repertoire of the Mexican American social mechanism. What real "liberty" might look like is the subject of yet another poem, "La libertad" (1942), that also speaks to the Rooseveltian "Four Freedoms":

| | |
|---|---|
| Raza morena y mestiza | Dark, mestizo race |
| ¡oh, semilla de grandeza! | Oh, seed of grandness! |
| llevas en ti la entereza | you bear within you the integrity |
| que te da la juventud. . . . | that youth gives to you. . . . |
| Indio descalzo, trigueño, | Barefoot, dusky Indian, |
| que llorando vas tu suerte, | who weeping bear your destiny, |
| indio, ¡qué diera por verte | Indian, what I wouldn't give to see you |
| soberano de verdad! | Sovereign in truth! |
| Con el estómago lleno, | With a full stomach, |
| bien vestido y bien calzado | well dressed and well shod |
| y en tu destino confiado— | and confident in your destiny— |
| ésa es la libertad. | that is liberty. (62) |

"Liberty" here is a material, concrete property of collective interactions, not an abstract reification from an assemblage of personal freedoms. Its features are solid, perceptible, attainable. Its blazon is a well-fed, well-dressed, well-shod *indio*, standing in the sovereignty of truth and the confidence of destiny. Beyond the myths of blood and tongue, the cause of la Raza's (the Folk's) cultural identity lies, as Paredes would have it, in the uneven development of history and world economy, situated on the margins of "cierta incertidumbre," figured in the subjective site of the *pocho*, the hybrid neo-culturo-mestizo, cross-cutting, crisscrossing the seemingly impermeable lines of cultural sovereignty.

The sovereignty of the *pocho*'s identity is by no means certified, however. Marked by the "certain incertitude" of local conditions, the *pocho* is undeniably subject to the barbarisms of history. Thus, the poem "Alma Pocha" (1936) was written in ironic response to the great and gaudy centennial celebrations of Texas's independence:

> En tu propio terruño serás extranjero
> por la ley del fusil y la ley del acero;
> y verás a tu padre morir balaceado
> verás a tu hermano colgado de un leño
> por el crimen mortal de haber sido trigueño.
> Y si vives, acaso, será sin orgullo,
> con recuerdos amargos de todo lo tuyo;
> tus campos, tus cielos, tus aves, tus flores
> serán el deleite de los invasores;
> para ellos su fruto dará la simiente,
> donde fueras el amo serás el sirviente.
> Y en tu propio terruño serás extranjero
> por la ley del fusil y la ley del acero. (35–36)

> In your native homeland a stranger you will be
> by the law of the rifle and the law of cold steel;
> and you'll see your father shot to death
> you'll see your brother strung from a limb
> for the mortal crime of having been born dark.
> And if perhaps you should happen to live, without pride it will be,
> with bitter remembrances of what once was yours;
> your lands, your skies, your birds, your flowers
> will be the delight of the invaders;
> for them your fruit will sprout,
> where once a master a servant now you will be.
> And in your homeland a stranger you will be
> by the law of the rifle and the law of cold steel.

The poem counterposes the grim reality of present conditions, "la jornada tejana" ("the arid Texan wastelands"), with the utopian memory of long-lost days. Nature's former beauty, its panoramic vistas, the land's living richness are another's and mock the former master, now a servant, with their fecundity. Calling the "Alma pocha" (the feminine soul of the *pocho*)[6] a stranger in her own homeland, Paredes's speaker, "destiny" ("el destino"), echoes here what, in another poem, another voice describes as "A sad, sad longing / That is almost pain / For something that I one day was / And wish to be again" ("Rose Petals"). Assaulted by "the law of the rifle and the law of cold steel," the "alma pocha" remains, nonetheless, "la que sufre, / la que espera" ("she who suffers / she who hopes").

In another poem from this same period (1935), entitled "Ahí nomás" ("Just over There"), Paredes reminds us that the Mexican American's conditions of existence are not by any means unique but constitute a fundamental part of American history:

> "Indian, dark brother from whose ancestors
> Half of my father's fathers sprang,
> You who know all these ragged mountains,
> Up to the nests that the eagles hang,
> Where do your weary footsteps take you?"
>
> . . . . . . . . . . . . . . . . . .
>
> [W]ith a shrug and a smile he answered,
> "Just over there. *Sí ahí nomás.*"
>
> . . . . . . . . . . . . . .
>
> Should I encounter along my journey
> A sister soul that is drawn to me,
> Who rhymes with me in a perfect couplet,
> Whose voice is pitched on my selfsame key,
> Touching my arm, she will stop me, ask me,
> "Where are you going? *¿A dónde vas?*"

And with a shrug and a smile I'll answer,
I too shall answer, "*Ahí nomás.*" (22)

The "alma pocha" here finds kindred souls among native peoples, and among women, all of whom have trod with "weary footsteps" the ages of "bitterness and despair." The "sister soul," in fact, is the very mediator of the alliance among the "dark brother," the poet, and the one "Who rhymes with me." The construction of the phrase "alma pocha" is a highly unusual one, but the exigencies of the grammatical rule allow for a great deal of figural free play concerning the fecundity, fruitfulness, and erotic destinies of Mexican American life, as this poem makes plain.

## The Borders of Modernity

The "new" Mexican consciousness that Paredes fiercely underwrites in his bilingual poems, a consciousness that resides in the cognitive, social, and political-economic space "between two worlds" and that speaks this bilingual tongue, now arises to contest other discourses for the authority to create new meanings and to assign different meanings and different directions to both the progressivist modernity of Roosevelt's New Deal rhetoric and the assimilative, pluralistic ideology of other Mexican American reformers of the day. In this, as in other matters, Paredes anticipated analytical formations and discursive strategies that lay decades in the future.

Situated on the border, a discursive site of heterogeneity and multiaccentual articulations, Paredes's poetry doubles the signs of "modernity" and the "national" to investigate the nation-space "in the process of the *articulation* of elements" (Bhabha, 3) and to set the scene for a new stage of Mexican American/Chicano cultural and social history. What Paredes will amply accomplish a half century later in his enthnographic and literary studies, he is already working out here in lyrical forms as snippets of cultural critique and social analysis to show how culture, knowledge, and power are interlinked as social constructions that might be challenged and reconfigured. Like Antonio Gramsci, another contemporaneous philosopher of working-class culture, Paredes "grasped the idea that culture serves authority, and ultimately the national State, not because it represses and coerces but because it is affirmative, positive, and persuasive" (Said, 171).

Unlike J. Frank Dobie, Walter Prescott Webb, and other official state intellectuals—Paredes's discursive antagonists, who in their mythological renderings of the American West and Southwest sought to legitimize one particular vision of American culture—and unlike even those oppositional Mexican American writers who sought to pluralize that legitimacy under the sign of assimilation, Paredes sought instead precisely to *de*-legitimize it by showing the production of a modern American "nation-space" in process, in medias res, half-made, "caught in the act of 'composing' its powerful image" (Bhabha, 3), as it were, and whose modernity was thus subject to a critical reproduction. As Homi Bhabha, in another context, has written:

> The marginal or "minority" is not the space of a celebratory, or utopian, self-marginalization. It is a much more substantial intervention into those justifications of modernity—progress, homogeneity, cultural organicism, the deep nation, the long past—that rationalize the authoritarian, "normalizing" tendencies within cultures in the name of the national interest or ethnic prerogative. In this sense, then, the ambivalent, antagonistic perspective of nation as narration will establish the cultural boundaries of the nation so that they may be acknowledged as "containing" thresholds of meaning that must be crossed, erased, and translated in the process of cultural production. (4)

Perhaps nowhere else than in Paredes's poetry of the 1930s and early 1940s is the future possibility of a Chicano national subject most unambiguously projected. Like Matthew Arnold in "Stanzas from the Grande Chartreuse" (1855)—the source of the title and epigraph to Paredes's collection of lyrics—retracing the poetic lines of Wordsworth's Alpine journey in *The Prelude,* Paredes returns to his own undiscovered country, the borderlands of South Texas. In this poetic return he repeats the symbolic phrases of his community's master narrative in the *corrido* but without the historical amnesia of the original score and in full knowledge of its possible self-negations.

A word about Arnold's poem is appropriate in conclusion. Arnold's "Grande Chartreuse" is not so much a lament for former times and beliefs as it is an expression of his hopelessness over the impotence to which melancholy stoicism reduces us (DeLaura, 20):

> Wandering between two worlds, one dead,
> The other powerless to be born,
> With nowhere yet to rest my head,
> Like these, on earth I wait forlorn.
> Their faith, my tears, the world deride—
> I come to shed them at their side.

In "Grande Chartreuse," Arnold poetically considers and rejects various historical attitudes: Christian faith, now simply "gone" (l. 84); his own "outworn" and "out-dated" (ll. 100, 106) code learned from his former "rigorous teachers," whom he calls the "masters of the mind" (ll. 67, 73); and the attitude of "the kings of modern thought," who are silent, dumb, passive, and merely "wait to see the future come" (ll. 116, 119). But Arnold allows of another historical possibility, one that he wistfully acknowledges is unavailable to him: the vision of a future country, now "powerless to be born."

This vision of what we might call, paraphrasing Arnold, the country of the kings of *postmodern* thought is unmistakably that which animates Paredes's modernist revolution. Arnold, "between two worlds," resigns himself at the beginning of modernism to his former ethical codes, judging himself totally unfitted for the life of "action and pleasure" (1.194) offered by the burgeoning modern world (DeLaura, 21). Paredes, in contrast, at the end of modernism, embraces this undiscovered country, figured in the liminal, differential status of living "between two worlds." It is a place that demarcates a spatiotemporal zone of critical deconstruction, and constitutes the very possibility of "action and pleasure" for his community. In a poem from 1950, entitled "Esquinita de mi pueblo" ("My community's corner"), Paredes reflects exactly on this process of living an imaginative cartography:

> At the corner of absolute elsewhere
> And absolute future I stood
> Waiting for a green light
> To leave the neighborhood.
> But the light was red.
> . . . . . . . . . . . .
> That is the destiny of people in between
> To stand on the corner
> Waiting for the green. (114)

With this poem, Paredes brings us to the present problematic of the post-contemporary. This is the era after World War II, during which, as Raymond Williams puts it, the modern shifts its reference from "now" to "just now" or even "then," and for some time has been a designation with which "contemporary" may be contrasted for its presentness (32). "All that is left us," adds Williams, "is to become post-moderns." To become postmodern, however, in this sense at least, is to remain modern, to keep in step, to be contemporary, to make of modernity an incomplete project.

What Paredes maps in "Esquinita de mi pueblo" as "the corner of absolute elsewhere / And absolute future" is precisely the marker and the substitute of the limits of the modern. Between the emergence of a properly modernist style and the representational dilemmas of the new imperial world system, Paredes's verses exploit their contingency to history—"the destiny of people in between" and the utopian glimpses of achieved community, "Waiting for the green," that this contingency allows. Indeed, in exploring its styles and testing its ethics, Paredes offers us something very like what

Fredric Jameson calls a "cognitive mapping" (1988) of the social spaces of the imaginary borders of modernity within the real conditions of existence. The achievement of his symbolic cartography is confirmed in its prefigurative tropes, tracing out in aesthetic patterns relationships that turn out to be all too real social realities. It is perhaps in this vein, as the anticipatory precursor of the postcontemporary, that we should read the concluding lines of Paredes's "Prologue": "I am aware that if this volume finds any favor with the reader it will be mostly as a historical document. It is thus that I offer it, as the scribblings of a 'proto-Chicano' of a half-century ago" (11).

## Notes

1. For further biographical information on Américo Paredes and excellent indications of his preeminent role in the foundation of Chicano Cultural Studies, see José E. Limón, "Américo Paredes: A Man from the Border" (1980); Héctor Calderón, "Reinventing the Border: From the Southwest Genre to Chicano Cultural Studies" (forthcoming); and José David Saldívar, "Chicano Narratives as Cultural Critique" (1991) and "Américo Paredes and Decolonization" (1993).

2. The problematic of "border writing" deserves an essay unto itself. Nonetheless, as idiosyncratic, not to say self-indulgent, initial explorations of the postmodern quality of contemporary Chicano discourse, see the essay by D. Emily Hicks, "Deterritorialization and Border Writing," and an interview conducted by Coco Fusco with Guillermo Gómez-Peña and Emily Hicks on "The Border Art Workshop/Taller de Arte Fronterizo."

3. On Gómez-Peña, in addition to the interview cited in note 2, see John Phillip Santos, "A Latin Quest for Identity: Performance Artist Guillermo Gómez-Peña Unveils New Work following 'Genius' Award," 19–20.

4. As early as March 1929, Roosevelt had already claimed that "modern social conditions have progressed to a point where such demands [as basic human rights] can no longer be regarded other than as matters of an absolute right" (Greer, 14).

5. Paredes has mentioned to this writer that at one point he considered entitling his collection *The Four Freedoms*. Concerning the claims of Roosevelt's "Four Freedoms," Paredes comments dryly in a footnote to his poem: "Some people were skeptical." Translations of the Spanish are my own.

6. "Alma" ("soul") is a feminine noun, requiring the corresponding feminine ending of the adjectival modifier, "pocha." On the derivation and meaning of the Mexicanism "pocho/a," Santamaría notes (s.v. "pocho/a") that it is "a name designating the northamerican descendents of Mexicans"; it also suggests "someone of limited abilities"; and it can also refer to the "corrupted Castillian tongue, mixture of English and poor Spanish, spoken by northamerican descendents of Mexican origin." Paredes activates all valences of the term and converts their pejorative quality into an honorific.

## References

Anderson, Benedict. *Imagined Communities: Reflections on the Origin and Spread of Nationalism.* Rev. ed. London: Verso, 1983, 1991.

Arendt, Hannah. *The Human Condition.* Chicago: University of Chicago Press, 1958.

Arnold, Matthew. "Stanzas from the Grande Chartreuse." In *The Norton Anthology of English Literature,* vol. 2. 4th ed. Ed. M. H. Abrams et al. New York: W. W. Norton, 1979.

Baker, Houston, Jr. *Blues, Ideology, and Afro-American Literature: A Vernacular Theory.* Chicago: University of Chicago Press, 1984.

Benjamin, Walter. "Theses on the Philosophy of History." In *Illuminations,* ed. Hannah Arendt. New York: Schocken Books, 1969.

Bhabha, Homi K., ed. *Nation and Narration.* London and New York: Routledge, 1990.

Calderón, Héctor. "Reinventing the Border: From the Southwest Genre to Chicano Cultural Studies." In *Chicano Cultural Studies,* ed. Mario T. García. Los Angeles: University of California Press, forthcoming.

DeLaura, David J. *Hebrew and Hellene in Victorian England: Newman, Arnold, and Pater.* Austin: University of Texas Press, 1969.

Foucault, Michel. *The History of Sexuality.* Vol. 1: *An Introduction.* Trans. Robert Hurley (New York: Pantheon Books, 1978).

Fusco, Coco. "Interview" with Guillermo Gómez-Peña and Emily Hicks in "The Border Art Workshop," *Third Text* 7 (summer 1989): 53–76.

Greer, Thomas H. *What Roosevelt Thought: The Social and Political Ideas of Franklin D. Roosevelt.* East Lansing: Michigan State University Press, 1958.

Habermas, Jürgen. "Modernity—An Incomplete Project." In *The Anti-Aesthetic: Essays on Postmodern Culture,* ed. Hal Foster. Port Townsend, Wash.: Bay Press, 1983.

Hicks, Emily. "Deterritorialization and Border Writing." In *Ethics/Aesthetics: Postmodern Positions,* ed. Robert Merrill. Washington, D.C.: Maisonneuve Press, 1988. 47–58.

Jameson, Fredric. "Cognitive Mapping." In *Marxism and the Interpretation of Culture,* ed. Cary Nelson and Lawrence Grossberg. Urbana: University of Illinois Press, 1988. 347–57.

———. "Modernism and Imperialism." In Terry Eagleton, Fredric Jameson, and Edward W. Said, *Nationalism, Colonialism, and Literature.* Intro. Seamus Deane. Minneapolis: University of Minnesota Press, 1990. 43–66.

Nairn, Tom. "The Modern Janus." In *The Break-up of Britain: Crisis and Neo-Nationalism.* 2d ed. London: Verso, 1981.

Paredes, Américo. *Between Two Worlds.* Houston: Arte Público Press, 1991.

———. *Folklore and Culture on the Texas Mexican Border.* Ed. Richard Bauman. Austin: Center for Mexican American Studies Publications and University of Texas Press, 1993.

———. "Folklore, Lo Mexicano, and Proverbs." *Aztlán* 13:1–2 (1982): 1.

———. *George Washington Gómez: A Mexicotexan Novel.* Houston: Arte Público Press, 1990.

———. "The Mexican *Corrido:* Its Rise and Fall." In *Madstones and Twisters,* ed. Mody C. Boatright. Dallas: Southern Methodist University Press, 1958. 91–105.

———. *A Texas-Mexican Cancionero: Folksongs of the Lower Border.* Urbana: University of Illinois Press, 1976.

———. *Uncle Remus con Chile.* Houston: Arte Público Press, 1993.

———. *"With His Pistol in His Hand": A Border Ballad and Its Hero.* Austin: University of Texas Press, 1958.

Roosevelt, Franklin Delano. "Annual Message to the Congress," January 3, 1940; and "Annual Message to the Congress," January 6, 1941. In *The Public Papers and Addresses of Franklin D. Roosevelt,* vol. 9: *War—and Aid to Democracies, 1940.* New York: Macmillan, 1941.

Said, Edward. "Reflections in American 'Left' Literary Criticism." In *The World, the Text, and the Critic.* Cambridge, Mass.: Harvard University Press, 1983.

Saldívar, José David. "Chicano Narratives as Cultural Critique." In *Criticism in the Borderlands: Studies in Chicano Literature, Culture, and Ideology,* ed. Héctor Calderón and José David Saldívar. Durham, N.C.: Duke University Press, 1991. 167–80.

———. "Américo Paredes and Decolonization." In *Cultures of United States Imperialism,* ed. Amy Kaplan and Donald E. Pease. Durham, N.C.: Duke University Press, 1993. 292–311.

Saldívar, Ramón. *Chicano Narrative: The Dialectics of Difference.* Madison: University of Wisconsin Press, 1990.

Santamaría, Francisco. Diccionario de Mejicanismos. 3d ed. Mexico City: Editorial Porrua, 1978.

Santos, John Phillip. "A Latin Quest for Identity: Performance Artist Guillermo Gómez-Peña Unveils New Work following 'Genius' Award." *San Francisco Chronicle* Datebook (November 3, 1991): 19–20.

Soja, Edward W. *Postmodern Geographies: The Reassertion of Space in Critical Social Theory.* London: Verso, 1990.

Williams, Raymond. *The Politics of Modernism: Against the New Conformists,* ed. Tony Pinkney. London: Verso, 1989.

⁓

# Telling the *différance*

## Representations of Identity in the
## Discourse of Indianness

JANA SEQUOYA-MAGDALENO

Insofar as American Indians have been taken apart as peoples and reinvented as discourse, the referent of the category "Indian" is a matter of much dispute.[1] The premise of this essay is that, first of all, this condition of disputation is an effect of the "Othering" province of the category itself.[2] Second, it is a paradoxical consequence of virtual American Indian acculturation to legal, political, and economic formations of an "Indian" difference, caught between differing and deferring, subject to regulation and administration. That administratively produced difference is, in turn, culturally inscribed as the standard of identity cohering American Indian diversity; strategic identity-in-difference is adopted as the political basis for nationalist claims to "self-determination" and tribal "sovereignty."

However, homogenizing criteria of Indianness-as-difference are simultaneously internalized as a lived process of self-othering through a network of symbolic signification—itself a cultural by-product of the historical dispossession of American Indian peoples. Iconically coded as a vanishing trace of the sacred at the horizon of the secular world, the Indian is (to paraphrase Jacques Lacan) a word in somebody else's conversation. And insofar as the terms of that conversation position contemporary American Indians ideally outside the time of representation, rather than in terms of shared histories of social rupture and cultural transformation, Indian-identified people themselves internalize a certain pressure to refrain from looking too closely at their constitution as representative subjects of the discourse of Indianness.[3]

Let us begin to look at the contentious conditions of Native American representation by articulating a distinction between the genealogical, territorial, symbolic, and cultural grounds of identity as a matter of identification with the category "Indian" and to ask the disturbing questions, "With what do we identify when we identify as Indian?" and "How does that positionality come to define a space of cultural production?" Both questions are linked to the stabilization of the literary production of American Indian cultures within the parameters of the figurative functions of Indianness in the late twentieth century.

While identification as Indian is more or less a function of indigenous descent, it is an effect, in turn, of a series of historical relationships to westward expansion and of the ideological and legal ramifications of that event. A theoretical distinction between biological, cultural, and political perspectives allows us not only to foreground the crosscutting conditions of Indian representation, but to displace the legalistic problem of right to such representation that haunts cultural producers of mixed Native American descent. The problem of "right" is in part a matter of evidence, or the lack thereof, of a paper trail that many of our forebears felt compelled to erase, and, in part, a consequence of those paradoxical imperatives of the discourse of Indianness constituting Indian identity as, by definition, subject to question.[4] The strategy adopted by this essay engages the issue of "identification" rather than of "identity" in order to focus upon the function of the category "Indian" to produce a subject that it claims to represent.[5]

## What Is (an) Indian?

The first twist in the productive logic of the category "Indian" is the question, "What is an Indian?" officially posed in the report by the U.S. Commissioner of Indian Affairs in 1892.[6] Answers have been sought in ontological terms codified as "blood-quantum," or alternately ascribed on the basis of the dominant culture's perceptions of "Indian" ways of life. The problem with both notions, of course, is that these criteria of Indianness do not necessarily coincide; the categorical logic of identity is countered by the possibility of being officially non-Indian while being genealogically a "full-blood" living in a traditional Indian community.

Thus the Pueblo could be declared non-Indians by the Supreme Court of New Mexico Territory in 1869 and again in 1877 by the U.S. Supreme

Court because they were observed to be "a peaceable, industrious, intelligent, and honest and virtuous people . . . , Indians only in feature, complexion, and a few of their habits."[7] However, this legal determination was less in recognition of common humanity than of federal and state economic interests in opening the land to settlement and development under the Homestead Act; for if the Pueblo were not Indians, then they were not protected by rights of dependency established by John Marshall's Supreme Court decision (*Cherokee Nation v. Georgia*, 1831). Although well meaning, Marshall's decision that the Indian's relation to the United States "resembles that of a ward to its guardian" was the first premise leading to the institutionalization of a paradoxical injunction for American Indians: if they were insufficiently "other" in relation to the dominant society, then they may be disqualified as Indians.

The production of Indianness as the timeless negative of a self-evident historical development is exemplified in the work of the late nineteenth-century photographer Edward Curtis. The original plate of one of his iconographs of "The Vanishing American" shows that the object the Piegan men display for the camera is a clock.[8] Their facial expressions indicate that their possession of this artifact is a matter of pride, and as such it competes for the narrative logic of the photograph. Precisely because the clock is at once symbol, product, and regulator of modern society, it reveals the discrepancy between their symbolic positioning as Other to the modern world and their lived experience of acculturation to it. For all that the presence of the clock belies the ahistorical image of Indianness, it is exactly what they, as the representative subjects of that image, cannot exhibit without forfeiting their unique symbolic value as anachronism—indeed, their very identity—in the eyes of the Euro-American observer. Therefore, Curtis erases the object from the plate, leaving the picture of the Piegan vacant at its very center.[9] That vacancy—a condition that is itself emblematic of the discourse of Indianness—marks the particularity of the betrayal behind their backs of the social contract under which the Piegan posed for the photo.

## Man Manqué: Orality as Text

Just as the Indian has been icongraphically depicted as outside the time of representation and therefore as, by definition, out of place, so the ideological connections between notions of wilderness and of Indians legitimate Native American cultural production in terms that are preliterate, if not precognitive. Thus, the second paradox of the discourse of Indianness is that while its conditions of change are presumed to be negated by a persistence "in the blood" of an ontological ahistoricity, traces of its signifying orality are deposited in textual literary forms and recuperated under the auspices of academic culture. As an effect of the individuated conditions of literary production, the communal foundations of oral cultures are at once hypostasized and represented according to the categorical imperatives of the discourse of Indianness. Hence, without a trace of irony, essays of cultural reclamation inform readers that Indians use words differently, more carefully, than non-Indian word-users: unlike "white" words, Indian words bear the concentrated force of the real.[10] Yet in the interests of incorporating this uniquely signifying Word into the American literary canon, the cultural logic of its conditions of representation is generally suppressed: the real change that might be effected by positing "Indian words" as a sort of textual Aladdin's lamp is precisely the transference of values from oral to textual structures of legitimation and the corresponding reterritorialization of "the Indian" in textual space. That "reterritorialization" (to invert Deleuze and Guattari's paradigm) is the condition of possibility for an emergent class of Indian-identified writers to chart, to redefine, and, in so doing, to intervene in hegemonic culture.[11]

Although (and because) the authors of Native American novels are often among the most marginal members of those Indian communities on which their imaginative works draw, they retain dual configurations of identity, which are thematically elaborated in their works. However, in their role as cultural representatives, Indian-identified writers are charged with a moral imperative that places them in a double bind: one condition of their newly privileged position as the West's ontological other is their critical perspective on the dominant culture; a second is their function as bridge between archaic and modern ways of knowing. These conditions of representation constitute the terms of legitimation that an emergent class of writers must negotiate in order to signify their Indianness; they also entail claims of authority vis-à-vis tribal traditions that transgress the customary modes of self-representation based on those traditions. Because the bicultural (or, initially, the not-yet-cultural) protagonist represents a mediating principle between contesting social formations—as it does in the notion of the "mixed-blood" as "bridge"—the Native American protagonist reprises the historic role of the bicultural translator.

And insofar as the figure of the "mixed-blood" or "half-breed" functions tropologically in accord with the aesthetic ideal of transition from the local to the universal, it mirrors hegemonic modes of assimilation to ever more universal, or canonical, cultural forms. By the same token, despite the generally adversarial stance of Native American literary criticism toward "Western" society, its oppositional rhetoric reflects residual Romantic currents in popular culture, conventional discourses inherited from the context in which both the figure of the Indian and the interpretive project of literary criticism have their historical ground.

Popular identification with Indianness as a symbolic site of resistance conceptually linked to idealisms of the organic revived with the countercultural movement of the 1960s, creating a receptive climate for Leslie Marmon Silko's first novel, Ceremony, in 1977. The author, of Laguna Pueblo, Anglo, Mexican, and "mixed-blood Plains" heritage, was acclaimed by Frank MacShane in the New York Times Book Review as "the most accomplished Indian writer of her generation." Ceremony is a syncretic work characterized by the incorporation of fragments from traditional Pueblo and Navajo clan stories that signify at once a home base to which the pathologically decentered protagonist may return and the Indianness of the genre.[12] However, at the same time that it redefines Indianness in terms of cultural syncretism, Ceremony novelizes the "residue of a broken ensemble" (Lacoue-Labarthe and Nancy, The Literary Absolute, 39–58) in keeping with the metynomic "model . . . of fragmented antiquity, the landscape of ruins" (50). Thus, the formal method of Silko's justly celebrated work is that of a double appropriation of disparate evaluative codes that are in some respects complementary and in others incommensurable:[13] it adapts the secular form of the modern novel to reproduce elements of sacred Pueblo and Navajo oral cycles at the same time that it invokes the stylistic form of the oral tradition (a device that is one of the earliest conventions of the novel form) to represent the dramatic conflict and resolution most characteristic of Western narrative.

The dual positioning of the work in mainstream (assimilative) and tribal (exclusive) societies creates a number of problems for its critical reception; yet, rather than being addressed, those problems are generally circumvented by the essence-seeking project of multicultural canon formation. Although Silko ostensibly writes against the grain of the "Vanishing American" motif of North American Indian iconography, the premise of the unreformed Indian as the residue of history enters Ceremony under cover of a binary relationship between "mixed-blood" and "full-blood"; the former signifies survival of tradition in adaptive developmental forms, and the latter its stagnation, degeneration, and corruption—thus inverting the nineteenth-century North American motif of the "tragic mixed-blood."

However, insofar as Silko's compensatory strategy defines as residual a population already "minorized," that is, construed by the mainstream imagination as categorically "minor" (an effect of its prior representation in terms of a primitive stage in the universal history of civilization), it not only reproduces the conventions of discourse of Indianness but legitimates those conventions as a Native American revitalization movement.[14] Hence, despite a proliferation of commentary on *Ceremony*, there has been substantial resistance to critiquing its form of representation.[15]

## Strategies of Legitimation

*Ceremony* is a canonical work in the sense not only that it is one of the most frequently assigned novels in university classes today (in both "literary" and "nonliterary" courses that need to cite/site "Indianness"), but also that it has generated within Native American literary criticism a sort of parallel universe, reproducing within the academic arena the primary concern of the text—a struggle between contesting systems of power and knowledge. At issue in that struggle, as it is taken up by pedagogical multiculturalism, are the emergent institutional interests of Indian-identified cultural producers to define and control the signifier "Indian."[16]

That these interests only gesturally coincide with those of less privileged Native Americans is a contradiction that is generally suppressed by the legitimating strategies of national canon formation. To the extent that critical reception of Silko's *Ceremony* reenacts the novel's thematic concern to redefine Indian identity according to the interests of the most acculturated class, it can be read as an allegory of crises in contemporary culture arising out of confrontations between conflicting worldviews to which writers of Native American fiction are particularly sensitive.

The sophisticated reader may be aware of a discrepancy between the narrative persona and the social reality of the writer of "mainstream" fiction (a discrepancy understood as a function of the aesthetic predicates of the literary work), yet the distinction seems less obvious when that same reader encounters the narrative "voice" in Native American fiction (presumed to be predicated on premodern standpoints). Rather than recognizing essentialist inscriptions as a strategy to locate the work and to set the terms of its reception, many scholarly interpreters of Native American fiction seem to assume that the writer, however explicitly bicultural, however modern—as evidenced by appropriation of the novel form itself—is nevertheless transparent at some preconscious level, that is, really *is* the narrative position taken up for the sake of participating in the discursive conditions of the genre.[17]

Before proceeding with an analysis of the Prologue to Silko's *Ceremony*, a text that is emblematic of the most intense negotiations around American Indian identity and cultural production, it is important to delineate the dominant strategies of critical discourse to represent those negotiations in scholarly literature. An instructive example of the institutional pressure to read minority literature as an ethnographic document of the voice of the Other may be observed in a multifaceted essay by Arnold Krupat, a critic whose work has contributed enormously to the field and whose sympathies are evident, yet whose work sometimes cannot avoid the contradictions inherent in the historical and institutional production of discourse on "the Indian."

Although "The Dialogic of Silko's Storyteller" engages Silko's first major work "from a Bakhtinian perspective . . . as a social model which allows for the projection of a particular image of human community," that model tends to deconstruct itself despite Krupat's admirable attempts to (re)cover contradiction as intention: "for all the seeming irony of proposing that the highly place-oriented and more or less homogeneous cultures of indigenous Americans might best teach us how to be cosmopolitans, that is exactly what I intend to say."[18]

Krupat's statement of purpose is significant for the discrepancy it reveals between intention and "projection" as a consequence of his paradoxical attribution of homogeneity to indigenous Americans. Indeed, the passage signals that the discourse of Indianness is both subtly rewriting the Bakhtinian paradigm of polyvocality and collapsing distinct aspects of Native American worldviews, disparate forms of social organization, and multiple cultural practices in order to find a point of mutual legitimation and articulation.

Krupat's reduction of Native American cultures to a zero sum of identity, on the one hand, and his compensatory elevation of (a perhaps ersatz) heterogeneity under the sign of "cosmopolitanism," on the other, is mitigated by his citation of Paul Rabinow's warning that "the trick is to avoid 'reify[ing] local identities or construct[ing] universal ones'" (65).[19] If we are to proceed with the caution recommended by Rabinow, we might pause to consider the first condition, as posited by Krupat, of Silko's exemplary relationship to a tribal culture that can "best teach us how to be cosmopolitans." That precondition is our acceptance of his proposition that "having called herself a storyteller," Silko "thus places herself in a tradition of tellings" (60).[20] In consideration of the "trick" involved in negotiations between local identities and cosmopolitan identifications, we may want to factor into the equation the particularity of Silko's relationship to the Laguna tribal community—a relationship that is obscured by the terms of Krupat's discussion of her representative status.

Those terms not only dispense with the distinction between the subject of Silko's desire (to be a traditional Laguna storyteller) and its object (to place herself in that tradition), but dispose, as well, of the possible resistance offered by precisely those communal sanctions acknowledged in Krupat's prior statement that "to be known as a storyteller is to be known as one who participates, in a communally sanctioned manner, in sustaining the group" (59).

The latter condition would seem to contradict Krupat's second contention that Silko's literary mediation of the general store of traditional Laguna narratives is "always consistent with . . . attempts to liberate 'cultural-semantic and emotional intentions' from the hegemony of a single and unitary language" (61)—a hegemony posited by Bakhtin (in response to a historical-political context quite different from that of the Laguna Pueblo) as a characteristic of "officially sanctioned myth." In this instance, Krupat's judgment of Silko's literary motivation is at odds with his prior formulation of her relationship of continuity with "officially sanctioned myth," since in principle her "attempts to liberate" tribal stories from traditional communal sanctions would compromise her relationship to Laguna cultural traditions.

Most significantly, in the context of Krupat's discussion of Bakhtin's "meditations" on polyvocality as they might apply to Silko's representative status vis-à-vis the Pueblo storytelling traditions, he asserts not only that "Silko's stories are always consistent with—to return to Bakhtin—attempts to liberate," but "consistent with a ' . . . loss of feeling for language as myth' " (61). Perhaps as a function of his substitution of the linking phrase "consistent with" for Bakhtin's connecting clause "and consequently the simultaneous loss of a feeling for myth,"[21] Krupat is able to evade the contradictory implications for his hypothesis, which he would otherwise have to address.

For instance, the central claims that "The Dialogic of Silko's Storyteller" makes on behalf of Silko's writing—that it signifies "unabashed commitment to Pueblo ways as a reference point" (65) and furthermore, that "what keeps the polyvocality of her writing from entering the postmodernist or schizophrenic heteroglossic domain, is its commitment to the equivalent of a normative voice" (65)—would seem untenable in light of her contradictory "attempts to liberate" Pueblo stories from their traditional communal contexts. Insofar as we agree with the latter proposition, we might conclude that Silko *refuses* rather than accepts the traditional function of Pueblo storyteller to "participate in a communally sanctioned manner in sustaining the group."[22] For if Silko's narrative strategies do signify a commitment to Pueblo "ways," she cannot be simultaneously engaged in transgression of those ways, precisely because—according to Krupat's own definition— "commitment to Pueblo ways" entails "sustaining the group" (59), presumably in terms of its own cultural values and social goals.

The only way out of this logical impasse would be to redefine the "group" in terms of that "cosmopolitan" consciousness toward which we are (advisedly) striving, rather than in terms of the traditional tribal community. However, if the proceeds from the author's best-selling "tellings" of the Pueblo oral tradition are indeed returned to that community, Krupat's characterization of Silko as simultaneously subversive and committed to "Pueblo ways" would again have a different meaning. Her social duality, in that case, would reflect structural and ideological shifts in those "ways." And insofar as she may be representative of the historical transformation of traditional structures of identity, the "communally sanctioned manner" of Silko's storytelling then has a meaning closer to that of contemporary Western culture as commodity, with Laguna community profit substituting for that of individuals.

To return to our hesitation over the posited equation between Silko's desire to be a traditional storyteller and Krupat's assumption that "she thus places herself in a tradition of tellings," his subordinate clause is sufficiently self-evident to suspend our caution for the moment: that "her stories cannot strictly be her own" (60) is a commonsense statement in that no stories can "strictly" be one's own given the fact of modern cultural literacy. Yet rather than deciding that therefore Silko is a modern writer informed by diverse cultural influences, as one might expect (particularly in light of Bakhtin's predication of "loss of feeling for myth" as a simultaneous consequence of liberation from tradition—a key indicator of modern consciousness), Krupat's interest in legitimating Silko in terms of Pueblo traditions leads him to affirm her "tellings" as continuous with premodern forms of literacy: "nor will we find in them what one typically looks for in post-Rousseauian, Western autobiography or . . . a uniquely personal voice" (60).

The convention of temporal inequality in the discourse of Indianness influences Krupat to foreclose on Silko's participation in the literary present (a present, it must be remarked, in which the "cosmopolitan" participates) via a prior "acknowledgment" that "it is the distinction between truth and error rather than that between fact and fiction that seems more interesting to native expression; and indeed, this distinction was also central to Western thought prior to the seventeenth century" (59). Thus Krupat's theoretical application of Bakhtin's dialogic positions Silko's writing in terms of "a return to that time when the line between history and myth was not very clearly marked," adding the conventional wisdom of the discourse of Indianness: "but this is the way things have always been for Native American literatures" (59).

Krupat's invocation of "always" marks a tendency that is one of the most common problems for Native American criticism—the reification (despite his own warning) of some facet of tribal culture in the interests of analyzing that fictional real in terms of hypothetically parallel instances of Euro-American theory. Thus a paradoxical condition of Krupat's analogy between Bakhtin's polyvocality and Silko's representative status vis-à-vis the Laguna storytelling tradition is the model's lack of engagement with the material history of Pueblo cultures.[23] In order to dispose of the latter, he not only must efface the circumstances of Silko's bicultural heritage and suppress her particular relationship to the heterogeneous traditions she mediates, but must ignore the positive sanctions and the negative limits entailed in her mediation of those traditions for the majority culture.[24]

Moreover, his omission of those considerations is sustained despite Silko's own denial—originally recorded in Kenneth Rosen's *Voices of the Rainbow*—of any unequivocal claim on her part to the Pueblo storytelling tradition: "The way we live is like Marmons . . . somewhere on the fringes . . . our origin is unlike any other" (68). (At a more subtly articulated level of that qualification however, Silko's self-perception of marginality simultaneously confirms her connection with the Pueblo archetype on which the Yellow Women stories are based. For the relationship between the Yellow Women stories and marginality see Paula Gunn Allen, *The Sacred Hoop*, 227.) Silko's account of her "fringe" relationship to Pueblo traditions is relegated to Krupat's endnotes, where he acknowledges that "as glossed from Alan Velie . . . this means like 'mixed-blood[s] from a ruling family.'"

Thus, despite Silko's own "telling" of the ambivalent relationship between her own "ruling family" and the more traditional (egalitarian?) Laguna in the village, her equivocation does not alert Krupat to a contradic-

tion that might compromise his contention that "for all the polyvocal openness of Silko's work, there is always the unabashed commitment to Pueblo
ways as a reference point," constituting an "authority . . . always to be reck-
oned with" (65)—a statement that itself contradicts the decentering mode
of his Bakhtinian connection.

Yet Krupat's elision of Silko's self-description is reflective of more than
inadvertency on the part of a critic whose project is precisely to call for theoretical sophistication in the interests of the canonical production of representative Native American subjects. The categorical requirements of the
canon itself tend to reduce the hybrid positions most characteristic of Native American writers to the pattern of a generic identity, a pattern discernible in his characterization of Native Americans as "the highly place-oriented and more or less homogeneous cultures of indigenous Americans"
(65). Most crucially, then, Krupat's construction of an imaginary identity
that displaces to the margins of his essay the lived complexity that Silko herself affirms is emblematic of the double-bind prescriptions for the field of
Native American literary criticism. That theoretical aporia reflects, in turn,
the general pressures on the representative Native American writer to make
a claim for authority vis-à-vis traditional tribal "ways," a claim that itself
defies traditional modes of self-representation.

The generic roles available as the constituting conditions of racially
marked "minority" literature subordinate the complexity of Silko's self-
characterization to the homogenizing discourse of "Indianness" that can be
extrapolated from her statements despite her protest against that reduction.
(It is interesting to note in this context that Silko insists, in an interview entitled "Predicting a Revolt to Reclaim the Americas," that she became a
writer "because I felt I wasn't that good as a storyteller at the Laguna
Pueblo" (January 3, 1992). I would like to suggest by the foregoing critique
that a strategy more reflective of the relationships between the disparate
factions within Native American communities (and between that internal
diversity and the relationship of those ideological and pragmatic tensions
to literary-aesthetic representations of Indianness) might consist, in the instance under consideration, in tracking the shifting standpoints of Silko's
own statements about herself.

Each standpoint in the series of her self-representation is a response to the
prevailing discursive conditions that solicit her narrative; each narrative position reflects upon the institutional interests particular to those conditions;
each representation has its own story to tell about the network of relationships out of which it is articulated. Not only might the thematic record of

Silko's self-representation tell a story about the system of forces sanctioning and constraining the constitution of Native American subject positions, and in turn contribute to a critical grasp of the conditions of possibility afforded emergent subject positions within the contesting but asymmetrical relations of power to be negotiated as a self, but it would enable us to better understand Silko's strategies of intervention in the hegemonic cultural field in which her work circulates as representative of the discourse of Indianness.[25]

This is to propose that a materially grounded critical response to Native American authors first of all acknowledge their changing representations of positionality as indications of pragmatic engagement with, and intervention in, canonical demands for a coherent identity. Accordingly, the reader who wishes to clarify Silko's actual relationship to the multiple traditions on which she draws might more productively consider the shifting emphasis of her early equivocation and the assertion one year later, included in Krupat's endnotes, that although she is "of mixed-breed ancestry," what she knows is "Laguna."

Rather than imposing on Silko a representative status that her own self-descriptions deny, critics might want to consider what forms of experience are selected as representative in constituting the writer's public persona (or in accommodating such constitution) as a legitimating condition of Native American canon formation; or again, out of the multiplicity of self-representations for the official record, consider why some experiences of identity and difference become more articulate than others—for example, what categorical pressures are signaled by Silko's stance as one who may speak for Laguna as if it were a unified object of knowledge; and then, as indicated by her subsequent hesitation, what communal sanctions are discernible in the following quote, even as the substance of those sanctions remains outside official representation:

> I suppose at the core of my writing is the attempt to identify what it is to be a half-breed or mixed blooded person; what it is to grow up neither white nor fully traditional Indian. It is for this reason that I hesitate to say that I am representative of Indian poets or Indian people, or even Laguna people. I am only one human being, one Laguna woman. (From Hymes 1981; in Lincoln 1983, 233)

By remarking the trajectory from collective to individuated sources of validation typified by such statements, one might engage the conditions of Native American self-formation in relationship to the sanctions and limits of legitimating traditions and discourses. On the other hand, consideration of the connection between affirmation and equivocation of communal identity would allow its theorization in terms more subtly articulated than those of the ironic mode to which it is reduced as an epochal signature of modernity. Critical engagement with the modes of externalization of conflicted structures of identity would, in turn, enable a connected understanding of corollary modes of internalization of institutional prescriptions in the production of canonical literature. And Silko, as in fact a modern writer rather than a "premodern" storyteller, has left ample record of the canonical literary influences that inform her writing.[26]

In light of the foregoing discussion, it would seem that Krupat's legitimation of Silko in the imaginary terms of Indianness paradoxically suppresses the very conditions that would support his appropriation of Rabinow's version of Bakhtin's cosmopolitan paradigm.[27] Not only are the dialogic conditions of her subjectivity, and therefore of her writing, returned to the rule of identity by Krupat's equation of Pueblo oral traditions with Silko's literary mediation of them, but the non-Indian influences on her work are discounted in the interests of a critical enterprise that seeks to celebrate the voice of the temporal, ontological, and epistemological Other. Nevertheless, it is exactly the dual (or multiple) cultural grounds of Silko's writing that constitute the material context of her work (a matter of particular interest, one might expect, for a "materialist" approach to Native American literature) just as it is her negotiation of traditional tribal and secular humanist ways of having stories that structures Silko's formal experiments. These conditions of representation provide at once the substance of Silko's literary position as a "canonical" Native American author and an anecdote to the idealistic tendencies of Krupat's cosmopolitan model of literary canon formation.

## Cultural Transformation: *Ceremony's* Prologue

Although Silko's many biographical statements complicate the categorical imperatives of Indianness by which she has been inducted into the American literary canon, the multiple narrators of *Ceremony's* Prologue nevertheless announce themselves as speaking for "Pueblo ways." In so doing, they offer a condensed version of the novel's system of representation:

> Thought-Woman, the spider,
> named things and
> as she named them
> they appeared.
> She is sitting in her room
> thinking of a story now.
> I'm telling you the story she is thinking. (1)

This seemingly transparent framing device mirrors the historical emergence of the ego or centered Renaissance subject from the dissolution of, in Fredric Jameson's words, "the older organic or hierarchical social groups" (*The Political Unconscious*, 153–54). In so doing, it positions the reader at the crux of traditional Pueblo and interpellating modes of cultural legitimation. (By interpellation I intend Althusser's sense of a hegemonic "hailing" and response, of the penetration and appropriation of Pueblo sacred forms by the secular-humanist ideology of the autonomous individual.) Secularization of the sacred archetype, Thought-Woman, is signaled at the outset by the narrative transference from collective ground to author function; yet rather than constituting an object of critical inquiry in relation to its ostensible referent—the traditional Laguna—the transitive procedure is received in the normative terms of Western individuation.[28] Similarly, despite the second narrator's admonition regarding the clan stories—"They aren't just entertainment. . . . They are all we have, you see, all we have to fight off illness and death"—the contradiction of "telling" these sacred story fragments within the recreational context of the novel form not only is masked by the allegory of orality conveyed by the verb "to tell," but the mode of appropriation is so fully taken for granted that its hegemonic character is, indeed, invisible.

Thus, the unmarked irony of the narrator's reproach is that insofar as tribal and commodified narratives are founded on disparate forms of cultural legitimation and produce very different modes of subjectivity, they are incommensurable *except* at the level of entertainment.[29] The conditions of bicultural mediation are particularly complex, then, when the dual sets of referentiality are those of sacred and secular modes of culture, or, more pointedly in the context of literary representations of traditional paradigms, creational and recreational constructions of identity.[30] Consequently, a critical understanding of *Ceremony* depends on where one stands in relation to the disparate evaluative systems underlying quite distinct modes of social organization. On the one hand, the Prologue's transition from Pueblo communal structures of legitimation to the individualist modes of the majority society betrays the former in its resistance to the latter. On the other hand, it reflects the heterogeneity of possible subject positions among the mixed population at the cultural periphery (in Silko's metaphor, at "the fringes") of Laguna. Yet, despite the basis of Silko's work in the latter standpoint, the Prologue reduces the conflicts between traditional and acculturated identities within the Laguna community (and, in turn, the conflicts between Pueblo and majority structures of legitimation) to a

JANA SEQUOYA-MAGDALENO 102

Manichean allegory of good and evil, and in so doing exerts pressures against readings that might escape those terms.

However, by opening the interpretive frame to include those standpoints at once implied and foreclosed by invocation of the clan stories, we may ground the Prologue's imaginary web of identity and identification in the ongoing struggles of the Laguna community to determine its own ethos. In order to do so, we might begin by accepting provisionally the hypothesis of Fredrick Barth's seminal study of ethnicity: "identification as a member of a traditionally bounded group implies a willingness to be judged by the codes relevant to that group."[31] Accordingly, from the perspective of those for whom the clan stories structure identification with traditional forms of social organization, Silko's narrative assumption of the persona of the Pueblo creatrix entails a corresponding accountability to the customary communal sanctions associated with those traditional Pueblo "ways."

If we are to approach *Ceremony* simultaneously in its relation to the split subject attributed to the social conditions of modernity in general and historical experiences of colonialism in particular, we must consider the relevant proscriptions attending traditional Pueblo worldviews in light of the limits they impose on the mediations of secular humanism encoded in the novel form.[32] As noted by Al Logan Slagle in "The Native American Tradition," the topographical referents of the clan stories "explain the powers and functions associated with those sites as actual geographic possessions and as sacred places."[33] Those geographic referents are constitutive rather than incidental to the significance of the clan stories; they are a matter of foreground rather than of background. The material referentiality of the clan stories restrains the centrifugal tendencies of modern economic organization and encourages reintegration of deculturated Indians with ancestral community. Literary texts, on the other hand, substitute typographic for geographic sites of knowledge and power. Their relations of production and distribution, as well as their modes of legitimation, tend to produce culture as commodity fetish, corresponding to economic principles of expansion and incorporation, in contrast to the subordinated social principles of identity founded on relationships to place.

Confrontation between contradictory forms of selfhood produced by these different modes of cultural legitimation is reflected in *Ceremony*'s motif of *Y Volveré* (the Mexican love song that marks a characteristic theme of "return" theorized by William Bevis in "Native American Novels: Homing In"). The efforts of American Indian communities to retain their dynamic relationships to the land base of culture (and hence their viability as

distinct peoples) is articulated at Laguna as an issue of communal bound-
aries and traditional role allocations of which a member of the Santa Clara
Pueblo speaks in anthropologist Nancy Scheper-Hughes's "The Best of Two
Worlds, the Worst of Two Worlds":

> The young people, who know little, will talk. The old, who know all that is
> worth knowing, will remain silent. That is our protection. This knowledge is
> codified in our myths. This kind of cultural knowledge is not for casual
> use. . . . If the information is distributed casually, power goes out of it, and
> Destruction Day comes closer.[34]

In one of the few instances in which tribal attitudes can be generalized, the
more traditional among Native American peoples consider it foolish to approach sacred power without ritual preparation and commitment.[35] Such
commitment has no bearing on a reader's access to literature about those
practices.

Moreover, the consequence of unsanctioned "tellings" of the sacred stories is the cumulative loss of that power for the community. When considered from this perspective, a problem with the mediation of the clan stories
for mainstream culture is evident: the writer who proclaims an analogy between her novelization of clan story fragments and the collective archetype
upon which those clan stories are based, legitimating by the force of that
analogy the assimilation of the latter to the majority culture (and hence re-
inforcing the breakdown of traditional sources of identity), undermines the
interests most acutely set forth in the Prologue's admonishment: "They are
all we have, you see, all we have to fight off illness and death."[36]

Just as the Prologue simultaneously posits and effaces the antagonism
between the competing narratives of identity and identification produced
out of divergent social histories and modes of cultural organization, so politicized readings of the cultural issues raised by *Ceremony* are constrained
by the values and expectations of the popular novel form as it articulates,
responds to, and resists, majority structures of legitimation. And because
the novel's self-reflexive critique of its paradoxical position between disparate legitimating codes tends to be alternately suppressed by its *Bildung* narrative and deflected by its motif of spiritual transcendence, a critical approach to this complex work must consider its representations of origins
and its corollary strategies to consolidate identity through an imaginary
community of interests.

Despite the framing terms of *Ceremony* according to the interpretive set
defined by Barre Toelken as the "medicinal level" of tribal story, the coun-
terstory of secular humanism historically encoded within the novel form

tends to delegitimate its metaphysical worldview. However, the conflict between the Pueblo sacred oral traditions and the individualistic and commodified aspects of modern recreational culture is further complicated from the standpoint of the former in that Thought-Woman (by her nature as creatrix) is thinking up the contest between incommensurate ways of having stories.

Because the secular context in which we read a novel that forbids such a reading entails a degree of cognitive dissonance, critical engagement with Silko's first novel depends upon our recognition of the multidirectional character of the accusatory sign producing identity and difference in the transaction of bicultural mediation:

> Their evil is mighty
> but it can't stand up to our stories.
> So they try to destroy the stories
> let the stories be confused or forgotten. (2)

Although the dual functions of the inclusive and exclusive pronouns are an expression of Thought-Woman's generative powers, their attributed values of good and evil construct the reader's identification with the role of cultural guardian. Yet in light of the foregoing discussion, identification with the possessive "our" entails an unstated conflict for the reader: the recreational context in which our position as defender of the clan stories is constituted is a context in many respects emblematic of precisely those appropriations against which we are to guard them. Consequently, for all that the Prologue's lure of identification appears to comprise an ethic of resistance to "they" who would "let the stories be confused or forgotten," upon closer inspection we see that our imaginary positioning as the privileged term of an opposition between insiders/defenders versus outsiders/destroyers effects a referential transference that disarticulates, rather than articulates, the relationship between preserving and "confusing" the clan stories.

Although the narrator's identification with Thought-Woman would seem to signal her authority to proffer the clan stories as our rightful property (in the dominant society's sense of culture as a common property of the more representative or universal subject), from the standpoint of those interests with which the Prologue ostensibly addresses the reader—the interests, specifically, of the more traditional among the Laguna—the reader's access to novels about the lifeways of cultural others is a function of the split condition of the production of knowledge of and discourse about colonized cultural objects. From the standpoint of the exclusively organized Pueblo, then, the first narrator's identification with Thought-Woman refers most concretely to the prerogatives assumed by the cross-cultural mediator to reverse through Western aesthetic traditions those collective social relations the Prologue appears to defend. From that standpoint, the accusatory "they" points *back* to us readers.

Along one axis of the web of identity and identification, we become "they" who would "confuse" Pueblo sacred traditions with the commodified relations of Western literature; along a second axis, the accusatory sign points to those traditionalists who would resist expropriation of their sacred stories by us cultural outsiders. Insofar as the reader takes up the imaginary position of centrality proposed by the self-validating system of identifications, we become enmeshed in a process of substitution in which our own interests as readers of novels about cultural "others" displaces those "Pueblo ways" that exclude us precisely in the interests of Pueblo identity. However, from the point of view of those who have been ritually initiated into the traditional Pueblo institutions, the clan stories are indeed protected from the alienation of the social resources of communal identity against which the Prologue warns. They are protected by kinship role allocations and the corresponding communal restrictions on the conditions of their mediation.

Nevertheless, while the clan stories themselves constitute the narrated continuity of Pueblo institutions, just as those entities do not consist in a static system, so tribal community is not a homogeneous identity. The ideological gaps and pragmatic factions generated by living social matrices produce and reflect incremental changes in the institutions (i.e., communities) of the historically various Pueblos, as in any society. That structural and ideological shifting of a traditional culture is reflected in the protest of a woman from the Santa Clara Pueblo quoted by Scheper-Hughes:

> There are just a few old men left who know the prayers and the ceremonies. They would rather see the prayers die and be forgotten, than share them with young women like myself or even with grandmothers, so that we could pass them on to our sons and daughters. I don't know if it does any good in the world if in every generation there are fewer and fewer people who know our Pueblo truths and who are willing to take the risk of sharing them.[37]

The woman's despair for the cultural continuity of her community expresses, in part, the sociological consequences of a philosophic contradiction: the traditional sanctions and limits concomitant with the transmission of the clan stories confront egalitarian aspects of Pueblo social organization with a structural elitism encoded as "the way things have always been." Although one must not project onto the variety of Native

American traditions those democratic models developed in response to Euro-American histories, nevertheless the internal constraints on access to the clan stories would seem (from the perspectives of those who experience exclusion, as did Silko) to mark a functional schism that is itself a condition of cultural change. And it is precisely in the openings afforded by the contesting forces of cultural change and continuity that Silko's creative work is forged.

Because of its interstitial position in relation to those contesting forces, *Ceremony* simultaneously attests to and mediates not only the aesthetic requirements of secular humanism for representations of individuality socialized to the interests of family and state, not only the conflicting interests within a given tribal community—conflicts attributable, in part, to its political, economic, and ideological penetration by dominant values and institutions—but also the reconfiguration of Laguna structures of identity and identification, which, of course, include increasingly exogamous marriage practices.[38]

Nevertheless, as I have argued, Silko's novelized "telling" of those changing conditions has become the pretext for pseudosacred "auratic" interpretive criticism in the universities. Despite the explicit stress of *Ceremony's* framing device on the conflict of interests entailed in such mediations, many scholars of Native American literature neglect consideration of an appropriate cross-cultural ethics. Perhaps, because we ourselves have internalized the presumptive rights of the dominant culture (however critical we may imagine ourselves to be of such presumptions), in our enthusiasm for the exotic—a Western tradition of sorts—we fail to account for the fact that the conditions of production that enable Silko's reframing (and our own!) of ancestral stories (but whose?) in the contemporary popular novel challenge the very "ways" it evokes for the mainstream reader.

Perhaps we are disposed to ignore the incorporative tendency of the bicultural position in order to make up a good story of our own about the secret life of the "subaltern." It is worth considering in conclusion why an "Orientalist" (Indianist) celebration of *Ceremony* as an exemplary recuperation of the storytelling traditions of cultural Others has become the conventional approach to this novel even though the Prologue itself has indicated the paradoxical situation of the bicultural mediator.[39]

If, indeed, Native American communities no longer attempted to constitute themselves as resistant formations within the dominant society, one might dispense with a critique of the processes by which the Indian fetish object is produced in the interests of an appetite for the auratic trace. But because such disposal is an effect of the representational code of the "Vanishing American," Silko's *Ceremony* is read more acutely as metacommentary on the author function vis-à-vis both traditionally exclusive tribal societies and the national iconography of Indianness. The competing interests of the bicultural position are reflected in the novel's conflicting systems of legitimation and motivation. Those aporetic structures confront the reader as an experience of the sublime that finds its analogy in the figure of the culturally dislocated protagonist. At the narrative level, the contradictions personified by the protagonist are resolved in terms of his accommodation within the sacred traditions of the Laguna (Tayo's entrance into the society of the Kiva); at the performative level of reader reception, the repositioning of the sacred clan story within the secular terms of the literary market generates new framing conditions that accommodate the canonization of *Ceremony* as a representative text of pedagogical multiculturalism.

*Ceremony*'s narrative strategy reproduces the terms of the academic reception of contemporary Native American literature in that both are predicated upon paradoxical structures of legitimation: both are affirmed in consonance with the postulates of canonical aesthetics—as they instruct, entertain, and forge identification with a common culture; conversely, both are allied with postcolonial discourse as they confirm a generally adversarial disposition toward "Western" culture. For all that Native American literature is grounded simultaneously in histories of confrontation and accommodation between colonizer and colonized—at once in lived experiences of social rupture and reformation based on fragments of cultural survival—these texts must negotiate multiple positionings in relation to the iconography of Indianness. The rhetorical nostalgia effected by the figure of the Indian must be critiqued by material history, however effaced its record, rather than internalized as the standard of Native American identity—for to place oneself nostalgically is to misplace oneself.

## Notes

1. The disputed conditions of Native American representation have most recently been given the added force of law by "The Indian Arts and Crafts Act of 1990" (Public Law 101–644) under which artists of Indian descent who are not enrolled tribal members can be fined two hundred and fifty thousand dollars or face five years in prison for a first offense, that is, for claiming to be Indian despite lack of documentation. According to *News from Native California*, "The Act has the potential to do more harm than good in California because of the way in which it defines Indian art and Indian artists. The new law appears to exclude Indian artisans who cannot prove they are Indian because their tribe lacks the mandatory federal or state recognition, and those who have not become enrolled members of their tribe for politi-

cal, religious or personal reasons, including early adoption and/or removal from their families" (vol. 12 [fall 1991]: 12). In response to a recent *Wall Street Journal* editorial protesting that the act "criminalizes the selling of Indian art not made by Indians," the *Lakota Times* admonishes the "arrogance and ignorance on Wall Street," contending that "it is inevitable when fighting for specific Indian rights that some individuals will fall through the cracks. But should the entire Indian art community be shortchanged and placed in jeopardy because of these few?" The issue that "falls through the cracks" of that question, of course, concerns the "jeopardy" in which undocumented Indians are placed "because of these few" imposters "who have been making life difficult for genuine, enrolled Indian artists" (November 26, 1992: A 4). A corollary move to disqualify as "Indian" those of undocumented "blood" was enacted at the February 1992 conference on Native American issues in higher education at Arizona State University in the form of a contract entitled "Mission Statement of the American Indian Professoriate" proposed by Dr. Karen Gayton Swisher: "The Association of the American Indian Professoriate is founded for the purpose of nurturing and sustaining an American Indian Professoriate." Among the criteria for determining the "validity" of its objects of "aid in the development, evaluation, and accreditation of American Indian Studies Department[s], related curriculum, and faculty within higher education institutions" are listed "certification of student as American Indian"; its "Suggestions for Voting Member" specifies "American Indian heritage" (*Wicazo Sa Review* 8; no. 1 [spring 1992]: 103).

2. Although not addressed as such, the function of the figure of "the Indian" as a compensatory Other for the modern middle class is theoretically confirmed by Jochen Schulte-Sasse in "The Prestige of the Artist under Conditions of Modernity" (*Cultural Critique* 12 [spring 1989]). In his discussion of the emergence of "art in the second half of the eighteenth century as a privileged space of cultural activities," Schulte-Sasse contends that modern alienation "is structurally connected with an 'other' site of modernity in which [alienation] is allegedly suspended; the most common specifications of this site were nature, the savage, and art" (86)—categories cathected as a realm of reconciliation and redemption, imagined as being at once inside and outside representation, that is, ineffable, and thus "able to suspend the negative side-effects of the structural interdependencies created by the functional differentiation of society."

3. See Johannes Fabian's discussion of the ideological nature of temporal concepts informing such discourses in *Time and the Other: How Anthropology Makes Its Object* (New York: Columbia University Press, 1983): "The Other's empirical presence turns into his theoretical absence, a conjuring trick which is worked out with the help of an array of devices that have the common intent and function to keep the Other outside the time of anthropology" (xl).

4. Attempts to limit and control the conditions of Indian identification (see note 1) respond to the current proliferation of such identifications as indicated by N. Scott Momaday's oft-repeated line, "An Indian is an idea a given man has of himself" ("The Man Made of Words," originally in *Indian Voices: The First Convocation of American Indian Scholars* [San Francisco: Indian Historian Press, 1970], 49–62). Appropriation of "Indian" identification is theorized by Walter Benn-Michaels in "The Vanishing American" (*American Literary History* 2, no. 2 [summer 1990]: 220–41) as being predicated on the need of North American immigrants for a national ancestor. Fredric Jameson's discussion of style in *Marxism and Form* (Princeton, N.J.: Princeton University Press, 1971) can be applied to Momaday's idea of "an Indian" as a figure for a primitive sort of style: "Style . . . is the very element of individuality itself, that mode through which the individual consciousness seeks to distinguish itself, to affirm its incomparable originality" (334). Jameson continues his meditation on style (quoting Roland Barthes's *Writing, Degree Zero*): "Its references are on the level of biology or of the past, rather than of history" (58–59). Similarly, insofar as the referent of "Indian" style is an imagined past, it is an idea that is continually reinvented according to the changing social conditions and needs of the major culture; "Indian" style, then, is one of the cultural options available to Momaday's

"given man"—an option derived from mainstream literary and pictorial images, an accessory of the rebellious self, and a whole system of signifying gestures, regardless of that "man's" historical antecedents. While such a style may constitute an inversion of Homi Bhabha's colonial "mimicry," as disidentification, it may also be, in Barthes's words, "a phenomenon of density, for what persists in solidity and depth beneath the style, harshly or tenderly assembled in its figures, are the fragments of a reality absolutely alien to language." In Barthes's sense, "Indian" style can be a sort of afterimage attending the creative production of bicultural Native Americans; its referent is the residual cultural practices that sound beneath contemporary commodified relations of aesthetic production.

5. Judith Butler's formulation of the distinction between sex and gender in *Gender Trouble: Feminism and the Subversion of Identity* (New York: Routledge, 1990) poses a very similar problematic. My thesis is that the category "Indian" is historically developed in North America as the mystified term of the generalized self/other structure of identity and identification. Both the material and ideological processes entailed in the development of the category "Indian" accord precisely with Lukács's theory of reification discussed in Fredric Jameson's *Political Unconscious* (Ithaca, N.Y.: Cornell University Press, 1981), in which "traditional or 'natural' unities, social forms, human relations, cultural events, even religious systems, are systematically broken up in order to be reconstructed more efficiently, in the form of new post-natural processes or mechanisms" (63). The figure of the "Indian" both exemplifies the subjectively lived experience of those processes of modernity and is "taken" (literally and figuratively) to illustrate them as a contesting site. Although Native American peoples have been variously subjected to processes of colonial domination that fit Jameson's description of reification, the symbolic values associated with the postfrontier development of the category "Indian" compensate for global experiences of objective and subjective fragmentation that are functions of the relations of modern capitalism. Thus, while the category "Indian" is projected as an ontological "other" to the normative development of society, it is paradoxically a paradigmatic figure for North American identity.

6. Russell Thornton, *American Holocaust and Survival: A Population History since 1492* (Norman: University of Oklahoma Press, 1987).

7. Thornton comments on the prescribed conditions of Indian identity: "Members of Indian tribes . . . must behave as non-Indians think they should, in order to be treated as Indian, no matter how unflattering whites make the definition." Hence, the Bureau of Indian Affairs, the administrative branch of federal Indian policy, rallied to identify the Pueblo as authentically "Indian" by filing lengthy reports of drunkenness, debauchery, dancing, and communal life. The court concluded that its earlier information was incorrect: the Pueblo were Indians after all, for they were "a simple, uninformed and inferior people" (ibid., 189).

8. For an analysis of the photographic construction of "Indianness," see Christopher Lyman's *Vanishing Race and Other Illusions* (New York: Pantheon Books, 1982).

9. Elision of the material conditions of representation is a symptomatic condition of discourses of otherness. For example, in "The Vanishing American," Benn-Michaels discusses the anthropological notion that Indians are at once exemplary of a peoples who have culture and seen as proof that culture is something that can be lost. The paradox is that Indianness is at once something to be inherited (by virtue of American birth and U.S. citizenship, i.e., the tropological relationship of the Indian to "place" through which biological descent is irrelevant, as in Momaday's dictum that "an Indian is an idea that a given man has of himself") and an idea whose cultural codes are available as a counternarrative to canonical Western culture while formally confirming canonical discourses. Thus Indianness provides a generic framework stucturally similar to classical education in that both are reified forms bearing no intrinsic relation either to living "Indians," in the former instance, or to living Greeks and Romans, in the latter. The paradox is that, for Indianness to be appropriated in "ancestral" terms—as a paradigm of belonging to the geographical place—living Indians must be perceived to be im-

posters, not the "real" Indians. In its various expressions, the discourse tends to displace the immediate—embodied—concerns of contemporary Indian people by imagining the real Indian as always receding in time and consequently inherently inaccessible to the present moment in which the symbol is ever being reconstituted according to the requirements of its function for the dominant imagination.

10. Among many such examples is Linda Hogan's essay on Momaday's *House Made of Dawn,* "Who Puts Together," in which she argues that Indians use words in a direct and powerful relationship to referents (in *Studies in American Indian Literature,* ed. Paula Gunn Allen [New York: Modern Language Association, 1983], 169–77); and Kenneth Lincoln, who contends in *Native American Renaissance* (Berkeley: University of California Press, 1983) that "words do not come after or apart from what naturally is, but are themselves natural genes, tribal history in the bodies of the people" (47), and moreover that "a word has the magical power to actualize spirits" (53).

11. See Gramsci's discussion of the hegemonic process in "The Study of Philosophy": "Culture . . . unifies, in a series of strata, to the extent that they come in contact with each other, [those] who understand each other's mode of expression" (*Selections from the Prison Notebooks,* ed. Quintin Hoare and Geoffrey Nowell Smith [New York: International Publishers, 1971], 349).

12. Relevant to this aspect of Silko's syncretic method is the statement from Jameson's *Political Unconscious* quoted in note 5, which continues: "These now isolated broken bits and pieces of the older unities acquire a certain autonomy of their own, a semi-autonomous coherence which, not merely a reflex of capitalist reification and rationalization, also in some measure serves to compensate for the dehumanization of experience reification brings with it, and so to rectify the otherwise intolerable effects of the new process" (63).

13. For a discussion of the "incommensurable" aspects of Native and Anglo-American worldviews, see Murray L. Wax, "The Ethics of Research," *American Indian Quarterly* 15, no. 4 (fall 1991): 431–56. Focusing on cross-cultural ethical evaluations of anthropological research among rural Indian communities (location unspecified in order to protect the identities of the participants), he notes the priority of collective bases of assessment among the latter. Because the ultimate evaluative criterion of traditional Native American communities is "the subsequent well-being of the people" (434), Wax concludes that "the investigators and the Indians do not share a common framework [for evaluative judgments] for the parties do not share a common moral vocabulary nor do they share a common vision of the nature of human beings as actors within the universe" (432). Similarly, Norma Alarcón, in "Chicana Feminism: In the Tracks of the Native Woman" (*Culture Studies* 4, no. 3 [October 1990]), draws upon Lyotard's concept of the "differend"—"a case of conflict, between (at least) two parties, that cannot be resolved for lack of a rule of judgment applicable to both arguments" as a metonym for both the figure and material referent of the Chicana in order to locate and articulate the sites of ideological and discursive conflict (353). Émile Durkheim, in his investigations of mythical representation and ritual, observed that the sacred "cannot, without losing its nature, be mixed with the profane. . . . There is between them no common measure, they are heterogenous and incommensurable" (quoted in Jürgen Habermas's *Theory of Communicative Action,* vol. 2: *Lifeworld and System: A Critique of Functionalist Reason,* trans. Thomas McCarthy [Boston: Beacon Press, 1987], 49).

14. In their Introduction to *The Nature and Context of Minority Discourse* (London: Oxford University Press, 1990), David Lloyd and Abdul R. JanMohamed develop a praxis-based theory of minority literature underscored by the subtitle, "What Is to Be Done?" In setting forth the project of minority discourse founded on the political relationship between *minor* and *major* literary categories, they explain that "becoming minor is not a question of essence (as the stereotypes of minorities in dominant ideology would want us to believe) but *a question of position:* a subject-position that in the final analysis can be defined only in political

terms—that is, in terms of the effects of economic exploitation, political disenfranchisement, social manipulation, and ideological domination on the cultural formation of minority subjects and discourses" (9). A theoretical framework firmly grounded in this critical position offers a much-needed corrective to the interpretive excess that simultaneously plays to an appetite for exoticism and dulls the critical edge of those contemporary works legitimated in terms of an essentialized "Native American" worldview. Thus, my concern is to recuperate the critical potential of Indian-identified cultural production in what Lloyd and JanMohamed argue is "*the* central task of the theory of minority discourse": to systematically articulate "the implications of that [critical] subject-position—a project of exploring the strengths and weaknesses, the affirmations and negations that are inherent in that position" (ibid.).

15. For a full analysis of this representational discourse, see David Lloyd's "Race under Representation," *Oxford Literary Review* 13 (1991).

16. The best description of multiculturalism that I have seen appears in a collectively authored article "How 'the West' Was One," by Brian Bremen, Ann Cvetkovich, Michael Hanchard, Barbara Harlow, Anne Norton, Gretchen Ritter, and Ramón Saldívar: "Multiculturalism . . . is an attempt to understand how and why cultures are developed, organized and used as they are. Multiculturalism, as an intellectual and practical project, seeks to interrogate manufactured categories and boundaries across history in order to assess their integrity and their utility in the understanding of multiple social realities" (*Images* [November 8, 1990]: 12–13).

17. That the "fictionalization of the self" constitutes the most salient characteristic of modern forms of social organization, of its discourses in general, and of the essay form of literacy in particular is the argument of ethnologists Ron and Suzanne B. Scollen in *Narrative, Literacy and Face in Interethnic Communication*, ed. Roy O. Freedle (Norwood, N.J.: Ablex, 1981).

18. Arnold Krupat, "The Dialogic of Silko's Storyteller," in Gerald Vizenor, ed., *Narrative Chance: Postmodern Essays on Native American Literature* (Albuquerque: University of New Mexico Press, 1989), 58–59, 60, 65.

19. Krupat defines his use of the term "cosmopolitanism," against its imperialist implications noted by Gramsci (as elaborated in Timothy Brennan's "Literary Criticism and the Southern Question" [*Cultural Critique* 11 (winter 1988–89), 87–114]), in accordance with Rabinow's usage as "the projection of heterodoxy not to the level of the universal, but, rather, to the level of the inter-national" (*Voice in the Margins* [Berkeley: University of California Press, 1989]). In light of the unavoidable associations of the cosmopolitan paradigm with structures of global capitalism, it is a problematic model for theorizing the entrance of Native American subjects into the field of representation. (Krupat acknowledges this problem in his *Ethnocriticism: Ethnography, History, Literature* [Berkeley: University of California Press, 1992].) In the spirit of "the Emperor's new clothes," perhaps we might acknowledge as well that social models derived from literary works are not so much a new form of criticism as a variation on canonical theories, substituting the legitimating premises of an autonomous aesthetic sphere for those of social relevance.

20. Krupat follows Momaday in characterizing Silko's writing as "tellings"; see N. Scott Momaday, "The Man Made of Words."

21. M. M. Bakhtin. *The Dialogic Imagination: Four Essays*, ed. Michael Holquist (Austin: University of Texas Press, 1981), 367.

22. This is not to suggest that Silko does not perform as a communally sanctioned storyteller under conditions in which community is conceived in the "cosmopolitan" sense advocated by Krupat—at the permeable borders between cultural traditions and within the institutional sites of their syntheses, rather than in the exclusive sense of tribal communities.

23. For a discussion of the "multicultural" foundations of Laguna Pueblo identity, see A. LaVonne Ruoff, "Ritual and Renewal: Keres Traditions in the Short Fiction of Leslie Silko"

(*MELUS* 5, no. 4 [winter 1978]: 2–3). Silko's great-grandfather and uncle were responsible, according to anthropologist Elsie Clews Parsons (quoted by Ruoff), for "the Great Split" between traditional and modernizing factions of the Laguna Pueblo. The two Marmon brothers worked for the federal government under contract "to set out the boundary markers for Laguna," and led the movement to suppress the practice of Pueblo traditions. Consequently, around 1860–70 the conservative faction removed its altars from Laguna to Mesita and then to Isleta. This is a matter of official historical record. However, according to tribal member Ruth Hopper of the University of California at Berkeley, not everyone departed. A traditional core of Laguna religious practice (as well as traditional forms of self-government) continued underground and was undiminished in its influence. Parsons was perhaps unaware of the continuing traditional presence at the Pueblo because she studied Laguna from the 1920s through 1939 as a site not of Pueblo tradition, but as a culture in radical transition, observing that it presented "unrivaled opportunity to study American acculturation and the important role played by miscegenation" (*Pueblo Indian Religion*, 888–90; quoted in Ruoff, 3).

24. Although cultural outsiders are excluded from observation of traditional Pueblo institutions (as suggested in note 23), it is important to emphasize that those institutions continue to be vital for those who live according to their codes. The traditional forms of government, religion, and clan relationships constitute the determining structures of Laguna subject formation and cultural practice despite peripheral interpellations by the majority culture and the formal overlay and observance of federal stuctures of government and Catholic forms of ritual. Just because scholars and others who do not "believe in them," as Ruth Hopper comments, "are not allowed to see Pueblo sacred institutions in action, doesn't mean they aren't there." See also Silko's "Language and Literature from a Pueblo Perspective," a transcript of her oral presentation to the English Institute in 1979, in *English Literature: Opening up the Canon. Selected Papers from the English Institute*, ed. Leslie A. Fiedler and Houston A. Baker Jr. (Baltimore: Johns Hopkins University Press, 1981).

25. It might be interesting to consider why Silko insists (without a trace of irony), in an interview reported in the Los Angeles weekly, *Village View* (January 24–30, 1992), that her 1991 novel *Almanac of the Dead* "has no political intent," even though it is a narrative in the epic mode of the last five hundred years of the Americas. As well as reflecting Silko's deconstruction of the exotic representations under which she has been canonically legitimated, her protest against being read for "political intent" indicates not only a corollary resistance to the minority status consequent on being so represented, but an internalization of the ideology of "majority" aesthetics that posits normative universal criteria of judgment. Silko's metaphysical desire is further suggested by her self-characterization in another article as "the archetypal character of the New Age" (*Los Angeles Times*, January 13, 1992: E1). Insofar as her most recent statements implicitly refute the politics of multiculturalism in favor of a universal notion of aesthetic criteria of judgment (e.g., her assertion that the "creative realm is androgynous and is beyond culture" as well as her protest that "I just see myself as a writer"), they perhaps evince resistance to the categorical imperatives of the emerging American multicultural canon.

26. For instance, in the *Village View* interview cited in note 25, Silko emphasizes that, as an English major at the University of New Mexico, her literary influences range from Milton through McMurty, and that Shakespeare was a "really important [influence on her writing] especially in the way he used imagery and metaphor" (21). For Silko's account of the literary influences on her work, see Leslie Marmon Silko and James Wright, *The Delicacy and Strength of Lace: Letters of Leslie Marmon Silko and James Wright*, ed. Anne Wright (1986), and Per Seyersted, "Two Interviews with Leslie Marmon Silko," *American Studies in Scandinavia* 13 (1981).

27. Although the multicultural history of the contemporary Laguna Pueblo consist of historically syncretic traditions well suited to serve Krupat's "cosmopolitan" discourse, at the same time it defies Krupat's homogenizing claim. Moreover, the multicultural influences at

Laguna and the resulting hegemonic struggles within the community create a multilayered system of discrete social and cultural contexts that entails differential negotiations of the Laguna political nexus as well as of traditional oral and commodified ways of having stories.

28. An exception to this tendency is Paula Gunn Allen's "Special Problems in Teaching Leslie Marmon Silko's *Ceremony*," *American Indian Quarterly* 14, no. 4 (fall 1990).

29. The problem of assimilating minority cultures through forms of entertainment is critiqued by David Lloyd in *Ethnic Cultures, Minority Discourse and the State* (London: Oxford University Press, 1993). Lloyd argues that the liberal pluralist strategy that underlies multiculturalism's project in the universities entails the displacement of "the dynamic social matrix of social relations which permit a specific form to emerge and within which . . . it makes sense" (13), "by divorcing culture(s) from the material grounds of their existence and appropriating them as cultures on the model of what has traditionally been termed Culture: namely, as a separate, recreationary sphere whose political significance derives precisely from its apparent autonomy from either economic or political considerations" (15). Similarly, Native American writer Sherman Alexie, in an interview, criticizes publishers' biases toward the "sanitized and simple" representations of Indianness produced by writers such as Tony Hillerman: "All that appropriation, not just the writing, but New Age culture, the men's movement . . . take all the good of Native culture or Native images or Native spirituality, without accepting any of the bad. The good has to be earned" (*Bloomsbury Review* [May–June 1994]: 15).

30. The problem of mediation between secular and sacred worldviews is evident in the Salman Rushdie case.

31. Fredrik Barth, *Ethnic Groups and Boundaries: The Social Organization of Cultural Difference* (Boston: Little, Brown, 1969), 17. Barth continues with the observation that "ethnic identity implies a series of constraints on the kinds of roles an individual is allowed to play . . . is superordinate to most other statuses, and defines the permissible constellations of statuses, or social personalities, which an individual with that identity may assume" (ibid.); he specifies that "belonging to an ethnic category implies being a certain kind of person [and] a claim to be judged, and to judge oneself, by those standards that are relevant to that identity" (14).

32. Application of the category "Native American fiction" is problematic for Indian-identified writers of fiction aimed at the mainstream reading public. Arnold Krupat's *Voice in the Margin* discusses the problems of category in American literature, and argues convincingly for inclusion of Indian-identified literature under the category "indigenous literature" (Berkeley: University of California Press, 1989, 202–32). Krupat cites Brian Swann's definition "that Native Americans are Native Americans if they say they are, if other Native Americans say they are and accept them, and (possibly) if the values that she held close and acted upon are values upheld by the various native peoples who live in the Americas" (208). However, as I have noted, there is a growing movement on the part of documented tribal members to deny "Indian" identification to undocumented people of Native American descent, despite the fact of the historical circumstances that generated such conditions. A further complication of categories of indigenousness to contemporary Indian-identified writers, however well-meaning, is the historical decontextualization it implies.

33. Al Logan Slagle, "The Native American Tradition and Legal Status: Tolowa Tales and Tolowa Places," *Cultural Critique* 7 (1987): 113.

34. Nancy Scheper-Hughes, "The Best of Two Worlds, the Worst of Two Worlds: Reflections on Culture and Field Work among the Rural Irish and Pueblo Indians," *Comparative Studies in Society and History* 29 (1987): 74.

35. Both Paula Gunn Allen, in "Special Problems in Teaching Leslie Marmon Silko's *Ceremony*" (379–86), and Barre Toelken, in "Life and Death in the Navajo Coyote Tales" (in *Recovering the Word: Essays on Native American Literature*, ed. Brian Swann and Arnold Krupat [Berkeley: University of California Press, 1987], 388–401), discuss the problems of unsanc-

tioned access to tribal sacred culture. Insofar as such access is a form of power over the "Other," however disguised as sympathy, the implications of this transition of values for multicultural-ism as a pedagogical project might be considered here. Cf. Michel Foucault's discussion of sympathy in *The Order of Things: An Archaeology of the Human Mind* (New York: Vintage Books, 1973) as an instance of the Same so strong and pressing that it does not rest content with being one of the forms of the similar; it has the dangerous power of assimilation, of making things identical to each other, of making them disappear in their individuality—thus sympa-thy has the power of making them alien to what they were. Sympathy transforms. It alters, but in the direction of the identical, in such a way that if its power were not counterbalanced, the world would be reduced to a point, to a homogeneous mass, to the mournful figure of the same (23–24). This danger seems remote, though it exerts a certain homogenizing pressure on the celebrations of difference, for, as Foucault adds, "Sympathy is counterbalanced by antipa-thy, which is why the world remains what it is" (24).

36. It is of interest, in this context, that Silko reprises the Prologue's prohibition in Geary Hobson's *The Remembered Earth,* contending that "the second racist assumption still abound-ing is that the prayers, chants, and stories weaseled out by the early white ethnographers, which are now collected in ethnological journals, are public property. Presently a number of Native American communities are attempting to recover religious objects and other property taken from them in the early 1900's that are now placed in museums. Certainly, the songs and stories which were taken by ethnographers are no different" ("An Old-time Indian Attack Conducted in Two Parts: Part 1: Imitation 'Indian' Poems," 212). See Paul Gunn Allen's criti-cism of Silko on precisely these grounds in "Special Problems in Teaching Leslie Marmon Silko's *Ceremony.*"

37. Nancy Scheper-Hughes, "The Best of Two Worlds, The Worst of Two Worlds," 74.

38. In "Intermarriage and Assimilation: The Beginning or the End?" Sandy Gonzales writes, "Despite whatever allegiances Native Americans in mixed marriages hold for their cul-ture, virtually all native partners will become absorbed into the dominant culture to a greater or lesser degree. Many believe that intermarriage will accomplish what the colonists and fed-eral governmental policy failed to achieve. . . . " However, she concludes that "continuance of the tribal culture and stressing the importance of the family unit remain vital to their survival as a group. This can be accomplished in intermarriages as well as traditional ones" (*Wicazo Sa Review* 8, no. 2 [fall 1992]: 51, 52).

39. In "Romance and Reification," Fredric Jameson comments upon "aesthetic religion" as "the sacred perceived from the outside" (*The Political Unconscious,* 252). The discourse of Indianness functions in much the same way: "Because we can no longer think the figures of the sacred from within, we transform their external forms into aesthetic objects . . . presumed to have an inside, yet housing powers that will forever remain a mystery to us."

# References

Alarcón, Norma. "Chicana Feminism: In the Tracks of the Native Woman." *Culture Studies* 4, no. 3 (October 1990).

Allen, Paula Gunn. *The Sacred Hoop: Recovering the Feminine in American Indian Traditions.* Boston: Beacon Press, 1986.

———. "Special Problems in Teaching Leslie Marmon Silko's *Ceremony.*" *American Indian Quarterly* 14, no. 4 (fall 1990).

Allen, Paula Gunn, and Kenneth Lincoln, eds. *Studies in American Indian Literature: Critical Essays and Course Designs.* New York: Modern Language Association, 1983.

Bakhtin, M. M. *The Dialogic Imagination: Four Essays.* Ed. Michael Holquist. Austin: Univer-sity of Texas Press, 1981.

Barth, Fredrik. *Ethnic Groups and Boundaries: The Social Organization of Cultural Difference.* Boston: Little, Brown, 1969.

Benn-Michaels, Walter. "The Vanishing American." *American Literary History* 2, no. 2 (summer 1990).

Bevis, William. "Native American Novels: Homing In." In *Recovering the Word: Essays on Native American Literature,* ed. Brian Swann and Arnold Krupat. Berkeley: University of California Press, 1987.

Brennan, Timothy. "Literary Criticism and the Southern Question." *Cultural Critique* 11 (winter 1988–89).

Butler, Judith. *Gender Trouble: Feminism and the Subversion of Identity.* New York: Routledge, 1990.

Coltelli, Laura. *Winged Words: American Indian Writers Speak.* Lincoln: University of Nebraska Press, 1990.

Fabian, Johannes. *Time and the Other: How Anthropology Makes Its Object.* New York: Columbia University Press, 1983.

Fiedler, Leslie A., and Houston A. Baker Jr., eds. *English Literature: Opening up the Canon. Selected Papers from the English Institute* (1979). Baltimore: Johns Hopkins University Press, 1981.

Foucault, Michel. *The Order of Things: An Archaeology of the Human Sciences.* New York: Vintage Books, 1973.

Gonzales, Sandy. "Intermarriage and Assimilation: The Beginning or the End?" *Wicaso Sa Review* 8, no. 2 (fall 1992).

Gramsci, Antonio. *Selections from the Prison Notebooks.* Ed. Quintin Hoare and Geoffrey Nowell Smith. New York: International Publishers, 1971.

Habermas, Jürgen. *The Theory of Communicative Action.* Vol. 2: *Lifeworld and System: A Critique of Functionalist Reason.* Trans. Thomas McCarthy. Boston: Beacon Press, 1987.

Hohendahl, Peter Uwe. *The Institution of Criticism.* Ithaca, N.Y.: Cornell University Press, 1982.

Hymes, Dell. *"In Vain I Tried to Tell You": Essays in Native American Ethnopoetics.* Philadelphia: University of Pennsylvania Press, 1981.

Jameson, Fredric. *Marxism and Form.* Princeton, N.J.: Princeton University Press, 1971.

———. *The Political Unconscious: Narrative as a Socially Symbolic Act.* Ithaca, N.Y.: Cornell University Press, 1981.

Krupat, Arnold. *Ethnocriticism: Ethnography, History, Literature.* Berkeley: University of California Press, 1992.

———. *The Voice in the Margin: Native American Literature and the Canon.* Berkeley: University of California Press, 1989.

Lacoue-Labarthe, Philippe, and Jean-Luc Nancy. *The Literary Absolute.* Albany: State University of New York Press, 1988.

Lincoln, Kenneth. *Native American Renaissance.* Berkeley: University of California Press, 1983.

Lloyd, David. *Ethnic Cultures, Minority Discourse and the State.* London: Oxford University Press, 1993.

———. "Race Under Representation." *Oxford Literary Review* 13 (1991).

Lloyd, David, and Abdul R. JanMohamed. *The Nature and Context of Minority Discourse.* London: Oxford University Press, 1990.

Lyman, Christopher. *The Vanishing Race and Other Illusions.* New York: Pantheon Books, 1982.

Momaday, N. Scott. "The Man Made of Words." In *Indian Voices: The First Convocation of American Indian Scholars.* San Francisco: Indian Historian Press, 1970. 49–62.

Moss, Marilyn. "Storyteller." *Village View Weekly,* Los Angeles (January 24–30, 1992).

*News from Native California* (fall 1991).

Rosen, Kenneth. *Voices of the Rainbow: Contemporary Poetry by American Indians.* New York: Seaver Books, 1974.

Ruoff, A. LaVonne. "Ritual and Renewal: Keres Traditions in the Short Fiction of Leslie Silko." *MELUS* 5, no. 4 (winter 1978).

Scheper-Hughes, Nancy. "The Best of Two Worlds, the Worst of Two Worlds: Reflections on Culture and Field Work among the Rural Irish and Pueblo Indians." *Comparative Studies in Society and History* 29 (1987): 56–75.

Scollon, Ron, and Suzanne B.K Scollon. *Narrative, Literacy and Face in Interethnic Communication.* Vol. 11: *Advances in Discourse Processes.* Ed. Roy O. Freedle. Norwood, N.J.: Ablex, 1981.

Seyersted, Per. "Two Interviews with Leslie Marmon Silko." *American Studies in Scandinavia* 13 (1981).

Silko, Leslie Marmon. *Ceremony.* New York: Viking Press, 1977.

———. "Predicting a Revolt to Reclaim the Americas." Interview, *Los Angeles Times* (January 3, 1992).

———. *Storyteller.* New York: Seaver Books, 1981.

Silko, Leslie Marmon, and James Wright. *The Delicacy and Strength of Lace: Letters of Leslie Marmon Silko and James Wright.* Ed. Anne Wright. Saint Paul, Minn.: Graywolf Press, 1986.

Slagle, Al Logan. "The Native American Tradition and Legal Status: Tolowa Tales and Tolowa Places." *Cultural Critique* 7 (fall 1987).

Thornton, Russell. *Indian Holocaust and Survival: A Population History since 1492.* Norman: University of Oklahoma Press, 1987.

Toelken, Barre. "Life and Death in the Navajo Coyote Tales." In *Recovering the Word: Essays on Native American Literature,* ed. Brian Swann and Arnold Krupat. Berkeley: University of California Press, 1987.

Vizenor, Gerald, ed. *Narrative Chance: Postmodern Essays on Native American Literature.* Albuquerque: University of New Mexico Press, 1989.

Wax, Murray L. "The Ethics of Research." *American Indian Quarterly* 15, no. 4 (fall 1991).

~

# The Politics of Carnival and Heteroglossia in Toni Morrison's *Song of Solomon* and Ralph Ellison's *Invisible Man*

## Dialogic Criticism and African American Literature

ELLIOTT BUTLER-EVANS

This essay will explore the appropriateness of applying interpretive strategies suggested by dialogic criticism to the interpretation of African American narrative texts. By dialogic criticism I refer to that critical approach that is informed by theoretical constructs largely identified with the writings of Mikhail Bakhtin and members of his circle.[1]

I am particularly interested in the manner in which concepts such as *carnival, heteroglossic, dialogic,* and *polyphony* might be useful in enabling broader dialogue focused on the interpretation of African American literature and result in more nuanced readings of those texts.

I first considered the possibility of conducting such an investigation in the fall of 1989 while teaching an upper division seminar on the African American novel. It struck me that what distinguished novels of the modern period—which, I would argue, began with the publication of Arna Bontemps's *Black Thunder* in 1937—from those written in the late nineteenth and early twentieth century was the emergence of more complex narrative forms. These novels marked a movement away from the African American novel as a product of an eminently commodifiable classic realism to a textual construct with a far more complicated and indeterminate structure. The distinction here is somewhat akin to that which Stanley Fish makes in his discussion of "two kinds of literary presentation":

> A presentation is rhetorical if it satisfies the needs of its readers. The word "satisfies" is meant literally here; for it is characteristic of a rhetorical form to mirror and present for approval the opinions its readers hold. . . . A dialectical presentation, on the other hand, is disturbing, for it requires of its readers a searching and rigorous scrutiny of everything they believe in and live by. It is didactic in a special sense; it does not preach the truth, but asks that its readers discover the truth for themselves.[2]

Interpretive strategies that would simply attempt to elucidate some totalizing racial narrative or presume a monolithic "Black experience" or an evolving Black tradition are likely to be wholly inadequate for a thorough critique of these later narratives. Their very complexity invites the applications of more recent critical and theoretical constructs that seek to tease out the polyvalent, heteroglossic elements of modern narrative. However, I did not want to blindly scaffold African American texts with theories simply because they are in vogue. My primary interest in this course was to test the suitability of specific theoretical constructs for the productive teaching and interpreting of African American texts. It was out of this interest that the present essay was generated.

Here I have chosen to examine Ralph Ellison's *Invisible Man* and Toni Morrison's *Song of Solomon,* not only because of their centrality to every attempt to advance the concept of a Black literary canon or tradition, but also because they are paradigmatic modern texts that demand rethinking of both our critical approaches to African-American narratives and the way we teach such texts in the classroom. In their extensive carnivalizing of the novel form and their extensive uses of polyphony, these novels lend themselves to Bakhtinian interpretive strategies.

## The Spirit of Carnival

Morson and Emerson argue that Bakhtin views the novel as "inspired by a laughing truth, indebted to parodic genres and the spirit of carnival."[3] For Bakhtin, this "spirit" of carnival, elaborated extensively in *The Problems of Dostoevsky's Poetics* and *Rabelais and His World,* displaces hierarchies and subverts the dominant order. What is presented in carnival might be described as a "minimally ritualized antiritual, a festive celebration of the other, the gaps and holes in all the mappings of the world laid out in systematic theologies, legal codes, normative poetics, and class hierarchies."[4]

The centrality of the role of such carnivalesque discourse in both Ellison's *Invisible Man* and Morrison's *Song of Solomon* is quite evident. Although the approaches undergirding carnivalesque inscriptions and representations might differ significantly, they attain roughly the same results. Both texts, foregrounding ethnic and racial identity through their semiotic strategies and modes of narration, function as alternatives to dominant, canonical, literature. For Ellison, this celebration of ethnicity lay in the recognition of one's self within the context of Western culture. Consequently, what one finds in Ellison is not necessarily a contestatory relationship between the African American self and Western culture, but a dialogic encounter between the African American self and its other, which thus suggests the Duboisian notion of double consciousness. Morrison, on the other hand, strongly influenced by the Black Aesthetic movement of the 1960s, emphasizes the dialectical aspect of the encounter between African American and non-African American cultures. She speaks of finding a distinct African American voice directed toward an imaginary Black reader, or more specifically, to the village or tribe.

This difference between Ellison and Morrison does not preclude their texts' achieving similar outcomes. Although the writers situate themselves quite differently in relation to the discourse of the West, they both subvert the novelistic genre. Both revise the novel form, opening it to the inclusion and celebration of a previously excluded set of African American cultural discourses.

This is particularly manifested in the manners in which both narratives employ the carnivalesque. My analysis of the carnivalesque in these two novels follows two stages: in each instance, I first address the use of the carnivalesque to subvert the novelistic genre; then I examine the way each novel reproduces a world in which the carnivalesque becomes dominant.

## Carnivalizing the Novel Form

Considerable attention has been devoted to exploring the ways Ellison's novel incorporates references to canonical writers, including Dostoevsky, Joyce, Dante, and Melville. Less frequently analyzed, however, are the specific strategies of intertextualization involved in those incorporations. Ellison's text engages in a radical appropriation and rearticulation of the sources rather than merely quoting or citing them. It would be useful to re-explore the intertextual project of *Invisible Man* bearing in mind Bakhtin's description of the process of intertextuality:

The author can only use the discourse of the other toward his own ends, in such a way that he imprints on this discourse, that already has, and keeps, its own orientation, a new semantic orientation. Such a discourse must, in principle, be perceived as being another's. A single discourse winds up having two semantic orientations, two voices.[5]

Strategies of intertextuality that focus on precisely this appropriation of the discourse of the other permeate *Invisible Man.* The evocation of Dostoevsky's underground man metamorphosed into a Black man in a hole in Harlem needing 1,369 lights to illuminate his hole, the Dantean descent facilitated by the protagonist's smoking marijuana and absorbing himself in the music of Louis Armstrong, and the unexpected intrusion of Beethoven's Fifth Symphony in the hospital scene all bespeak this particular mode of intertextualization. One subdued but brilliant use of this strategy occurs when the narrator attempts to come to terms with his identity crisis during the first speech that he gives for the Brotherhood:

> What had I meant by saying that I had become "more human"? Was it a phrase that I had picked up from some preceding speaker, or a slip of the tongue? . . . Perhaps it was something Woodridge had said in the literature class back at college. I could see him vividly, half-drunk on words and full of contempt and exaltation, pacing before the blackboard chalked with quotations from Joyce and Yeats and Sean O'Casey; thin, nervous, neat, pacing as though he walked a high wire of meaning upon which no one of us would dare venture. I could hear him: "Stephen's problem, like ours, was not actually one of creating the uncreated conscience of his race, but of creating the *uncreated features of his face.* Our task is that of making ourselves individuals. The conscience of the race is the gift of its individuals who see, evaluate, record . . . "[6]

This reification and incorporation of the voice of Joyce's discourse in an African American context is a striking example of Ellison's intertextuality. Although the traces of Joyce are apparent in the passage, what Bakhtin identifies as "a new semantic orientation," "a single discourse . . . with two voices" is evident here. It is a dialogic instance in which the voices of Joyce and the narrator fuse to an alternative epistemology that is distinctly African American. Here is not a blind and passive echoing of the dominant text but a reconceptualization of it through a dialogic encounter between a canonical work and a specific African American narrative logic. The strategy of intertextuality here is somewhat akin to that recently posited by Barbara Johnson, who argues that intertextuality

> tends to speak of misreading or infiltration, that is, violations of property. Whether such violations occur in the oedipal rivalry between a specific text

and its precursor . . . or whether they inhere in the immersion of any text in the history of its language and literature . . . intertextuality designates the multitude of ways a text has of not being self-contained, of being traversed by otherness.[7]

Because Morrison's political emphases differ from those of Ellison, she conceptualizes her relationship in a significantly different manner. The quest for authentic Black voices precludes the approach that Ellison employs. While the concept of dialogism is important to her text, her focus is on the heteroglossia of the Black community, and excludes that which lies outside. Addressing this issue, Morrison argued:

> It is important that what I write not be merely literary. I am most self-conscious about making sure that I don't strike literary postures. I avoid, too studiously perhaps, name-dropping, lists, literary references, unless oblique and based on written folklore. . . .
>     In the Third World cosmology as I perceive it, reality is not already constituted by my literary predecessors in Western culture. If my work is to confront a reality unlike that received reality of the West, it must centralize and animate information discredited by the West—discredited not because it is not true or useful or even of some racial value, but because it is information held by discredited people, information dismissed as "lore" or "gossip" or "magic" or "sentiment."[8]

The subversion here is similar to that which Bakhtin maintains is characteristic of Rabelais's text. The privileged discourse is subordinated—in the case of Morrison, actually excluded—and an alternative reality is presented.

For Ellison, the act of writing involves the reformulation of the dominant discourse; Morrison would omit it altogether. Hence, in *Song of Solomon* one encounters within the framework of the novel multiple stories involving personal histories of members of the mythical Black community, African and African American folklore, the flying motif of the novel, the evocation of the social rituals of this mythic community, such as those in the barber shop and in Mary's bar and lounge. The text remains primarily focused on the "inner world" of Blacks. Although their agendas differ significantly, however, both *Invisible Man* and *Song of Solomon* carnivalize the novel form.

## The Carnivalesque in Ellison

Similar to their carnivalizing of form, in both novels the thematic of the carnivalesque is central to the symbolic construction of communities. Once again, however, Ellison's and Morrison's approaches are dissimilar. *Invisible Man* inscribes the carnivalesque in a world in which the major focus is on an "outer world." The thematics behind the perception of these conflicts are couched in an optic tropology—a series of conflicts that involve struggles for power between sight and blindness, seeing and not seeing—and leads to a series of situations in which the carnival element triumphs.[9] *Song of Solomon,* focusing more intensely on the "inner world" of Black communities, presents the carnivalesque as normalized in those communities and therefore a part of the existential modalities of Black life.

The most striking narration of the carnivalesque in Ellison's novel occurs in the Golden Day episode, in which the discourse of madness assumes a privileged position, assuming primacy over sanity, as does disorder over order—hierarchies are demolished and deferences to authority transformed into parodic gestures. One fascinating example of this textual strategy is evident in the parody of medical discourse:

> Two men stood directly in front of me, one speaking with intent earnestness: " . . . and Johnson hit Jeffries at an angle of 45 degrees from his lower left lateral incisor, producing an instantaneous blocking of his entire thalamic rine, frosting it over like the freezing unit of a refrigerator, thus shattering his autonomous nervous system and rocking the big brick-laying creampuff with extreme hyperspasmic muscular tremors which dropped him dead on the extreme tip of his coccyx." (75)

This statement by an unidentified speaker early in the scene establishes the tone that will characterize the entire episode, and forms part of a cluster of carnivalesque moments that punctuate the novel. The bar patrons' physical triumph over Supercargo signifies a radical displacement of authority; Mr. Norton becomes "only a man" and the object of vulgarities and jeers; and the vet's insights into the real relationship between the protagonist and Norton undermines whatever idealistic notions the latter had of that relationship. Moreover, as an alternative reality to the rigidly disciplined social and political world of the college, the Golden Day episode represents an even more compelling example of the carnivalesque.

Carnival, of course, is also central to Ellison's depiction of the Harlem riot. Upon entering the riot zone, the protagonist remarks that it reminds him of a Fourth of July celebration; the description of the riot evokes a sense of ritual. A grave atmosphere reflected by "the footfalls of running boy," fire trucks, shootings, and "the steady filtering of shattered glass" signifies the displacement of order by disorder, law by anarchy. It is in this episode that the text inscribes what Bakhtin identifies as grotesque realism.

For Bakhtin, grotesque realism celebrates the "material bodily principle." He identifies its essential principle as "degradation, that is the lowering of all that is high, spiritual, ideal, abstract; it is a transfer to the material level, to the sphere of earth and body in their indissoluble unity."[10]

Two scenes in the novel spectacularly develop this thematic. The first occurs when the protagonist describes the experience of eating a yam while walking the streets of Harlem:

> I took a bite, finding it as sweet and hot as any I'd ever had, and was overcome with such a surge of homesickness that I turned away to keep my control. I walked along, munching the yam, just as suddenly overcome by an intense feeling of freedom—simply because I was eating while walking along the street. It was exhilarating. I no longer had to worry about who saw me or about what was proper. To hell with all that, and as sweet as the yam actually was, it became like nectar with the thought. If only someone who had known me at school or at home would come along and see me now. How shocked they'd be! I'd push them into a side street and smear their faces with the peel.(264)

What the protagonist experiences verbally and intellectually in this episode resonates with the experiences of the folk who later participate in the riot. His detailed description of the riot invokes a moment of the eruption of the bodily, a celebration of the physical and the bodily:

> And I saw a crowd of men running up pulling a Borden's milk wagon, on top of which, surrounded by a row of railroad flares, a huge woman in a gingham pinafore sat drinking beer from a barrel which sat before her. The men would run furiously a few paces and stop, resting between the shafts, run a few paces and rest, shouting and laughing and drinking from a jug, as she on top threw back her head and shouted passionately in a full-throated voice of blues singer's timbre:
>
> > *If it hadn't been for the referee*
> > *Joe Louis woulda killed*
> > *Jim Jefferie*
> > *Free beer!!*
>
> —sloshing the dipper of beer around. (544)

The description continues with the protagonist's observing "a crowd rushing a store that faced the intersection, moving in, and a fusillade of canned goods, salami, liverwurst, hogs heads and chitterlings belching out to those outside and a bag of flour bursting white upon them" (554). The huge woman consuming beer, the ritual laughter of the crowd, the store's "belching" out varied foodstuffs all give the scene a strong sense of carnival. This celebration of the physical and the sensual marks a momentary triumph of the culture of the folk over that of established order.

These two moments of carnival in *Invisible Man* are representative of the discourse of carnival that permeates the novel. Similar representations can be found in the battle royal scene, the hospital scene, and the depiction of Rinehart. Collectively they contribute to the construction of a symbolic world in which chaos reigns supreme and a persistent folk culture always threatens the hegemonic or established order.

## The Carnivalesque in Morrison

Morrison's use of the carnivalesque is informed by a different aesthetic and political vision from that of Ellison. She seeks to create a Black form that will challenge traditional perceptions of what constitutes the novel. As I indicated earlier, one of her major goals is the deconstruction of dominant fictional discourse and the creation of a space for narratives that are traditionally "discredited." Of equal significance is the incorporation of "the major characteristics of Black art." For example, she wishes

> the ability to be both print and oral literature: to combine those two aspects so that the stories can be read in silence, of course, but one should hear them as well. It should try deliberately to make you stand up and make you feel something profoundly in the same way that a Black preacher requires his congregation to speak, to join him in sermon, to behave in a certain way, to stand up and to weep and to cry and to accede to change and to modify—to expand on the sermon that is being delivered.[11]

What Morrison proposes here is similar to Bakhtin's elaboration of the concept of *skaz*. Bakhtin amends Eikhenbaum's definition of *skaz* as "an orientation toward the oral form of narration," arguing that *skaz* is "above all an orientation toward *someone else's speech*, and only then as a consequence, toward oral speech." Bakhtin's further elaboration helps one to better appreciate Morrison's approach to narrative:

> It seems to us that in most cases, *skaz* is introduced precisely for the sake of *someone else's voice*, a voice socially distinct, carrying with it precisely those points of view and evaluations necessary to the author. What is introduced here, in fact, is a storyteller, and a storyteller, after all, is not a literary person; he belongs in most cases to the lower social strata, to the common people (precisely this is important to the author)—and he brings with him oral speech.[12]

Although Bakhtin's formulation of *skaz* cannot be applied to Morrison's text without some modification, its emphasis on the role of orality and storytelling is clearly related to her positions on both.[13] Therefore, in Morrison's novel the preconditions for carnivalization are clearly present: the foregrounding of "discredited" knowledge and the written reproduction of African-American oral culture are enabling toward that end.

In spite of its apparent primary focus on Milkman's quest, *Song of Solomon* is above all a narrative that contains numerous embedded narratives. Each major character has a story to tell or to be told. Macon Dead reveals his personal history and the basis of his hostility toward Ruth through his narrative; Ruth provides Milkman, as well as the reader, with insight into her character by setting forth a personal narrative focused on her relationship with Macon and her father. Guitar gives significant illumination to his character through the story he tells; and the town of Shalimar is the source of the numerous stories and myths that lead Milkman to self-discovery. These autonomous narratives coalesce to create the novel, and the experience of reading *Song of Solomon* is less one of decoding a linearly constructed text than it is of encountering varied and numerous stories. This strategy of multiple storytelling is made even more complicated when the same incident is narrated by two persons with entirely different perspectives—for instance, the manner in which Macon depicts the deathbed scene between Ruth and her father and Ruth's narration of the same scene. Although the two reports conflict, the narrative makes no effort to resolve the issue, but merely presents them to the reader. What is dialogically significant here is the manner in which individual consciousnesses present themselves as autonomous voices unmediated by either the narrator or Morrison, thereby opening the novel to numerous interpretive possibilities.

*Song of Solomon* is saturated with evocations of African American folk culture. The myth of "flying to Africa," the very clever processes of naming that are endemic to African culture (e.g., the naming of Not Doctor Street, individual characters' names, such as Milkman, Guitar, Railroad Tommy, Hospital Tommy, Empire State), the nursery rhymes and children's melodies, as well as the tales of the fantastic all contribute to the dominance of folk culture and the oral in the novel.

Morrison's uses of discourses drawn from African American cultural practices are analogous to certain practices in Ellison's novel—for example, his extensive use of Black folklore, and his references to African American rituals and Black music. They directly relate to the narrative's inscription of the community as the embodiment of carnival. There is, however, a significant distinction between Ellison's and Morrison's strategies of representing the carnivalized aspects of the community. As I have argued, carnival in

Ellison seems to be related primarily to "outer world" concerns and thematized in terms of the subversion of dominant hierarchies. It encodes a world that implicitly laments the disintegration of order. In Morrison, conversely, the carnival moment is incorporated into the quotidian experiences of the community. This is brilliantly depicted in the description of the response to Robert Smith's promise to fly:

> Mr. Smith didn't draw as big a crowd as Lindbergh had four years earlier—not more than forty or fifty people showed up—because it was already eleven o'clock in the morning, on the very Wednesday he had chosen for his flight, before anybody read the note. At that time of day, during the middle of the week, word-of-mouth news just lumbered along. Children were in school; men were at work; and most of the women were fastening their corsets and getting ready to go see what tails or entrails the butcher might be giving away.[14]

What is striking here is the way the narration of the fantastic (Robert Smith's attempt to fly from Mercy Hospital) is linked to a "real" historical event (the Lindbergh flight) and incorporated into the mundane aspects of daily life (children at school, men at work, women fastening their corsets).

A similar mode of narration is employed when Susan Byrd relates the story of Solomon to Milkman. When asked why she called Solomon a flying African, she responds:

> "Oh, that's just some old folks' lie they tell around here. Some of those Africans they brought over here as slaves could fly. A lot of them flew back to Africa." (323)

When Milkman inquires whether she meant "ran away" or "escaped" she continues:

> "No, I mean flew. Oh, it's just foolishness, you know, but according to the story he wasn't running away. He was flying. He flew. You know, like a bird. Just stood up in the fields one day, ran up some hill, spun around a couple of times and was lifted up in the air. Went right on back to wherever it was he came from." (322–23)

Both episodes represent Morrison's strategy of valorizing "discredited" knowledge. More importantly, she shows how these modes of knowing are integrated into the community. In *Song of Solomon,* narrative strategies thus depart significantly from the modes of narration associated with the novel of classic realism. The primary thrust is to present the lived experiences of a "real" Black community. Morrison's representation of "the real," however, is strongly grounded in the discourse of magic realism, and folk knowledge is given the same status as valorized knowledges.

In *Song of Solomon*, as in *Invisible Man*, then, two modes of carnivalization exist. Both Ellison and Morrison position themselves in specific manners regarding dominant Western discourse. Ellison fuses it with Black folk culture to construct an alternative textual modality. Morrison displaces it with folk culture. Ellison inscribes carnival largely as a subversion of hierarchies in a nihilistic social system, whereas Morrison sees the carnivalesque as integrated into the existential fabric of Black life.

## Polyphony as a Narrative Strategy

We have observed how the carnivalesque is textualized and inscribed in both novels. I will now turn to examination of the manner in which each work employs polyphony as its primary narrative strategy. Bakhtin's identification of what he sees as the dominant feature of Dostoevsky's oeuvre provides a useful point of departure:

> A plurality of independent and unmerged voices and consciousnesses, a genuine polyphony of fully valid voices. . . . What unfolds in his works is not a multitude of characters and fates in a single objective world illuminated by a single authorial consciousness; rather a *plurality of consciousnesses, with equal rights and each with its own world*, combine but are not merged in the unity of the event.[15]

It is somewhat risky to suggest that a narrative that employs first-person point of view might be read as polyphonous; however, I would contend that although there is an apparent privileging of the narrator's angle of focalization in Ellison's novel, the dialogic nature of the narrative often leads to a subversion of that point of view. We might gain insight into that process by examining specifically those instances in the narrative in which an *apparent* polyphonic strategy is used, for ideological purposes, to reify the discourse of the other, when a subordinate voice emerges to displace and call into question the narrator's discourse, and those moments in which the narrator attempts to construct a self while facing contradictory and conflicting voices.

Scholarly attention has not focused on Ellison's *Invisible Man* as a polyphonic text. There is compelling evidence, however, that both polyphony and heteroglossia were central to Ellison's concerns when he wrote the novel. Two statements, roughly thirty years apart, are illuminating in this regard. On receiving the National Book Award, Ellison argued that in choosing a form for *Invisible Man*, he found both "the tight well-made Jamesian novel, which . . . was too concerned with 'good taste' and stable

areas" and "the forms of the hard-boiled novel, with its dedication to physical violence, social cynicism, and understatement" inappropriate models
for the narrative he wished to write. He was particularly dissatisfied with
what he identified as the monosyllabic utterances that characterized the
language of the "hard-boiled" novel. Dismissing that language as "embar-
rassingly austere," he called for recognition of a more vibrant diversity in
American expression:

> Our speech I found resounding with an alive language swirling with over
> three hundred years of American living, a mixture of the folk, the Biblical,
> the scientific and the political. Slangy in one stance, academic in another,
> loaded poetically with imagery at one moment, mathematically bare of im-
> agery in the next.[16]

In his Introduction to the thirtieth anniversary edition of *Invisible Man*,
Ellison also refers to the novel as a text that has as its dominant characteristic an interplay of heterogeneous voices. Comparing the process of writing
*Invisible Man* with that of some of his earlier short stories, he speaks of a
"voice" that demanded incorporation into the narrative:

> While I had structured my short stories out of familiar experiences and pos-
> sessed concrete images of my characters and their backgrounds, now I was
> confronted by nothing more substantial than a taunting disembodied voice.
> And while I was in the process of plotting a novel based on the war then in
> process, the conflict which that voice was imposing upon my attention was
> one that had been ongoing since the Civil War. Given the experiences of the
> past, I had felt on safe historical grounds even though the literary problem
> of conveying the complex human emotions and philosophical decisions
> faced by a unique individual remained. It was, I thought, an intriguing idea
> for an American novel but a difficult task for a fledgling novelist. Therefore,
> I was most annoyed to have my efforts interrupted by an ironic down-home
> voice that struck me as being irreverent as a honky-tonk trumpet blasting
> through a performance, say, of Britten's *War Requiem*. (xiv–xv)

For Ellison, then, heteroglossia and polyphony may be said to be intrinsic
to American culture. He envisions the American scene as one that derives
its vitality from the juxtapositions of these various voices that represent different ethnic, class, and political locations. Moreover, in his reference to the
"taunting disembodied voice," later described as having "echoes of blues-
toned laughter," that surfaced in his writing, he implies a repressed presence
suggestive of Houston Baker's concept of a vernacular voice.

In contrast to this recognition of and engagement in actual polyphonic
discourse, however, Ellison employs narrative strategies that produce an apparent polyphony that serves an implicit ideological agenda. In those in-

stances, the voices of the others are ventriloquized and made the object of parody. Two significant examples are the representation of Ras as the embodiment of the extreme forms of Black nationalism and the discourse of the members of the Brotherhood as a metaphor for scientific Marxism. In both instances, the representations are largely rearticulations of recognizable clichés, so that the voices largely function semiotically to reinforce an implicit ideological position. We have here what Darko Suvin describes as characters who function as "exempla . . . and shifting nodes of narration."[17] This particular strategy of representation is, at bottom, directly related to the ideology of the narrative that would hold both the nationalist and the Marxist positions to be inimical to the development of personal identity.

In these instances the first-person point of view is doubtlessly a strategy of containment, whereas at other moments alternate voices erupt with such force as to either bracket the narrator's voice or totally displace it. These might be described as moments of epistemological crisis in which the political and moral premises entertained by the narrator are either problematized or challenged. Two incidents representative of this emergence of the voice of the other are Trueblood's act of self-fashioning and Bledsoe's revelation of the manner in which he exercises power.

For the narrator—and, one might assume, the reader—Jim Trueblood represents one of the least desirable members of the Black community. Even when describing Trueblood in retrospect, the narrator sees him primarily as a somewhat primitive and exotic black peasant who, before "[bringing] disgrace upon the black community," had been a source of entertainment and amusement. The attitude toward Trueblood later changes to one of "contempt blunted by tolerance," eventually becoming "a contempt sharpened by hate" as a result of the sharecropper's "sin."

Trueblood, however, provides a different reading of his experience, which he narrates directly to Norton and indirectly to the reader. Through his story, he engages in an act of self-mythologizing that is at odds with the Invisible Man's construction of him, and this allows him to emerge as a rather exotic folk figure. After describing his incestuous moment with Matty Lou, the violent encounter with Kate, and the ostracism he faced both from within and from outside the Black community, Trueblood reflectively continues his tale:

> Finally, one night, way early in the mornin', I looks up and sees the stars and I starts singin'. I don't mean to, I didn't think 'bout it, just start singin'. I don't know what it was, some kinda church song, I guess. All I know is I *ends up* singin' the blues. I sings me some blues that night ain't never been

sang before, and while I'm singin' them blues I makes up my mind that I
ain't nobody but myself and ain't nothin' I can do but let whatever is gonna
happen, happen. I made up my mind that I was goin' back home and face
Kate; yeah, and face Matty Lou too. (66)

One has here a dialogic encounter in which the primordial, vernacular
Black voice erupts and disrupts the "literariness" of the protagonist's voice.
The voice demands of Ellison's hero, as well as the reader, a nonjudgmental,
sympathetic reading of what would be considered a sordid act in normal
circumstances. The Invisible Man's perspective, therefore, is both displaced
and subverted.

A similar subversion occurs during the encounter between the protagonist and Bledsoe. When the young student threatens to report Bledsoe's actions to Norton, the college president responds:

"Tell anyone you like," he said. "I don't care. I wouldn't raise my little finger
to stop you. Because I don't owe anyone a thing, son. Who, Negroes? Negroes don't control this school or much of anything else—haven't you
learned even that? No, sir, they don't control this school, nor white folk either. True they *support* it, but *I* control it. I's big and black and I say 'Yes,
suh' as loudly as any burrhead when it's convenient, but I'm still the king
down here. I don't care how much it appears otherwise. Power doesn't have
to show off. Power is confident, self-assuring, self-starting and self-stopping,
self-warming and self-justifying. When you have it, you know it. Let the Negroes snicker and the crackers laugh! Those are the facts, son. The only ones
I even pretend to please are *big* white folk, and even those I control more
than they control me. This is a power set-up, son, and I'm at the controls.
You think about that. When you buck against me, you're bucking against
power, rich white folk's power, the nation's power—which means government power!" (142)

As in the Trueblood episode, through an act of self-narration, a morally
ambiguous character presents himself in a light significantly different from
that in which the narrator presents him. In the protagonist's discourse,
Bledsoe is characterized by servility and buffoonery. In Bledsoe's own presentation, he projects himself as a very cynical yet shrewd man capable of
exercising a Machiavellian sense of power. Again, as in Trueblood's case, the
stronger act of self-narration creates a broader context for understanding
the character. The reader's response, therefore, becomes problematic, as the
subversive voices of Trueblood and Bledsoe demand to be heard.

It is in the protagonist's construction of self, however, that the underpin-
ning concepts of heteroglossia and polyphony are most dramatically revealed. This construction of self is akin to Bakhtin's description of such a
construction in the midst of surrounding discourses. Addressing the rela-

tionship of the problematic of self-construction to one's existential position in the world, he writes:

> When someone else's discourse is internally persuasive for us and acknowledged by us, entirely different possibilities open up. Such discourse is of decisive significance in the evolution of individual consciousness: consciousness awakens by independent ideological life precisely in a world of alien discourse surrounding it, and from which it cannot initially separate itself. The process of distinguishing between one's own and another's discourse, between one's own and another's thought, is activated rather late in development. When thought begins to work in an independent, experimenting and discriminating way, what first occurs is a separation between internally persuasive discourse, along with a rejection of those congeries of discourses that do not touch us.[18]

Bakhtin's theory of the construction of the self is clearly relevant to the dominant thematic of Ellison's *Invisible Man*. The protagonist's quest for self is conducted in a world in which he is confronted with the presence of multiple discourses. His flaw is that he uncritically incorporates the voices of others in his vain search for identity. His identification of himself as a future Booker T. Washington, as an heir to Bledsoe's position, and as a leader in the Brotherhood is generated by his encounters with "the internally persuasive discourse" of others. Addressing what for him is an existential crisis, he reflects:

> If only all the contradictory voices shouting inside my head would calm down and sing a song in unison, whatever it was I wouldn't care as long as they sang without dissonance; yes, and avoided the uncertain extremes of the scale. (259)

The strongest voice, however, is that of a primordial Black culture, which manifests itself in the folkloric utterances that inform Black culture. This voice functions as the return of the repressed to the protagonist's life. It is this voice that shatters his illusions and continues to keep him anchored in a racially defined self. This is illustrated in his description of a bus ride home after the younger Mr. Emerson reveals the contents of Bledsoe's letter:

> In the seat in front of me a dark man in a panama hat kept whistling a tune between his teeth. My mind flew in circles, to Bledsoe, Emerson, and back again. There was no sense to be made of it. It was a joke. Hell, it couldn't be a joke. Yes, it is a joke . . . Suddenly the bus jerked to a stop and I heard myself humming the same tune that the man ahead was whistling, and the words came back:
>
> > *O well they picked poor Robin clean*
> > *O well they picked poor Robin clean*

> *Well they tied poor Robin to a stump*
> *Lawd, they picked all the feathers round*
> *from Robin's rump*
> *Well they picked poor Robin clean.* (193)

It is this folkloric voice that becomes the part of the Invisible Man's identity that must be recognized and to which he must be reconciled. It is ubiquitous, manifesting itself in the form of memory, the chants of peddlers, and the rhythms of the street, and encoded semiotically in images of food or objects such as the possessions of the evicted couple. This voice is always present as a challenging, contestatory one. It may also appear elliptically, depending upon the reader to infer its presence. The conversation between the protagonist and Brother Jack when the former is being disciplined for conducting an authorized funeral oration for Tod Clifton illustrates this:

"So we went ahead on my personal responsibility."

Brother Jack's eyes narrowed. "What was that?" he said. "Your what?"

"My personal responsibility," I said.

"His personal responsibility," Brother Jack said. "Did you hear that, Brothers? Did I hear him correctly? Where did you get it Brother?" he said. "This is astounding, where did you get it?"

"From your ma—" I started and caught myself in time. (463)

The final phrase of the passage—"From your ma—"—again represents the spontaneous emergence of the voice of the folk that surfaces in moments of crisis. The intratextual reference is to act of "playing the dozens" in the hospital scene:

WHO WAS YOUR MOTHER?

I looked at him, feeling a quick dislike and thinking, half in amusement, I don't play the dozens. And how's *your* old lady today? (241)

## Morrison and the Inscription of Women's Issues

Although Ellison's novel is exceptional in its inscription of and deployment of polyphony, its ideological trajectory precludes allowing the voices of women to be heard. In *Invisible Man*, women are generally denied agency or subjectivity: we see them only through a male gaze. Kate and Matty Lou, for example, are presented only as they are seen through the eyes of Trueblood. Emma and Sybil are seen as disruptive of the political goals of the Brotherhood and largely as sexual outlaws. Mary Rambo, depicted as asexual, is represented as an archetypal Black matriarch. The politics of this text, as in similar works that it echoes, constructs the existential quest as an inherently male pursuit.

In Toni Morrison's novel, we witness an equally extensive use of polyphony and heteroglossia, with a significant supplement: the emergence of the voices of women.

In *Song of Solomon,* the primary focus seems to be on Milkman's quest. The narrative explores extensively his complex relationship with Ruth and Macon, his friendship with Guitar, his involvement with Hagar, and, above all, his search for meaning in his life. Hence, it would seem logical to view him as protagonist and read the novel as primarily narrating his story. I would argue, however, that the presence of multiple stories and the interplay of diverse voices in the novel preclude such a reductionist approach.[19] Examination of several representations of characters in the novel reveals its complexity and polyphonic density.

Macon Dead is initially presented as superficial, patriarchal, and abusive. His primary concern seems to be the possession of both persons and material goods. His reification of human relationships is dramatically illustrated in the description of his sexual encounters with Ruth:

> There had been a time when he had a head full of hair and when Ruth wore lovely complicated underwear that he deliberately took a long time to undo. When all of his foreplay was untying, unclasping, unbuckling the snaps and strings of what must have been the most beautiful, the most delicate, the whitest and softest underwear on earth. . . .
> When Ruth was naked and lying there as moist and crumbly as unbleached sugar, he bent to unlace her shoes. That was the final delight, for once he had undressed her feet, and peeled her stockings down over her ankles and toes, he entered her and ejaculated quickly. She liked it that way. So did he. And in almost twenty years during which he had not laid eyes on her naked feet, he missed only the underwear. (16)

The strategy employed in this passage is akin to the mode of narration that Dorrit Cohn describes as narrated monologue, "the technique for rendering a character's thought in his own idiom while maintaining the third-person reference and the basic tense of narration."[20] Cohn further contends that "no matter how 'impersonal' the tone of the text that surrounds them, narrated monologues themselves tend to commit the narrator to attitudes of sympathy or irony."[21] In the cited passage, the third-person narrator presents the erotic, or, more appropriately, antierotic encounter as it is filtered through Macon's mind.

However, the references to the "lovely uncomplicated underwear" and Ruth's "lying there as moist and crumbly as unbleached sugar," and the return of the focus to the underwear at the end of the passage, not only illuminate Macon's character but undermine him as well. The passage functions as an extended metaphor for the total range of Macon's interpersonal involvements. He is presented as a person whose personal relationships are reified and whose self-definition is inextricably linked to the symbolic value of objects. Ruth, Lena, and Corinthians are all like "keys to all the doors of his houses," which he kept curled around his fingers, and the 1936 Packard, which he would use to vulgarly display his family.

Yet this negative portrayal of Macon is balanced by his telling his own story. When he describes the idyllic scenes evoked by memories of his boyhood days sharing farming chores with his father, Milkman noticed that his "voice sounded different. . . . Less hard, and his speech was different. More southern and comfortable" (52). His description of his father's murder elicits a sympathetic response, and the hostility he encounters from Ruth's father because of caste and class differences provides a context for an understanding of their troubled marriage. Like Trueblood and Bledsoe in *Invisible Man*, Macon, empowered by his act of narration, subverts any reading of his character that would reduce him to being simply villainous. Through our encounter with his narrated personal history, we appreciate him as a complex human being.

The representation of Guitar provides another instance of the effective use of polyphony. Guitar is committed to an ideology grounded in retribution and revenge. Embracing the old adage of an eye for an eye, a tooth for a tooth, he holds that the appropriate response to murder is murder. Although his position is one that could be read as ideologically problematic, the use of direct dialogue without intrusion by an external narrator allows his voice to be heard without interruption or censure. The position is simply presented by Guitar, forcing readers to arrive at their own conclusions.

In comforting Hagar, Guitar reveals a more tender side to his character. Here the voice is one of wisdom and compassion, as he lectures Hagar on the dangers of clinging and possessive love:

> You think he belongs to you because you want to belong to him. Hagar, don't. It's a bad word "belong." Especially when you put it with somebody you love. Love shouldn't be like that. Did you ever see the way the clouds love a mountain? They circle all around it; sometimes you can't even see the mountain for the clouds. But you know what? You go up on top and what do you see? His head. The clouds never cover the head. His head pokes through, because the clouds let him; they don't wrap him up. They let him keep his head up high, free, with nothing to hide him or bind him. (306)

The expression of compassion, as well as the eloquence and poetic quality of the voice, illuminate a dimension of Guitar's character that is suppressed in his earlier political discourse. Like Macon, Guitar is humanized by having his own voice rather then being represented as an ogre.

It is when we turn to the inscription of the voices of women in *Song of Solomon* that we observe remarkable differences between it and Ellison's novel. Morrison's novel enters into the subjective worlds of women; their psychic realities are presented with the same detailed attention given to those of men. In *Song of Solomon*, are there not only unfoldings of the personal consciousnesses of individual women, but explorations of intersubjective relationships between women. Ruth, Hagar, Pilate, Lena, and Corinthians, through having their voices heard, assume full, complex existences in a way the women in Ellison's novel do not.

For example, while Macon presents Ruth's relationship with her father as perverse, Ruth, through her narration, illuminates that relationship in its greater complexity. Responding to his inquiry about her visits to her father's grave, she explains:

> I am a small woman. I don't mean little; I mean small, and I am small because I was pressed small. I lived in a great big house that pressed me into a small package. I had no friends, only schoolmates who wanted to touch my dresses. . . . I was small but he was big. The only person who ever really cared whether I lived or died . . . He was not a good man, Macon. Certainly he was an arrogant man and a foolish and destructive one. But he cared whether and he cared how I lived, and there was and is, no one else in the world who ever did. (124)

As in similar acts of storytelling by male characters, Ruth's narration gives the reader insight into her total character. The peculiar oral quality of the passage lends it poignancy and elicits compassion while fleshing out her personality.

Lena's confrontation with Milkman after he has told Macon of Corinthians's involvement with Porter provides a dramatic moment—an angry female voice erupts in the text and asserts itself. The reader's earlier understanding of the two sisters was that they were passive and ineffectual. In Lena's outburst, however, a suppressed rage is revealed, indicating a level of awareness of which they appeared to be incapable. In constructing her narrative of the abuse she and Corinthians suffered in the Dead household, Lena finds a voice that empowers her to rebel. The reader, who may have been misled into accepting the implied characterization of the two women as weak, is forced to revise his/her position. Lena's final rejection of Milkman reveals a heretofore repressed aspect of her character:

"You are a sad, pitiful stupid, selfish, hateful man. I hope your little hog's guts stands you in good stead, and that you take care of it, because you don't have anything else. But I want to give you notice. . . . I don't make roses anymore, and you have pissed your last in this house." (216)

With the exception of the opening pages that depict Guitar's comforting of Hagar, the entire thirteenth chapter is devoted to the voices of women. The framing narrative is bracketed, and the focus is on Hagar's disintegration and death, and Pilate's grief. Hagar's grief and anguish are presented in detail; the intensity of her pain is reinforced through the extensive use of narrated monologues in which the external narrator is sympathetic with her. The episode involving Hagar's ordeal in the fitting room is, in spite of its apparent trivial nature, quite significant in illuminating Hagar's thoughts and representing her pain:

> She carried an armful of skirts and an Evan-Picone two-piece number into the fitting room. Her little yellow dress that buttoned all the way down lay on the floor as she slipped a skirt over her head and shoulders down to her waist. But the placket would not close. She sucked in her stomach and pulled the fabric as far as possible, but the teeth of the zipper would not join. A light sheen broke out on her forehead as she huffed and puffed. She was convinced that her whole life depended on whether or not those aluminum teeth would meet. (311)

What we experience in this passage, particularly the last sentence, is an insight into Hagar's desperation. It resonates with those later passages in which she reflects on the possibility that Milkman rejects her because of the texture of her hair and her complexion. It is Hagar's voice, then, that leads the reader to an empathetic response to her pain.

After Hagar's death, the focus of the chapter shifts to an almost exclusive representation of the voices of Pilate and Reba. In Pilate's and Reba's crying out for "Mercy," and in Pilate's singing out the songs that had served as a bond between her and Hagar when the latter was a child, the grief experienced by the women is made concrete for the reader. Most importantly, at that moment the novel creates a space in which the voices of women are heard exclusively.

It is this animation of the voices of women that distinguishes *Song of Solomon* from *Invisible Man*. The uses of carnival, polyphony, and heteroglossia in both narratives arguably serve aesthetic and ideological agendas. Their evocations of African American cultural practices, and foregrounding of discourses of race and ethnicity, establish them as alternatives to Western narratives. *Invisible Man*, however, still shares with Western narratives a focus on male heroic quests and the erasure of the voices of women. *Song of Solomon*, produced by a different agenda, places the sphere of the domestic and the voices of women in a narrative space in which their voices are clearly heard.

I intended this essay as an intervention in the areas of African American literature and literary theory. I particularly want to demonstrate that thoughtful application of critical constructs derived from dialogic criticism can prove useful in enabling richer and more nuanced readings of African American narrative. Although passing applications of Bakhtinian concepts have been made in the past, no critical projects have been involved in extensive or sustained application of dialogic criticism to African American texts.[22]

I would argue that with the emergence of more complex texts dialogic criticism will become an extremely useful tool to aid the reading, discussion, and interpretation of African American narratives. As we move away from a politics informed by a single identity to one that addresses multipositionalities and locations, we might expect to encounter narratives such as those postnationalist narratives that address gender, class, sexual orientation in a contestatory relationship with race. Here, it would seem, dialogic criticism would be extremely useful.

## Notes

1. For an extensive discussion and thorough survey of dialogic criticism, see Don Bialostosky, "Dialogic Criticism," in *Contemporary Literary Theory*, ed. G. Douglas Atkins and Laura Morrow (Amherst: University of Massachusetts Press, 1989), 214–28.

2. Stanley E. Fish, *Self-Consuming Artifacts: The Experience of Seventeenth-Century Literature* (Berkeley, Los Angeles, London: University of California Press, 1974), 1.

3. See Gary Saul Morson and Caryl Emerson, *Mikhail Bakhtin: Creation of a Prosaic* (Stanford: Stanford University Press, 1990), 433.

4. Katerina Clark and Michael Holquist, *Mikhail Bakhtin* (Cambridge, Mass.: Belknap, Harvard University Press, 1984), 300.

5. Cited in Tzvetan Todorov, *Mikhail Bakhtin: The Dialogical Principle*, trans. Wlad Godzich (Minneapolis: University of Minnesota Press, 1984). Laurent Jenny, in his discussion of "strong" strategies of intertextualization, speaks of the author's need to reify the discourse of the other, making it the object of a metalanguage and allowing for the possibility of a new parole (see Laurent Jenny, "The Strategy of Form," in *French Literary Theory Today: A Reader*, ed. Tzvetan Todorov, trans. R. Carter [Cambridge: Cambridge University Press, 1982], 59).

6. Ralph Ellison, *Invisible Man* (New York: Random House, 1954; repr. 1981), 354. Further references to this work will be cited in the essay followed by page numbers.

7. Barbara Johnson, "Les Fleurs du Mal Armé: Some Reflections on Intertextuality," in *A World of Difference* (Baltimore and London: Johns Hopkins University Press, 1987), 116.

8. Toni Morrison, "Memory, Creation, and Writing," *Thought*, vol. 59, no. 235 (December 1984): 387, 388.

9. My use of the inner world/outer world construct is borrowed from Juri Lotman's topological model of the literary text. Ann Shukman describes that model as follows: "The inner/outer opposition may be variously interpreted in different cultures and different texts as 'one's own people/other people,' 'believers/heathens. . . . The inner world/outer world opposition may also be interpreted as 'this world/the other world'" (Ann Shukman, *Literature and Semiotics: A Study of the Semiotics of Yuri M. Lotman* [Amsterdam: North Holland Press, 1977], 95–96).

10. Mikhail Bakhtin, *Rabelais and His World*, trans. Helene Iswolsky (Bloomington: Indiana University Press, 1984), 19–20.

11. Toni Morrison, "Rootedness: The Ancestor as Foundation," in *Black Women Writers at Work (1950–1980): A Critical Evaluation*, ed. Mari Evans (New York: Anchor Press, 1984), 341.

12. Mikhail Bakhtin, *Problems of Dostoevsky's Poetics*, ed. and trans. Caryl Emerson, introd. Wayne C. Booth (Minneapolis: University of Minnesota Press, 1984), 191–92.

13. Bakhtin establishes here an axiological opposition between a "storyteller" and a "literary person," as well as between the author or narrator and "common people." It seems to me that those distinctions are nonexistent not only in *Song of Solomon* but in all of Morrison's texts. What one sees in her narratives is a fusion of the various voices, and more important, a common existential identity.

14. Toni Morrison, *Song of Solomon* (New York: Alfred A. Knopf, 1977), 3–4. Further references to this work will be cited in the essay followed by page numbers.

15. Bakhtin, *Problems of Dostoevsky's Poetics*, 6.

16. Ralph Ellison, "Brave Words for a Startling Occasion," in *Shadow and Act* (New York: Random House, 1963), 102–3.

17. Darko Suvin, "Can People Be (Re)Presented in Fiction: Toward a Theory of Narrative Agents and a Materialist Critique beyond Technology or Reductionism," in *Marxism and the Interpretation of Culture*, ed. Cary Nelson and Lawrence Grossberg (Urbana and Chicago: University of Illinois Press, 1988), 690.

18. Mikhail Bakhtin, "Discourse in the Novel," in *The Dialogic Imagination: Four Essays by M. M. Bakhtin*, ed. Cary Emerson and Michael Holquist (Austin: University of Texas Press, 1981), 345.

19. For an excellent treatment of a similar strategy of narration employed by Morrison in *Sula*, see Deborah E. McDowell's "Boundaries: Or Distant Relations and Close Kin," in *Afro-American Literary Study in the 1990s*, ed. Houston A. Baker Jr. and Patricia Redmond (Chicago and London: University of Chicago Press, 1989), 51–70. McDowell argues that Morrison "implicitly criticizes such concepts as 'protagonist,' 'hero,' and 'major character' by emphatically decentering and deferring the presence of Sula, the title character. Bearing *her* name, the narrative suggests that she is the protagonist, the privileged center, but her presence is constantly deferred. We are first introduced to a caravan of characters . . . before we get any sustained treatment of Sula. Economical to begin with, then, the novel is roughly one-third over when Sula is introduced, and it continues that long after her death" (61). I am not, of course, suggesting that the presentation of Milkman in *Song of Solomon* follows exactly the same pattern. I do maintain, however, that as the numerous stories begin to unfold in the novel, his simply becomes one of several.

20. Dorrit Cohn, *Transparent Minds: Narrative Modes for Presenting Consciousness in Fiction* (Princeton, N.J.: Princeton University Press, 1978), 100.

21. Ibid., 117.

22. Two impressive early critical references to applications of Bakhtinian constructs to African American narratives can be found in Houston A. Baker Jr., *Blues, Ideology, and Afro-*

*American Literature: A Vernacular Theory,* and Henry Louis Gates Jr., *The Signifying Monkey: A Theory of Afro-American Literary Criticism.* Baker suggests that Richard Wright's autobiography might be read within the context of Bakhtin's "carnivalesque discourse," and Gates utilizes Bakhtin's "double-voiced discourse," particularly the use of the parodic, to illuminate African American literature in general and Ellison's *Invisible Man* in particular.

# Tropology of Hunger

## The "Miseducation" of Richard Rodríguez

NORMA ALARCÓN

The historical condition of our times is to have "ethnicity," albeit reconfigured and remapped in the aftermath of the civil rights movement in the
United States. The Marxist mandate to acquire a class consciousness has
been too limited to account for all the elements in the formation of raced
ethnic groups in the context of the Americas. It increasingly appears as well
that in the Euro-American terrain the formation of a proletarian class consciousness has become more of a step on the way to the formation of an un-
stable bourgeois liberal subject, given the hegemony of the ideology, than to
becoming the "subject of history." Consequently, the contemporary en-
twinement of modernism (in the guise of aesthetics, positivism, enlightenment capitalist liberalism, and their conditioned Marxist contestations)
and postmodernism (marking the refractedness and sinister side of the enlightenment project of progressive rationality, the multiplicity of life-world
group formations, and the crisis of the male-biased liberal, political subject) gives rise to complex questions with respect to the cartography of culture and politics pertinent to the so-called ethnic canon, especially in its
currently subordinated position to the nation and its canon (Harvey 1989;
Jameson 1991; Laclau and Zac 1994). Thus, the primary questions before us
are, What is an American? What is America? What are the Americas?

It is not enough to assume ethnic identity in the context of the nation. One must pursue the conditions of its production and constitution and the structural and rhetorical forms engaged in the process. The extent to which ethnicity (raced or not) and gender can or cannot be refused is also of paramount importance given the constitutive contradictions to which the speaking/writing subject is subjected with respect to questions of identity-in-difference (Trinh 1989; Anzaldúa 1987; Spivak 1988). For the "aesthete" like Richard Rodríguez, contradictions emerging from sociopolitical inequalities and spheres of institutional power may be turned into biting, (un)witty, and playful ironies as he insists in the too absolutist separations of the public and the private in classical liberal terms. The boundaries and traffic between the aesthetic and the political are a debatable nexus of analysis and discourse through the structures produced.[1]

Perhaps no other U.S. writer of Mexican descent has simultaneously embraced and undermined the political subject of bourgeois classical liberalism as has Richard Rodríguez. Indeed, Rodríguez's salient critical apparatus entails the deployment of the extremely dichotomized political categories of the private and the public, such that the private pertains to culture and experience, and the public to the (unquestioned) institutional or public political sphere of the nation-state. It is clear that his anti-affirmative action and antibilingual education positions assume a bourgeois classical liberal understanding of the public sphere. In the words of Nancy Fraser, such understanding of the public sphere assumes "that it is possible for interlocutors in a public sphere to bracket status differentials and to deliberate 'as if' they were social equals . . . and that a single, comprehensive public sphere is always preferable to a nexus of multiple publics" (Fraser 1994, 80). The call for "as if" they were social equals requires the construction of a "public persona" with a greater or lesser degree of dissonance with the "private" one. Under these conditions, the demand for group representation as people of Mexican descent (that is, as an ethnicized group) in the public sphere makes no sense, must be subsumed under the private and thereby rendered irrelevant—along with non-English languages—to the public sphere. English becomes, then, the common denominating language of the public sphere and all differences may be erased. The mandate, under these conditions, is for the formation of bourgeois classical liberal political subjects devoid of difference, devoid of (produced or constructed) "ethnic" trappings, indeed of gender and sexuality. In the liberal political context of Euro-America, then, it is no accident that the most sustained critique and challenge of the domains of the private and the public continue to emerge from feminist theorists, since it is what counts as private and/or public that becomes a salient issue in contemporary politics and demands for radical democracy (Pateman 1989; Fraser 1994; Eisenstein 1994).[2]

In a sense, then, Rodríguez's deployment of these political categories in his work is part of a noncritically acquired education that in effect leads him to the (unsustainable) refusal of ethnicity, except as a private phenomenon that is then opposed to his construction of a public persona. Notwithstanding the historical naïveté of his political positions—which make him a popular public speaker in neoconservative spheres—it is the structural and rhetorical traffic between experienced culture and politics, which he cannot neatly sever into the private and the public, that undermines the political public persona to which, in his view, we should all aspire.

Rereading *Hunger of Memory* and other of his works from the hierarchical structure and discourse generated through the pivotal scene in the section "Complexion" enables us to track the double binds, which are often played for ironic effects, and the political economy's constitutive contradictions, which become inescapable for people of Mexican descent in the United States on the one hand, and for the (im)migrant's location on the other. A simultaneous reading of the constitutive contradictions of (im)migrants from the point of view of a Mexican location requires a reading of the displacement of campesinos/Indians from the economy and their exclusion from forming a public persona under Mexican conditions. In effect, the Chiapas neo-Zapatista movement is a recent dramatic example, in Mexico, of the political economy's productive processes and the displaced people's claims to citizenship in the Mexican nation-making history (Burbach 1994).

The section titled "Complexion" in Rodríguez's *Hunger of Memory* may be said to be structured by the mediating category of (im)migration. This analytical manuever enables the displacement of a reading of the work as "merely" that of an emblematic passage into a self-making, self-determining Anglo-American political liberal subject and brings into relief the salient constitutive contradictions that (im)migrants of Mexican descent undergo as they cross and recross the geopolitical border Mexico-United States (Rouse 1991). Moreover, it offers the possibility of reading Rodríguez's "ironic" mapping since his clear intentions are often enunciated by marking his privileged difference from (im)migrants, whom he wittily calls *los pobres*. (The only other Spanish term used is *los gringos*.) He points to his entry into the public sphere as a citizen-subject who "could act as a public person—able to defend my interests, to unionize, to petition, to speak up—to challenge and demand" (138). On the other hand, Rodríguez situates the (im)migrant as silent: "Their silence is more telling, they lack a public identity. They remain profoundly alien. Persons apart. People lacking a union obviously, people without grounds" (138). As (im)migrants subject to the waged-work realm of private capital and cultural spaces, Rodríguez underlines their lack of a "public identity" through which to defend their "rights" as workers. If they have a "public persona" at all it is as *collectivized* (im)migrants, displacing the possibility of *individualized* "rights" claims, thus highlighting the liberal justice system's vexed question of the rights of individuals versus the rights of (raced, gendered, and ethnicized) groups, as groups, a tension that is deeply implicated in the formation of the nation. As if proximity to (im)migrants bespoke a contagious disease, Rodríguez claims his "rights" as citizen-subject, reconfirming liberal ideology, and declares, "I would not shorten the distance I felt from *los pobres* with a few weeks of physical labor. I will not become like them. They were different from me" (135–36).

By marking the economic difference in Spanish-language terms, the (im)migrants are not just any (im)migrants but Mexican ones (or Latino ones), making as much the point that citizenship is as dependent on economic well-being as on speaking English. As a result, through the substitution of *los pobres* for (im)migrants, Rodríguez undermines the liberal "as if" proposition of social equality; that is, economic inequality becomes a sociopolitical one as well. By reversing the substitution of the ideological romanticization of the U.S. formation, (im)migration narrative is put on trial as it is revealed that (im)migrants are impoverished people with virtually no rights. In this scenario, *los pobres* as (im)migrants are constituted as the other of the bourgeois classical liberal political subject. Thus the political economy's constitution of this grouping (i.e., immigrants) is rejected for the pleasures of the hyperindividualized citizen-subject. On the one hand, it is precisely the tension between groupings (via the processes of the political economy) and individuals that historically overdetermined minoritized subjects put in evidence; on the other hand, Rodríguez's "refusal" to recognize this tension leads him to forget his (im)migrant status via the father, which, interestingly enough for us as readers, produces the unintended "irony" that undermines his claimed grounds. Moreover, the very "Complexion" that produces the relationality to the (im)migrants (discussed shortly) and undermines his separationist politics may well have the effect of turning him into an alien in Governor Pete Wilson's California. The separatist's politics are double and simultaneous (1) from (im)mi-

grants, (2) between the private and the public, such that (im)migrants become part of the private sphere and silenced.(See note 2.)

Yet Rodríguez's marking of his difference works not only in the direction
of the (im)migrant worker but also in the direction of the "authentic" (i.e.,
Anglo-American) nonalien, without much grasp of the production of an
alie(n)ation insofar as the (im)migrant has no "grounds" for a "public persona."The autobiographical impulse moves toward dis-alie(n)ation through
the desire not to be ethnicized as "Chicano" or "Mexican American" but
rather one who is an "American," as Rodríguez claims in his essay "An American Writer." Terms such as Mexican American often function in his work as
"merely" sociological categories unrelated to the practice of aesthetic writing—which again is a hyperindividualized project in Rodríguez—and
bound to compete as aesthetic object in the aesthetic sphere of debate.

Euro-American liberal "rhetoric, in its Americanizing power to interpel-
late selfhood along consensual lines of upward mobility, social regenera-
tion, and affirmative self-making," has often been the critical reading par
excellence of autobiography (Wilson, 118). Given the fact that such is the salient self-identity narrative in *Hunger of Memory*, the work implicitly falls in
line with the "Americanist discourse, which no matter how critical it gets of
existing society, only is granted professional legitimacy and social currency
if it can evoke an affirmative relation to 'America' as the process of national
self-affirmation and international self-assertion" (ibid., 124). This form of
critical reading becomes the corresponding partner to notions of the public and the private in liberal political discourse, which calls for the homogeneous making of the citizen-subject. Rodríguez follows the ideology of
what Wilson refers to as "the master-narrative of Americanization" (ibid.,
109), through the mediating categories of the public and the private, thus
promoting the (hyper)individuation of liberal political philosophy, which
has often found its ideal discursive genre in autobiography on the one
hand, and capitalist formation on the other (Sprinker 1980).

Nevertheless, as mentioned earlier, Rodríguez is aware of his undeniable,
metonymically articulated relation to the (im)migrant via racialization and
language. Through this evident relation, "White America" would want him
to "claim unbroken ties with [the] past" (*Hunger of Memory*, 5). What he
would relegate to the past is constantly present in the figure of the dark-
complected (im)migrant. A "clean" break with the past becomes impossible
in a nation whose very formation has been constituted through racializa-
tions. Thus, he is actually trapped in-between the "past" that is not past and
the "future" that is not present. Desire, which is ever the future, is "misrec-

ognized" by Rodríguez in the salient ideology of "Americanization." It has been the "misrecognition" of choice for many (prima facie male) (im)migrants. Rodríguez, however, does not consciously seize the historical entrapment, which is the one that often pertains to minoritized intellectuals in the United States.

Wit, with its concomitant use of inversions, irony, sarcasm, parody, and contradiction, is even more salient in Rodríguez's more recent work. Having learned the difference in socioeconomic class from the British, who until recently believed themselves a pale island, he has also learned the racist difference in Anglo-America, but he is too polite to say so. Mexico, whose "melting-pot" ideology has called for miscegenation, becomes, in his wit-producing grammar, an assimilationist country, while the United States, with its myth of assimilationism, becomes the country of criminalized miscegenation. He does not have to use an imaginary past—which in any case he cannot remember—as a shield because he carries it on his face—"Look at this Indian face!" ("An American Writer," 10). Indeed, he is not supposed to remember, since just about the time of the Anglo-America of Manifest Destiny Mexicans began to make much of their *mestizaje*, or what Rodríguez calls their assimilationist policy. Thus, if the Anglo-American nation-state formation is murderously manifested, the Mexican one is forcefully miscegenated and vice versa. One can very well ask what might be Rodríguez's aim through this baroque wit, characterized in literature by complexity of form and bizarre, ingenious, and often ambiguous imagery; characterized as well by grotesqueness, extravangance, or flamboyance.

The cover of the November 1991 issue of *Harper's* promotes Richard Rodríguez's essay "Mexico's Children" (subsequently collected in *Days of Obligation: An Argument with My Mexican Father*), as "The end of cultural and racial purity: Mixed Blood—a celebration of our *mestizo* world." Between covers, Rodríguez proclaims: "I have come at last to Mexico, the country of my parents' birth. I do not expect to find anything that pertains to me" (51). (A Mexican national anonymous reader said he did not read much that pertained to him; in fact, the essay seemed to him a form of "Chicano" writing!) Rodríguez, however, concludes his tourism by remarking that "the Indian stands in the same relation to modernity as she [*sic*] did to Spain: Willing to marry, to breed, to disappear in order to ensure her inclusion in time; refusing to absent herself from the future. . . . I take it as an Indian achievement that I am alive, that I am Catholic, that I speak English, that I am an American" (56). Indian, Catholic, English, American are four trope-producing terms that Rodríguez employs for the concatenation of his cultural and political persona. To round out the visit to Mexico, he states: "Mexico City: Europe's lie. . . . Each looks like mine. . . . where, then, is the famous conquistador? We have eaten him . . . we have eaten him with our eyes. I run to the mirror to see if this is true. It is true" (56). (Rodríguez plays here with a Mexican idiom applied to those that look too directly at another: "Comérselo con los ojos.") These observations bind two transformative effects—masculine into feminine and conquistador into Indian, respectively—turning through the consuming eyes.

In this later work, where he works tropes through the Indian face, Rodríguez contradicts an earlier position. In "Late Victorians," for example, he had elected—"barren skeptic" that he is—to be a "reader of St. Augustine, curator of the earthly paradise, inheritor of the empty mirror." As curator, he administers by and large a rhetorical museum, and the mirror is empty. He has chosen the role of spectator, "shift[ing] my tailbone upon the cold, hard pew" (66). This "American Writer" does not fail to remind us that he too is a professional (ironic) Aztec: "God it must be cool to be related to Aztecs" ("An American Writer," 10). In the course of everyday transactions the body is textualized by others. He observes to his Anglo-American audience, "I am one of you" (11), as he exclaims, "Look at this Indian face!" (10). He is told by both San Francisco and Berkeley liberals, as well as his grandmother, to maintain his culture, "whatever that means" (10). Americans end up sounding like one another, he observes, and "We do not, however, easily recognize our common identity" (4). But he claims to retain "aspects of culture, the deepest faiths, and moods of my ancestors, an inheritance deeper sometimes than I dare reveal to you, formal you" (11). The theme of secretive, in this instance, privatization continues, and the clue to the put-down of his Anglo-American audience is in that "formal you." If Americans do not differentiate linguistically between an informal "private" you and a formal "public" you, he begs the privilege to invoke the Hispanic usage, albeit embroiled in the baroque effects of colonization. He distances himself from "you" through linguistic practices that are alien to the "egalitarian" linguistic mask of Anglo-America.

Rodríguez's baroqueness is not book-learned from Indo-Hispanic America but from his orally rooted and disenfranchised father who learned the proper grammatical address, and from the British from whom he learned about manners, socioeconomic class, and the forms appropriate to it—especially those that deploy the wit/conceit of the upper classes or the aristocracy. The implication is that the colonized servants learn "conceit" from the aristocrats or upper classes and subsequently hold up a mirror, albeit rhetorical. In a sense, this accounts for Rodríguez's fondness for the pastoral, the form of impersonation "felt to imply a beautiful relation between rich and poor," where the elite get to be shepherds for a day and conduct a "courtship between contrasted social classes" (Burke, 123). According to Burke, William Empson's *Some Versions of Pastoral*, which Rodríguez read, was a "response to a vogue for 'proletarian' literature," and thereby "profoundly concerned with the rhetoric of courtship between contrasted social classes" (ibid.). Thus, it should be no surprise that Rodríguez would use the conceits of the form as the devices to propel his rejection of self-proclaimed Chicano "proles" on the one hand, and the "egalitarian" mask of Anglo-America on the other, through the very fulcrum of middle-class America, the "universal" class and its bourgeois liberal subject.

In many ways, Rodríguez places in question those who are fond of claiming citizenship by saying "I am an American" and think they know what they mean. To this Rodríguez replies implicitly, "so am I"—though most of his book learning has been English/British through education (recently he has added Octavio Paz and Carlos Fuentes to the list), his socioeconomic and political life is (Anglo)American, and his affective life is represented through working-class Mexican Spanish (which he cannot write). If the aristocrats can play at being shepherds, Rodríguez can play at being an aristocrat. He acts the aristocrat and simultaneously courts him. But he can also play at being an American and fly east from California, "against the grain of America, into the dark" ("An American Writer," 3). Rodríguez's rhetorical impersonations involve what Butler has called a complex "double inversion that says appearance is an illusion" (Butler, 337). In Rodríguez's vocabulary, the outside appearance is Indian/feminine but the "essence" inside the body is aristocratic/masculine. At the same time, it symbolizes the opposite: the appearance outside is aristocratic/masculine but the "essence" inside is Indian/feminine, operating via the tropes produced as a result of "eating through the eyes." Enacted impersonations place the truth of identity in question while simultaneously producing other possibilities as in the case of "neoethnicity" gambits. For example, a book by Danny Santiago *(Famous All over Town)*, an Anglo whose name was James, won a Casa de las Américas Prize as a Chicano book. More recently, the Cherokee tale *The Education of Little Tree* was discovered not to have been written by a Cherokee but by Asa (Ace) Carter, a white supremacist who wrote speeches for former Alabama governor George C. Wallace and worked for the Ku Klux Klan.

The complicity between the demand for authenticity and its subsequent commodification, and the ease with which we can pass as "authentic" by learning the "right" things, come with the territory of having "ethnicity" in the Americas today. In a sense it is an additional aspect of its production in advanced capitalist nations. Richard Rodríguez says with Trinh T. Minh-ha "Like you/not you," the "in-between zones are the shifting grounds on which the (doubly) exiled walk" (Trinh, 70). And to mark this duplicity, Rodríguez translates the style of the drag queen through the rhetorical museum of the Indian. Much, one might say—as Derrida's Nietzsche in *Spurs*—translates the style of the man through the rhetorical museum of the feminine. In the Trinh T. Minh-ha citations, the exile is double because the Insider is Outsider, the Outsider is Insider, "Outside in Inside Out." Further in the never-ending play of the rhetorical, Rodríguez reveals his "ethnicity" because he is an American, and he reveals his Americanness because he is an "ethnic." "I suspect," he says, "ethnicity is only a public metaphor, like sexuality or age, for a knowledge that bewilders us" ("An American Writer," 9). But in the United States, for example, those that continue to be "ethnic" (or in Mexico, "Indians") are those who are unable to miscegenate, that is, they could not actually pass for or impersonate an "Anglo-American." Manifest Destiny is the move of Anglo-America toward the South and then the West, and from both we read America against the grain: "Undercutting the Inside/Outside opposition, her intervention is necessarily that of both a deceptive insider and a deceptive outsider" (Trinh, 70). In the rhetorical museum of (wo)man, the impersonator is virtually always feminine (ibid., 74). Yet this baroque wit, which we insist on calling "postmodern," is an inversion of the pastoral for Rodríguez, for we have the "shepherd" playing at the "aristocrat," or, shall we say the Caliban playing at Prospero: "I have taken Caliban's advice. I have stolen their books. I will have some run of this isle" (*Hunger of Memory*, 3). Rodríguez's performance of raced ethnicities finds resonance in the Supreme Court's nation-defining statement in the Bakke decision, which claims that "all groups in the United States are a minority, each of which so far as 'racial and ethnic distinctions' go is rooted in our Nation's constitutional and demographic history" (*Regents of University of California v. Bakke*, 1221). According to this vision, the United States is a "nation of minorities," each of which had to struggle "to overcome prejudices not of a monolithic majority, but of a 'majority' composed of various minority groups of whom it was said—perhaps unfairly in many cases—that a shared characteristic was a willingness to disadvantage other groups" (ibid.). Since the civil rights movement puts in crisis the myth of the "melting pot" of nation-making Anglo-America, ethnic raconteurs and "disadvantaging majorities" from all academic disciplines including jurisprudence are all now embroiled in "identity" formation discourses.

Is a bourgeois pastoral subject all a "true" American can have? Rodríguez's fascination with the pastoral is due to the paradigmatic and ideological function that he saw in the form. However, since the form itself is ironically mannered, he is drawn deeper into its wit, very self-conscious of the fact that not all is as is, perhaps a variation on the *ser/parecer* theme of the Spanish baroque itself. Tomás Rivera observed of *Hunger of Memory* that Rodríguez's use of the verb *to be* is one of locatedness, of place, rather than of predication. Rivera gets at this by noting that in Spanish there are two verbs to signify *to be, ser* and *estar* (contrast this with *ser/parecer*—that is, *ser* pivots two contrastive verbs). Rivera theorizes that the first reflects interiority and the second exteriority, and that the core of "our" life is the family, the interiority, the intimate—completely the reverse of what Rivera assumes that Rodríguez claims. Rivera sees Rodríguez as claiming that the core of his life is the "public" one because he silences his immediate family, refusing to educate himself on Hispanic culture, his genealogical family as well. I think Rivera is preliminarily on the right track on his observations of the use of *to be*—as *being* and as *situatedness*. It is the play between those possibilities, including *ser/parecer*, that Rodríguez puts into play through his usage of tropes in the English language. However, Rivera glides too easily from individual interiority to the family to the private and presumes that they correspond in too symmetrical a fashion to *ser*, leaving *estar* to designate the "public." No assessment has been made of Rivera's linguistic claims on *Hunger of Memory;* at this point this becomes an instance of the traffic between Spanish and English.

For Rodríguez the use of the Spanish language is something to savor. The contrast of Spanish and English is a contrast between gliding and stumbling, mellifluous sliding and screeching. He sentimentalizes the working-class users of Spanish (shepherds?) from the point of view of English usage (aristocrats?). Spanish, for Rodríguez, represents his parents, who betrayed him by insisting that he do as the nuns say and learn English. He does so with a vengeance (as we have come to learn) in order to hurt his parents— and, in a childish way, both to keep the intimacy of what his parents offered and to distance himself from them. Through this emotionally charged relationship, he privatizes Spanish, relegating it to the domestic sphere, and severs it (unsuccessfully) from English, which is relegated to the public sphere. His rage at the break—the discontinuity between home and school, past and present that every Spanish-speaking child experiences in the United States—is displaced toward Chicanos who demand bilingual education. Moreover, he refuses to claim, as Rivera would want him to, a heritage that is not his, playing on the finer point of possession/dispossession—the political displacement and dispossession of his father from Mexico. To claim a heritage is to use it as a shield, yet simultaneously he relegates his (im)migrant father to silence.

Insofar as judicial affirmative action narratives have hitched constitutional consistency and coherence to the privileged rights of the individual who is above "political and social judgments" pertinent to groups, Rodríguez is in complete agreement with the system. According to the Supreme Court, "Nothing in the constitution supports the notion that individuals may be asked to suffer otherwise impermissible burdens in order to enhance the societal standings of their ethnic groups" (*Regents of University of California v. Bakke,* 1223). It will not be suffered that the individual's worth be tarnished by "stereotypes of groups"; moreover, "innocent individuals should not be forced to bear the burdens of redressing grievances not of their making" (ibid.). The pursuit of self-possessed individuality in Richard Rodríguez takes place according to the Constitution of the United States as coded in the Fourteenth Amendment. Yet he also demonstrates, unwittingly, the limits of the refusal to play the Anglo-American ethnic game. Anglo-America's politics continue to be predicated on acquiring visibility through ethnicity, not race, a factor that makes the justices shutter as it may imply a "two-class theory." It was the incorporation of race into the Constitution that henceforth made denial impossible, yet that is eroded through the ethnic dance. In my view, the hidden episteme in Rodríguez's pastoral is the rage at our embodied history, for while his wit may pass muster, his face does not. As a result, the face becomes a weapon along with wit. How else can he tell us that his body is as textualized as his speech? Yet he knows what he is about as he asserts, "There are those in America who would anoint me to play out for them some drama of ancestral reconciliation. . . . But I reject the role" (*Hunger of Memory,* 4). Who are the ancestors? Who are those?

Richard Rodríguez's "bad faith," if I may use such an antiquated existential phrase, and even on occasion his egregious politics, lie in the silencing of the disenfranchised—(im)migrant labor. He does so politically by continuing to allow his bioexemplum to serve as the preferred citation of right-wing liberals. In some sense, Rodríguez demonstrates that neoconservative liberal cynicism knows no bounds, as it rhetorically feeds its own trope machine by the selective filtering of the discourses of emancipation. In *Hunger of Memory,* as George Yúdice has observed, "arguments against affirmative action and bilingual education, because these policies construct a certain minority identity, are a significant indictment of liberal morality (or hypocrisy to be more exact)" (Yúdice, 222). Rodríguez's unsustainable refusal of a minoritized identity blunts the edge of his anger, as he prefers to advance his "public" and "scholarship boy" persona, which has become a carbon copy of the literate dominant even as he admits that such an obedient and imitative persona voids him of critical thinking. He has discovered, however, that totalizing self-construction is elusive.

Caught within the limitations of a self-avowed spectatorship, the demands of participatory democracy, the textualization of the body, and the will to conserve some notion of the "American" way, Rodríguez has been as much silenced by some criticism as he has silenced the Mexican (im)migrant. Displacement and dislocation are at the core of the invention of the Americas. However, it is not the dispossessed (im)migrant laborer or Indian as presence but her absence from the public sphere, as citizen-subject, that continues to drive the nation-making processes. Rodríguez's major unintended question may well be, "Can the Subaltern Speak?" (Spivak 1988). To which his answer is no because she lacks a public persona. Yet he would deprive her of the possibility of a public persona by insisting on an identitarian figuration of the public sphere, while simultaneously performing the tropology of differences as aesthetic project closed off from the sociopolitical sphere. Thus, in Rodríguez's writing trajectory, difference is aesthetic and private, identity is political and public and must be subordinated to prevailing hegemonic views of the public sphere. One might well say, from this point of view, that not even the Supreme Court justices agree completely!

## Notes

1. It is interesting to note that Richard Rorty's *Contingency, Irony, and Solidarity* relegates irony to privatized aesthetic spheres, blocking off questions of its sociopolitical implications. For further comment on Rorty, see also Honi Fern Haber's *Beyond Postmodern Politics: Lyotard, Rorty, Foucault.* I would question, however, the feasibility of leaping to beyond. In his work *Chicano Narrative: The Dialectics of Difference,* Ramón Saldívar also pursues the too absolute a separation between the private and the public in Rodriguez's work and attendant problems.

2. The political twists and turns of the private and the public are being played out in California through its Proposition 187, which was passed in the 1994 elections. The Proposition would have schools report undocumented (im)migrant children to the Immigration and Naturalization Service, which goes against children's protected educational rights under the Family Educational and Privacy Act. See the *San Francisco Chronicle,* August 13, 1994: A1, A15.

# References

Anzaldúa, Gloria. *Borderlands/La Frontera: The New Mestiza*. San Francisco: Spinsters/Aunt Lute, 1987.

Burbach, Roger. "Roots of the Postmodern Rebellion in Chiapas." *New Left Review* 205 (1994): 113–24.

Burke, Kenneth. *A Grammar of Motives*. Berkeley: University of California Press, 1969.

Butler, Judith. "Gender Trouble, Feminist Theory and Psychoanalytic Discourse." In *Feminism/Postmodernism*, ed. Linda Nicholson. New York: Routledge, 1990.

Eisenstein, Zillah R. *The Color of Gender: Reimaging Democracy*. Berkeley: University of California Press, 1994.

Fraser, Nancy. "Rethinking the Public Sphere: A Contribution to the Critique of Actually Existing Democracy." In *Between Borders: Pedagogy and the Politics of Cultural Studies*, ed. Henry A. Giroux and Peter McClaren. New York: Routledge, 1994.

Jameson, Fredric. *Postmodernism or, The Cultural Logic of Late Capitalism*. Durham, N.C.: Duke University Press, 1991.

Haber, Honi Fern. *Beyond Postmodern Politics: Lyotard, Rorty, Foucault*. New York: Routledge, 1994.

Harvey, David. *The Condition of Postmodernity*. Cambridge, Mass.: Basil Blackwell, 1989.

Laclau, Ernesto, and Lilian Zac. "Minding the Gap: The Subject of Politics." In *The Making of Political Identities*, ed. Ernesto Laclau. New York: Verso, 1994.

Pateman, Carole. *The Disorder of Women: Democracy, Feminism and Political Theory*. Stanford: Stanford University Press, 1989.

*Regents of University of California v. Bakke*, 438 U.S. 265, 98 S.Ct.2733, 57 L.ed.2d 750 (1978).

Rivera, Tomás. "Richard Rodriguez's *Hunger of Memory* as Humanistic Antithesis." *MELUS* 11:4 (winter 1984): 5–13.

Rodriguez, Richard. "An American Writer." In *The Invention of Ethnicity*, ed. Werner Sollors. New York: Oxford University Press, 1989. 3–13.

——. *Days of Obligation: An Argument with My Mexican Father*. New York: Viking, 1992.

——. *Hunger of Memory: The Education of Richard Rodriguez*. Boston: Godine, 1982.

——. "Late Victorians: San Francisco, AIDS, and the Homosexual Stereotype." *Harper's* (October 1990): 57–65.

——. "Mixed Blood, Columbus's Legacy: A World Made Mestizo." *Harper's* (November 1991): 47–56.

Rouse, Roger. "Mexican Migration and the Social Space of Postmodernism." *Diaspora* 1:1 (1991): 8–23.

Spivak, Gayatri Chakravorty. "Can the Subaltern Speak?" In *Marxism and the Interpretation of Culture*, ed. Cary Nelson and Lawrence Grossberg. Urbana: University of Illinois Press, 1988.

Sprinker, Michael. "Fictions of the Self: The End of Autobiography." In *Autobiography: Essays Theoretical and Critical*, ed. James Olney. Princeton, N.J.: Princeton University Press, 1980.

Trinh T. Minh-ha. *Woman/Native/Other*. Bloomington: Indiana University Press, 1989.

Wilson, Rob. "Producing American Selves: The Form of American Biography." *Boundary 2* (summer 1991): 104–29.

Yúdice, George. "Marginality and the Ethics of Survival." In *Universal Abandon? The Politics of Postmodernism*, ed. Andrew Ross. Minneapolis: University of Minnesota Press, 1988.

~

# Calculated Musings

## Richard Rodríguez's Metaphysics of Difference

ROSAURA SÁNCHEZ

In the realm of culture, outsideness is a most
powerful factor in understanding.
—M. M. Bakhtin, *Speech Genres and Other Late Essays* (7)

In his work on *Exiles and Émigrés*, Terry Eagleton poses the notion that the great literary achievements of the First World War period in modern English fiction were those of foreigners and émigrés: James, Conrad, Eliot, Yeats, Joyce, Pound, and Lawrence (who was English but working-class) (Eagleton 1970, 14–15). In contrast, the two dominant English strands of literature, that of the "upper class" and the "lower middle class," are described as being "too tied, at crucial points, to the dominant orthodoxy they opposed" (13). Both traditional modes, according to Eagleton, were "incapable of embracing, or transcending, the society to which they represented a critical reaction, and yet with which they shared a common basis of assumptions" (14). The work of foreigners and émigrés, on the other hand, presented frameworks that allowed for an analysis of the "erosion" of their time and space in a rather creative manner and from a broader perspective, given their "immediate access to alternative cultures and traditions" (15), that is, to other than the dominant national culture, whether that of another country or that of a nondominant English class, as in the case of Lawrence. All of these writers were tied to the English center they inhabited, yet their perspective retained an alien component. It is this estrangement (which Eagleton discusses later in his essay "Nationalism: Irony and Commitment"), this sense of being an outsider/insider, in the culture but not wholly of it, this alienation and disidentification in the face of social and political oppression, and the distinct awareness of being part of an alternative community, an "imagined community" (B. Anderson) with its own cultures and traditions, that characterize our best ethnic literature.

It is an ambiguous, contradictory position, being both inside and outside, offering both interior and exterior ways of perceiving social reality, allowing as much for strategies of accommodation to hegemonic discourses as for contestatory practices from an alternative position. It is a difficult position, considering that the danger is, of course, always there that the literature of the "social exile" in the United States may in fact succumb to what Eagleton has noted in "lower middle-class" English literature and offer only a representation of spaces of marginalization within American society. The reconstruction of "submerged social realities," generated out of a sense of oppression and frustration, without transcending "the direct pressures of that experience to evaluate it as a whole" (Eagleton 1970, 14), is, however, not the only stumbling block faced by ethnic writers. There is always the equally powerful pressure to filter all constructs of marginality through hegemonic ideological frameworks, in the end legitimating the perspective of the dominant society. Faced with the aggressive onslaught of late capitalist ideological leveling that is seemingly inevitable in the contemporary text, ethnic writers will have to do more than employ kitsch and simulated "nostalgia" to deal with and express what West calls "the ragged edges of the Real" and "that brutal side of American capital," racism, and sexism that is often forgotten amid the rhetoric of pluralism (West in Stephanson, 277, 281).

It is indeed curious that during a period of retrenchment of the political right and global fears concerning the incursions of Third World (and now Eastern bloc) immigrants into European and American metropolitan areas, multiculturalism and ethnic literature should gain currency even as concerns over the risks of uniformity across the globe emerge. Thus, while some scholars mourn the fragmentation of Western culture, others, like Feyerabend, lament the "new and powerful uniformities" that are leading to the disappearance of cultural difference and the replacement of "indigenous crafts, customs and institutions" by "Western objects, customs, organizational forms" (Feyerabend, 2). Feyerabend is in fact concerned that multinational capital and technological development are threatening the globe with "monotony and dullness" (3). It is the threat of "sameness" rather than concern over economic policies promoting the exploitation of the Third World for its cheap labor and natural resources that has—in some quarters, at least—triggered a call for diversity and difference and yet, given the function of culture during this period of late capitalism, the threats are clearly inseparable.

The premise of impending global uniformity needs to be contextualized, however, for it is predicated not only upon the impact of multinational capital, technology, and cultural penetration but upon mass consumption of consumer goods. Thus, given social stratification, that is, class-divided societies, and a global market that sells primarily to the upper classes, not everything in the Third World has been reduced to wholesale "sameness," despite the tremendous impact of consumer culture; not even within U.S. borders is this the case. In the Third World, the uneven development produced by transnational capital and incomplete modernization is in fact paralleled by cultural heterogeneity and fragmentation, despite the *Northamericanization* of dominant bourgeois culture, as in the case of Mexico (Monsiváis). It is this uneven development that concerns Samir Amin, for example, who argues for a reorganization of the world on the basis of polycentrism and difference. The task, he says, calls for delinking peripheral Third World nations from externally imposed capitalist development policies. Each nation would follow the "imperatives of the complex stages of its internal development" (Amin, ix). Amin's interesting formulation of delinking would in effect counter shifts toward merging or uniformity and promote a break in the chain, that is, a rupture in dependency, and allow for an independently determined economic policy.

For ethnic minorities in this country, however, interlinked as they are by the national economic and political system, delinking is not now plausible, for, despite social fragmentation and stratification, the links between minority and majority populations, between the marginal and the dominant, are vital, organic. Ruptures like the Los Angeles uprising, for example, do, however, occasionally occur, fraying the variable linkages in the chain, in view of the nature of the linkage itself, which is not one of equals but of dominant/dominated classes and collectivities, constituted and reproduced through strategies of exclusion (Mouzelis, 59). Thus, in this society, characterized by unequal access to the means of production, linkages not only bind and contain culturally but also govern and constrain, creating frictions, antagonisms, and the potential for struggle. Notwithstanding, then, the leveling power of hegemonic ideologies to create consensus, antagonistic class, race, and ethnic relations and the center's domination through strategies of exclusion and segregation have in fact ensured and propitiated alternative "imagined communities" (B. Anderson) within this country, giving rise to a form of polyculturalism often reinforced by spatial segregation and linguistic diversity. Thus, despite hegemonic claims for a common "American culture," concrete social configurations continue to generate discourses of social difference and nourish an emergent literature produced within the center but from the perspective of inside outsiders, "social exiles" (Eagleton 1970, 18) within the belly of the monster (Martí, 3). As Bercovitch indicates, "'America' is many forms of ethnicity, many patterns of thought, many ways of life, many cultures, many American literatures" (Bercovitch 1968a, 438).

Recent calls for decentering the canon from a multicultural perspective with an attendant call for "pluralism" while seemingly evidencing a recognition of the cultural heterogeneity within this country have only provoked virulent attacks and apocalyptic admonishments from conservatives arguing for the maintenance of Eurocentric culture. In these heated debates, the notion of "pluralism" itself is often used as if it were equivalent to polycentrism, that is, to a plurality of equal cultural "centers" rather than what in fact it reconstructs: a center and several marginal sites. For this reason, "pluralism" threatens to become a new myth of equality. Equally troubling is the exclusive focus on culture, micropolitics, and discourses of "difference," which have proliferated to the point that everything and nearly everyone is deemed potentially "different" or "marginal" in some measure. As difference is naturalized and made into a topical discourse, the more crucial and immediate issues of class and race are displaced from critical analyses in the name of cultural representation and inclusion. In effect, as "difference" becomes a meaningless "universal," it also becomes a powerful ideological discourse masking social relations embodied within distinct spheres of difference.

But that is precisely what antagonists of multiculturalism, along the lines of Shelby Steele and Richard Rodríguez, seek to do. The latter, in his latest work, *Days of Obligation: An Argument with My Mexican Father*, allays the fears of defenders of a Eurocentric "common culture" by reminding them that the children of immigrants all eventually become "stranger[s] to [their] parents, stranger[s] to [their] own memory of [themselves]" (161). In the ten essays that comprise the book, Rodríguez focuses on his own estrangement from his parents' place of origin, Mexico, and scoffs at educators who propose to celebrate "diversity" as if it were a "solution to itself." After all, he insists, the term "diversity" "admits everything, stands for nothing" (169). What is at issue for Rodríguez is not the term's concealment of racial/ethnic oppression and class exploitation but rather the celebration of multiethnic diversity itself. From his vantage point, America is full of immigrant populations but they all gradually acculturate and appropriate the dominant discourses and practices ("how shall we describe Americanization, except as loss?" [164]). Sameness always counters and eliminates difference, exotic as it may be, except of course at a metaphysical level, where traces of difference, it seems, always remain. That, at least, is Rodríguez's "American dream." The discourses of "difference" with which he plays in these essays are not the product of social relations but rather mythic/metaphysical and fetishistic "differences" that entering college students in English 1A will be asked to consume as examples of "ethnic" literature. Selectively ethnicizing the canon cannot, then, be our objective, at least not while the power to establish that canon is not our prerogative.

Rodríguez's text offers a cross between the discourses of the confessional and the travelogue: disparate, fragmentary, disjointed, and contradictory memories of a gay Catholic man of Mexican origin in search of icons and signs, posts to tell him who and where he is, whether in Sacramento, San Francisco and Los Angeles, Mexico City, the Tijuana-San Diego border, the California missions, Santa Rosa, the East Coast, London, or Rome. Each icon or representational space (Lefebvre, 39) focused upon—be it the Virgen de Guadalupe, a Victorian house, the missions, the head of Joaquín Murrieta, his quintessential Mexican village—gives rise to a chain of meanings that form his metaphysical imaginary (Kellner, 153) and allow him to extrapolate and interpret "national character," ostensibly both Mexican and American. Each fetishized space evokes a particular resonance in him, a man of multiple identities, each one in tension with the others but none crucial enough to affect his overriding self-satisfaction with his upper-middle-class trappings, his chaste gay existence (in consonance with the Catholic church's encyclical censure of active homosexuals as sinners), and his self-conscious role as a "professional Mexican American." It is from this space of self-righteousness and dilettantism that he marks off distances, initiating his conversation or dialogue rarely with his Mexican father or Mexicans in general, more often with "you," the majority population in the United States ("We didn't have an adequate name for you. In private you were the gringo" [Rodríguez 1992, 63]). Although he is well aware of a larger audience beyond that includes Chicanos and other minorities, who serve as an impetus for positioning and repositioning himself throughout the text, for the most part the text solipsistically focuses on Rodríguez and his particular circumstances and personal demons. In a work that raises a number of polemical issues, he enjoys bantering and contradicting himself continuously as if his primary strategy were to escape being pigeonholed (as he was after his publication of *Hunger of Memory*). But his "straw subjectivities" do not conceal the claims he makes to the majority population of being the new all-American ethnic wonder: "When I was a boy who spoke Spanish, I saw America whole. I realized that there was a culture here because I lived apart from it. I didn't like America. Then I entered the culture. I entered the culture as you did, by going to school. I became Americanized. I ended up believing in choices as much as any of you do" (172).

*Days of Obligation* is undoubtedly a rebuttal of criticism to his earlier book, *Hunger of Memory*, in which the narrator revealed his estrangement from his ethnic collectivity (he is now, ten years later, metaphysically Mexican), his incapacity to see Spanish as more than a "private" language (he now recognizes Spanish to be a "great metropolitan language" [64]), his pathetic self-loathing for having dark skin (his newly found Indian blood is now a mark of distinction), his intellectual snobbishness and his reactionary assessment of bilingual education (he was just playing devil's advocate, playing "America"), and his repudiation of affirmative action (he now sarcastically recognizes that he may be one of those who have profited from affirmative action ("those of us with access to microphones because of affirmative action" [70]). We are, of course, to revel in how much Rodríguez has evolved and is coming to grips with his "identities." For his good services, following the publication of his first book of essays, the author became the darling of right-wing politicians and conservative groups. In time he was tapped by mainstream media as if he were the official representative of the very population that he views in the text with disdain; his opinions have since been published in the *Los Angeles Times* and he has appeared on the *MacNeil/Lehrer Newshour* to provide the "Mexican American" perspective. His privileged status and appeal to the political right are, of course, not unrelated to his "ethnic difference," one that he can make palatable to the dominant society at a moment of crisis when it feels threatened by waves of immigrants from the Caribbean, Asia, Mexico, and Central America as well as by urban upheaval within its cities. Here for the world to behold is a Mexican American who identifies primarily as an "American," defends the notion of a common culture, and takes to task educators for "instill[ing] in children a pride in their ancestral pasts" (169). For Rodríguez, multicultural education and American history are mutually exclusive, and in fact the former implies "a curtailing of education": "Gay studies, women's studies, ethnic studies—the new curriculum ensures that education will be flattering. But I submit that America is not a tale for sentimentalists" (ibid.).

Rodríguez deprecates the teaching of ethnic history and literature for being "flattering," presumably to the minority group, but the teaching of European history and literature, ostensibly the only heritage pertinent to American history and culture, is held up as the sine qua non of the American persona:

> If I am a newcomer to your country, why teach me about my ancestors? I need to know about seventeenth-century Puritans in order to make sense of the rebellion I notice everywhere in the American city. Teach me about mad British kings so I will understand the American penchant for iconoclasm. Then teach me about cowboys and Indians; I should know that tragedies created the country that will create me. (Ibid.)

Rodríguez does not seemingly oppose ethnicizing the canon ("To argue for a common culture is not to propose an exclusionary culture nor a static culture" [170]), yet he would not teach ethnic culture in relation to the nation of origin ("why teach me about my ancestors"). His proposal is not as contradictory as it may seem, however, given his political stance. What Rodríguez deems acceptable is the inclusion of ethnic history or literature *within* dominant culture programs, ensuring thereby a hegemonic reading of ethnic cultural production. His approach ignores historically specific struggles for ethnic studies, women's studies, and gay studies programs and departments, and negates our right to present a reading of our history, struggles, and literature from our own vantage point and, equally important, to devise our own curriculum and select our own texts. Multicultural curricula are for Rodríguez a threat, a harbinger of "the dismantlement of national culture. The end of history" (171). He resents what he calls "the university's" use of the immigrant as a "convenient national excuse" to "undo America," to "untie the cultural knot," to "sever memory" (ibid.). Ironically, if for Fukuyama "the end of history" is what Perry Anderson calls "the exhaustion of any viable alternatives" to Western liberal democracy (P. Anderson, 282), for Rodríguez it is exactly the opposite; the end of history is the positing of cultural alternatives to the canon: "Now the American university is dismantling the American canon in my name. In the name of my father, in the name of Chinese grocers and fry cooks and dentists, the American university disregards the Judeo-Christian foundation of the American narrative" (Rodríguez 1992, 171).

What Rodríguez fails to see is that multicultural concerns may in fact reinject history into the curriculum. He prefers consenting to the myth of a common American identity traceable to New England and the Puritans. Instead of dealing with the Puritan cultural myth as an ideological construct, he sets it up as a transcendental truth (Jehlen, 14), forgetting that, far from a "common culture," there always was cultural diversity in this society, despite efforts of the dominant class to gain the consensus of the middle classes. Economic and political conflicts, racism and slavery, xenophobia, expansionism and imperialism, class struggles—all have ensured that the posited consensus has always been subverted to some extent. Even in the face of dissensus (Bercovitch 1986b, viii), however, rather than examine the historical and material conditions that disarticulate the construct of an "all-encompassing American identity" (see Jehlen, 4), Rodríguez will prefer to cling to the notion of a transcendental truth to explain why white Anglo-Saxon Protestants could, by any stretch of the collective imagination, be proponents of multicultural education, as we shall see.

Rodríguez's metaphysical imaginary is based on a selectively posited grid of categories that allow him to explain differences between American culture and Mexican culture on the basis of dichotomies. For example, he ascribes feminine gender to Mexico to oppose it to the masculinity of the United States. This gendering of Mexico as feminine counters notions of Mexico as a nation of machos but it does, on the other hand, follow the Octavio Paz metaphysical mode, which analyzes social problems in Mexico on the basis of essential ethnic and cultural attributes. For Rodríguez, Mexico is a whore ("Mexico lay down and the gringo paid in the morning" [88]), "Mother Mexico" (58) who calls out to her blood children (57), and la Malinche, Cortés's Indian translator and lover, symbol of betrayal ("Mexico? The country that had betrayed them?" [53]). Among his set of binary oppositions positing essentialist distinctions are the following: Protestants versus Catholics, feminine versus masculine, communal versus individualistic, loyalty versus betrayal, matriarchal/maternal versus patriarchal/paternal-uncle, secular time versus religious time, past versus future, tragedy versus comedy, Europe versus Asia/India, public versus private, reproduction versus nonreproduction, gay versus straight, American versus immigrant, intimate/formal versus informal, memory versus failure of memory, sin versus forgiveness. In each case he privileges one side as American and dominant, the other side as subordinate and Mexican, although he does suggest that Mexico is increasingly Americanized and given to consumer culture in view of the large numbers of immigrant workers that cross and recross the U.S.-Mexico border; their returns to Mexico "in style" are described as "celebration[s] of American desire" (79). There is obviously a major confusion here between nation and class, as there is throughout the work, for it is their economic "improvement," their higher wages vis-à-vis Mexican workers, that they celebrate, rather than a newly found "American" taste for consumerism.

With this essentialist baggage in tow, Rodríguez sets out to interpret "the American mind" and explain what to him is untenable support for multiculturalism. It is, he will argue, precisely individualism that characterizes Americans (163–64), as well as independence of thought (167). For this reason, he concludes, "no belief is more cherished by Americans, no belief is more typical of America, than the belief that one can choose to be free of American culture" (171). It is the Puritan spirit in Americans, "the antisociability of American Protestantism," their "fear of the crowd" (167) that rejects the communal and ironically favors an immigrant nation: "America became a multiracial, multireligious society precisely because a small band of Puritans did not want the world" (165). Thus Rodríguez would explain sociohistoric changes on the basis of cultural myths and twisted logic, for only by the farthest stretch of the imagination could the Puritans be seen as anything but the most exclusionary and xenophobic of societies, as evident, for example, in their massacre of the Pequot Indians (Zinn, 15). In Rodríguez's essays, individualism is seen not as a discursive construct generated during a period of capitalist development but as a transcendental truth, inherent in the very genes of Americans and already traceable to the Puritans, who, he forgets, punished any sign of individualism, any antinomianism, any challenge or sign of deviance from the communal norm, to the point of burning "witches" and ostracizing "sinners."

It cannot be that Rodríguez ignores the fact that immigration is historically tied to this country's economic interests in attracting a labor force for its growing industries and for its westward expansionism. No, in a separate discussion he demonstrates awareness that "America wanted cheap labor. American contractors reached down into Mexico for men to build America" (52). But this type of information, noted in passing, is never valorized by Rodríguez, nor does it play a role in his analysis. It is "national character," good old Puritan individualism, rather than capitalism and imperialism, that explains this immigrant nation. The binary opposition "communal/individualistic" affords him the opportunity to shift from one side to another, whenever the posited dominant side proves unworkable, and to "go beyond" historical specificity. Thus we are informed that these essential features are sometimes temporarily set aside in time of crisis. Rodríguez will grudgingly acknowledge that when they feel threatened, individualist

Americans resort "to the idea of a shared culture" (164), that is, to a notion of the communal. This "imagined community" is, however, exclusionary, leaving out all those considered different, like Catholics and Jews (ibid.). He admits that the latter have now been replaced by "Hispanics and Asians," who, though still feared by "nativists," are also welcomed for bringing "diversity" to America and for reintroducing the absent yet desired communal spirit. Rodríguez's binary model thus ensures that any opposition can be reversed and subsumed to the overriding greater good; the closure is nevertheless always the same; exclusion (social), seen from this vantage point, is another form of inclusion (imaginary), but so too were "separate but equal" facilities. Thus, when individualism is threatened by a failing economy ("Americans are no longer sure that economic invincibility derives from individualism. Look at Japan!" [171]), Americans reach out to "diversity" and begin to eat Chinese, Japanese, and Mexican food since they see ethnic minorities as "the alternatives of communal cultures at a time when [they] are demoralized" (ibid.). The essays are rife with similar types of convoluted and inane circular arguments that flit from one side of a dichotomy to another, as if a curve in time made all oppositions one and the same thing and dissolved all social antagonisms.

Having explained American contradictions through this individualist-communal dialectic, Rodríguez proceeds to show that he has the inside track on Mexico as well. It is important, however, to ensure that his position as an insider in America is clear. He will therefore assert his "American identity" through the "othering" of Mexico, depicted as an alien social space that produces nausea. The work itself tellingly begins with a scene of a typical American tourist in Mexico vomiting out his guts, but here the tourist is none other than Rodríguez and his nausea is not a result of consuming hot and spicy dishes or even dubious water, but an effort to purge out of the body that which is perceived as alien to the body: Mexico and its discourses. His attempt to expurgate the Spanish text that he has been force-fed during his stay in Mexico ("All the badly pronounced Spanish words I have forced myself to sound during the day, bits and pieces of Mexico spew from my mouth. . . . I am crying from my mouth in Mexico City" [xv]), on the very first page of this work, serves as an introduction to a second session of catharsis. Unable to expunge Mexico fully, the task of "ethnic cleansing" too daunting a task, he devises a metaphysical scheme that allows him to explain his dilemma in terms of timeless essential features from which he is unable to wholly free himself. Thus Mexico, the tragic but happy feminine Catholic country, stands in contrast to the sad masculine Protestant United

States/California of comedy ("a state where children run away from parents, a state of pale beer, and young old women, and divorced husbands living alone in condos" [xvii]) and is presented as a nation-state *"llorona"* crying out for her children and even the children of her children, the Chicanos, so near and yet so far. Although economically, politically, and culturally distant, the narrator intimates that he fears finding himself attracted by transcendental forces that incline him more toward tragedy, he says, as he reaches middle age, as if the catharsis were incomplete and his susceptibility increased with age.

What becomes increasingly clear is that the narrator's search is constantly for a simulacrum of Mexico, one initiated by his parents, and later one of his own making. There is for him no historical Mexico, only a pastiche, like the Victorian homes restored in San Francisco that so draw him. At other times, it becomes a fetishized space: Mexico is its miscegenation. Its social relations, its class and ethnic struggles, its dependent and uneven development, none of that matters in the face of genetic forces. Assuming that age-old miscegenation is a new phenomenon, he declares *mestizaje* itself the very sign of modernity (24–25). Who better, then, to "present" a documentary on Mexico to a British television audience? Who better than Rodríguez to remark the timelessness and transcendence of Mexico, to posit romantic notions of Mexican villages? Who better to dehistoricize Mexico? Mexican voices questioning his lack of social analysis ("Where do you get your ideas about Mexico? From Graham Greene? You have the opportunity to say something in public, and you go on and on about old churches and old mothers. You do a disservice with your reactionary dream of Mexico. Here, we are trying to progress . . ." [74]) are condescendingly acknowledged, tolerated in silence, and reduced to the level of trivia ("I smile./I feel I know them all; recognize the way their faces crease into smiles; recognize the ease of irony in a language so extravagant. Nothing is meant all that seriously, I suppose" [ibid.]), for nothing that the narrator sees or hears in Mexico, for example, in relation to the *maquiladoras* (the U.S. sweatshops along the border), leads to a reassessment of his tourist perspective ("Do I have it all wrong? Was the Mexico I had imagined—the country of memory and faith—long past?" [75]). His questioning, his studied self-reflection, is part of the simulacrum itself. Symptomatic of this is his planned filmic reconstruction of an imaginary Mexican village, for example, one from which his father would have wished to escape and one for which his mother longed, an imaginary bubble burst by the reality of a concrete village funeral. But is it? In fact, the funeral itself is staged textually to make his point about Mexico as a darkly romantic land of tragedy and death, of women in dark shawls and children "with preternaturally large eyes" (xix). It is a Goyaesque construction, postcard material, meant to make Rodríguez's point about the intimate and ultimately unfathomable relation between Mexico and tragedy.

To project his metaphysics of nation, sexuality, and religion, Rodríguez often focuses on cultural signs, icons, and symbols. If San Francisco reconstructs its own simulacrum of domesticity in the restored Victorian houses inhabited by gay couples, California, like America without memory, Rodríguez argues, creates its own pastiche of the past, its "fantasy heritage," with the restoration of the missions. The history of Indian oppression and exploitation is not of particular interest to the narrator (the Indians were not innocent, he says; were they not the "spiritual equals of Europeans"? [115]), but he is fascinated by the thought of finding traces of European culture in the California missions. Signs and myths are all he sees being exchanged by Catholics and Protestants, American Puritans and Mexicans, gays and nongays, signs whose exchange, divested of historical specificity, serves to buttress his cultural transactions, his metaphysics of difference.

His reconstruction of the legend of the Virgen de Guadalupe, for example, serves for a projection of his imaginary investment of Mexico as maternal, Catholic, mestizo, and communal. In recounting the tale of her miraculous apparition on the hill of Tepeyac to the Indian Juan Diego, the imprint of her image on his mantle, and the subsequent mass conversion of Indians, Rodríguez does not pause, even if only momentarily, to analyze the restructuring of Indian religious symbols within dominant religious frameworks; any remark on the astuteness of the missionaries to produce an apparition on the hill of Tepeyac—already the site where an Indian goddess was adored—as an ideological strategy of domination is dismissed ("Why do we assume Spain made up the story?" (19) he asks straightfacedly). No, for Rodríguez there is no imposition of a European religion through both coercion and consensus, but rather the appropriation of Catholicism by the Indians: "Catholicism has become an Indian religion" (20). ("Indian," for Rodríguez, is equivalent to "brown skin.") Catholicism itself (herself?) is deemed to be responsible for this *mestizaje* ("The success of Spanish Catholicism in Mexico resulted in a kind of proof—a profound concession to humanity: the *mestizaje*" [20]). The foregoing is, of course, only true if by Spanish Catholicism one means Spanish conquest and colonialism. Here, however, specific historical relations of colonialism, enslavement, oppression, and exploitation are glossed over and explained, at best, by Catholic faith. In his eager effort to defend the church against historians who have always noted her willing participation in the enslavement and exploitation of the Indian population, particularly in eighteenth- and nineteenth-century California, Rodríguez reconstructs Catholicism in an image more to his liking—not as an ideological and economic force that sought to maintain the Indians as a separate republic and thus as an unfree caste (Góngora, 162), but as a proponent of *mestizaje*. Of course, one might—if Rodríguez is to be followed—view the contribution of Catholic priests to *mestizaje* as ever more forceful and direct, if we consider, as Góngora explains, that "all the Spanish officials, priests, soldiers and travellers acted as agents of biological miscegenation and of acculturation" (ibid.). But, then, it is not history but ideological discourses that Rodríguez seeks to reconstruct. He prefers to view *la Guadalupana* fetishistically as a totem, ranking higher than any political construct of nation:

> Unique possession of her image is a more wonderful election to Mexicans than any political call to nationhood. Perhaps Mexico's tragedy in our century, perhaps Mexico's abiding grace thus far, is that she has no political idea of herself as compelling as her icon. (19)

Beyond the nonsensical drift of statements of this ilk and his condescending attitude toward Mexico, Rodríguez fails to mention, for example, that *la Guadalupana* has, in fact, since 1810, been a political image, part of the discourses of Mexican nationalism since Hidalgo's *grito* for independence while waving a banner of the Virgin. In fact, what was created by the church to subdue the Indians and gain their consent to their own subordination was turned into an instrument of revolt by the father of Mexican independence, Hidalgo, a priest denounced by the Inquisition. Since then the image has unrelentingly been manipulated by all political contenders to attract the support of the masses.

The binary opposition of Catholic Mexico versus Protestant America as an essential difference distinguishing the two nation-states is based on Rodríguez's peculiar concepts of Catholicism and Protestantism, both sects that he asserts to know in depth, given his religious studies at the Union Theological Seminary and Columbia University (188). The primary distinctions between the two, in the script (Scripture?) according to Richard Rodríguez, are, as indicated earlier, agential (communal/individualistic) and gendered (feminine/masculine). Despite this national-religious opposition, he detects an encroachment upon Latin American communal Catholicism by individualistic evangelical Protestantism throughout the continent. The success of fundamentalist/evangelical sects in areas previously dominated by Catholics is, however, not analyzed in relation to economic restructuring or cultural imperialism but rather to abstracted power relations that ultimately lead to the subordination of the feminine, Catholicism (181): "The Catholic part of me—ancient, cynical, feminine—is appalled by the nakedness, the humorlessness, the sweetness of evangelical conversion narratives" (180). Because Protestantism—Rodríguez continues—is individualistic and male and represents a "call to manhood" (182) and success ("American Protestants came to their villages dressed in suits and ties. The evangelical appearance advertises an end to failure" [183]), evangelicals in Latin America have succeeded in their proselytism.

Gender and individualism thus serve Rodríguez to explain what might be more uncomfortable to analyze: the ties of Protestant churches to U.S. economic and political interests in Latin America and their recruitment strategies, as well as the role of the Catholic church in Latin America, especially of its upper clergy, historically and now. A few pages later, however, he proceeds to deconstruct his own binary argument when he refers to an invitation to speak on "multiculturalism" to a group of priests in California facing growing numbers of Asian and Latino parishioners who want Mass in their own languages. Rodríguez's advice to the priests, far from appealing to the communal, is arrogant and elitist. He again assumes an antibilingual stance and proffers the suggestion that they preach in English or in Latin. That parishioners might be further alienated is of no concern to Rodríguez, who views the objectives of the church metaphysically rather than socially: "the Catholic knowledge of union, the mystical body of Christ" (196). Rather than meeting the needs of the parishioners that are presently attending, he, pretending to be more truly Catholic than the priests themselves, more theologically adept, in fact, proposes that they seek to attract the grandchildren, a proposal that flies in the face of the willingness of Latino priests to preach in Spanish, suggesting rather that they "invest" in the future and minister to the future, probably wealthier, generation:

> Fine, I say (Asshole), have your Spanish masses and your Vietnamese masses. But realize the Church is setting itself against inevitability; the inevitable Americanization of the grandchildren. You are going to lose the grandchildren; in fact, you've lost them already. You are papering your churches with poverty. You are using the poor to distract you from your failing enterprise. (195)

In his contradictory assessment of goals and necessary readjustments, Rodríguez becomes blind to the obvious (without grandparents in the church there are no grandchildren), while his entire binary scheme about differences between Catholics and Protestants begins to disintegrate. In his exposition to the priests, his worst fears are revealed: now Protestants, described earlier as individualistic, in this discussion are said to have the capacity to enjoy "intensely communal worship." They have, in fact, taken over the communal function of the Catholic church: "In the small evangelical church, people who are demoralized by the city turn to the assurance of community. In the small church, each soul has a first name again. One hand grips another's hand against anonymity" (198). Wait, that was what Catholics offered over Protestants. This deconstruction of his essentialist binary model does not, however, signal a reevaluation of his ideological constructs, for we are asked to assume that this is an earlier episode, since, as he indicates at the beginning of the book, the work is written from the present to the past (it is not). Thus his earlier (end of book) enlightenment (198), which leads him to disarticulate his essentialist metaphysical matrix, has not affected his continual binary assessment of differences between Mexico and the United States in terms of religion and blood (13), which appears at the beginning of the book—that is, in the most recent past. In fact, the binary framework at the beginning includes additional equally stereotypical concepts of space and time. Spatially, Rodríguez goes on to argue, the two countries differ in a ranking of the private and public ("In America, one is most oneself in public. . . . In Mexico, one is most oneself in private" [54]). This of course is a continuation of Rodríguez's essentialist gender scheme, unlike the temporal dichotomy that places Mexico in either mythic or natural time and the United States in historical time. Mexico is thus presented as timeless, as the past; there time is circular. The United States, on the other hand, is the future; here time is linear.

This time/space distinction is partly applied and at the same time deconstructed in his discussion of the U.S.-Mexico border. Although not entirely rejected, the time/space construct also reveals its shortcomings, but these are glossed over flippantly. After a weeklong visit to Tijuana during the Easter holidays, Rodríguez comes again—like his pronouncements on Mexico—to profound conclusions about the essence of the two border cities:

> Tijuana and San Diego are not in the same historical time zone. Tijuana is poised at the beginning of an industrial age, a Dickensian city with palm trees. San Diego is a postindustrial city of high-impact plastic and despair diets. And palm trees. San Diego faces west, looks resolutely out to sea.
>
> Tijuana stares north, as toward the future. San Diego is the future, secular, soulless. San Diego is the past, guarding its quality of life. Tijuana is the future. (84)

Tijuana is, of course, not poised at the beginning of an industrial age, as Rodríguez claims; it is already very much linked to the present phase of U.S. late capitalism and has been dependent on the U.S. economy since its establishment. San Diego, never highly industrialized, stares west because it is a port and its future is undoubtedly tied to research and development and trade in the Pacific Rim. Tijuana, on the other hand, is the urban space where California's reserve labor pool, its potential labor force of undocumented workers, many of whom have been displaced by U.S. agribusiness in the Mexican Northwest, assembles. Rodríguez recognizes that Tijuana is a by-product of San Diego and is well aware that it is one of many border sites for foreign assembly plants, the *maquiladoras*. Nor can he ignore that Tijuana is the epitome of dependent development initiated by multinational capital, for he has been dutifully informed by a San Diego anthropologist (93) and a professor at the Colegio de la Frontera (96), and he is quick to repeat the information on pp. 94 and 95, but without making the necessary connections, perhaps because it is not the economic relations between the two countries that concern him, but rather his personal safety, his total sense of alienation, and his fear of the Mexican masses.

In his review of mutual stereotypes, he identifies with the Americans: "We are an odorless, colorless, accentless, orderly people, put upon and vulnerable to the foreign." Mexicans, on the other hand, are "carriers of chaos—their backs are broken with bundles of it: gray air, brown water, papacy, leprosy, crime, diarrhea, white powders, and a language full of newts and cicadas" (91). As he moves through the city, in fact, we perceive his own disgust. He is the typical tourist afraid to drink the water; he puts the glass of juice to his lips but does not drink (92). He fears the crowd, and when his friend, a priest, invites him to a neighborhood in Tijuana and asks him to assist in the food distribution, he is shocked by their "zombielike" advances and their eagerness to grab: "An old hag with chicken skin on her arms grabs for my legs—extravagant swipes, lobsterlike, or as if she were plucking a harp—trying to reach the boxes behind me" (98). For him the people are animalesque, lobsterlike; they are nocturnal ("Mexicans move as naturally and comfortably in the dark as cats or wolves or owls do" [87]); they refuse to be limited by time; they are cynical, patient, and tolerant of corruption ("Public officials tread a path to corruption, just as men need their whores" [88]). Glaringly overlooked, however, are the parallels in this country. The United States, with all its corruption at every level—evidenced since the nineteenth century and including the more recent Iran-contra affair, the junk-bond fiasco, the savings and loan scandal, and an infinite number of such cases, including California's own Stanford and Huntington episode—has traveled the very same path; moreover, considering the light "country-club" prison sentences and pardons given to public officials and wealthy corporation executives, Rodríguez would do well to admit to a high level of tolerance for corruption in the upper strata of this country. One facile comment does not, of course, undo the other, but it does serve to underscore the vacuity of many of his remarks in this work.

Throughout, Rodríguez is quick to mark the distance and distinguish himself from the Mexicans he is describing. After touring through Tijuana, he is finally free to return to his hotel on the U.S. side of the border ("Because Mexico is brown and I am brown. I fear being lost in Mexico" [96]); the best way to insure that he will not be swallowed up in their brown or confused with a Mexican is to stay on the American side. But right before he rushes off to have brunch in tony La Jolla, he makes one last run across the border for "local color" to attend Mass at the "aquamarine" cathedral, where he notes the "thick hair" of the family of four sitting in front of him (106). "See, dear reader," he seems to be saying, "I see them exactly as you do, even if I may choose to commune with them once in a while in their garish 'aquamarine' cathedral. I note their coarse, uncared-for Indian hair. I share your prejudices, your tastes. I have more in common with you than with 'those people.' I am just like you, an American."

Apparently, Rodríguez's greatest fear, which he communicates to his American readers, is the mass of young Mexicans posed at the border ("the anticipatory, desperate city massing beyond the cyclone fence is not going to dissipate into ether at the sound of the five o'clock whistle" [95]); like all Americans, he too fears the crowd ("This nation was formed from a fear of the crowd" [163]). He dreads the inevitable invasion: "Tijuana is here. It has arrived. Silent as a Trojan horse, inevitable as a flotilla of boat people, more confounding in its innocence, in its power of proclamation, than Spielberg's most pious vision of a flying saucer" (106). Aliens, space invaders, U.S. space invaders, or is it a retaking of Mexican space? Rodríguez is ever hopeful, however, that, whether as one city or two, this urban metropolis will remain stratified: "The theme of city life is the theme of difference. People living separately, simultaneously" (105). Diversity is thus all right as long as everyone stays within the lines and adjusts to a "diverse but separate" policy. It is this same concern that leads him to scoff at the idea of Latinos in the United States uniting as a group (they have nothing in common, he protests [69]). Perhaps he knows that as individuals they are more likely to consent to their own subordination, but as a united group they might no longer remain silent.

Ironically tripped up by his own binary dilemma, his erstwhile musings on community notwithstanding, Rodríguez opts to be (his kind of) good Puritan, an individualist, an iconoclast who, after the death of Martin Luther King, defects from the left (where he claims to have been positioned earlier [189]), all in the name of community, that is, of the political right: "After his death, the Pauline vision of a society united is undermined by hack radicals like Stokely Carmichael, proclaiming a conventional protestant separatist line" (ibid.). The presence of riot police in the Columbia University cafeteria will lead student activists and others to sit as a group apart. But not Rodríguez; no, he will sit with the men in blue—on principle (192–93). His iconoclasm falls on its face when up against dominant values and authority. Order and the "common good" are paramount even at the risk of the individual. Note what he says about Galileo. If the Inquisition condemned him for heresy, perhaps the church had its good reasons: "If the Church was wrong it may have been wrong for a valid reason. The Church sought to protect the communal vision, the Catholic world—a rounded, weighted, lovely thing—against an anarchy implicit in the admission of novelty. Novelty should only come from within the Church: a question not of facts but of authority" (190). Need we say more? Even the Vatican has recanted its position on Galileo—almost four hundred years late—but not so Richard Rodríguez, ever the stalwart, principled Catholic.

Rodríguez's essays call for a more extensive analysis than is possible here, particularly his comments on Chicanos or Mexicanos in the United States. The binary scheme contrasting the United States and Mexico is, of course, the same one employed to contrast Chicanos vis-à-vis the majority white Anglo-Saxon population. For example, he finds that Mexicans in the United States are "notorious . . . for their skepticism regarding public life" (61). He cites as a case in point the fact that they drop out of school and do not vote. Considering the high dropout rate among other ethnic minorities and the fact that only 50 percent (54 percent in the 1992 elections) of the entire voting population generally votes in the United States, that would classify a large number of Americans as very "private," Mexican skeptics. Rodríguez's work is full of these nuggets of fool's gold. He considers that it was not a Mexican thing to submit to the draft and fight in World War II: "Not a very Mexican thing to do, for Mexico had taught us always that we lived apart from history in the realm of *tú*" (62). Does he not know that even young men residing in Mexico signed up to fight for the United States during World War II? Has he bothered to find out that as early as the American Civil War, Salvador Vallejo led a group of Californios and Mexicanos who signed up to fight for the Union Army? Is he not aware of the disproportionate number of Chicano and Latino veterans and corpses that came back from Korea and Vietnam?

Rodríguez is here to tell us that "Mexican Americans" are really just upper-middle-class Americans of Mexican origin. He, of course, is our enlightened Mexican tour guide, who has discovered that the whole story of oppression is a myth: "Without the myth of victimization—who are we? We are no longer Mexicans. We are professional Mexicans. We hire Mexicans. After so many years spent vainly thinking of ourselves as exempt from some common myth of America, we might as well be Italians" (70). Rodríguez may be a journalist, but he is blind to the social conditions faced by millions, not only of Chicanos/Mexicanos and Latinos, but of other minority, elderly, and even white men, women, and children in this society: rising unemployment and underemployment, poverty, homelessness, a lack of medical attention and other health services, low educational attainment, and violence. As conditions worsen for Chicanos and others alike, it is rather senseless, if not cynical, to continue to brandish the myth of the American dream from an ivory Victorian tower.

Why devote so much attention and so much paper to a writer who has clearly been groomed and strategically deployed by the political right? Given what undoubtedly will be the uncritical inclusion of his work in many American English freshmen classes, he needs to be taken to task for every one of his reactionary, frivolous statements. Equally important is the task of bringing to the forefront the importance of a historicized ethnic canon and a voice in determining what ethnic texts are considered in general American English classes. Who, for example, decides on the women writers to be incorporated as representatives of Chicana literature? Who determines that it is Rodríguez's texts that will be read? Clearly, ethnic status alone does not imply an alternative perspective. Rodríguez's book of essays, for example, is not so much a disingenuous cliché-ridden, hodgepodge of clever-sounding, self-reflective, self-absorbed musings as it is a calculated compendium of manipulations geared, on the one hand, to assuage mainstream fears of diversity and, on the other, to set down directions for a more "effective" incorporation of minority discourses in what promises to be a time of increasing conflict and upheaval in these United (but not unified) States. Culturally, although not socially and economically, the shift from the margins to the center may be at hand, but whose margins, what outsiders, what perspective will be ethnicizing the canon is still not clear. Perhaps it will be the likes of Richard Rodríguez, a blatant example of an insider in the clothing of an outsider, of an ethnic writer estranged more from his own collectivities than from dominant society. Ethnic works like his, "politically correct" discourses of the political right, only serve to perpetuate dominant fantasies about marginalized populations and to legitimate the status quo.

## Note

I wish to thank Beatrice Pita for her suggestions and comments on this paper.

## References

Amin, Samir. 1990. *Delinking: Towards a Polycentric World*. London: Zed Books.

Anderson, Benedict. 1983. *Imagined Communities*. London: Verso.

Anderson, Perry. 1992. "The Ends of History." In *A Zone of Engagement*. London: Verso.

Bakhtin, M. M. 1986. *Speech Genres and Other Late Essays*. Trans. Vern W. McGee. Austin: University of Texas Press.

Bercovitch, Sacvan. 1986a. "Afterword." In *Ideology and Classic American Literature*, ed. Sacvan Bercovitch and Myra Jehlin. Cambridge: Cambridge University Press.

———. 1986b. "Preface." In *Reconstructing American Literary History*. Cambridge, Mass.: Harvard University Press.

Eagleton, Terry. 1970. *Exiles and Émigrés: Studies in Modern Literature*. New York: Schocken Books.

———. 1990. "Nationalism: Irony and Commitment." In Terry Eagleton, Fredric Jameson, and Edward W. Said, *Nationalism, Colonialism, and Literature*. Intro. Seamus Deane. Minneapolis: University of Minnesota Press.

Feyerabend, Paul. 1987. *Farewell to Reason*. London: Verso.

Góngora, Mario. 1975. *Studies in the Colonial History of Spanish America*. Trans. Richard Southern. London: Cambridge University Press.

Jehlen, Myra. 1986. "Introduction: Beyond Transcendence." In *Ideology and Classic American Literature*, ed. Sacvan Bercovitch and Myra Jehlen. Cambridge: Cambridge University Press.

Kellner, Douglas. 1989. *Jean Baudrillard: From Marxism to Postmodernism and Beyond*. Stanford, Calif.: Stanford University Press.

Lefebvre, Henri. 1991. *The Production of Space*. Trans. D. Nicholson-Smith. Cambridge, Mass.: Basil Blackwell.

Martí, José. 1975. *Inside the Monster: Writings on the United States and American Imperialism*. Ed. Philip S. Foner. New York: Monthly Review Press.

Marx, Karl. 1959. "Manifesto of the Communist Party." In Karl Marx and Frederick Engels, *Basic Writings on Politics and Philosophy*, ed. Lewis S. Feuer. Garden City, N.Y.: Anchor Books.

Monsiváis, Carlos. 1984. "Cultura urbana y creación intelectual. El caso mexicano." In *Cultura y creación intelectual en América Latina*, ed. Pablo González-Casanova. Mexico City: Siglo Veintiuno.

Mouzelis, Nicos P. 1990. *Post-Marxist Alternatives: The Construction of Social Orders*. London: Macmillan Press.

Rodriguez, Richard. 1992. *Days of Obligation: An Argument with My Mexican Father*. New York: Viking.

————. 1981. *Hunger of Memory: The Education of Richard Rodriguez.* Boston: David R. Godine.

Stephanson, Anders. 1988. "Interview with Cornel West." In *Universal Abandon,* ed. Andrew Ross. Minneapolis: University of Minnesota Press.

Zinn, Howard. 1990. *A People's History of the United States.* New York: Harper Perennial.

~

# "Sugar Sisterhood"

## Situating the Amy Tan Phenomenon

SAU-LING CYNTHIA WONG

The sensational success of Amy Tan's first novel, *The Joy Luck Club* (1989), is the stuff of publishing legend. Before the shrewd eye of agent Sandra Dijkstra spotted a potential winner, Tan was entirely unknown to the literary world. But lavish advance praise—the dust jacket of the hardcover edition bears enthusiastic blurbs by Alice Walker, Alice Hoffman, and Louise Erdrich—and postpublication rave reviews instantly propelled *The Joy Luck Club* onto the *New York Times* best-seller list, where it stayed for nine months. The hardcover edition was reprinted twenty-seven times and sold 275,000 copies (J. Simpson, 66); frenzied bidding by corporate publishers pushed the price for paperback rights from a floor of $100,000 to an astonishing $1.2 million (Holt). *The Joy Luck Club* was a finalist for the National Book Award and the National Book Critics Circle Award, and a recipient of the 1990 Bay Area Book Reviewers Award for Fiction.

Tan's second novel, *The Kitchen God's Wife* (1991), has not duplicated *Joy Luck*'s blockbuster success. However, it too is a highly acclaimed best-seller, with most reviewers declaring it as good as, if not better than, its predecessor (e.g., Dew; Gillespie; Howe; Humphreys; Iyer; James; Perrick; Romano; Yglesias).[1] The $4 million advance that Putnam reputedly paid on it (Solovitch, 18) has apparently been money well spent.[2] The Amy Tan phenomenon continues its momentum with a new children's book, *The Moon Lady*, spun off from an episode in *The Joy Luck Club*; a third novel in the works (Rothstein); and a film adaptation of *The Joy Luck Club* made by noted Chinese American director Wayne Wang.[3]

Like Maxine Hong Kingston's *Woman Warrior* (1976), *The Joy Luck Club* is a crossover hit by a female ethnic writer; it also straddles the worlds of "mass" literature and "respectable" literature, stocking the shelves of airport newsstands as well as university bookstores, generating coffee table conversations as well as conference papers. Tan's stellar status in the publishing world, further assured by *The Kitchen God's Wife,* causes one to wonder: wherein does the enormous appeal of her fiction lie?

To say that book buyers and readers are simply responding to Tan's good writing—briskly paced, easy to follow, by turns poignant and hilarious—is to give a naive and decontextualized, if partially true, answer. It goes without saying that the history of literary reputations abounds with instances of "good" writing belatedly recognized, or else of "bad" writing amply rewarded in the marketplace. (Without getting into a general disquisition on the social construction of taste, I use the "good"/"bad" distinction here to refer to either a disjuncture between academic/critical opinion and popular success, or else a revision of judgment over time.) To narrow the consideration to contemporaneous Asian American women's writing alone, the year *The Joy Luck Club* appeared also saw the polished novelistic debut of another young writer, Cynthia Kadohata (*The Floating World*), as well as new books by two established figures: Kingston's *Tripmaster Monkey: His Fake Book* and Bharati Mukherjee's *Jasmine.* All three works show remarkable artistry and garnered strong reviews, but none became a commercial triumph. That elusive element, "timing" or "luck," usually summoned to explain cases of overnight celebrity, must be restored to historicity: What is it about the subject matter of *The Joy Luck Club* and its treatment that somehow "clicked" with the times? What prompts Tan's following to come back loyally to *The Kitchen God's Wife*? Where is her fiction positioned in the multiple discourses that make up American writing? What discursive traditions does it participate in, and to what ideological effect, to create Tan's trademark fictional world and a niche market?

Tan has often been presented in the media as a meteoric individual talent, bursting full-blown from obscurity onto the literary scene (e.g., Kepner). She has even been implicitly credited with singlehandedly ushering in an Asian American literary renaissance (J. Simpson), even though Tan herself takes pains to point out that many of the writers of the 1991 "wave" named by the mainstream media (David Wong Louie, David Mura, Gish Jen, Gus Lee, Laurence Yep, Frank Chin) had been writing and publishing before—

some, like Chin and Yep, long, long before—she became known, and that they represent very different, unique voices (Fong-Torres, B4). The media account of Tan's singularity, based on tacit meritocratic assumptions and a late twentieth-century variation on the myth of the original romantic artist, obscures the role of politics in the making (and breaking) of Asian American and other ethnic minority writers. Demythologizing this kind of portrayal, this essay situates the appeal of Amy Tan's fiction in its sociohistorical context and analyzes the discursive demands and contradictions experienced by Chinese American (and to some degree other Asian American) writers at this juncture in American history.

## Feminist/Matrilineal Discourse and China Mama's Revenge

One of the most obvious reasons for the success of *The Joy Luck Club* and *The Kitchen God's Wife* is the centrality of the mother-daughter relationship in these books. This subject matter places them squarely in a tradition of matrilineal discourse that has, as a part of the feminist movement, been gathering momentum in the United States over the last ten to fifteen years. In 1976, Adrienne Rich wrote that the "cathexis between mother and daughter—essential, distorted, misused—is the great unwritten story" (225; quoted in Hirsch, "Maternal Narratives," 415). In 1984, Tillie Olsen was still able to lament, "Most of what has been, is, between mothers, daughters, and in motherhood, daughterhood, has never been recorded" (275; quoted in Pearlman, 1). But a scant five years later, as Mickey Pearlman notes, the profusion of creative writing as well as social-science scholarship on the "linked lives" of mothers and daughters had become overwhelming.[4]

That the success of Amy Tan's fiction is a product of, and testimony to, the strength of the feminist movement is easy to see. Both her books capture the contradictions that have been identified as characteristic of the "literature of matrilineage" in Nan Bauer Maglin's simple but convenient schema:

> 1. the recognition by the daughter that her voice is not entirely her own;
> 2. the importance of trying to really see one's mother in spite of or beyond the blindness and skewed vision that growing up together causes;
> 3. the amazement and humility about the strength of our mothers;

4. the need to recite one's matrilineage, to find a ritual to both get back there and preserve it;

5. and still, the anger and despair about the pain and the silence borne and handed on from mother to daughter. (258)

Any number of pithy quotations from *The Joy Luck Club* and *The Kitchen God's Wife* can be culled to illustrate these interconnected themes. What is harder to determine than Tan's place in American matrilineal discourse is the reason why her fiction has so conspicuously eclipsed works by Euro-American writers on similar subject matter,[5] as Kingston's *Woman Warrior* did over a decade ago. The white feminist reading public appears to have an unusually keen appetite for mother-daughter stories by and about people of color.[6] In particular, as one British reviewer wryly observes from across the Atlantic, "Whether by a quirk of literary fate or because it is their psychological destiny, Chinese American women seem to have won the world rights to the mother/daughter relationship" (Perrick). Why? Why this privileging of Chinese American mothers and daughters in literature while no equivalent is forthcoming in the realm of, say, employment opportunities or provision of child care?

I suggest it is neither literary fate nor psychological destiny that has conferred favored status on the Chinese American mother-daughter relationship, but rather a convergence of ethnic group-specific literary tradition and ideological needs by the white-dominated readership—including the feminist readership—for the Other's presence as both mirror and differentiator.

Contrary to popular belief, Kingston did not invent Chinese American matrilineal discourse, and Tan, creating something of an accessible "*Woman Warrior* without tears" in *Joy Luck,* is not so much revisiting Kingston territory as sharing a concern long of interest to many other Chinese American women writers. Antecedents for Kingston's strong Chinese women can be found in the female-centered household in Su-ling Wong and Earl Cressy's little-known collaborative autobiography, *Daughter of Confucius* (1952). Even propatriarchal Chinese American autobiographies from the pre-1965 period,[7] such as Helena Kuo's *I've Come a Long Way* (1942) and Jade Snow Wong's *Fifth Chinese Daughter* (1945), like *Daughter of Confucius,* show occasional inruptions of matrilineal consciousness, as in Kuo's anecdote of mother-daughter complicity in novel reading (24), or Jade Snow Wong's descriptions of hours spent with her grandmother and mother learning about Chinese customs—at once mother-daughter bonding and induction into the woman's submissive role in the culture (28–33; 48–60). That is to say, even earlier male-identified Chinese American women writers are, at some level, aware of the precariousness of their place in a patriarchal society—an awareness also reflected in the virtually obligatory opening explanations of how they come to receive a decent education, thanks to generous fathers willing to mitigate prevailing gender norms (e.g., Kuo, 21, 33–44; J. Wong, 14–15).[8] Chinese American interest in matrilineage continues in the post-1965 period; examples range from Chuang Hua's recurrent image of the majestic matriarch in *Crossings* (1968) (again in spite of an overt obsession with the father's approval);[9] to Alice P. Lin's combined ethnic/matrilineal root-seeking journey in *Grandmother Has No Name* (1988); to the fiction of younger writers like Sarah Lau (1990), Wen-Wen C. Wang (1990), and Fae Myenne Ng (1993), who, like Kingston, explore their bond with immigrant mothers simultaneously tough and vulnerable.

Chinese American preoccupation with the mother-daughter bond can be further situated in a broader Asian American discourse of matrilineage, both pre- and post-*Woman Warrior* (Lim). Hisaye Yamamoto's classics, "Seventeen Syllables" (1949) and "Yoneko's Earthquake" (1951), predate *The Woman Warrior* by over two decades; apparent inspiration for "The Handkerchief" (1961) and "Songs My Mother Taught Me" (1976) by Wakako Yamauchi, Yamamoto's literary disciple, these stories depict the ambivalent and largely unspoken emotional exchanges between unhappily married mothers and daughters on the verge of womanhood, in ways again reminiscent of Maglin's schema. Despite the protagonists' expressed yearning for the father's love, the presence of abrasive, abusive, but irrepressibly vigorous grandmothers is indelible in Burmese American Wendy Law-Yone's *Coffin Tree* (1983) as well as Japanese American Cynthia Kadohata's *Floating World* (1989); the grandmother/matriarch figure, coupled again with an absent mother, resurfaces in Singaporean American writer Fiona Cheong's *Scent of the Gods* (1991). The resilient spirit of female ancestors embodied in the Vietnamese legend of the woman warrior, along with the support of living women relatives, is lovingly recalled in Le Ly Hayslip's account of her life during and after the Vietnam War, *When Heaven and Earth Changed Places* (1989). Merle Woo's "Letter to Ma" (1981) articulates a radical, lesbian perspective on Asian American mother-daughter relationships. Ronyoung Kim's *Clay Walls* (1987) chronicles the strong ties between a Korean immigrant woman and her daughter. Short fiction such as South Asian Appachana's (1989) and Dhillon's (1989), and Japanese American Sasaki's

(1989), continue the exploration of matrilineage. If we broaden the Asian American canon to include Asian Canadian works, then Joy Kogawa's *Obasan* (1982) offers a distinctly matrilineal text, in which themes like the search for the absent mother, surrogate motherhood (or maternalistic aunthood), silence breaking, and rituals of reclamation are woven into an account of the uprooting of Japanese Canadians during the Second World War. More recently, South-Indian Canadian writer Mara Rachna's *Of Customs and Excise* (1991) places the story of the "immigrant daughter's revolt" in a multigenerational, postcolonial global context to deepen one's understanding of matrilineage.[10]

This quick survey of the literature of matrilineage in the Chinese American and Asian American traditions is meant to contextualize Tan's work more precisely: to dispel the notion that her fiction is simply riding on the coattails of white feminism, tapping directly into "universal" concerns from the vantage point of individual insight.[11] Even if there had been no white buyers of *The Joy Luck Club* and *The Kitchen God's Wife*, there would still have been a readership for these books among Asian American women, many of whom are hungry for validation of their own experiences as daughters of immigrant mothers (e.g., Fong and Sit; compare Suzi Wong on Kingston's *Woman Warrior*).

Identifying a matrilineal Asian American tradition is important in terms of not only racial politics within feminism, but also gender politics within cultural nationalism. The kind of rehabilitation of Asian American literary patrilineage undertaken by the *Aiiieeeee* group,[12] essential as it is, is attained at the expense of the female perspective (Cheung). In the influential Introduction to *Aiiieeeee!* (Chin et al. 1974), the numerical superiority of Asian American women writers is categorically denounced as a sign of the literature's emasculation by white society, while not one living Chinese American woman writer is included in *The Big Aiiieeeee!* (Chan et al. 1991), the sequel to the first anthology.[13] Frank Chin's *Year of the Dragon* (1981), a play about a disintegrating Chinatown family in the 1960s, is emblematic of this suppression of the woman's voice. In addition to a scatterbrained American-born mother humming inherent snatches of song, the play features China Mama, the patriarch's first wife left in China because of immigration restrictions and suddenly transported to San Francisco to assuage the dying man's cultural and familial guilt. This *gum sahn paw* (Cantonese for "Gold Mountain wife") is portrayed as totally devoid of subjectivity: a recalcitrant, alien presence unceremoniously deposited in the Eng family's living room, mute except for sporadic attempts to communicate with the children in gibberish-like Cantonese. In Chin's play, the old immigrant woman from China is just a convenient symbol, not a human being with decades' worth of experiences and grievances to recount.[14] In this context, *The Joy Luck Club* and *The Kitchen God's Wife* are China Mama's revenge: the Joy Luck aunties get not only their own voices back but equal time with their American offspring. And when Winnie in *The Kitchen God's Wife* holds forth about her past, she is allowed to do so endlessly, for more than 330 pages, until her daughter Pearl nearly falls off the chair from surprise at revealed secrets (397), and we the readers from sheer fatigue.

It is vital to recognize the Asian American discursive context for Amy Tan's fiction, but the Asian American readership for matrilineal discourse is simply not large enough to support the kind of sales that Tan's fiction has enjoyed. Today's book-buying readers of literature are predominantly white and female (Zill and Winglee).[15] The question thus remains: what do these readers—some with conscious feminist leanings, some without—find so engrossing in Tan's stories of the mother-daughter bond?

## "Sugar Sisterhood": The Persistent Allure of Orientalism

This brings me to the odd-sounding title of this essay, "Sugar Sisterhood," derived from the phrase "sugar sister" used by Winnie in *The Kitchen God's Wife*. Winnie is explaining to Pearl, her English-speaking daughter, her closeness to cousin Peanut. Peanut has found a face-saving way to reveal that she has given up Wen Fu, a charming, wealthy, but as it turns out abusive, young man, for Winnie to marry; the emotionally orphaned Winnie is grateful for Peanut's generosity:

> And that's how we came to be as close as sisters once again for the rest of the time I had left with my family. In fact, from that day forward, until I was married, we called each other *tang jie*, "sugar sister," the friendly way to refer to a girl cousin. (154)

*Tang jie*, again presented with the "sugar sister" translation for Pearl's benefit, is repeated in a later scene, when Winnie and Peanut are temporarily reunited (350). The phrase "sugar sister" is an egregious mistranslation based on Amy Tan's confusing two Chinese homophones, while the accompanying explanation of how the two young women come to address each other by that term betrays a profound ignorance of the Chinese kinship system. What is most remarkable about this passage is its very existence: that

Amy Tan has seen fit to include and elaborate on such a "gratuitous" detail—gratuitous in the sense of not functioning to advance the plot or deepen the characterization, of which more later—on something of which she has little knowledge. Furthermore, this putative clarification issues from the mouth of Winnie, a native Chinese-speaker born and raised in China for whom it should be impossible to make such mistakes.

I use the term "sugar sisterhood," then, to designate the kind of readership Amy Tan has acquired, especially among white women, through acts of cultural interpreting and cultural empathy that appear to possess the authority of authenticity but are often products of the American-born writer's own heavily mediated understanding of things Chinese. By examining the "sugar sister" solecism and related uses of Chinese or Chinese-seeming details, by analyzing the stylistic features and narratological design in both of Tan's works, and by uncovering the culturalist reading practices that such novelistic elements encourage, I argue that the "Amy Tan phenomenon" must ultimately be situated in quasi-ethnographic, Orientalist discourse. Occasional anti-Orientalist statements made by the characters, and the opportunities for anticulturalist interpretation provided by Tan's keen observations of Chinese American life, do not negate my assessment. In fact, they are functional in that they enable Orientalism to emerge in a form palatable to middle-class American readers of the 1980s. Specifically, for the feminist audience, the Chinese American mother/daughter dyad in *The Joy Luck Club* and *The Kitchen God's Wife* allegorizes a Third World/First World encounter that allows mainstream American feminism to construct itself in a flattering, because depoliticized, manner—an outcome unlikely to be delivered by mother-daughter stories penned by writers from Euro-American traditions.

Since the "sugar sister" phrase provides the entering wedge for my thesis, I will dwell a moment longer on its significance. Besides the confusion of two different characters for *tang*, there are several other implausibilities in this passage. The term *tang jie* does exist and can be used in the relationship between Winnie and Peanut. (Peanut is the daughter of the younger brother of Winnie's father.) But *tang jie* is a descriptive label and a term of address defined stringently by one's position in a patrilineal system of blood ties; it is not, as Tan suggests, a friendly term of endearment, to be assumed at will when two girl cousins feel close to each other. Moreover, in the thoroughly hierarchical, age-conscious Chinese kinship system, *jie*, or "older sister," is always complemented by *mei*, or "younger sister": two women cannot simultaneously be the *jie*—not even in "courtesy" situations where blood ties are not involved, such as *xuejie/xuemei* (fellow students) or *qijie/qimei* ("sworn sisters") relationships.

In citing the "sugar sister" passage, I am not practicing an idle and mean-spirited "Gotcha!" school of criticism. Something larger is at issue: what is sought is a more precise determination of Tan's stance toward her audience(s) and the types of discourses her works participate in, leading to a clearer understanding of her popularity. To readers who protest that Tan is just writing fiction, I concede that a phrase like "sugar sister" does little to detract from her overall achievements as a writer—from the page-turning narrative drive of her novels, or the general contours of Winnie's vivid character. Given this, the question arises, then, of what function is served by this kind of detail—a romanized Chinese phrase with an appositive explanation, tossed off as an aside by a Chinese-speaking character to her English-dominant daughter—or other similar details of language and custom, minimally warranted by the immediate narrative context but providing occasions for elucidating an exotic Chinese culture.

A list can easily be compiled of such highly dubious or downright erroneous details: Lindo Jong's first husband in Taiyuan is described as yanking off her red veil at the wedding ceremony (59)—a suspiciously Western practice, since traditionally the bride's red veil is removed only in the privacy of the wedding chamber, before the consummation of the marriage;[16] in Ying-Ying St. Clair's childhood reminiscences, the customs that are allegedly part of Moon Festival celebrations—burning the Five Evils (68) and eating *zong zi* (73)—actually belong to the *Duanwu* or "Dragon-Boat" Festival on the fifth day of the fifth lunar month; the operatic version of the Moon Lady-Hou Yi story witnessed by Ying-Ying includes a detail from another legend about another festival—the annual meeting of two star-crossed lovers on the seventh night of the seventh month (80); the mother-in-law's rebuke to the young bride Lindo, "*Shemma bende ren!*" rendered in English as "What kind of fool are you!" (55), sounds like a concoction by some first-year Chinese student and necessitates a quiet emendation by the Chinese translator of *The Joy Luck Club* (Tan, *Xifuhui*, 46); the warning Rose Hsu Jordan remembers from her mother, shortly before her younger brother's drowning, likewise sounds gratingly unidiomatic in Chinese—"*Dangsying tamende shenti,*" translated by Tan as "Watch out for their bodies" (123); except for the first one, the characters used for the Chinese version of McDonald's name, *mai dong lou,* are not what Lindo Jong says they are, "wheat," "east," and "building" (259); in *The Kitchen God's Wife*, the Chinese pilots allegedly give General Chennault a good Chinese name, *shan,* "lightning," and *nao,* "noisy," but his name actually has a well-known standard Chinese translation, *Chen Naide.* The list goes on.

The function of such insertions of "Chinese" cultural presence is worth investigating not only because a history of controversy exists in Asian American cultural politics concerning issues of authenticity, but also because Tan's books have been showered with praise precisely for their *details.*

## Detail and Myth

*The Joy Luck Club* is repeatedly applauded by reviewers for the specificity of its descriptions—entire "richly textured worlds" (Shapiro, 64) evoked by details "each . . . more haunting and unforgettable than the one before" (Bernikow). The book is called "dazzling because of the *worlds* it gives us"; the word "tapestry" is used to describe this effect of intricacy and richness (Sit). This view of Tan's distinctive gift is carried over to reviews of *The Kitchen God's Wife:* "The power of literature over sociology lies in particularization, and it is in details that *The Kitchen God's Wife* excels"; "it is through vivid minutiae that Tan more often exercises her particular charm" (Yglesias, 1, 3); "what fascinates in *The Kitchen God's Wife* is not only the insistent storytelling, but the details of Chinese life and tradition" (Romano); *The Kitchen God's Wife's* "convincing detail" is said to give her fiction "the ring of truth" (Humphreys, 1), and Dew urges her readers to give themselves over to Tan's "Tolstoyan tide of event and detail."

This emphasis on details as a main source of Tan's appeal is intriguing because it coexists with a seemingly opposite type of commendation: that details do *not* matter that much in *The Joy Luck Club,* and to a lesser extent *The Kitchen God's Wife,* since they are lyrical, mythical, dreamlike: "full of magic" (See), "rich in magic and mystery" (Fong). Of Tan's second book, Perrick writes, "There is something dizzyingly elemental about Tan's storytelling; it melds the rich simplicities of fairytales with a delicate lyrical style." Fairy tales, we may note, are "generic" stories stripped of historical particulars, and lyricism is generally associated with moments of inwardness set apart from the realm of quotidian social facts.

*The Joy Luck Club* draws comparisons with myth even more readily. One reviewer calls it "almost mythic in structure, like the hypnotic tales of the legendary Scheherazade" (Bernikow). In the eyes of some readers, the lack of differentiation between the rapidly alternating narrative voices in *Joy Luck,* far from betraying a limited artistic repertoire, is in fact an asset: the mark of universal appeal to women (Sit) or a more capacious sensibility (E. Kim, "'Such Opposite Creatures,'" 82). Orville Schell, who wrote a widely quoted glowing review of *The Joy Luck Club*, acknowledges that the book's segmented structure, with its abrupt transitions in time and space, may be confusing, but argues that "these *recherches* to old China are so beautifully written that one should just allow oneself to be borne along as if in a dream." Juxtaposed with the daughters' "upwardly mobile, design-conscious, divorce-prone and Americanized world," the mothers' vanished world in China seems "more fantastic and dreamlike than real," a product of "memory" and "revery" (28)—and herein, Schell seems to suggest, lies its peculiar charm.

Is there any necessary incompatibility between these two views of Tan's fiction, one lauding her mastery of details, the other deeming them relatively inconsequential in its overall effect? Not at all, if one takes into account another recurrent theme in reviews of the two novels: their value as anthropological documents, giving the non-Chinese reader access to an enigmatic culture.[17] A review of *The Kitchen God's Wife* finds it a convenient lesson in Chinese history and sociology:

> As a backdrop . . . we learn more about the nature of arranged marriages in Chinese societies and also about the kind of inter-wifely accommodation arranged by second or third wives and their offspring. It is like being invited into a dusty room full of castoffs, and being given a chance to reapprehend them in their former richness. We get to understand how, why, and from where Chinese-American society evolved. . . . Tan is handing us a key with no price tag and letting us open the brass-bolted door. (Gillespie, 34)

In view of the inaccurate cultural details we have seen, this coupling of Tan's fiction with anthropological discourse, which carries with it implicit claims of credibility and factual verifiability, may be ironic. But the issue is not so much how Tan has failed as a cultural guide; it is, rather, the text- and reception-oriented question of how and why the American reading public has responded so eagerly to her writings as faithful chronicles of things Chinese. Tan's fiction has apparently been able to hold in colloidal suspension two essential ingredients of quasi-ethnographic Orientalist discourse on China and the Chinese, which both have a long genealogy in this country (E. Kim, *Asian American Literature*, 23–32). These ingredients are "temporal distancing" and "authenticity marking." Tan's ability to somehow keep both details and "nondetails," as it were, in busy circulation allows readers with culturalist propensities—that is to say, a large proportion of the American reading public—to recognize the genre and respond accordingly, with enthusiastic purchases as well as a pleasurable mixture of respect and voyeurism, admiration and condescension, humility and self-congratulation.

## Temporal Distancing and Other "Othering" Maneuvers

Johannes Fabian, in his *Time and the Other: How Anthropology Makes Its Object*, suggests that "temporal distancing" is a means of constructing the Other widely employed in ethnographic discourse. He proposes the term "Typological Time" to refer to a use of time "almost totally divested of its vectorial, physical connotations": "instead of being a measure of movement, it may appear as a quality of states" presumably "unequally distributed among human populations of this world." The concept of Typological Time produces familiar distinctions attributed to human societies such as preliterate versus literate, traditional versus modern, peasant versus industrial (23), the term with which the anthropologist identifies himself/herself invariably being the privileged one. The contrast between some such binary states—traditional versus modern, superstitious versus secular, elemental versus materialistic, communal enmeshment versus anomie—is, we may note, precisely what *The Joy Luck Club* and *The Kitchen God's Wife* are engaged in exploring.

Whereas the ethnographer relies on the temporalized protocols of the "field method" to achieve Othering—field notes in the past tense, subsequent generalizations about the culture in the "ethnographic present" tense—Tan's two novels effect it through a number of narratological and stylistic means. (Whether Tan consciously employed them is another matter: *means* here refers not to goal-oriented artistic choices but an after-the-fact reconstruction of how the reader is affected.) Chief among these is the way the stories about old China are "framed" by reference to the present time of America. In *The Joy Luck Club*, except for the short chapter entitled "Scars," all the mothers' narratives open with some kind of time signature in the United States of the 1980s, in the form of a silent addressing of the daughter as "you" or some mention of "my daughter" in her present predicament. In *The Kitchen God's Wife*, of course, Winnie's entire tale is framed by the "now" of Pearl's dealings with her mother in connection with cousin Bao Bao's wedding and Grand Aunt Du's funeral; periodically, too, within what amounts to a lengthy monologue, Winnie supplies answers to queries (unrecorded), rhetorical questions, proleptic allusions, and philosophical musings for the benefit of her daughter.

The temporal distancing that makes possible the Othering of the Chinese mothers does not consist in locating their stories in elapsed time—after all, the daughters too tell about their childhood. Instead, it works through a subtle but insistent positioning of everything in the mothers' lives to a watershed event: arrival in the United States. Like using the arrival of the white man to demarcate two modes of being, the later one redeeming the earlier from cyclical repetition as a matter of inevitable "progress," this practice bears the unmistakable traces of a hegemonic cultural vantage point vis-à-vis a "backward" Third World. The Typological Time in both novels revolves around an unstated aporetic split between the static, ritual-permeated, mythical Time of a China past, where individuals' lives are deprived of choice, shaped by tradition and buffeted by inexorable "natural" circumstances (in terms of which even wars are described), and the unfolding, enlightened, rational, secular Time of contemporary America, where one can exercise decision making and control over one's life and where learning from the past is possible (Dew). The mothers, who are portrayed as fixated on old hurts and secrets and obsessed with cultural transmission in the form of aphorisms, and whose transformation in America from young refugees to stolid matrons is never delineated, belong to the mythical time so beloved of many a non-Chinese reader.

The Othering accomplished by temporal distancing is augmented by the stylistic uniformity of the Joy Luck mothers' voices when recounting their lives in China, which has the effect of constructing the Third World women's experiences as interchangeable and predictably constrained, because so overwhelmingly determined by culture (Ong, 85). As Renato Rosaldo observes, "social analysts commonly speak . . . as if 'we' have psychology and 'they' have culture" (202). The content of one set of stories is no doubt distinguishable from the next, but the manner of presentation is not. In The Kitchen God's Wife, despite Tan's claim of a new departure (Gillespie, 33), her stylistic range can hardly be said to be noticeably extended, and Winnie's voice inevitably recalls Lindo Jong's or An-mei Hsu's.

Both The Joy Luck Club and The Kitchen God's Wife contrast a "low-resolution" picture of the mothers' lives in China with descriptions of high material specificity or informational density in the daughters' sections. The American-born and -bred daughters—whose world Tan shares—are able to name things in their world to a high degree of topical and local precision: a scroll-length calendar from the Bank of Canton hangs on Auntie Hsu's wall; candy is not just candy but See's Nuts and Chews or M&M's (35); Shoshana's outing is to not just any science museum but to the

Exploratorium; the trendy restaurants Rose dreams of asking Ted to go to are Cafe Majestic and Rosalie's. In contrast, the items in the mothers' stories are much more "generic": the fish in the Fen River are not identified; the variety of lanterns at the Moon Festival is not differentiated; the bicycle on which An-mei Hsu's little brother rides has no brand name.

This lack of elaboration cannot be explained away as merely a realistic mirroring of the mothers' memory lapses. In the minds of many older people, recollections of remote childhood events often surpass, in clarity and specificity, those of more proximate occurrences. And young children are not nearly as oblivious to culturally meaningful distinctions as retrospective idealization makes them out to be. Finally, while the consumer orientation of present-day American society may partly account for the profusion of named objects in the daughters' narratives, it would be ignorant and condescending to attribute a preindustrial simplicity to the mothers' China. Whether uneven distribution of authorial knowledge about the two worlds is a factor in the textural fluctuation in the novels, or whether Tan is consciously manipulating the degree of resolution, remains an open, perhaps unanswerable, question. However, from the point of view of reception analysis, the leveling of descriptive details in the "Chinese" segments is an important source of pleasure for white readers, who accept and appreciate it as a "mythic" treatment of a remote but fascinating China.

## Markers of Authenticity: "The Oriental Effect"

Are the reviewers simply misguided then when they laud Tan's "convincing details"? Not at all. The details are there, but their nature and function are probably not what a "commonsense" view would make them out to be: evidence of referential accuracy, of the author's familiarity with the "real" China. Rather, they act as gestures to the "mainstream" readers that the author is familiar with the kind of culturally mediated discourse they have enjoyed, as well as qualified to give them what they expect. I call these details "markers of authenticity," whose function is to create an "Oriental effect" by signaling a reassuring affinity between the given work and American preconceptions of what the Orient is/should be.

The term "Oriental effect" borrows from "the reality effect" posited by Roland Barthes.[18] In an essay of that name, Barthes investigates the function of apparently "useless" descriptive details in realist fiction—details that are "scandalous (from the point of view of structure)" or "allied with a kind of narrative *luxury*" (11), lacking "predictive" power for plot advancement

(12), and salvageable only as a cumulative indicator of "characterization or atmosphere" (11). Citing epideictic discourse in classical rhetoric, in which "plausibility [is] not referential, but overtly discursive"—"it [is] the rules of the discourse genre which laid down the law" (13)—Barthes goes on to argue that in the modern aesthetic of *vraisemblance,* the function of apparently superfluous details is to announce "*we are the real*" and produce a "reality effect." "It is the category of the 'real,' and not its various contents, which is being signified" (16).[19] Extending Barthes's analysis, I argue that, in both *The Joy Luck Club* and *The Kitchen God's Wife,* there are many details whose existence cannot be justified on structural or informational grounds, but whose function seems to be to announce "We are Oriental" to the "mainstream" reader. These are the details for which reviewers have praised Tan. Marking the discourse as "authentic," but in a discursive rather than referential dimension, they are in a sense immune to revelations that "real" Chinese cultural practices are otherwise.

An important class of such details is made up of romanized words of limited, at times nonexistent, utility in structural or informational terms. Their usage ranges from "redundant" romanization (such as the appearance of *pai* in the same sentence where the standard English name for mahjong pieces, *tiles,* also appears (24); or adding "bad *pichi*" to "bad temper" (50), when the latter is a perfectly serviceable equivalent of the Chinese term); to correct renditions of Chinese based on a sophisticated knowledge of the language and culture (such as the clever pun on Suyuan's name); to plausible and justifiable uses of Chinese for concepts without full English equivalents (such as *shou* for filial piety), or for representing the Americanized daughters' cultural gropings (as when Rose remembers the term *huli-hudu* during her postdivorce disorientation). Errors of the "sugar sister" type, like the ones listed earlier in this essay, actually constitute only a small percentage of Tan's handling of Chinese matters. But whether "gratuitously" deployed or not, whether informed or not, the very insertion of italicized words in a page of roman type, or of explanatory asides about what the Chinese do and think in a story, is a signal that the author has adopted a certain stance toward the audience. She is in effect inviting trust in her as a knowledgeable cultural insider and a competent guide familiar with the rules of the genre in question: quasi ethnography about the Orient.

We can extend the concept of authenticity marking to a peculiar variety of prose Amy Tan has developed, which has the effect of announcing "Chineseness" in the speakers. The preponderance of short, choppy sentences and the frequent omission of sentence subjects are oft-used conventions whereby the Chinese can be recognized as Other. In addition to these, Tan employs subtle, minute dislocations of English syntax and vocabulary— jolting the language out of whack just enough—to create an impression of translation from the Chinese even where no translation has taken place. For example, in Ying-Ying's recollections of her childhood trauma at the Moon Festival, an old woman's complaint about her swollen foot takes this form: "Both inside and outside have a sour painful feeling" (71). This is neither an idiomatic English sentence nor a direct English equivalent of an idiomatic Chinese sentence; it cannot be attributed to Ying-Ying's poor command of English, for the mothers' laborious, grammatically mangled, often mala- propric English appears only in "real life," that is, when they are in the United States, speaking with their daughters. Elsewhere, when telling their own stories, they are given a different kind of English, fluent if simple, by Tan's own avowal designed to better articulate their subjectivities, do full justice to their native intelligence, and restore them to the dignity they de- serve (Tan, "Mother Tongue"). This cause is decidedly not well served by such slight linguistic skewings, which in the American popular imagination have been associated with the "comic," pidginized "Asian English" found in Anglo-American writing on Asians (E. Kim, *Asian American Literature*, 12–14). However, reading exactly like the kind of quaint, circumlocutious literal translations, or purported literal translations, in the tradition of self- Orientalizing texts (e.g., by Lin Yutang and Pardee Lowe), they indicate the comforting presence of cultural mediation to the "mainstream" reader. Thus it is not surprising to find white reviewers like Miner (567) and Schell (28) praising the *authenticity* of the immigrant women's diction. This valo- rized "Oriental effect" exists independent of Tan's sincerity in wanting to give voice to first-generation Chinese women, which we have no cause to doubt.[20]

If, as Todorov maintains in *The Poetics of Prose*, verisimilitude in litera- ture is less a relation with "reality" than "what most people believe to be re- ality—in other words, with public opinion," and with "the particular rules of [a] genre" (82), then the reviewers' satisfaction with Tan's details is en- tirely consistent with their assessment of *The Joy Luck Club* and *The Kitchen God's Wife* as "mythic" or "lyrical." Tan's details may lack referential preci- sion, but what shapes the reviewers' expectations is verisimilitude in Todorov's second and third senses. The reviewers' dual emphases—on a timeless mythic realm and on presumably authentic details—are ultimately Orientalist in spirit. It is a certain image of what China must be like ("pub- lic opinion"—here defined, of course, as the opinion of the "mainstream") and familiarity with a certain type of writing about China ("rules of the genre") that have influenced their estimation of Tan's fiction. Paradoxical as it may seem, an author with more direct historical knowledge about China than Amy Tan may well be *less* successful in convincing the American reading public of the "truthfulness" of her picture, since, in such a case, the element of cultural mediation would be correspondingly weaker.[21]

## Counter-Orientalist Gestures

It is fair to say that gestures of cultural mediation are an important component in Amy Tan's novels and are responsible, in no small part, for their popularity. But it is also fair to say that the variety of Orientalism informing *The Joy Luck Club* and *The Kitchen God's Wife* is far from simple-minded or unproblematized. It is not the knowingly exploitative misrepresentation described by Peanut in *The Kitchen God's Wife*:

> They sell *Chinese* garbage to the foreigners, especially people from America and England. . . . They sell anything that is broken, or strange, or forbidden. . . . The broken things they call Ming Dynasty. The strange things they say are Ching Dynasty. And the forbidden things—they say they are forbidden, no need to hide that. (156; italics in original)

After all, Tan, born in racially heterogeneous Oakland, California, in 1952 (albeit in a predominantly white neighborhood), grew up in the 1960s; however peripherally or obliquely, her works cannot but bear traces of the ethnic consciousness movement of that era. These traces range from relatively inconsequential information about the characters[22] or satirical observations on ethnic chic (and its cousin, prole chic),[23] to the pervasive, if often implicit, presence of the vocabulary and concepts of identity politics in *The Joy Luck Club*—what does it mean to be Chinese? to be an ethnic minority? to be American? The white middle-class book-reading and book-buying public of the post-civil rights era, likewise touched, has learned to enjoy its exotica flavored by the rhetoric of pluralism and an awareness of domestic and global interethnic connectedness. An unself-consciously ingratiating invitation to the cultural sightseer, such as the tourist brochure-style, zoom-in description of San Francisco Chinatown in the opening paragraph of Jade Snow Wong's *Fifth Chinese Daughter* (1), has a decidedly old-fashioned ring to it and no longer carries the persuasiveness it once possessed.[24] Indeed, this type of writing is no longer produced by any Asian American writers of note. A credible cultural middleman for the contemporary "mainstream" reader needs to demonstrate, in addition to access to

an authentic originary culture (or the appearance thereof), some sophistication regarding the limitations of monologism.

On this score Amy Tan fits the bill well. Again, whether by design or not,
she manages to balance on a knife edge of ambiguity, producing texts in
which Orientalist and counter-Orientalist interpretive possibilities jostle
each other, sometimes within the same speech or scene. The complex, un-
stable interplay of these possibilities makes for a larger readership than that
enjoyed by a text with a consistently articulated, readily identifiable ideological perspective. The nonintellectual consumer of Orientalism can find much
in *The Joy Luck Club* and *The Kitchen God's Wife* to satisfy her curiosity about
China and Chinatown; at the same time, subversions of naive voyeurism can
be detected by the reader attuned to questions of cultural production.

## Contending Interpretive Possibilities

That Tan's works have a little bit of something for everyone can be illustrated by a few examples from *The Joy Luck Club*. (*The Kitchen God's Wife*,
which is fashioned from the same range of elements as its predecessor but
contours them differently, will be discussed at greater length in a later section.) Waverly Jong's first chapter, "Rules of the Game," contains a portrayal
of the young Chinatown girl as hit-and-run cultural guerrilla: to get back at
a Caucasian tourist who poses her with roast ducks, Waverly tries to gross
him out with the disinformation that a recommended restaurant serves
"guts and duck's feet and octopus gizzards" (91). An anti-Orientalist impulse animates this incident; in Tan's account of daily routines among bak-
eries, sandlots, and alleyways, one recognizes a desire to demystify the tourist mecca and evoke a sense of Chinatown as home, not spectacle. However,
this effect is undermined by what appears to be a retroactive exoticizing
reading of an everyday detail: Waverly, now seeming to have adopted the
tourist's mentality, recalls that her meals used to begin "with a soup full of
mysterious things I didn't want to know the names of" (89). Furthermore,
the chapter opens with language highly reminiscent of fortune cookie wisdom, Charlie Chan aphorisms, and the kind of Taoist precepts scattered
throughout Lin Yutang's *Chinatown Family* (1948):[25]

> I was six when my mother taught me the art of invisible strength. . . .
> [S]he said, "Wise guy, he not go against wind. In Chinese we say, Come back
> from South, blow with wind—poom!—North will follow. Strongest wind
> cannot be seen." . . . My mother imparted her daily truths so she could help
> my older brothers and me rise above our circumstances. (89)

At times, the characters in *The Joy Luck Club* articulate a historicized under-standing of their situation and an awareness of the perils of essentializing ethnicity. For example, as her marriage deteriorates, Lena St. Clair begins to appreciate the advice of her friend Rose, herself a disappointed divorcée:

> "At first I thought it was because I was raised with all this Chinese humility," Rose said. "Or that maybe it was because when you're Chinese you're sup-posed to accept everything, flow with the Tao and not make waves. But my therapist said, Why do you blame your culture, your ethnicity? And I re-membered reading an article about baby boomers, how we expect the best and when we get it we worry that maybe we should have expected more, be-cause it's all diminishing returns after a certain age." (156)

Coexisting with such insights into Chinese American exigencies, and in-deed outnumbering them, are statements encouraging a culturalist view of Chinese American life. Much is made of the so-called Chinese horoscope with the twelve animal signs: Ying-Ying St. Clair emphasizes the mystical, quasi-genetic cultural transmission from her "tiger lady" self (248) to her "tiger girl" daughter (251), while Waverly Jong attributes her conflicts with her mother to incompatible horoscope signs, horse and rabbit (167).[26]

Given the mutually subverting and qualifying copresence of contradic-tory tendencies in *The Joy Luck Club*—Orientalist, culturalist, essentialist, and ahistorical on the one hand, and counter-Orientalist, anticulturalist, constructionist, and historicist on the other—the same narrative detail may yield widely divergent readings. Lindo Jong's mother, in response to her daughter's mock-innocent question about "Chinese torture," answers, "Chinese people do many things. . . . Chinese people do business, do med-icine, do painting. Not lazy like American people. We do torture. Best tor-ture" (91). How is this statement, delivered "simply" (91), to be read? Is it a straightfoward expression of the mother's ethnocultural pride? Or is it an ironic gesture of exasperation at, and resistance against, the daughter's early induction into hegemonic discourse? Has she already seen through the daughter's "wickedness" in transforming a personal irritation and minor filial rebellion into an ideological struggle? (If so, then even the mother's air of matter-of-factness is suspect; Waverly could have been simply insensible of her parodic inflection.)

The reader's quandary parallels Jing-mei Woo's puzzlement in the face of her mother's explanation about Jewish versus Chinese mahjong: "Jewish mah jong, they watch only for their own tile, play only with their eyes. . . . Chinese mah jong, you must play using your head, very tricky" (33). For all intents and purposes, Mrs. Woo could be just describing the difference between novice and expert playing—in which case the scene affords an intriguing glimpse of culturalism in action: the mother mobilizing ethnicity xenophobically to reinforce the exclusivity of her cultural authority. But if, like Jing-mei, one is brought up on reified ethnic categories and has an emotional investment in believing the speaker's cultural knowledge-ability, the purported insider's explication might leave one in a curious state of suspended judgment (which could be mistaken for cultural sensitivity and respect for the mysteries of the Other's life).

The temptation to galvanize this uncertainty into a definite interpretation is strong, and, given the current voguishness of multiculturalist rhetoric, the safest course for the befuddled non-Chinese reader might be to take the fictional "insider" speaker at face value. This spells the ultimate, if circuitously achieved, victory of Orientalist readings at the expense of other approaches. A handful of scholars of Asian American literature have argued emphatically against a one-dimensional view of *The Joy Luck Club* as a tale of intergenerational cultural confrontation and resolution. Melani McAlister, for example, has provided compelling evidence that socioeconomic class is as much a factor as culture in the mother-daughter conflicts in *The Joy Luck Club*—that, in fact, "cultural difference" can function as a less volatile or more admissible surrogate term for class anxieties. When the yuppie daughters are embarrassed by their mother's color-mismatched outfits or "un-American" restaurant manners, McAlister observes, they are consumed by the fear of being déclassé, even though they may, in all sincerity, be experiencing their distancing from the mothers *in terms of cultural conflict*. Like McAlister, Lisa Lowe, as part of a larger theoretical project on the "heterogeneity, hybridity, and multiplicity" of Asian American identity, has warned against reductionist readings of *The Joy Luck Club* that leave out class concerns ("Heterogeneity," 35–37; "Rethinking Essentialisms"). Nevertheless, voices such as McAlister's or Lowe's, already a minority in the academy, are unlikely to reach the "airport newsstand" readership of Tan's works.

Furthermore, McAlister's thesis that culturalist readings of *The Joy Luck Club* are *mis*readings—implying that a class-informed reading is somehow closer to Tan's intentions—may itself be a simplification. It is true that, as McAlister points out, when reviewer Orville Schell poses the Americanized daughters against the Joy Luck mothers wearing "funny Chinese dresses with stiff stand-up collars and blooming branches of embroidered silk sewn over their breasts" (28), he is betraying a binarist mind-set. (The Joy Luck mothers have been wearing slacks, print blouses, and sturdy walking shoes for years. "Tonight, there is no mystery" [ibid.].) Schell's telescoping of historical moments—the late 1940s and the late 1980s—freezes the mothers at their moment of immigration, absolutizes the foreign-American distinction, and reproduces the American myth that intergenerational strife is the inevitable price of assimilation. To that extent, one is justified in speaking of a *misreading*. However, in another sense, Schell is not "wrong," for *The Joy Luck Club*, as we have seen, is filled with features that would amply support the spirit if not the letter of his reading. The ending of the novel itself offers a powerful essentialist proposition: despite much wavering throughout the crisscrossing narratives, "family" and "blood" (288) eventually triumph over history. When Jing-mei travels to China to meet her long-lost half sisters, she discovers "what part of [her] is Chinese" and is able to "let [it] go" (288). This ostensible reconciliation presupposes the reality of a self-alienating ethnic malaise (without considering how it could be an ideological construction in the service of monoculturalism), then locates redemption in origin, thus in effect nullifying or at least discounting the "American" temporality of the Chinese American experience.

*Joy Luck Club* is not a misunderstood, co-opted ethnic text that has been unfortunately obscured by a culturalist haze and awaits recuperation through class- or gender-based readings. To suggest so risks explaining away the persistence of Orientalism as a matter of the individual reader's ignorance, inattention, or misguidedness. It is more defensible to characterize *The Joy Luck Club* as a multidimensional cultural product, one whose many ideological layerings, reflections, and refractions are aligned, for a broad cross section of the American reading public, with the contending needs and projections of the times. The book's popular success—and the "Amy Tan phenomenon" in general—cannot be fully understood apart from its *equivocation* vis-à-vis issues of culture and identity, allowing a profusion of interpretive claims to be made with seemingly equal cogency.

## The "Declarative Modality" and Its Implications

Many of the issues raised in the foregoing discussion of how to "read" Amy Tan recall the controversy surrounding Maxine Hong Kingston's *Woman Warrior*. Some Chinese American critics have accused Kingston of distorting traditional myths and cultural practices to capitalize on the Orientalist inclinations of the white reader (Sau-ling C. Wong, "Autobiography as Guided Chinatown Tour?"). Indeed, *The Woman Warrior*, like its successor *The Joy Luck Club*, has excited many reviewers who single out its picturesque details about old China for praise. The tacit assumption, as Kingston notes in an exasperated complaint about many of her so-called admirers ("Cultural Mis-readings"), is that the author's Chinese blood is a natural and sufficient guarantor of reliable knowledge; thus the questions Kingston raises in the book about the very cultural ignorance and confusion of the American-born Chinese are casually brushed aside. The question of Kingston's possible complicity in her own misreading is too vast to examine here; her relationship to Orientalism cannot be summed up in few senten- ces. And in a way, any ethnic writer who takes on the issue of stereotyping is caught in a bind: like the man in the Zen parable who holds on to a tree branch with his teeth and is asked the way by a straying passer-by, he is lost whatever he does. If he opens his mouth to give the "right" answer, he falls and gets hurt; but if he keeps silent he only deepens the surrounding con- fusion. How does one protest a problem without mentioning it? But in mentioning it, does one not risk multiplying its visibility and potency, through reiteration if nothing else? Generalization aside, confining our- selves to *The Woman Warrior* and *The Joy Luck Club*, we may note a crucial difference between the two works: in modality of presentation.

According to Elliott Butler-Evans, *The Woman Warrior* is distinguished by an "interrogative modality"—it ceaselessly deconstructs its own narra- tive authority and overtly thematizes the epistemological difficulties of the American-born Chinese. Its governing rhetorical trope is the palinode, or the taking back of what is said (Sau-ling C. Wong, "Ethnic Dimensions"). In other words, despite the first-person form, the narrator/protagonist lays no claim to referential advantage: the negotiations of her consciousness are foregrounded. In Naomi Schor's terms, she is an *interpretant* (interpreting character; as opposed to the interpreter, or interpreting critic/reader of the book) (122), constantly aware of the hazards of under- or overreading, yet unable to refrain from trying to wrest cultural meanings from bewildering details. Through the interpretant, the author Kingston "is trying to tell the interpreter something *about* interpretation" (Schor, 122). In contrast, *The Joy Luck Club* is epistemologically unproblematized—in Butler-Evans's view, its narrative modality is "declarative." The mothers' narratives about their Chinese life are displayed as im-mediate, coming directly from the source, and, for that reason, are valorized as correctives to the daughters' unenlightened or biased outlook. The intervention of a narrating con- sciousness is thus erased. This is what creates the space for equivocation about culture and identity: one is never entirely sure when a reinsertion of this mediation is necessary, and whether attribution of a Chinese American cast to such mediation is justified. Whereas the conflation of Chinese and Chinese American is explored in *The Woman Warrior* as a perilous legacy of Orientalism—the need to sort out the conflation defines the narrator/protagonist's lifelong act of self-creation—it is never actively interrogated in *The Joy Luck Club*.

The "declarative modality" of *The Joy Luck Club* is arguably appropriate for the project of giving voice to the immigrant mothers. Of course, this project is not the only one inferable from Tan's first novel. The "four-by-four" structure of the work—four sections each with four chapters, so that, except for the deceased Mrs. Woo (whose story is told through Jing-mei), each mother-daughter set gets to speak twice—allows the alternating accounts to resonate with, balance out, and qualify each other. The daughters' worlds, if depicted as flawed by greed and small-mindedness, are at least fleshed out enough to be counterpoised against the mothers'. Despite the compromised nature of the voice Tan assigns to the mothers, with its many Orientalist stylistic maneuvers, the narrative design does not draw overwhelming attention to the issue of the voice's truthfulness.

## The Valorization of Origin

Yet a question remains, one whose ramifications do not become fully evident until *The Kitchen God's Wife*. Unlike *The Woman Warrior*, whose narrator/protagonist has to outgrow the illusion that talking to mother will resolve cultural disorientation and crystallize truth, *The Joy Luck Club*, while posing subjectivities "declaratively" against each other, does not push the relativistic implications of this move to their limit. The ending of *The Joy Luck Club*, as well as the tentative dramas of mother-daughter reconciliation within the body chapters, suggest there is indeed a locus of truth, and that locus is origin. The daughter's task is to break through the obfuscation caused by her American nativity and upbringing. Certainly there is poignancy in the picture of the mother whose voice is not heard by her daughter:

> Because I remained quiet for so long now my daughter does not hear me. She sits by her fancy swimming pool and hears only her Sony Walkman, her cordless phone, her big, important husband asking her why they have charcoal and no lighter fluid. (67)

But there is also an asymmetry in the poignancy of this isolation *à deux*: the burden is on the daughter to educate herself into truth, to put aside her fears and needs, so that she can see her mother for what she is (183–84). The China trip—planned by Waverly, actually undertaken by Jing-mei—is in some ways an extended trope for this embrace of origin. Origin stays put, long-suffering but autotelic, awaiting rediscovery and homage.

But if there is a privileging of origin—which, in the context of Tan's books, means privileging China and the Chinese (whether "native" or diasporic)—does it not run counter to the colonialist tenor of Orientalism?

This question becomes even more pertinent when we examine *The Kitchen God's Wife*, in which both the "declarative modality" of narration and the valorization of the mother's life in China are far more pronounced than in *The Joy Luck Club*. The broad shape of characters and story types from the first novel is preserved—the assimilated, upwardly mobile daughter married to a white husband and living in the suburbs; the immigrant mother in Chinatown with a thing or two to teach her daughter about life; sufferings in China recounted; secrets revealed, old grievances banished, blood ties reaffirmed. But much more explicitly than in *The Joy Luck Club*, the daughter's role is ancillary. The staggered framework has given way to a sandwiching of the mother's tale, which forms the bulk of the novel, between two thin slices of the daughter's life. The daughter's presence, its countervailing function almost reduced to irrelevance, is now little more than a conduit for the True Word from mother, a pretext for Winnie's outpouring.

What is accomplished by this accordion-like redistribution of narrative and thematic priorities? Judging from the way they concentrate on Winnie, most reviewers of *The Kitchen God's Wife* would probaby answer "Not much." Humphreys considers Pearl's opening segment merely a "long prologue" making for a "late start" of the "central story," which gathers "energy and momentum" only when Winnie begins speaking (1). Dew bemoans the novel's "slow start" (9), and Howe feels that whenever Pearl and her husband appear the novel "bogs down" (15). To these critics, Pearl's presence might be the result of an artistic miscalculation, a nuisance one has to get past to reach the good stuff, or else a residue from the successful formula of *The Joy Luck Club*. Yet in the context of repackaging Orientalism—considered again as de facto impact on the reader—this apparently awkward or primitive narrative convention in fact serves useful functions for *The Joy Luck Club* and especially for *The Kitchen God's Wife*.

## The Americanized Daughter's Functions

The Americanized daughter, who needs to be enlightened on things Chinese, serves as a convenient, unobtrusive stand-in for the mainstream reading public. White readers, their voyeurism concealed and their curiosity in-

dulged by "naturalized" explanations, are thus relieved of possible historical guilt, free to enjoy Chinese life as a depoliticized spectacle. In such a
spectacle, the interesting localness of nomenclature and custom overshad-
ows larger historical issues. The "sugar sister" statement, besides being a
"marker of authenticity" establishing the author's credentials, is thus also a
cultural demonstration addressed simultaneously to the Americanized
daughter and the mainstream American reader, overtly in one case, covertly
in the other. Working in much the same way are Winnie's asides about linguistic trivia, such as her remarks on the formulaic expression *yi wan* (ten
thousand) ("That is what Chinese people always say . . . always an exagger-
ation" [89]), or the distinction between *syin ke* (literally, "heart liver"), a
Chinese term of endearment, and English *gizzard* (93). The phrase *taonan*
elicits the following from Winnie:

> This word, *taonan?* Oh, there is no American word I can think of that
> means the same thing. But in Chinese, we have lots of words to describe all
> kinds of trouble. (207)

The English language can hardly be guilty of lacking words for "all kinds of
trouble"—a quick flip through Roget's Thesaurus would show that readily.
What Winnie gives Pearl is not empirically grounded contrast but the kind
of cultural tidbits Orientalist readers enjoy—decontextualized, overgener-
alized, speculative, and confirmative of essential difference.

   In the larger scheme of China on display, the propositional content of
any specific comparison is relatively immaterial. At times the United States
seems to come out ahead, portrayed as institutionally more advanced, such
as when Lindo Jong of *The Joy Luck Club* speaks of flood damage: "You
couldn't go to an insurance company back then and say, Somebody did this
damage, pay me a million dollars" (53). At other times commonality seems
to be stressed, such as when Lindo compares herself to an American wife on
a TV detergent commercial in terms of eagerness to please the husband
(56). What matters more is that, by setting up the Americanized daughter as
the one to whom Chinese life has to be explained, while at the same time
endowing the mother with ancestral wisdom born of the sheer vastness of
her life experiences, the edge is taken off the suffering of the Chinese people
(in particular, Chinese women). The enormity of Chinese suffering is now
made safe for literary consumption. As Rey Chow remarks of what she calls
the "King Kong syndrome," the "Third World," as the "site of the 'raw' material that is 'monstrosity,' is produced for the surplus-value of spectacle,
entertainment, and spiritual enrichment for the 'First World'" (84).[27]

This is the process that enables *Newsweek* reviewer Pico Iyer to apply an adjective like *glamorous* to Winnie in *The Kitchen God's Wife:* "the dowdy, pinchpenny old woman has a past more glamorous than any fairy-tale, and more sad." The American-born daughters and the readers they stand in for, from the secure distance of their material privilege, can glamorize suffering as ennobling. They can have their cake and eat it too, constructing the Chinese woman—as a type of Third World woman—in such a way that their own fundamental superiority vis-à-vis the foreigner, the immigrant, is not threatened. The Third World woman is simultaneously simpleminded and crafty, transparent and unfathomable, capable of surviving unspeakable victimization but vulnerable in the modern world. She may be strong and resourceful in privation—a suitable inspiration for those grown soft from the good life—but ultimately she still needs the validation and protection of the West (in the form of immigration, a white husband, or, in the case of Winnie, Jimmy Louie—an American-born Chinese who speaks perfect English, dances, wears an American uniform, and has God on his side).[28] Superficially, to concede that women such as Winnie, Lindo Jong, even Ying-Ying St. Clair could hold the key to truth and be teachers to the Westernized or Western woman may seem a sign of humility before the Third World. But such a concession does not really threaten the Western(ized) woman's image of herself as "secular, liberated, and having control of their own lives" (Mohanty, 81). Rather, the mothers' repeated message to the daughters is that the latter have frittered away their chance to enjoy what women in the West take for granted—freedom, choice, material plenty. The harrowing accounts of arranged marriages, sadistic mothers-in-law, sexual humiliation, floods and famines, bombings and dead babies, government corruption, technological backwardness, and other assorted bane for the Third World woman are meant to bolster, not undermine, the incontrovertible desirability attributed to the Western(ized) woman's station. (The exaltation of origin is not incompatible with this message, for it removes the Chinese American's proper arena of struggle from material and political concerns in the United States, relocating in privatized psychology and dehistoricized geography.) In fact, to those readers with feminist sympathies, the books' emphasis on sexist oppression as the basis for cross-cultural, cross-generational female bonding invites a facile sense of solidarity (e.g., Miner). A reassuring projection of universal Woman obscures the role of the West in causing the very historical catastrophes from which Tan's mothers so gladly escape.

In setting tales of personal tribulation against a Chinese historical backdrop, the mothers' chapters in *The Joy Luck Club* and Winnie's recitation in *The Kitchen God's Wife* overlap the discursive space occupied by a proliferating number of English-language works in which the upheavals of "recent"—meaning post-Western contact (Fabian's Typological Time is again at work here)—Chinese history are used as a foil for personal dramas, often those of women from prominent, Westernized families, or women marrying prominent white Americans. Constituting a subgenre that might be called "the Chinese *Gone with the Wind*,"[29] these works are billed sometimes as memoirs (of varying degrees of fictionalization), sometimes as historical fiction. Virtually all involve a multigenerational family saga interwoven with violent historical events (the "Boxer Rebellion," the Republican Revolution, the Nationalist-Communist Civil War, the Cultural Revolution, the Tiananmen Square massacre), as well as a culminating personal odyssey across the ocean to the West, signaling final "arrival" in both a physical and an ideological sense.[30] From these works of epic sweep about China in turmoil, American readers can derive the concomitant satisfaction of self-congratulation and limited self-flagellation: "Thank heavens we natives of the democratic First World don't have to go through that kind of suffering; but then again, we miss out on the opportunity to build character and we lose touch with the really important things in life—Roots, Culture, Tradition, History, War, Human Evil." So the equation is balanced after all.

### The "Psychospiritual Plantation System" in the Reagan Era

Thus the daughters' presence in the narratological apparatus of *The Joy Luck Club* and *The Kitchen God's Wife* serves another vital purpose: it tempers the novels' critique of Reagan-era rapacity and hedonism, rendering it temporarily chastening but ultimately undemanding. After listening with appropriate awe, empathy, and "culture envy" to her mother, the daughter returns to yuppiedom (to which Chinese Americans have been allowed qualified access) and continues to enjoy the fruits of assimilation. In the same manner, the "sugar sisterhood" among Tan's readership returns edified from the cathartic literary excursion, but its core of historical innocence remains undisturbed.

A kind of "psychospiritual plantation system"—a stratified world of privileged whites and colored servers/caregivers—is at work in Amy Tan's novels as well as films from roughly the same period such as Bruce Beresford's *Driving Miss Daisy* (1989), Woody Allen's *Alice* (1990), and Jerry

Zucker's *Ghost* (1990).[31] All these products of popular culture make indictments against the shallow, acquisitive, image-conscious (read "middle- and upper-middle-class white") world of wealth and institutional power by putting selected members of this world in physical and/or emotional crisis, and by engineering their education/rescue by a person of color. Tan's mothers, the African American chauffeur in *Driving Miss Daisy,* the Chinese herbalist in *Alice,* and the African American medium in *Ghost* all surpass their uptight, disaffected protégés in vitality, vividness of personality, instinctual wisdom, integration of self, cultural richness, interpersonal connection, and directness of contact with elemental presences (love, death, spirituality). At the same time, these Third World healers, like loyal Black slaves of the past, are remarkably devoid of individual ambition and content with a modest piece of the American pie. If, like the frugal Joy Luck mothers or the flamboyant small-time crook in *Ghost,* they value money, that interest has an almost childlike forthrightness to it, dissociated from the "rational" pursuit of status that is the forte of their overcerebral, impeccably schooled charges. In short, the world is neatly stratified into those who have wealth and power but no soul, and those who have soul but neither wealth nor power. The latter group nurtures the former but is not interested in displacing or replacing it.

What Renato Rosaldo says of the discipline of anthropology is a good gloss on "psychospiritual plantation" discourse:

> Social analysts . . . often assert that subordinate groups have an authentic culture at the same time that they mock their own upper-middle-class professional culture. In this view, subordinate groups speak in vibrant, fluent ways, but upper-middle-class people talk like anemic academics. Yet analysts rarely allow the ratio of class and culture to include power. Thus they conceal the ratio's darker side: the more power one has, the less culture one enjoys, and the more culture one has, the less power one wields. (202)

Both *The Joy Luck Club* and *The Kitchen God's Wife* tacitly subscribe to a worldview in which the inverse relationship between political power and cultural visibility is deemed natural. Despite its chatty, upbeat tone and inspirational effectiveness, Tan's fiction, too, has a darker side.

## Conclusion

Judging from the frequency with which *The Joy Luck Club* has been anthologized and adopted for courses during the brief period since its publication, and the way Amy Tan has been chosen to perform the Asian American

spokeswoman/figurehead function once assigned to Maxine Hong Kingston, Tan currently occupies a place of substantial honor in the "mainstream" literary canon. The movement for curricular diversification in the
academy has created a demand for fairly accessible ethnic works of a multiculturalist, preferably also feminist, bent, and *The Joy Luck Club*, whatever
its other complexities, fits the bill well. Tan's place in the Asian American
canon is less clear: there has been some academic interest in *The Joy Luck
Club* (less so for *The Kitchen God's Wife*), but hardly comparable in amount
and intensity to what *The Woman Warrior* generated. Only time will tell
what the staying power of the "Amy Tan phenomenon" is.

The fortunes of once-popular, now overlooked cultural interpreters in
Chinese American literary history, such as Lin Yutang and Jade Snow Wong,
suggest that cultural mediation of the Orient for the "mainstream" readership requires continual repackaging to remain in sync with changing times
and resultant shifts in ideological needs. It will be interesting to see whether
Tan will be superseded by another "flavor of the month" (Streitfield, F8),
and if so, when, how, and to what degree. Unlike Lin Yutang's and Jade
Snow Wong's, Amy Tan's books appeared *after* the Asian American consciousness movement, at a time when Asian American cultural production
is burgeoning, Asian American literary studies has been instituted as a force
(albeit still a weak one) in cultural politics, and Asian American critics are
busily engaged in defining a canon dissociated as much as possible from
Orientalist concerns, through teaching, practical criticism, and other professional activities if not conscious, explicit theorizing. Although there is
obviously no end point in the canon-formation process, there are already
signs that the "Asian American" canon, the one arising from contestations
within the community, differs considerably from the one shaped by the
publishing industry and the critical establishment. It would be intriguing to
study how these two canons are related and how they act upon each other.

Whatever the future holds, the extent of Amy Tan's sensational success
becomes somewhat more comprehensible when we see her works as standing at the confluence of a large number of discursive traditions, each carrying its own history as well as ideological and formal demands: "mainstream" feminist writing; Asian American matrilineal literature; quasi
ethnography about the Orient; Chinese American "tour-guiding" works;
post-civil rights ethnic soul-searching; the "Chinese *Gone with the Wind*"
genre; multiculturalist rhetoric; and Reagan-era critiques of materialism—
to name only those touched on in this essay. (The literature of immigration
and Americanization is an obvious tradition that has been omitted in this

discussion; the literature of New Age self-healing might be another [Palumbo-Liu].) This heteroglossic situation, where discourses press against each other, generating now synergy, now conflict, is what makes possible the intriguing equivocation in *The Joy Luck Club* and *The Kitchen God's Wife* and allows readers of differing persuasions to see what they expect (or desire) in the texts.

## Notes

I would like to thank Victor Bascara, Elliott Butler-Evans, Juliana Chang, Samuel Cheung, Cynthia Liu, Melani McAlister, Fae Myenne Ng, Angela Pao, Catharine Stimpson, Henry Zhao, John Zou, and members of the Asian American Reading Group at the University of California, Berkeley, for suggestions, permission to cite unpublished work, and other types of assistance. In particular, David Palumbo-Liu's comments have helped me refine some of the key arguments in this essay.

1. Shapiro is among the few dissenting voices, noting that in *The Kitchen God's Wife* "all the excitement is on the surface" (64).

2. The most recent sales estimate for Tan's novels that I could find, said to be based on publishers' figures, gives 253,000 hardcover (note the difference from J. Simpson's figures) and over two million paperback for *The Joy Luck Club* and nearly 392,000 for *The Kitchen God's Wife* (Sun).

3. The film was released, to generally enthusiastic reviews, just as the final revision of this essay was completed in the fall of 1993. Some of the issues raised about the book are addressed in the film version, some not, but a comparison cannot be undertaken here because of space limitations.

4. The extent of the growth in mother-daughter discourse can be gauged by comparing the bibliographies in Broner and Davidson's review essay (1978), Davidson and Broner's anthology (1980), Hirsch's review essay (1981), and Hirsch's book-length study (1989). This phenomenon can be placed in a larger context of changing motherhood discourse in American popular culture (Kaplan).

5. For example, Brown (1976); Oates (1986); M. Simpson (1987). Most of the works surveyed in Pearlman ("Introduction") fall into this category.

6. For example, Toni Morrison's *Sula* (1987) and *Beloved* (1987), Terry Mcmillan's *Mama* (1987), and others. See Hirsch ("Maternal Narratives") on the matrilineal tradition in African American literature.

7. 1965 was the year immigration legislation was reformed to end decades of exclusion and restriction and allow Chinese to enter on an equal footing with immigrants from other countries.

8. This immediately recalls the pivotal role of literacy acquisition in African American slave narratives. Autobiographies by Chinese American men from the same period, such as Huie Kin's (1932; alphabetized under Huie) or Pardee Lowe's (1943), do not show this feature.

9. Chuang Hua is a pseudonym; alphabetization is under Chuang.

10. This list does not even include works like Ruthanne Lum McCunn's *Thousand Pieces of Gold* (1981) and Yoshiko Uchida's *Picture Bride* (1987), which, though not depicting mother-daughter relationships, may be construed as part of matrilineal literature in that they reconstruct the lives of heroic female ancestors who crossed the ocean to come to America. In addition, there is a large body of Asian American poetry dealing with matrilineage, such as Jessica Hagedorn (1975: "Cristina," pages unnumbered), Nellie Wong (1977: 7, 12, 14, 18, 40–41), Janice

Mirikitani (1978: "Desert Flowers" and "Lullabye," pages unnumbered), Fay Chiang (1979: 26), Kitty Tsui (1983: 4–8), Cathy Song (1983: 2–6, 43–48).

11. In a *Washington Post* story on the success of *The Joy Luck Club,* David Streitfield notes: "According to one theory, Tan inadvertently tapped into the mentality of the baby boomer female—who also, coincidentally, forms a huge chunk of the book-buying public. Heading toward and through that crucial dividing line of age 40, these women are realizing, as Tan did, that their mothers won't be with them forever" (F9). The context suggests that the reference here is to "mainstream" female readers.

12. "The *Aiiieeeee* group" refers to writers Frank Chin, Jeffery Paul Chan, Lawson Fusao Inada, and Shawn Wong, who edited *Aiiieeeee!* (1974) and later *The Big Aiiieeeee!* (1991). Though not the first anthology of Asian American literature, *Aiiieeeee!* has been the most influential in that its Introduction sets forth a sort of declaration of independence for Asian American writers. Frank Chin, the informal leader of the group, has been the most vocal spokesman for the cultural nationalist and masculinist position articulated in the 1974 anthology. The 1991 sequel contains both a general Introduction, signed by all four editors, and a lengthy prefatory essay, "Come All Ye Asian American Writers of the Real and the Fake," signed by Frank Chin alone, in which the effeminization of Chinese American literature continues to be bemoaned and Maxine Hong Kingston, Amy Tan, and David Henry Hwang are attacked for producing "fake" Chinese American literature.

13. Works by Japanese American women writers are included. No explicit explanation for this discrepancy is provided.

14. Yung (80–83, esp. 80) provides a woman-centered account of Chinese women married to "Gold Mountain men" who were affected by decades of family separation.

15. I am indebted to Catharine R. Stimpson for this reference.

16. Given China's sheer size and regional variations in cultural practices, it is of course impossible to rule this out entirely, especially since the novel is set in a period of increasing Western influence. However, the inland location of the episode and the lack of corroboration in the ethnographic literature (e.g., Shizhen Wang) make the kind of veil lifting and bride kissing described by Tan an extremely unlikely occurrence. In the film version, the red veil is removed in the wedding chamber.

17. One of the first academic papers I heard on *The Joy Luck Club* borrows anthropologist Clifford Geertz's term, "thick description," to refer to Tan's renditions of Chinese places and mores (Butler-Evans).

18. I am indebted to David Palumbo-Liu for referring me to this highly useful theoretical piece, as well as to Schor.

19. This view is disputed by Schor (141–47), but for our purposes Barthes's framework is quite sufficient.

20. Dasenbrock and Ashcroft, Griffiths, and Tiffin (64–66) offer alternative views of how untranslated words function in "minority" writing. I have no quarrel with their theoretical positions but find Tan's case to constitute a significant complication of them.

21. A good example of this phenomenon is Eileen Chang's (Chang Ai-ling's) masterful "Golden Canque," which deals with the kind of milieu depicted in parts of *The Joy Luck Club* and *The Kitchen God's Wife:* the protagonist is a concubine trapped in a decaying Chinese family in a Westernizing city, much like An-mei Hsu's mother. Filled with precise details of dress and decor, highly respected by Chinese readers as a classic of short fiction, and available in English translation, "The Golden Canque" is yet little known to the American reading public.

22. For example, Lena St. Clair majors in Asian American studies, a field that did not exist prior to the 1969 Third World student strikes in San Francisco and Berkeley.

23. See, for example, in *The Joy Luck Club,* Lindo Jong's complaint, "Now she wants to be Chinese, it is so fashionable" (253), and Jing-mei's attitude toward her jade pendant (197); in

*The Kitchen God's Wife,* Pearl's changing attitude toward the once detested "art deco" dressing table in her mother's house (17).

24. *Fifth Chinese Daughter* enjoyed immense popularity in the 1940s and 1950s; in 1952 Jade Snow Wong was sent on a State Department-sponsored tour of Asia to speak on behalf of American democracy (E. Kim, *Asian American Literature,* 60).

25. See, for example, the Confucian and Taoist dicta in chap. 7, sec. 3; chap. 12, sec. 1; chap. 18, sec. 2 and sec. 3. Lin Yutang is alphabetized under Lin.

26. It might be noted that the Chinese horoscope, in China proper, was used more for reckoning than for fortune-telling, which more often called for information not only about the year of birth but also the date and hour (*shichen bazi*). The fascination with the twelve animals of the horoscope appears to be the combined effect of American cultural appropriation and Chinese American cultural evolution/accommodation. Although it is plausible for the American-born Waverly to have internalized this fascination, China-born Ying-Ying St. Clair is less likely to be as preoccupied with "tiger attributes" as Tan makes her out to be.

27. Interestingly, Amy Tan links the writing of *The Kitchen God's Wife* to the bloody events in Tiananmen Square; of both the abused Chinese wife (her mother) and the repressed Chinese students, she wanted to know why rising-up did not take place sooner (Fong-Torres, B4).

28. It might be instructive to relate this process to what Chandra Mohanty calls the production of "third-world difference" in Western feminist discourse: "Third-world women as a group or category are automatically and necessarily defined as: religious (read 'not progressive'), family oriented (read 'traditional'), legal minors (read 'they-are-still-not-conscious-of-their-rights'), illiterate (read 'ignorant'), domestic (read 'backward') and sometimes revolutionary (read 'their-country-is-in-a-state-of-war; they-must-fight!')" (80).

29. This is a promotional phrase used on the dust jacket of Linda Ching Sledge's *Empire of Heaven.*

30. In this category can be included Anna Chennault's *Education of Anna* (1980); Bette Bao Lord's *Spring Moon* (1981); Katherine Wei and Terry Quinn's *Second Daughter* (1984); Nien Cheng's *Life and Death in Shanghai* (1986); C. Y. Lee's *China Saga* (1987); Tsai Chin's *Daughter of Shanghai* (1988); Linda Ching Sledge's *Empire of Heaven* (1990); Bette Bao Lord's *Legacies* (1990); Jung Chang's *Wild Swans* (1991); Lillian Lee's translated *The Last Princess of Manchuria: A Novel* (1992); C. Y. Lee's *Gate of Rage* (1992); and Ching Yun Bezine's trilogy, *Children of the Pearl* (1991), *Empire of the Moon* (1992), and *On Wings of Destiny* (1992). C. Y. Lee is the author of *The Flower Drum Song* (1957), source of the notoriously Orientalist musical of the same name.

31. These and other films portraying physical and psychospiritual caregiving by people of color are analyzed in my "Diverted Mothering."

# References

Appachana, Anjana. "My Only Gods." In *The Forbidden Stitch: An Asian American Women's Anthology,* ed. Shirley Geok-lin Lim and Mayumi Tsutakawa. Corvallis, Ore.: Calyx, 1989. 228–34.

Ashcroft, Bill, Gareth Griffiths, and Helen Tiffin. *The Empire Writes Back: Theory and Practice in Post-colonial Literatures.* London: Routledge, 1989.

Asian Women United of California. *Making Waves: An Anthology of Writings by and about Asian American Women.* Boston: Beacon, 1989.

Barthes, Roland. "The Reality Effect." In *French Literary Theory To/day: A Reader,* ed. Tzvetan Todorov. New York: Cambridge University Press, 1982. 11–17.

Bernikow, Louise. Review of Amy Tan's *The Joy Luck Club. Cosmopolitan,* October 1989: 42.

Bezine, Ching Yun. *Children of the Pearl*. New York: Signet, 1991.

———. *Empire of the Moon*. New York: Signet, 1992.

———. *On Wings of Destiny*. New York: Signet, 1992.

Broner, E. M., and Cathy N. Davidson. *Mothers and Daughters in Literature*. Special issue. *Women's Studies* 6.1 (1978).

Brown, Rosellen. *The Autobiography of My Mother*. New York: Doubleday, 1976.

Butler-Evans, Elliot. "Strategies of Self-Fashioning in Amy Tan's *The Joy Luck Club*." Paper presented at "Reading Each Other: Cross-Cultural Perspectives on Literatures Other Than One's Own." Modern Language Association Convention, Washington, D.C., December 27–30, 1989.

Chan, Jeffery Paul, Frank Chin, Lawson Fusao Inada, and Shawn Wong, eds. *The Big Aiiieeeee! An Anthology of Chinese American and Japanese American Literature*. New York: Meridian, 1991.

Chang, Eileen (Chang Ai-ling). "The Golden Canque." Trans. author. In *Twentieth Century Chinese Stories*, ed. C. T. Hsia, with Joseph S. M. Lau. New York: Columbia University Press, 1971. 138–91.

Chang, Jung. *Wild Swans*. New York: Simon & Schuster, 1991.

Cheng, Nien. *Life and Death in Shanghai*. 1986. New York: Penguin, 1988.

Chennault, Anna. *The Education of Anna*. New York: Times Books, 1980.

Cheong, Fiona. *The Scent of the Gods*. New York: Norton, 1991.

Cheung, King-Kok. "The Woman Warrior versus the Chinaman Pacific: Must a Chinese American Critic Choose between Feminism and Heroism?" In *Conflicts in Feminism*, ed. Marianne Hirsch and Evelyn Fox-Keller. New York: Routledge, 1990. 234–51.

Chiang, Fay. *In the City of Contradictions*. New York: Sunbury Press, 1979.

Chin, Frank. *The Chickencoop Chinaman* and *The Year of the Dragon*. Seattle: University of Washington Press, 1981.

———. "Introduction." In *Aiiieeeee!* ed. Frank Chin et al. xxi–xlviii.

Chin, Frank, Jeffery Paul Chan, Lawson Fusao Inada, and Shawn Wong, eds. *Aiiieeeee! An Anthology of Asian-American Writers*. 1974. Washington, D.C.: Howard University Press, 1983.

Chin, Tsai. *Daughter of Shanghai*. New York: St. Martin's Press, 1988.

Chow, Rey. "Violence in the Other Country: China as Crisis, Spectacle, and Woman." In *Third World Women and the Politics of Feminism*, ed. Mohanty, Russo, and Torres, 81–100.

Chuang, Hua [pseud.]. *Crossings*. 1968. Boston: Northeastern University Press, 1986.

Dasenbrock, Reed Way. "Intelligibility and Meaningfulness in Multicultural Literature in English." *PMLA* 102.1 (1987): 10–19.

Davidson, Cathy N., and E. M. Broner, eds. *The Lost Tradition: Mothers and Daughters in Literature*. New York: Ungar, 1980.

Dew, Robb Forman. "Pangs of an Abandoned Child." Review of Amy Tan's *The Kitchen God's Wife*. *New York Times Book Review*, June 16, 1991, sec. 7: 9.

Dhillon, Kartar. "The Parrot's Beak." In Asian Women United, 214–22.

Fabian, Johannes. *Time and the Other: How Anthropology Makes Its Object*. New York: Columbia University Press, 1983.

Fong, Yem Siu. Review of Amy Tan's *The Joy Luck Club*. *Frontiers* 11.2–3 (1990): 122–23.

Fong-Torres, Ben. "Can Amy Tan Do It Again?" *San Francisco Chronicle*, June 12, 1991: B3, B4.

Gillespie, Elgy. "Amy, Angst, and the Second Novel." Review of Amy Tan's *The Kitchen God's Wife*. *San Francisco Review of Books*, summer 1991: 33–34.

Hagedorn, Jessica. *Dangerous Music*. San Francisco: Momo's Press, 1975.

Hayslip, Le Ly. With Jay Wurts. *When Heaven and Earth Changed Places: A Vietnamese Woman's Journey from War to Peace*. New York: Doubleday, 1989.

Hirsch, Marianne. "Maternal Narratives: 'Cruel Enough to Stop the Blood.'" In *Reading Black, Reading Feminist: A Critical Anthology,* ed. Henry Louis Gates Jr. New York: Meridian, 1990.
———. *The Mother/Daughter Plot: Narrative, Psychoanalysis, Feminism.* Bloomington: Indiana University Press, 1989.
———. "Mothers and Daughters." Review essay. *Signs* 7.1 (1981): 200–222.
Holt, Patricia. "The Shuffle over 'Joy Luck.'" *San Francisco Chronicle Review,* July 16, 1989: 2.
Howe, Joyce. "Chinese in America: Telling the Immigrant Story." Review of Gish Jen's *Typical American,* Gus Lee's *China Boy,* Amy Tan's *The Kitchen God's Wife,* David Wong Louie's *Pangs of Love,* and Frank Chin's *Donald Duk. Express Books,* a supplement to the East Bay *Express,* October 1991, 1: 14–15.
Huie, Kin. *Reminiscences.* Peiping [Beijing]: San Yu Press, 1932.
Humphreys, Josephine. "Secret Truths: Amy Tan Writes of Fate and Luck." Review of Amy Tan's *The Kitchen God's Wife. Chicago Tribune,* June 9, 1991, sec. 14: 1, 5.
Iyer, Pico. "The Second Triumph of Amy Tan." *Newsweek,* June 3, 1991: 67.
James, Caryn. "Relax, But Don't Leave Your Mind Behind." Review of Amy Tan's *The Kitchen God's Wife* and other works. *New York Times,* late ed., May 31, 1991: C1, C25.
Kadohata, Cynthia. *The Floating World.* New York: Viking, 1989.
Kaplan, E. Ann. *Motherhood and Representation: The Mother in Popular Culture and Melodrama.* London: Routledge, 1992.
Kepner, Susan. "Imagine This: The Amazing Adventure of Amy Tan." *San Francisco Focus,* May 1989: 58–60, 160–62.
Kim, Elaine H. *Asian American Literature: An Introduction to the Writings and Their Social Context.* Philadelphia: Temple University Press, 1982.
———. "'Such Opposite Creatures': Men and Women in Asian American Literature." *Michigan Review,* winter 1990: 68–93.
Kim, Ronyoung. *Clay Walls.* 1987. Seattle: University of Washington Press, 1990.
Kingston, Maxine Hong. "Cultural Mis-readings by American Reviewers." In *Asian and Western Writers in Dialog: New Cultural Identities,* ed. Guy Amirthanayagam. Hong Kong: Macmillan, 1982. 55–65.
———. *Tripmaster Monkey: His Fake Book.* New York: Knopf, 1989.
———. *The Woman Warrior: Memoirs of a Girlhood among Ghosts.* New York: Knopf, 1976.
Kogawa, Joy. *Obasan.* 1981. Boston: Godine, 1982.
Kuo, Helena. *I've Come a Long Way.* New York: Appleton, 1942.
Lau, Sarah. "Long Way Home." In Watanabe and Bruchac, 87–95.
Law-Yone, Wendy. *The Coffin Tree.* New York: Knopf, 1983.
Lee, C. Y. *China Saga.* New York: Weidenfeld, 1987.
———. *The Flower Drum Song.* New York: Farrar, Straus & Cudahy, 1957.
———. *Gate of Rage.* New York: William Morrow, 1991.
Lee, Lillian (Lee Pik-Wah). *The Last Princess of Manchuria: A Novel.* Trans. Andrea Kelly. New York: William Morrow, 1992.
Li, Leslie. *Bittersweet.* Boston: Tuttle, 1992.
Lim, Shirley Geok-lin. "Asian American Daughters Rewriting Asian Maternal Texts." In *Asian Americans: Comparative and Global Perspectives,* ed. Shirley Hune, Hyung-chan Kim, Stephen S. Fugita, and Amy Ling. Pullman: Washington State University Press, 1991. 239–48.
Lin, Alice P. *Grandmother Has No Name.* San Francisco: China Books and Periodicals, 1988.
Lin, Yutang. *Chinatown Family.* New York: John Day, 1948.
Lord, Bette Bao. *Legacies: A Chinese Mosaic.* New York: Fawcett Columbine, 1990.
———. *Spring Moon: A Novel of China.* New York: Harper, 1981.
Lowe, Lisa. "Heterogeneity, Hybridity, Multiplicity: Making Asian American Differences." *Diaspora* 1.1 (spring 1991): 24–44.

———. "Rethinking Essentialisms: Gender and Ethnicity in Amy Tan's *The Joy Luck Club*." Paper presented at the American Literature Association Conference, San Diego, June 2, 1990.

Lowe, Pardee. *Father and Glorious Descendant*. Boston: Little, Brown, 1943.

Maglin, Nan Bauer. "'Don't Never Forget the Bridge That You Crossed Over On': The Literature of Matrilineage." In Davidson and Broner, 257–67.

Mara, Rachna. *Of Customs and Excise*. Toronto: Second Story Press, 1991.

McAlister, Melani. "(Mis)reading *The Joy Luck Club*." *Asian America: Journal of Culture and the Arts* 1 (winter 1992): 102–18.

McCunn, Ruthanne Lum. *Thousand Pieces of Gold*. San Francisco: Design Enterprises, 1981.

Mcmillan, Terry. *Mama*. New York: Washington Square Press, 1987.

Miner, Valerie. "The Daughters' Journeys." Review of Amy Tan's *The Joy Luck Club* and Hisaye Yamamoto's *Seventeen Syllables and Other Stories*. *The Nation*, April 24, 1989: 566–69.

Mirikitani, Janice. *Awake in the River*. N.p.: Isthmus Press, 1978.

Mohanty, Chandra Talpade. "Under Western Eyes: Feminist Scholarship and Colonial Discourses." In *Third World Women and the Politics of Feminism*, ed. Mohanty, Russo, and Torres, 51–80.

Mohanty, Chandra Talpade, Ann Russo, and Lourdes Torres, eds. *Third World Women and the Politics of Feminism*. Bloomington: Indiana University Press, 1991.

Morrison, Toni. *Beloved*. New York: Knopf, 1987.

———. *Sula*. New York: Bantam, 1973.

Mukherjee, Bharati. *Jasmine*. New York: Weidenfeld, 1989.

Ng, Fae Myenne. *Bone*. New York: Hyperion, 1993.

Oates, Joyce Carol. *Marya: A Life*. New York: Dutton, 1986.

Olsen, Tillie. *Mother to Daughter, Daughter to Mother*. Ed. Tillie Olsen. New York: Feminist Press, 1984. 275. Cited in Pearlman, 1.

Ong, Aihwa. "Colonialism and Modernity: Feminist Re-presentations of Women in Non-Western Societies." *Inscriptions* 3.4 (1988): 79–93.

Palumbo-Liu, David. "Model Minority Discourse and the Course of Healing." Forthcoming in *Minority Discourse: Ideological Containment and Utopian/Heterotopian Potential*, ed. Abdul JanMohamed.

Pearlman, Mickey. "Introduction." In *Mother Puzzles: Daughters and Mothers in Contemporary American Literature*, ed. Mickey Pearlman. New York: Greenwood, 1989. 1–9.

Perrick, Penny. "Daughters of America." Review of Amy Tan's *The Kitchen God's Wife*. *Sunday Times Book Review*, July 14, 1991: 6.

Rich, Adrienne. *Of Woman Born: Motherhood as Experience and Institution*. New York: Norton, 1976. 225.

Romano, Nancy Forbes. "The Disorientation of Pearl and Kai." Review of Amy Tan's *The Kitchen God's Wife*. *Los Angeles Times Book Review*, June 16, 1991, home ed.: 2.

Rosaldo, Renato. *Culture and Truth: The Remaking of Social Analysis*. Boston: Beacon, 1989.

Rothstein, Mervyn. "A New Novel by Amy Tan." *New York Times*, June 11, 1991, late ed.: C13-C14.

Sasaki, Ruth. "The Loom." In Asian Women United, 199–214.

Schell, Orville. "Your Mother Is in Your Bones." Review of Amy Tan's *The Joy Luck Club*. *New York Times Book Review*, March 19, 1989: 3, 28.

Schor, Naomi. *Reading in Detail: Aesthetics and the Feminine*. New York: Methuen, 1987.

See, Carolyn. "'Joy Luck' Readers: Extraordinary Good Fortune." Review of Amy Tan's *The Joy Luck Club*. *Oakland Tribune*, March 15, 1989: D8.

Shapiro, Laura. "From China, with Love." Review of Amy Tan's *The Kitchen God's Wife*. *Newsweek* 117.25, June 24, 1991: 63–64.

Simpson, Janice C. "Fresh Voices above the Noisy Din." *Time*, June 3, 1991: 66–67.

Simpson, Mona. *Anywhere but Here*. New York: Knopf, 1986.

Sit, Elaine. "Taking 'My Mother's Place . . . On the East, Where Things Begin.'" Review of Amy Tan's *The Joy Luck Club*. *East/West News*, April 13, 1989: 6.

Sledge, Linda Ching. With Gary Allen Sledge. *Empire of Heaven*. New York: Bantam, 1990.

Solovitch, Sara. "Finding a Voice." *West*, June 30, 1991: 18–22.

Song, Cathy. *Picture Bride*. New Haven: Yale University Press, 1983.

Streitfield, David. "The 'Luck' of Amy Tan: Bestselling Writer Puts Newfound Fame in Perspective." *Washington Post*, October 8, 1989: F1, F8, F9.

Sun, Qingfeng. (In Chinese) "*Tan Enmei de ertongshu Yueniang*" [Amy Tan's children's book *The Moon Lady*]. *World Journal*, November 29, 1992: C8.

Tan, Amy. *The Joy Luck Club*. New York: Putnam, 1989.

———. *The Kitchen God's Wife*. New York: Putnam, 1991.

———. *The Moon Lady*. Illustrated by Gretchen Shields. New York: Macmillan, 1992.

———. "Mother Tongue." 1990. Repr. in *The Best American Essays 1991*. New York: Tickner & Fields, 1991. 196–202.

———. *Xifuhui [The Joy Luck Club]*. Trans. Yu Renrui. Tabei: Lianhe wenxue chubanshe, 1990.

Todorov, Tzvetan. *The Poetics of Prose*. Trans. Richard Howard. New Foreword by Jonathan Culler. Ithaca, N.Y.: Cornell University Press, 1977.

Tsui, Kitty. *The Words of a Woman Who Breathes Fire*. San Francisco: Spinsters, 1983.

Uchida, Yoshiko. *Picture Bride*. Flagstaff, Ariz.: Northland Press, 1987.

Wang, Shizhen. (In Chinese) *Zhongguo gesheng hunsu* [Wedding customs in various provinces of China]. Taibei: Xingguang chubanshe, 1981.

Wang, Wen-Wen C. "Bacon and Coffee." In Watanabe and Bruchac, 97–105.

Watanabe, Sylvia, and Carol Bruchac, eds. *Home to Stay*. Greenfield Center, N.Y.: Greenfield Review Press, 1990.

Wei, Katherine, and Terry Quinn. *Second Daughter: Growing up in China, 1930–1949*. 1984. New York: Holt, Rinehart and Winston, 1985.

Wong, Jade Snow. *Fifth Chinese Daughter*. 1945. Seattle: University of Washington Press, 1989. With a new Introduction by the author.

Wong, Nellie. *Dreams in Harrison Railroad Park*. N.p.: Kellsey Sreet Press, 1977.

Wong, Sau-ling C. "Autobiography as Guided Chinatown Tour? Maxine Hong Kingston and the Chinese-American Autobiographical Controversy." In *Multicultural Autobiography: American Lives*, ed. James Robert Payne. Knoxville: University of Tennessee Press, 1992. 248–79.

———. "Diverted Mothering: Representations of Caregivers of Color in the Age of 'Multiculturalism.'" In *Mothering: Ideology, Experience, and Agency*, ed. Evelyn Nakano Glenn, Grace Chang, and Linda Rennie Forcie. New York: Routledge, 1993. 67–91.

———. "Ethnic Dimensions of Postmodern Indeterminacy: Maxine Hong Kingston's *The Woman Warrior* as Avant-garde Autobiography." In *Autobiographie & Avant-garde*, ed. Alfred Hornung and Ernstpeter Ruhe. Tübingen: Gunter Narr Verlag, 1991. 273–84.

Wong, Su-ling [pseud.], and Earl Herbert Cressy. *Daughter of Confucius: A Personal History*. New York: Farrar, Straus & Giroux, 1952.

Wong, Suzi. Review of Maxine Hong Kingston's *The Woman Warrior*. *Amerasia Journal* 4.1 (1977): 165–67.

Woo, Merle. "Letter to Ma." In *This Bridge Called My Back: Writings by Radical Women of Color*, ed. Cherríe Moraga and Gloria Anzaldúa. Watertown, Mass.: Persephone Press, 1981. 140–47.

Yamamoto, Hisaye. "Seventeen Syllables." 1949. Repr. in *Seventeen Syllables*, 8–19.

———. *Seventeen Syllables and Other Stories*. Latham, N.Y.: Kitchen Table: Women of Color Press, 1988.

————. "Yoneko's Earthquake." 1951. Repr. in *Seventeen Syllables*, 46–56.
Yamauchi, Wakako. "The Handkerchief." 1961. Repr. in *Amerasia Journal* 4.1 (1977): 143–50.
————. "Songs My Mother Taught Me." *Amerasia Journal* 3.2 (1976): 63–73.
Yglesias, Helen. Review of Amy Tan's *The Kitchen God's Wife*. *Women's Review of Books* 8.12 (1991): 1, 3, 4.
Yung, Judy. *Chinese Women in America: A Pictorial History*. Published for the Chinese Culture Foundation of San Francisco. Seattle: University of Washington Press, 1986.
Zill, Nicholas, and Marianne Winglee. *Who Reads Literature? The Future of the United States as a Nation of Readers*. Foreword by Jonathan Yardley. Commissioned by the Research Division of the National Endowment for the Arts. Cabin John, Md./Washington, D.C.: 1990.

## PART THREE

# The Ethnic, the Nation, and the Canon

# In Search of Filipino Writing

## Reclaiming Whose "America"?

E. SAN JUAN JR.

... Fertilizer ... Filipinos ...
—From a letter dated May 5, 1908, by H. Hackfield and Company sent to
George Wilcox of the Grove Farm Plantation, Hawaii [1]

It must be realized that the Filipino is just the same as the manure that we
put on the land—just the same.
—From an interview of a secretary of an agricultural association in 1930 [2]

## Filipinos: Challenge and Enigma

Ever since the United States annexed the Philippine Islands in 1898, the discourse of capital (as these opening quotes testify) has always been reductive, monological, and utilitarian. Although luminaries such as Mark Twain, William James, and William Dean Howells denounced the slaughter of the natives during the Filipino-American War of 1899–1902, the Filipino presence was not registered in the public sphere until their singular commodity, labor power, appeared in large numbers in Hawaii and on the West Coast from 1907 to 1935. Until 1946, when formal independence was granted, Filipinos in the metropolis (numbering around 150,000) occupied the limbo of alterity and transitionality: neither slaves, wards, nor citizens. Carey McWilliams believed that these "others" belonged to "the freemasonry of the ostracized" (*Brothers*, 241). How should we address them, and in what language? Can they speak for themselves? If not, who will represent them?

Called "little brown brothers," barbaric "yellow bellies," "scarcely more than savages," and other derogatory epithets, Filipinos as subjects-in-revolt have refused to conform to the totalizing logic of white supremacy and the knowledge of "the Filipino" constructed by the Orientalizing methods of American scholarship. Intractable and recalcitrant, Filipinos in the process of being subjugated have confounded U.S. disciplinary regimes of knowledge production and surveillance. They have challenged the asymmetrical cartography of metropolis and colony, core and periphery, in the official world system. Interpellated within the boundaries of empire, Filipinos continue to bear the marks of three centuries of anticolonial insurgency. Given this indigenous genealogy of resistance, which I have traced elsewhere (San Juan, *Racial Formations*), the Filipino writer has functioned not simply as *porte-parole* authorized by the imperium's center but more precisely as an organic intellectual (in Gramsci's sense) for a people whose repressed history and "political unconscious" remain crucial to the task of judging the worth of the American experiment in colonial "tutelage" and to the final settling of accounts with millions of its victims.

Up to now, however, despite the Philippines' formal independence, the texts of the Filipino interrogation of U.S. hegemony remain virtually unread and therefore unappreciated for their "fertilizing" critical force. Not demography, but a symptomatic reconnaissance of contested territory seems imperative. An inventory of the archive (by a partisan native, for a change) is needed as an initial step toward answering the questions I raised earlier. Foremost among these is why the Filipino intervention in the U.S. literary scene has been long ignored, silenced, or marginalized. Although the Filipino component of the Asian-Pacific Islander ethnic category of the U.S. Census Bureau has now become preponderant—1,255,725 persons as of 1989 (O'Hare and Felt, 2), and in the next decade will surpass the combined total of the Chinese and Japanese population—the import of this statistical figure so far has not been calculated in the existing Baedekers of U.S. High Culture.

Literary surveys drawn up in this era of canon revision ignore the Filipino contribution. In the 1982 MLA (Modern Language Association) survey of *Three American Literatures* edited by Houston Baker Jr., the Asian American section deals only with Chinese and Japanese authors. This omission is repeated in the 1990 MLA reference, *Redefining American Literary*

*History;* no reference is made to Filipino writing except in a meager biblio-graphic list at the end under the rubric "Philippine American Literature" (Ruoff and Ward, 361–62). In this quite erroneous citation of ten authors' "Primary Works," three authors would not claim at all to be Filipino Amer-ican: Stevan Javellana, Celso Carunungan, and Egmidio Alvarez.[3] Nor would Jose Garcia Villa, the now "disappeared" inventor of modern Filipino expression in English, who is a permanent U.S. resident but not a citizen. The classification "Philippine American" may appear as a harmless con-junction of equal and separate terms, but in fact it conceals subsumption of the former into the latter. In everyday life, the combinatory relay of Ameri-can pragmatic tolerance easily converts the "Philippine" half into a routin-ized ethnic phenomenon, normalized and taken for granted. How, then, do we account for the absence, exclusion, and potential recuperability of Fili-pino writing in this society—at least that portion conceded recognition by institutional fiat?

### Expropriating Carlos Bulosan's Worldliness

In general, the production, circulation, and reception of texts are necessar-ily, though not sufficiently, determined by the dynamics of class and race. Everyone agrees that in this system numbers do not really count unless the community exercises a measure of economic and political power. Filipinos in the United States remain an exploited and disadvantaged group, not at all a "model" minority. A 1980 study of income distribution among Filipinos found that young men (80 to 86 percent of whom are employed in the sec-ondary sector in California) received only about two-thirds of the income of white males, while the older men get only half; women, on the other hand, receive one-half the income of white men. Such income disparities persist despite comparable investments in human capital (education, work experience, etc.), which generate low returns "suggestive of race discrimina-tion" (Cabezas and Kawaguchi, 99). Filipinos rank third among Asian Americans in median household income, behind Japanese and Asian Indi-ans. Another survey (Nee and Sanders, 75–93) concludes that although Fil-ipinos have a higher educational attainment than whites or recent Chinese immigrants, their average income is lower than Japanese Americans and Chinese Americans because they are confined to low-skilled, low-paying jobs.

Except in the last few years, Filipinos in the United States have not par-ticipated significantly in electoral politics (notwithstanding recent breakthroughs in California and Hawaii), a fact attributed by mainstream sociologists to the inertia of "provincial allegiances and personality clashes" (Melendy "Filipinos," 362). Collective praxis, however, is not a given but a sociohistorical construct. This implies that we have to reckon with the tenacious legacy of four centuries of Spanish and U.S. colonial domination to understand the Filipino habitus. What passes for indigenous music or architecture turns out to be a mimesis of Western styles; the refined skills of reading and writing needed for the production and distribution of the knowledge monopolized by the elite (compradors, landlords, bureaucrat capitalists) serve business interests. In brief, cultural literacy is geared to soliciting the recognition of American arbiters of taste and brokers of symbolic capital. We may have talented writers but certainly have had no sizable and responsive audience of readers and commentators up to now. And so this predicament of the community's powerlessness, together with its largely imitative and instrumentalized modality of cultural production/reception, may shed light on the invisibility of Filipino writing in the academy and in public consciousness. But its exclusion and/or marginalization cannot be grasped unless the irreducible historical specificity of the Philippines as a former colony, and at present as a virtual neocolony of the United States, and Filipinos as subjugated and conflicted subjects, are taken into full account.

This dialectical perspective explains the irrepressible centrality of Carlos Bulosan's oeuvre in the shaping of an emergent pan-Filipino literary tradition affiliating the U.S. scene of writing. What distinguishes Bulosan's role in this field of Filipino American intertextuality is his attempt to capture the inaugural experience of uprooting and bodily transport of Filipinos to Hawaii and the North American continent. In Bulosan's life history, the itinerary of the peasant/worker-becoming-intellectual unfolds in the womb of the occupying power (the United States) a narrative of collective self-discovery: the traumatic primal scene of deracination is reenacted in the acts of participating in the multiracial workers' fight against U.S. monopoly capital and valorized in interludes of critical reflection (San Juan, *Carlos Bulosan*, 119–43). This solidarity, forged in the popular-democratic crucible of struggling with whites and people of color against a common oppression, stages the condition of possibility for the Filipino writer in exile. In effect, writing becomes for the Filipino diaspora the transitional agency of self-recovery. It facilitates a mediation between the negated past of colonial dependency and a fantasied, even utopian, "America" where people of color exercise their right of self-determination and socialist jus-

tice prevails. Bulosan's historicizing imagination configures the genealogy
of two generations of Filipinos bridging the revolutionary past and the
compromised present, and maps out the passage from the tributary formation of the periphery to the West Coast's "factories in the fields" and canneries in *America Is in the Heart* (hereafter *America*), which cannot be
found in the sentimental memoirs of his compatriots.

History for Bulosan is what is contemporary and prophetic. In "How My
Stories Were Written," he evokes the childhood of Apo Lacay, the folk sage
who inspired his vocation of allegorical remembering chosen during "the
age of great distress and calamity in the land, when the fury of an invading
race impaled their hearts in the tragic cross of slavery and ignorance" (*If
You Want to Know What We Are*, 25). The allusion here is to the scorched-
earth tactics of U.S. pacification forces during the Filipino-American War
and the ruthless suppression of a nascent Filipino national identity—a foreign policy "aberration" in most textbooks, but recently vindicated by Stanley Karnow's apologia, *In Our Image* (1989). In stories like "Be American," in
the quasi-autobiographical *America*, and in his novel, *The Power of the
People*, Bulosan renders in symbolic forms of fabulation how the U.S. conquest exacerbated feudal injustice in the Philippines and accomplished on a
global scale an iniquitous division of international labor that transformed
the United States into a metropolis of industrial modernity and the Philippines into an underdeveloped dependency: a source of cheap raw materials
and manual/mental labor with minimal exchange-value.

Since it is impossible to ignore Bulosan's works in dealing with Filipino
"ethnicity"—recall how his essay "Freedom from Want" (*Saturday Evening
Post*, March 6, 1943), commissioned to illustrate President Roosevelt's "Four
Freedoms" declaration, was subsequently displayed in the Federal Building
in San Francisco—how does the Establishment handle the threat posed by
their radical attack on capitalism? In other words, how is Bulosan sanitized
and packaged to promote pluralist American nationalism? Instead of re-
hearsing all the possible ways, it will be sufficient here to give an example of
a typical recuperative exercise from *The American Kaleidoscope* (1991) by
Professor Lawrence Fuchs:[4]

> The life of Bulosan, a Filipino-American, illustrates the process by which the
> political struggle against injustice and on behalf of equal rights often turned
> immigrants and their children into Americans. . . . Disillusioned, Bulosan
> considered becoming a Communist; at another time, he became a thief. But
> his principal passions were American politics and American literature, and
> these stimulated him to organize the Committee for the Protection of Fili-
> pino Rights, and to start a small school for migrant workers, where "I traced

the growth of democracy in the United States" . . . recalling that his brother
had told him "America is in the hearts of men." . . . When, after months of
illness and debility, he finished his autobiography, he called it *America Is in
the Heart,* using words similar to those of President Roosevelt to Secretary of
War Stimson, "Americanism is simply a matter of the mind and heart," and
those of Justice Douglas, that "loyalty is a matter of the heart and mind."
    . . . Bulosan, the Filipino migrant worker, much more than Dillingham,
the scion of an old New England family, had proved to be a prescient interpreter of American nationalism. Those who had been excluded longest from
membership in the American civic culture had rushed to embrace it once
the barriers were lifted. (237–38)

Earlier, Fuchs paternalistically ascribes to Bulosan the fortune Blacks did
not have of being befriended by a half dozen white women. Somehow
Bulosan was also endowed with the exceptional gift of having access to a secret knowledge denied to other minorities: "When he spoke of the American dream he wrote of his migrant-worker students that 'their eyes glowed
with a new faith . . . they nodded with deep reverence.' . . . Bulosan identified with the experience of the Euro-Americans who had come to this
country as immigrants" (147–48). Shades of Andrew Carnegie, Horatio
Alger, the Godfather? As if that were not enough, Bulosan is lined up with
"Carl Schurz, Mary Antin, and tens of thousands of other self-consciously
Americanizing immigrants" (357). Bulosan is thus appropriated by official
discursive practice to hype a putative "civic culture" of "voluntary pluralism" by occluding the historical specificity of his anti-imperialist politics.
Both his materialist outlook and his paramount commitment to genuine
national sovereignty for the Philippines and to socialism are buried in the
abstraction of a "political struggle against injustice." The strategy of containment here is one of tactical omission, calculated redeployment, selective emphasis, and, more precisely, decontextualization. Its mode of uprooting certain words and phrases from their historical habitat of political
antagonisms recapitulates President McKinley's policy of "benevolent assimilation" and the duplicitous discourse of pacification from William
Howard Taft to the latest scholarship on U.S.-Philippines relations. It can
also be read as a textual analogue to the HSPA's (Hawaiian Sugar Planters'
Association) raid of peasant male bodies from occupied territory from 1906
to 1946. By such ruses of displacement and complicity, Bulosan is recruited
by his enemies, the imperial patriots, who celebrate his romantic naïveté at
the expense of his egalitarian principles and his repudiation of chauvinist-
fascist apartheid founded on wars of conquest and the dehumanization of
people of color.

We would expect a less distorting treatment of Bulosan from the revisionist anthology edited by Paul Lauter et al.: *The Heath Anthology of American Literature*, which was published in 1990. Unfortunately, this textbook disappoints us. Instead of using a more representative segment about migrant workers and socialist activism, the editors select one rather precious, introspective sketch that gives the impression that Bulosan is a neurotic existentialist from the tropics, a brown-skinned Wallace Stevens conjuring verbal fetishes from his head (1841–43). Moreover, Amy Ling's prefatory note (1840–41) compounds the problem by reproducing factual errors and misleading inferences derived from Elaine Kim's *Asian American Literature*. Kim might be chiefly responsible for the defusion of Bulosan's insurrectionary aesthetics, subscribing as she does to the immigrant paradigm of Euro-American success criticized long ago by Robert Blauner and others; for she claims that Bulosan "shares with the Asian goodwill ambassador writers a sustaining desire to win American acceptance" (57). (Because the term "America" denotes a complex overdetermined but not indeterminate relation of peoples and nationalities, I urge that its use should always be qualified, or replaced by other terms.) In spite of her good intentions, Kim's pedestrian conformism disables her from perceiving the deviancy of Bulosan's text. Like Fuchs, she fosters the instrumentalist prejudice that *America* is unilaterally "dedicated to the task of promoting cultural goodwill and understanding"(47), an opinion induced by her completely uncritical endorsement of the patronizing banalities of reviewers (46) and the damaged mentalities of her native informants (47). Indeed, Kim's prophylactic handling of Asian American authors for systemic recuperation and fetishism proceeds from the assumption that ethnic texts are produced by the minds of lonely, disturbed, and suffering immigrants, helpless and lost, but somehow gifted with inner resources capable of transcending their racial oppression and sundry adversities by way of hard work, genius, and luck. At best, in the spirit of a philanthropic liberalism shared by apologists of Anglo missionaries, Kim says that to become part of American society one can always rely on "the urge for good, for the ideal," which is "lodged permanently in the human heart" (51).

Reading (as Fuchs and his ilk practice it) turns out to be an act of violence in more ways than one. What all these reappropriations of Bulosan signify is the power and limits of the hegemonic consensus and its apparatuses to sustain its assimilative but ultimately apartheidlike project to absorb the Asian "Other" into the fold of the unitary hierarchical racial order. In the case of Filipinos settling in the United States, it forgets the original deed of conquest and elides the question, How did Filipinos come to find themselves in (as José Martí puts it) "the belly of the beast"? From a world-system point of view, it is the continuing reproduction of unequal power relations between the Philippines and the United States that is the matrix of the disintegrated Filipino whose subjectivity (more exactly, potential agency) is dispersed in the personae of migrant worker, expatriate intellectual (the major actant in Bienvenido Santos's fiction), cannery or service worker, U.S. Navy steward, and solitary exile. We should remind ourselves that Filipinos first appeared in large numbers in the landscape of an expansive military power not as fugitives (the "Manilamen" of the Louisiana bayous) from eighteenth-century Spanish galleons but as recruited laborers transported by the HSPA.[5] Reinscribed into this context of differential power relations, the Filipino imagination thus acquires its fated vocation of disrupting the economy of "humanist" incorporation by transgressing willy-nilly the boundaries of interdicted times and tabooed spaces.

## Who Represents Whom?

What is at stake is nothing less than the question of Filipino self-representation, of its articulation beyond commodity reification, postmodern narcissism, and paranoia. In lieu of the usual atomistic and hypostatizing view, I submit this principle of world-system linkage (the colony integrally situated as the double of the imperial polity) as the fundamental premise for establishing the conditions of possibility for apprehending Filipino creative expression in the United States. Lacking this cognitive/reconstructive mapping, one succumbs to sectarian fallacies vulnerable to the "divide-and-rule" policy of laissez-faire liberalism.

An instructive case may be adduced here. In their foreword to the anthology *Aiiieeeee!* Oscar Penaranda, Serafin Syquia, and Sam Tagatac fall prey to a separatist adventurism and thus inflict genocide on themselves: "No Filipino-American ('Flip'-born and/or raised in America) has ever published anything about the Filipino-American experience. . . . Only a Filipino-American can write adequately about the Filipino-American experience" (37–54). Writing in the early seventies, a time when Filipinos here born during or after World War II were undergoing the proverbial "identity crisis" in the wake of Third World conscientization movements that swept the whole country, our Flip authors contend that Santos and Bulosan, because of birth, carry "Filipino-oriented minds" whereas "the Filipino born and reared in America writes from an American perspective" (50). What exactly is "an American perspective"? Flawed by a crudely chauvinist empiricism, this position of identifying with the hegemonic order and its transcendent claims, which validates the "exclusively Filipino-American work," becomes supremacist when it dismisses Philippine literature produced in the former colony as inferior, lacking in "soul" (510).[6]

In contrast to this Flip manifesto, the singular virtue of the volume *Letters in Exile* (published two years later) lies in confirming the de-/reconstructive force of the premise of colonial subjugation I propose here. Its archival and countervailing function needs to be stressed. When the Philippine Islands became a U.S. colony at the turn of the century, its inhabitants succeeded the Africans, Mexicans, and American Indians as the "White Man's Burden," the object of "domestic racial imperialism" carried out through brutal pacification and co-optative patronage (Kolko, 41–43, 286–87). The first selection in *Letters in Exile*, "The First Vietnam—The Philippine-American War of 1899–1902," provides the required orientation for understanding the Filipino experience of U.S. racism culminating in the vigilante pogroms of the 1930s. Neither Chinese, Japanese, nor Korean history before World War II contains any comparable scene of such unrestrained unleashing of racial violence by the U.S. military (Vietnam later on exceeds all precedents). Without taking into account the dialogic contestation of American power (mediated in American English) by the Filipino imagination judging its exorbitance and "weak links," the critique of U.S. cultural hegemony worldwide remains incomplete.

Until 1934, when Filipinos legally became aliens as a result of the passage of the Tydings-McDuffie Independence Act, their status was anomalously akin to that of a "floating signifier" with all its dangerous connotations. Wallace Stegner described the breathing of their fatigued bodies at night as "the loneliness breathing like a tired wind over the land" (20). This index of otherness, difference incarnate in the sweat and pain of their labor, is the stigma Filipinos had to bear for a long time. Like it or not, we still signify "the stranger's" birthmark. Only in 1934 did the Filipino "immigrant" (at first limited to fifty) really come into existence; hence neither Bulosan nor Villa were immigrants. Nor were the laborers enraptured by dreams of success who were rigidly bound to contracts. In this context, the hyphenated hybrid called "Filipino-American" becomes quite problematic, concealing the priority of the second term (given the fact of colonial/racial subordination and its hallucinatory internalizations) in what appears as a binary opposition of equals. If the writings of Bulosan and Santos do not represent the authentic Filipino experience, as the Flips self-servingly charge, and such a privilege of "natural" representation belongs only to those born or raised in the U.S. mainland (which excludes territorial possessions), then this genetic legalism only confirms the Flips' delusions of exceptionality. It reinforces "the thoroughly racist and national chauvinist character of U.S. society" (Occeña, 35) by eradicating the rich protean history of Filipino resistance to U.S. aggression and thereby expropriating what little remains for Euro-American legitimation purposes.

By contrasting the polarity of ideological positions in the two texts cited, I intended to demonstrate concretely the dangers of systemic recuperation and the illusion of paranoid separatism. Even before our admission to the canon is granted, as Fuchs shows, the terms of surrender or compromise have already been drawn up for us to sign. Who, then, has the authority to represent the Filipino and her experience? Answers to this question and to the problem of how to define Filipino cultural autonomy and its vernacular idiom cannot be explored unless historical parameters and the totalizing constraints of the world system are acknowledged—that is, unless the specificity of U.S. imperial domination of the Philippines is foregrounded in the account. Since 1898, the production of knowledge of, and ethico-political judgments about, the Filipinos as a people different from others has been monopolized by Euro-American experts like W. Cameron Forbes, Dean Worcester, Joseph Hayden, and others. Consider, for example, H. Brett Melendy's discourse on "Filipinos" in the *Harvard Encyclopedia of American Ethnic Groups,* which offers the standard functional-empiricist explanation for Filipino workers' subservience to the Hawaii plantation system due to their indoctrination "to submission by the barrio political system known as *caciquismo*" (358). Melendy claims that their kinship and alliance system inhibited social adaptation and "militated against their achieving success in American politics" (362). Thus the Filipino becomes a "social problem." Not only does this expert blame the victims' culture, but he also acquits the U.S. state apparatus and its agents of responsibility for deepening class cleavages and instituting that peculiar dependency syndrome that has hitherto characterized U.S.-Philippines cultural exchange.[7]

## From Exile to "Warm Body" Export

One of the first tasks of a decolonizing Filipino critical vernacular is to repudiate the putative rationality of this apologia and replace it with a materialist analysis. I have in mind exploratory inquiries like Bruce Occeña's synoptic overview "The Filipino Nationality in the U.S."[8] Except for patent

economistic inadequacies, Occeña's attempt to delineate the historical, social, and political contours of the Filipino in the United States as a distinct
nationality can be considered a salutary point of departure.[9] According to
Occeña, two basic conditions have decisively affected the development of a
unique Filipino nationality in the United States: first, the continuing oppression of the Filipino nation by U.S. imperialism, and second, the fact
that as a group, "Filipinos have been integrated into U.S. society on the
bases of *inequality* and subjected to discrimination due both to their race
and nationality" (31).[10]

What follows is a broad outline of the sociopolitical tendencies of three
waves of migration needed to clarify the heterogeneous character of the Filipino nationality. The first wave (1906–46) covers 150,000 workers concentrated in Hawaii and California, mostly bachelor sojourners—crippled
"birds of passage"—forced by poverty, ill health, and so on, to settle permanently; the second (1946–64) is comprised of thirty thousand war veterans
and their families, conservative in general because of relative privileges; and
the third (since 1965, about 630,000 from 1965 to 1984) encompasses the
most numerous and complexly stratified group because of the fact that they
have moved at a time when all sectors of Philippine society were undergoing cataclysmic changes. This latest influx harbors nationalist sentiments
that help focus their consciousness on multifaceted struggles at home and
keep alive their hope of returning when and if their life chances improve
(although some will stay). Given the collapse of distances by the greater
scope and frequency of modern communication and travel, linguistic, cultural, and social links of the Filipino diaspora to the islands have been considerably reinforced enough to influence the dynamics of community politics and culture here, a situation "quite different from the previous period
when the Filipino community was in the process of evolving a conspicuously distinct sub-culture which was principally a reflection of their experiences in U.S. society and alien in many ways to the national culture of the
Philippines itself" (Occeña, 38).[11] Contradictory networks of thought and
feeling traverse this substantial segment of the community, problematizing
the evolution of a monolithic "Filipino American" sensibility not fissured
by ambivalence, opportunism, and schizoid loyalties. Recent immigrants
are composed of (1) urban professional strata exhibiting a self-centered
concern for mobility and status via consumerism, and (2) a progressive majority who occupy the lower echelons of the working class exposed to the
worst forms of class, racial, and national oppression. Occeña posits the
prospect that "the life options of many of these Filipino-Americans are

grim—the 'poverty draft' will push them into the front lines of the U.S. war machine or the life of low paid service workers. Consequently, this emerging generation promises to be the most thoroughly proletarianized section of the third wave" (41) and thus ripe for mobilization.

Although I think the last inference is mechanical and does not allow for the impact of changing political alignments, ideological mutations, and other contingencies in the "New World Order" of late "disorganized" capitalism, Occeña's emphasis on the unifying pressure of racial and national marginalization serves to rectify the narcosis of identity politics that posits a mystifying "Filipino American" essence. In addition, a focus on the overlay and coalescence of the key sociological features of the three waves in the extended family networks should modify the schematic partitioning of this survey and intimate a more dynamic, hospitable milieu within which Filipino heterogeneity can be further enhanced and profiled.

It becomes clear now why, given these nomadic and deterritorializing circuits of exchange between the (in our reinterpretation) fertilizing margin and parasitic center, the use of the rubric "Filipino American" can be sectarian and thus susceptible to hegemonic disarticulation. Should we then bracket "American" (not reducible to heart or mind) in this moment of analysis, mimicking the antimiscegenation law of the thirties?

Oscar Campomanes has tried to resolve the predicament of the intractable nature of Filipino subjectivity (I hesitate to use "subject position" here because it may suggest a shifting monad, a disposable lifestyle unanchored to specific times and places) by postulating three historical moments: colonial generation, ethnic identity politics, and political expatriation. Given the global constellation of forces I have drawn earlier, Campomanes hopes to synthesize multiple literary productions by subsuming it in the phenomenology of exile:

> Motifs of departure, nostalgia, incompletion, rootlessness, leave-taking, and dispossession recur with such force in most writing produced by Filipinos in the U.S. and Filipino Americans, with the Philippines as always either the original or terminal reference point. Rather than the U.S. as the locus of claims or "the promised land" that Werner Sollors argues is the typological trope of "ethnic American writing," the Filipino case represents a reverse telos, an opposite movement. It is on this basis that I argue for a literature of exile and emergence rather than a literature of immigration and settlement whereby life in the U.S. serves as the space for displacement, suspension, and perspective. "Exile" becomes a necessary, if inescapable, state for Filipinos in the United States—at once susceptible to the vagaries of the (neo)colonial U.S.-Philippine relationship and redeemable only by its radical restructuring. (5)

This approach is provocative, inviting us on one hand to test the validity of Edward Said's conceptualization of exile as a reconstitution of national identity (359) and, on the other, to contextualize Julia Kristeva's psychoanalysis of every subject as estranged, the "improper" Other as our impossible "own and proper" (191–95). But how does this protect us from the internal colonialism at work in High Culture's idealizing of the worldwide division of mental/manual labor?

Although Campomanes does foreground the fact of dependency and its libidinal investment in an archetypal pattern of exile and redemptive return, he indiscriminately lumps together migrant workers, sojourners, expatriates, pseudo-exiles, refugees, émigrés, and opportunists at the expense of nuanced and creative tensions among them.[12] The hypothesis of exile is heuristic and catalyzing, but it fails to discriminate the gap between Bulosan's radical project of solidarity of people of color against capital and the integrationist "melting pot" tendencies that vitiate the works of N. V. M. Gonzalez, Bienvenido Santos, and Linda Ty-Casper. Subjugation of one's nationality cannot be divorced from subordination by racial and class stigmatizing; only Bulosan and some Flip writers are able to grapple with and sublate this complex dialectics of Filipino subalternity and bureaucratic closure. In a typical story, "The Long Harvest," Gonzalez easily cures the incipient anomie of his protagonist by making him recollect the primal scene of his mother suturing his narcissism with artisanal commodity production at home (28). As long as those sublimating images of an archaic economy survive, the petit bourgeois expatriate can always resort to a conciliatory, accommodationist therapy of mythmaking and need never worry about class exploitation, racism, and national oppression.[13]

This is the caveat I would interpose. Unless the paradigm of exile is articulated with the global division of labor under the diktat of U.S. finance capital (via IMF-World Bank, United Nations, private foundations), it simply becomes a mock-surrogate of the "lost generation" avant-garde and a pretext for elite ethnocentrism. The intellectual of color can even wantonly indenture himself to the cult of exile à la Joyce or Nabokov. Bulosan also faced this tempting dilemma: stories like "Life and Death of a Filipino in the USA" and "Homecoming" (San Juan, *Bulosan,* 25–30, 105–11) refuse commodity fetishism by fantasizing a return to a healing home, a seductive catharsis indeed: "Everywhere I roam [in the United States] I listen for my native language with a crying heart because it means my roots in this faraway soil; it means my only communication with the living and those who died without a gift of expression" ("Writings," 153–54). But he counters this nostalgic detour, this cheap Proustian fix, by reminding himself of his vocation and its commitment to the return of symbolic capital expropriated from his people:

> I am sick again. I know I will be here [Firland Sanitarium, Seattle, Washington] for a long time. And the grass hut where I was born is gone, and the village of Mangusmana is gone, and my father and his one hectare of land are gone, too. And the palm-leaf house in Binalonan is gone, and two brothers and a sister are gone forever.
>
> But what does it matter to me? The question is—what impelled me to write? The answer is—my grand dream of equality among men and freedom for all. To give a literate voice to the voiceless one hundred thousand Filipinos in the United States, Hawaii, and Alaska. Above all and ultimately, to translate the desires and aspirations of the whole Filipino people in the Philippines and abroad in terms relevant to contemporary history. Yes, I have taken unto myself this sole responsibility. (Kunitz, 145)

Bulosan's transplantation from the empire's hinterland to the agribusiness enclaves of the West Coast coincides with his transvaluative mapping of the future—not the "America" of corporate business—as the space of everyone's desire and emancipated but still embodied psyche (San Juan, *Toward a People's Literature,* 119–43; "Beyond Identity Politics," 556–58). When the patriarchal family disintegrates, the narrator of *America* (unlike Melendy's "Filipino") discovers connections with Chicano and Mexican workers, finds allies among white middle-class women, and taps the carnivalesque life energies of folklore in *The Laughter of My Father,* Bulosan's satire of a money-obsessed society. He encounters the submerged genius loci of anti-imperialist solidarity in gambling houses, cabarets, labor barracks—sites of loss, excess, and expenditure that found a new social bond; points of escape that circumscribe the power of the American "dream" of affluence. Bulosan's strategy of displacement anticipates the insight that "a society or any collective arrangement is defined first by its points or flows of deterritorialization" (Deleuze and Guattari, *A Thousand Plateaus,* 220), by jump cuts, syncopations, and scrambling of positions.

Borderlines, of course, include by excluding. It might be surmised that when the conclusion of *America* reaffirms the narrator's faith in "our unfinished dream"—an "America" diametrically opposed to the nightmares of history that comprise the verisimilitude of quotidian existence—Bulosan suppresses history. One might suspect that he infiltrates into it a "jargon of authenticity" and forces art to fulfill a compensatory function of healing the divided subject. David Palumbo-Liu cogently puts the case against this kind of closure in ethnic textuality as capitulation to, and recapitalization of, the dominant ideology: "In ethnic narrative, the transcendence of the material via an identification with the fictional representation of lived life often suppresses the question of the political constitution of subjectivity, both within and without the literary text, opting instead for a kind of redemption that short-circuits such questions" (4). But, as Marilyn Alquizola has shown, a probing of *America*'s structure will disclose an ironic counterpointing of voices or masks, with numerous didactic passages and exempla critical of the system undercutting the naive professions of faith so as to compel the reader to judge that "the totality of the book's contents contradict the protagonist's affirmation of America in the conclusion" (216). Beyond this formalist gloss, an oppositional reading would frame the logic of the narrator's structuring scheme with two influences: first, the routine practice of authors submitting to the publisher's market analysis of audience reception (wartime propaganda enhances a book's salability) and, second, the convention of the romance genre in Philippine popular culture, which warrants such a formulaic closure. Further metacommentary on the subtext underlying *America*'s mix of naturalism and humanist rhetoric would elicit its Popular Front politics as well as its affinity with Bulosan's massive indictment of capital in "My Education," in the 1952 International Longshore and Warehousemen's Union *Yearbook* editorial, and in numerous letters, all of which belie his imputed role of servicing the behemoth of American nationalism. Ultimately, we are confronted once again with the masks of the bifurcated subject disseminated in the text, traces of his wandering through perilous contested terrain. Forgotten after his transitory success in 1944 with *The Laughter of My Father*, Bulosan remained virtually unknown until 1973 when the University of Washington Press, convinced of Bulosan's marketability and impressed by the activism of Filipino American groups opposed to the "U.S.-Marcos dictatorship," reissued *America*. My current acquaintance with the Filipino community, however, confirms Bulosan's lapse into near oblivion and the unlikelihood of the Establishment's initiating a retrieval to shore up the ruins of the "model minority" myth. This immunity to canonization, notwithstanding the possibility that the fractured discourse of *America* can lend itself to normalization by disciplinary regimes, is absent in the works of Bienvenido Santos, whose narratives cultivate a more commodifiable topos: the charm and hubris of victimage.

Santos's imagination is attuned to an easy purchase on the hurts, alienation, and defeatism of *pensionados,* expatriated *ilustrados,* petit bourgeois males marooned during World War II in the East Coast and Midwest, and other third-wave derelicts. His pervasive theme is the reconciliation of the Filipino psyche with the status quo.[14] Since I have commented elsewhere on Santos's achievement (*Toward a People's Literature*, 171–73; *Crisis in the Philippines*, 182–83), suffice it to note here its power of communicating the pathos of an obsolescent humanism such as that exemplified by David Hsin-Fu Wand's celebration of the universal appeal of ethnic writing, its rendering of "the human condition of the outsider, the marginal man, the pariah" (9) in his Introduction to *Asian American Heritage*. The patronage of the American New Critic Leonard Casper might be able to guarantee Santos's efficacy in recycling the ethnic myth of renewal, the born-again syndrome that is the foundational site of the hegemonic American identity. Casper's technique of assimilation differs from Fuchs's in its reactionary essentialism. Bewailing Filipino society's alleged loss of "agrarian ideals that guaranteed cultural uniformity and stability" (xiv), a loss that supposedly aggravates the traumatic impact of the "America of individualism" on poor tribal psyches, Casper superimposes his antebellum standard on his client: Santos is "offering an essentially timeless view of culture, which transcends history limited to the linear, the consecutive, and the one-dimensional" (xv). But read against the grain, Santos's *Scent of Apples*, and possibly his two novels set in San Francisco and Chicago, derive their value from being rooted in a distinctive historical epoch of Filipino dispossession. As symptomatic testimonies of the deracinated neocolonized subject, they function as arenas for ideological neutralization and compromise, presenting serious obstacles to any salvaging operation and any effort to thwart recuperation because they afford what Brecht calls "culinary" pleasure, a redaction of the native's exotic susceptibilities for tourist consumption and patronage.

So far we have seen how Fuchs's extortive neoliberalism can hijack the transgressive speech of Bulosan into the camp of "American nationalism" (!) and how Casper's paternalistic chauvinism can shepherd Santos up to the threshold of the Western manor of polite letters. Appropriated thus, our authors do not really pose any threat to the elite proprietorship of administered learning. Does that apply to Villa, the avant-garde heretic now *desaparecido*, who once scandalized the colony's philistines?

## Jose Garcia Villa: Masks and Legerdemain

When Villa arrived in the United States in 1930, he was already acclaimed as a modernist master by his contemporaries, a stature further reinforced when his two books of experimental and highly mannered poems, *Have*

*Come Am Here* (1942) and *Volume Two* (1949), came out and earned praise from the leading mandarins in the Anglo-American literary establishment, among them Edith Sitwell, Marianne Moore, e.e. cummings, Richard Eberhart, and Mark Van Doren. His poems were then anthologized by Selden Rodman, Conrad Aiken, and W. H. Auden (though, as far as I know, no textbook of American literature has included Villa). He has received numerous prizes, including the American Academy of Arts and Letters Award and the Shelley Memorial Award; he was nominated for the Pulitzer Prize in 1943. Villa claims that he was denied a Bollingen Prize because he was not an American citizen. On June 12, 1973, the Marcos government bestowed on Villa its highest honor, "National Artist of the Philippines." After the publication of his *Selected Poems and New* in 1958, however, Villa immediately sank into obscurity—an enigmatic disappearance that can be plausibly explained (apart from rapid changes in taste and fashion) by the immense reifying and integrative power of mass consumer society to flatten out diverse or antithetical visions and philosophies.[15]

Villa had no problems being hailed as an "American" poet by the celebrities mentioned earlier, including the editor of *Twentieth Century Authors*, Stanley Kunitz. For this reference guide, Villa confessed the reason why his poems were "abstract" and lacked feeling for detail and particularity:

> I am not at all interested in description or outward appearance, nor in the contemporary scene, but in *essence*. A single motive underlies all my work and defines my intention as a serious artist: The search for the metaphysical meaning of man's life in the Universe—the finding of man's selfhood and identity in the mystery of Creation. I use the term *metaphysical* to denote the ethic-philosophic force behind all essential living. The development and unification of the human personality I consider the highest achievement a man can do. (Kunitz, 1035–36)

Thirty years later, Werner Sollors tries to smuggle Villa back into the limelight by focusing on the poet's reactive idiosyncracy, not his metaphysical selfhood, that substantiates the myth of U.S. exceptionalism in which the languages of consent (to assimilation) and descent collaborate to Americanize almost any immigrant. Villa's indeterminate status in the United States motivated his fabrication of a new poetic language of "reversed consonance" (Sollors, 253–54). Positing the imperative of syncretic belonging, Sollors's pastiche of ethnic genealogy thoroughly cancels out Villa's descent. Meanwhile S. E. Solberg "naturalizes" Villa and so annuls Filipino collective self-determination, labeling the poet's spiritual quest a "personal and idiosyncratic fable, a protean version of the 'making of Americans'" (54).

Elsewhere I have argued that Villa's poems can be properly appraised as "the subjective expression of a social antagonism," which constitutes the originality of the lyric genre (Adorno, 376; San Juan, *Reading the West*). What preoccupies Villa is the phenomenology of dispossession or lack in general, a malaise that translates into the double loss of the poet's traditional social function and audience when exile overtakes the Filipino artist. What is staged in Villa's texts are scenarios for overcoming the loss by the discovery and ratification of the imagination as a demiurgic logos expressing the poet's godhood, a process that also reciprocally evokes the forces of alienation and reification the poet is wrestling with; in short, both the reality-effect and the domination-effect (Balibar and Macherey, 91–97) are fused in the grammar of poetic enunciation. Such contradictions, pivoting around the themes of revolt against patriarchal power, psychomachia, negativity, and bodily uprooting, elude the neocolonizing maneuvers of Villa's critics and the parodic mimicry of his epigones.

It is not too much, I think, to suggest that Villa has refused the "ethnic" trap by challenging imperial authority to recognize his authentic artist-self and so validate his equal standing with his white peers. But this also spelled his premature redundancy, since reconciliation via aestheticism is nothing but the hegemonic alternative of healing the split subject in a transcendental restoration of plenitude of meaning. We can observe this in the way the crisis of exile, rendered as metonymic displacement in "Wings and Blue Flame: A Trilogy" and "Young Writer in a New Country" (in *Footnote to Youth*), is dissolved by metaphoric sublimation: in his visionary re-presentation of the primal loss (exile as castration; expulsion by the father), the antinomic discourses of place, body, inheritance, and need converge in the self-exiled native's being reborn in the desert of New Mexico, where the oedipal trauma (the loss of the mother's/*patria*'s body) is exorcised by a transcendent trope of the imagination. Art, then, functions as the resolution of the conflict between solitary ego and community, unconscious drives and the fixated body, symbolic exchange and the imaginary fetish, between subjugated people and despotic conqueror.

In his sympathetic introduction to Villa's stories, Edward J. O'Brien intuits a "Filipino sense of race" or "race consciousness" embedded in the text, but this consciousness swiftly evaporates in the "severe and stark landscape of New Mexico" (Villa, 3). Such a gesture of alluding to difference acquires a portentous modality when Babette Deutsch, again with the best of intentions, apprehends something anomalous in Villa's situation only to normalize it as strange: "The fact that he is a native of the Philippines who comes to the English language as a stranger may have helped him to his unusual syntax" (56). But the stigmata of the alien is no hindrance to Villa's creation of "luminous and vibrant" poems "concerned with ultimate things," a sacrificial rite whose antiutilitarian telos may not be so easily instrumentalized as Bulosan's idealism for the sake of vindicating the ethos of the pluralist market. Even if difference as plurality is granted, it is only at the expense of its subsumption in the sameness/identity of the artist, whose self-contained artifices, predicated on the organic reconciliation of ego and alter, transcend the exigencies of race, nationality, class, gender, and all other segmentations integral to profit accumulation in the planetary domain of the late bourgeoisie.

At this juncture, the quest for Filipino self-representation reaches an impasse. Villa's "abject" response to the world of commodities and the cash nexus combines both acquiescence and nausea, given our hypothesis that the lyric form harbors social antagonisms and yields both reality- and domination-effects. His work might be read as a highly mediated reflection of the vicissitudes of the conscienticized Filipino who is driven from the homeland by economic crisis, alternatively nostalgic and repelled, unable to accommodate himself to his new environment. Villa's "disappearance" is but one episode in the allegory of the Filipinos' pre-postcolonial ethnogenesis. The group's persistently reproduced subordination arises from its belief that it owes gratitude for being given an entry visa, and that by imitating the successful models of Asians and other immigrants who made their fortune, it will gradually be accepted as an equal; at the same time, it cherishes the belief that it originated from a distinct sovereign nation enjoying parity with the United States. To salvage Villa, we have to read his work symptomatically for those absent causes that constitute its condition of possibility, even as those very same ruptures and silences betray the manifold contradictions that define the "American civic" consensus. Villa's agenda is integration of the personality, ours the reinscription of our subject-ion in the revolutionary struggle to forge an independent, self-reliant Philippines and in the resistance of people of color everywhere to the violence of white supremacy.

## From Totem Worshipers to Dogeaters and Other Nomads

In this emancipatory project to build the scaffolding of our cultural tradition, we can learn how to safeguard ourselves from the danger of reclamation by a strategy of retrospective mapping (performed in the preceding sections) and anticipatory critique. To advance the latter, I comment on two modes of narrating Filipino self-identification: Jessica Hagedorn's *Dogeaters* and Fred Cordova's *Filipinos: Forgotten Asian Americans.*

Conflating heresy and orthodoxy, Hagedorn's novel possesses the qualities of a canonical text in the making—for the multiculturati. It unfolds the crisis of U.S. hegemony in the Philippines through a collage of character types embodying the corruption of the Americanizing oligarchic elite (see San Juan, "Mapping the Boundaries," 125–26). In trying to extract some intelligible meaning out of the fragmentation of the comprador-patriarchal order that sacrifices everything to acquisitive lust, she resorts to pastiche, aleatory montage of diverse styles, clichés, ersatz rituals, hyperreal hallucinations—a parodic bricolage of Western high postmodernism—whose cumulative force blunts whatever satire or criticism is embedded in her character portrayals and authorial intrusions. This narrative machine converts the concluding prayer of exorcism and ressentiment into a gesture of stylized protest. Addressed mainly to a cosmopolitan audience, Hagedorn's trendy work is undermined by postmodern irony: it lends itself easily to consumer liberalism's drive to sublimate everything (dreams, eros, New People's Army, feminism, anarchist dissent) into an ensemble of self-gratifying spectacles. At best, *Dogeaters* measures the distance between the partisanship of Bulosan's peasants-become-organic intellectuals and the pseudo-yuppie lifestyles of recent arrivals. As a safe substitute for Bulosan and as one of the few practitioners of Third World/feminine "magic realism," Hagedorn may easily be the next season's pick for the Establishment celebration of its multicultural canon.[16]

Examining Cordova's photographic montage, we encounter again our otherness as "fertilizer" and "little brown brother." We discern here a symptom of the conflicted subaltern compensating for his lack by impressing the public with an overwhelming multiplicity of images of family/communal togetherness, simulacra of smiles and gestures that animate the rituals of the life cycle and whose repetition seems enough to generate illusions of successful adjustment and progress. Filipinos turn out to be "first" on many occasions. Despite the negative witness of parts of the commentary, the surface texture of those images serves to neutralize the stark evidence of a single photo (on page 42) that captured stooping, faceless workers caught in the grid of a bleak imprisoning landscape. Nothing is mentioned of why or how these alien bodies were transported and smuggled in. What is suppressed here can be gleaned from a comparable though abbreviated photographic discourse, *Pearls* (Bock, 38–47). Its section "Pinoy" offers an apologetic history and the usual documentary exhibits of Filipinos adapting to their new habitat, but the inclusion of newspaper cutouts headlining anti-Filipino riots serves to demystify the ideology of adjustment and compromise that informs officially funded enterprises such as Cordova's.[17] *Pearls* records a vestigial trace, a lingering effect, of what *Letters in Exile* strove to accomplish: a reconstruction of the historical conditions of possibility of the Filipino presence in the metropolis and their struggle to affirm their humanity by acts of refusal, solidarity, and remembering.[18]

The Marcos dictatorship interlude (1972–86) in Philippine history, which brought a flood of exiles and pseudorefugees to the United States at the same time that Washington amplified its military and economic aid to the national security state, has foregrounded again the reality of U.S. domination of the homeland that distinguishes the Filipino nationality from other minorities. Our neocolonial stigmata renews the signifiers of difference.[19] I reiterate my thesis that the creation of the vernacular résumé of the Filipino's experience of limits and possibilities here can only be theorized within the process of comprehending the concrete historical particularity of their incorporation in the U.S. empire and the ecology of this unequal exchange.

In the context of recent demography, Bulosan seems to be a "rural" misfit. The transplantation of recent Filipino immigrants to the urban wilderness of Los Angeles, San Francisco, Seattle, Chicago, and New York City has impelled young writers to conjecture the emergence of an "urbane" sensibility, adoptive and adaptive at the same time, born from the clash of cultures and memories. The trajectory of the proletarian imagination from Hawaii's plantations to California's Imperial Valley to Washington's Yakima Valley no longer crosses the paths of "dogeaters" and "Flips." Recent subaltern anxiety, however, seeks legitimacy from the universal archetypes found in archaic folklore and myth—an ironic aporia, indeed. How can this recover from the "backwaters" the writings of Serafin Malay Syquia, for example? And how can it valorize the paradigm of the *sakada*'s redemptive agon in *Istorya ni Bonipasyo: Kasla Gloria Ti Hawaii* for its lessons of inventing "history from below"?[20]

Only disconnect and recontextualize—that's our motto. What makes such disparate events as Fermin Tobera's killing in 1930 and the murder of Domingo and Viernes in 1981 the condensed turning points of the Filipino odyssey in the United States?[21] You have to conceive of both occurring in the space of the heterogeneous Other occupied by U.S. "civilizing" power. While the texts of the nationality's autochthonous tradition are interred in the imperial archive that cries for inventory and critique—I am thinking of the oral histories of the "Manongs"; interviews of veterans of union organizing; testimonies in letters and journals of immigrant passage; reportage and videofilms of various struggles, such as that over the International Hotel in San Francisco; and other nonverbal signifying practices—unfortunately there are few discerning and astute commentaries or informed reflections on these circumstantial texts. We need to disconnect them from the hegemonic episteme of Fuchs and Melendy, contextualize them in the resistance narrative of peasants and workers, and then reconfigure them in the punctual lived experiences of Filipinos today. Therefore I consider the production of transformative critical discourse a priority in the task of identifying, generating, and selecting the anticanon[22] of Filipino agency and praxis that in varying degrees have resisted co-optation and incorporation. Toward realizing this agenda of searching for our "representative" speech, I propose Bulosan's corpus of writings as central touchstone and researches like *Philip Vera Cruz: A Personal History of Filipino Immigration and the Farmworkers Movement* (Scharlin and Villanueva) as crucial linkages between popular memory and individualist dissidence. In this syllabus, we include Santos's and Gonzalez's fiction on the diaspora as loci for renegotiation, together with Villa's entire production as salvageable for counterhegemonic rearticulation in spite of his status as a legendary classic. Meanwhile, the prodigious creativity of a "third-wave" generation—among them Jessica Hagedorn, Marianne Villanueva, Michelle Cruz Skinner, the Flips, Peter Bacho, and many more who participated in the annual exodus from the Philippines in the last decade—remains a reservoir of practices for future hermeneutic appraisal and reader/writer empowerment.

To accomplish this project of discovery, rescue, and affirmation of Filipino agency against recolonizing strategies from above, we need a radical transformation of grassroots consciousness and practice, a goal addressed by Marina Feleo-Gonzalez's playbook, *A Song for Manong*. What is at stake here is a recovery of the inaugural scene of Filipino subject-ification and insurgency as a dialectical process. We find this event dramatized here when the script unfolds the figure of Pedro Calosa, a leader of the Tayug uprising in Pangasinan from whose milieu of sedition and dissidence Bulosan emerged, as one who learned the craft of resistance from the Hawaii interethnic strikes of the twenties. Feleo-Gonzalez chooses to circumvent any easy return to a pristine homeland by concluding the performance with the solidarity-in-action of Euro-Americans and Third World peoples in the campaign to preserve the site of the International Hotel from corporate modernization.[23] Feleo-Gonzalez's intervention reawakens the community's conscience and redeems its "collective assemblage of enunciation" (to use Deleuze and Guattari's phrase) from the fate of recoding by the celebrated "melting pot" religion.

One such assemblage is Manuel Buaken's neglected book *I Have Lived with the American People*. Indeed, Buaken returns to haunt us with the lesson that no fable of dredging up a coherent and synchronized identity through memory alone, no privileging of the therapeutic power of art, no sacred ceremony of reminiscence by itself can cement together the fragments of our uprooting from the ravished homeland and repair the tragic disintegration of the nation's spirit. In the breakdown of Buaken's "goodwill autobiography" as a teleological fable, we find a counterpointing discourse: our quest for linkage and autonomy encounters the testimonies of such early migrants as Francisco Abra (117–20) and Felipe Cabellon (121–24) soliciting empathy and justice, interrupting our pursuit of wholeness. With the Filipino nationality in the United States still mind-manacled and the islands convulsed in the fire of people's war for liberation, the practice of writing by, of, and for Filipinos in the United States remains nomadic, transitional, hybrid, metamorphic, discordant, beleaguered, embattled, "always already" in abeyance. Such a genre of "minor" writing, which I define as a praxis of becoming-what-is-other-for-itself, is (to quote Deleuze and Guattari) "the revolutionary force for all literature."

## Notes

1. Takaki, *From Different Shores*, 4.
2. Takaki, *Strangers*, 324.
3. Eric Chock, another name listed by Amy Ling, identifies himself as a Hawaiian writer and resident (Ruoff and Ward, 362). The Filipinos in Hawaii, condemned to almost castelike conditions, constitute a community significantly different from Filipinos on the mainland. For a survey of the writing by Hawaiian Ilocanos, see Somera.
4. Aside from having served as director of the Peace Corps in the Philippines (1961–63), Fuchs was executive director of the Select Commission on Immigration and Refugee Policy under President Carter. Another mode of recuperation is exemplified by Stanley, who insists on the "relatively libertarian character of U.S. rule" (4).
5. In 1946, six thousand Filipino workers were imported to Hawaii to counter the industrywide strike—proof once more that the Philippines is an "inside" factor in the U.S. imperial polity (Philippine Center, 6).
To the early contingents of Filipino workers belong the honor of spearheading the first and most resolute labor militancy in Hawaii in modern U.S. history. According to Sucheng Chan, after the 1882 Chinese Exclusion Act and the Gentleman's Agreement of 1907 limiting the entry of Japanese labor, Filipinos became the predominant agricultural labor force in Hawaii: "Not surprisingly, they became the main Asian immigrant group to engage in labor militancy."

Moreover, as Beechert has noted, they did so in politically repressive environments with crim-inal syndicalist laws" (87). Although Bulosan does not claim to describe, for instance, the epic strikes of 1924 in Hawaii's Hanapepe plantation and of 1937 in Puunene, the scenes of union organizing and strikes in *America* function as an allegorical emblem of all such instances of the sporadic or organized resistance of masses of people of color. Bulosan's life covers four major episodes in the Filipino workers' history: the action of the Agricultural Workers Industrial Union-Trade Union Unity League in 1930, the formation of the Filipino Labor Union in 1933, the affiliation of the Alaska Cannery Workers Union with the CIO in 1937, and the establish-ment of the Filipino Agricultural Workers Association in 1939.

In the late thirties, 25 percent of Filipinos were service workers, 9 percent were in the salmon canneries, and 60 percent in agriculture (Takaki, *Strangers*, 316–18; Catholic Insti-tute, 36).

6. Aside from Sam Tagatac's experimental "The New Anak" (Penaranda's "Dark Fiesta" deals with native rituals and folk beliefs in the Philippines), the Flips will only include the Flip poets—some of those in *Without Names* (Ancheta et al.) and some in Bruchac's collection. I will not repeat here the bibliographic data of Filipino American authors found in Cheung and Yogi's excellent reference guide.

In fairness to the Flips, I should state here that Serafin Malay Syquia's poems and his essay "Politics and Poetry" (Navarro, 87–89) represent a crucial intervention that seeks to reclaim an "America" reconstituted by people of color. At a time when leaders of the community were re-jecting Bulosan's socialist vision and the legacy of the Manongs, Syquia and his comrades were striving to reconnect via their ethnic rebellion with the insurgency in the neocolony—an emancipatory project of opening up the space prematurely closed by Santos's conciliatory ac-ceptance of the status quo, Gonzalez's myths of restoration, and Villa's patrician withdrawal.

7. I take issue with the bias of functionalist, positivist social science in my book *Racial Formations/Critical Transformations*. The assimilationist doctrine of the ethnic paradigm, with its ahistorical empiricism, has vitiated practically most studies of the Filipino community in the United States. Typical is Pido's *Pilipinos in America*, littered with such blanket pronounce-ments as "Pilipinos fear alienation" (35). Far more insightful are articles such as Aurora Fer-nandez, "Pilipino Immigrants," *East Wind* (fall–winter 1982): 34–36, and Teresita Urian (writ-ten by Mila de Guzman), "Into the Light," *Katipunan* 4.7 (October 1991): 10–11.

8. Occeña's pioneering effort can be supplemented and corrected by regional studies made by Barbara Posadas, Ruben Alcantara, Edwin Almirol, Antonio Pido, and original archi-val work now being done by Campomanes and others.

9. Although the term "Asian American" as an operational bureaucratic designation is misleading because of the now widely disparate historical experiences of the groups concerned and tends to covertly privilege one or two of its elements (as in the Modern Language Associ-ation surveys cited earlier), Occeña points out that the self-recognition and societal recogni-tion of the peoples involved stem from their integration into U.S. society "on the bases of in-equality vis-à-vis whites; subjected to various forms of racial and national discrimination and constituted as an oppressed strata of U.S. society" (29). However, because the Asian and Pacific peoples, from their arrival up to the present, have not amalgamated to form one distinct na-tionality, it is best to discard the label "Asian American" and use the particular names of each nationality to forestall homogenizing ascriptions like "superminority."

10. Until 1946, Filipinos did not have the right to be naturalized. Nor could they marry whites in California until 1948 or own land until 1956 (Philippine Center, 8–9, 15–16).

11. This trend is discernible in the Flips statement of identity politics. The Flips mainly de-scend from the relatively conservative formation of the second wave of Filipino immigrants (about thirty thousand) comprised of war veterans enjoying some privileges (Catholic Insti-tute, 41–42). Their code words registering anxiety toward "melting pot" miscegenation are

found in phrases like "cathartic stage of ethnic awareness" and "maintaining ethnic awareness." But by juxtaposing inside/outside, they replicate what they want to negate: including the Same/excluding the Other.

12. Although Solberg is correct in pointing out the interdependence of Filipino American writing and indigenous Filipino writing in English, his ascription of a mythmaking function to Bulosan and others (which explains, for instance, Buaken's failure to produce a unified narrative out of his own fragmented life) is misleading since the myth's regime of truth turns out to be a discourse of co-optation as "the Filipino dream of independence fades into the American dream of equality and freedom" (56).

13. Gonzalez's subaltern mentality typically contrives an apologia for the Cordova volume (xi) when he cites the white master's endorsement of his servant: "My servant was a Manilla man." In this way the stereotype of Filipinos in the thirties as "wonderful servants" (Takaki, *Strangers*, 317) is repeated and reinforced.

14. To illumine the deceptive stoicism of Santos's closure in his stories "The Day the Dancers Came" or "Scent of Apples," it would be instructive to compare the ending of J. C. Dionisio's "Cannery Episode" (413), where the narrator captures the discipline and strength of the "Alaskeros" on the face of a horrible mutilation of one of their compatriots. We also find in Pete's character (reflected by the choric narrator) an embodiment of revolt against the inhumane system, a subject position typically absent in Santos's and Gonzalez's fiction.

15. Elaine Kim dismisses Villa as nonethnic (288). Bulosan's judgment of Villa reflects my own earlier polemical evaluation (*Toward a People's Literature*, 73–76). For Bulosan, Villa "is somewhat in line with Baudelaire and Rimbaud, for these two appeared when French poetry had already reached its vortex and was on the downgrade. Naturally they were great apostles of the poetry of decay. When we speak of literature as a continuous tradition, a growing cultural movement, Villa is out of place and time." Villa does not represent "the growth of our literature"; rather he "expresses a declining culture after it has reached its height" ("Writings," 151).

16. Here I approximate the first mode of incorporation via commodity form that Hebdige outlines (94–96); the ideological mode of incorporation I exemplify in my remarks on Bulosan, Santos, and Villa.

17. Only two out of over two hundred photos depict Filipinos on strike (pages 76 and 81). Most are photos of families and relatives of the editor and the kin-related staff of the Demonstration Project. If one compares the text of the section "Alaska Canneries" with a contemporary account of the dismal conditions by Emeterio Cruz, one will notice the textual and iconographic techniques of neutralization and obfuscation deployed by Cordova's album, whose cutoff point is 1963, a revealing date that marks the initiation of radical activism in the Filipino community. In featuring Hilario Moncado (183), Cordova commits an act of partiality and censorship—one of many—when he fails to mention Moncado's notorious opposition to Filipino workers' demands for justice (Chan, 76, 89).

Cordova's inadequacies include his false generalizations on religion (167) and his eulogy for one million Filipinos who died during World War II for the sake of "Americanism" (221). But these amateurish mistakes descend to unwitting racism when he lumps together inter alia Lincoln, the Lone Ranger, Superman, Charlie Chan, and Martin Luther King Jr. (230).

A similar reservation can be made of otherwise instructive documentaries like *In No One's Shadow* where the cinematic sequence focuses on the normal adjustment of the Filipino immigrant despite all odds. This selective method of fetishizing individual success stories conceals the insitutional structures and historical contingencies that qualified and limited such individual lives. The ideology of the image and its system of verisimilitude need to be elucidated and criticized as a determining apparatus producing a deformed Filipino subjectivity ripe for hegemonic reproduction.

18. A modest attempt has been made by the Philippine Center for Immigrant Rights in New York City to revive the example of *Letters in Exile* with the publication of its pamphlet *Filipinos in the USA*. But no major initiative has been taken to organize the Filipino community on the basis of its nationality and its unique response to continuing U.S. domination since the demise of various socialist formations with Filipino leadership in the 1980s.

19. Except for Puerto Ricans. In another essay I argue that the cultural history of the United States cannot be fully inventoried and assayed without registering the symptomatic absence in it of Filipinos and Puerto Ricans as colonized subjects. Operating in the field of American English, the Filipino interruption of U.S. monologism is unique insofar as it demarcates the limits of the imperial episteme, its canonical inscriptions, and its reflexive frame of reference.

20. A play directed by Behn Cervantes, who adapted materials from Virgilio Felipe's M.A. thesis, "What You Like to Know: An Oral History of Bonipasyo," presented in Hawaii in late 1991. The assimilationist rationale for this event may be perceived from this statement in the program notes: "The Hawaii [the chief protagonist] was lured to as 'paradise' seems harsh and full of hardships, but is compensated for by Bonipasyo's rightful pride in the conviction that his toil and sacrifice made Hawaii." Whose Hawaii?

21. Fermin Tobera, a twenty-two-year old worker, was killed during the anti-Filipino riot in Watsonville, California, on January 22, 1930; his body was interred in the Philippines on February 2, marked as "National Humiliation Day" (Quinsaat, 55, 57; for a contemporary estimate of the Watsonville situation, see Buaken, 97–107). Silme Domingo and Gene Viernes were anti-Marcos union activists and officials of the International Longshore and Warehousemen's Union, Local 37, in Seattle, Washington, whose 1952 *Yearbook* Bulosan edited. They were slain on June 1, 1981, by killers hired by pro-Marcos elements and corrupt union operatives. Union sympathizers alleged that the FBI and the CIA were involved in this affair.

22. By "anticanon," I mean a mode of resisting standardization by the dominant Euro-American ideology and by the conservative aura of a comprador-bourgeois Filipino tradition. On the problematic of the canon, I have consulted Weimann, Guillory, Scholes.

23. Berger inflects the theme of exile in this century of banishment by suggesting that "only worldwide solidarity can transcend modern homelessness" (67).

# References

Adorno, Theodor. "Lyric Poetry and Society." *Telos* 20 (summer 1974): 56–71.

Alquizola, Marilyn. "The Fictive Narrator of *America Is in the Heart*." In *Frontiers in Asian American Studies*, ed. Gail Nomura. Pullman: Washington State University Press, 1989.

Ancheta, Shirley, et al., eds. *Without Names*. San Francisco: Kearney Street Workshop, 1985.

Balibar, Etienne, and Pierre Macherey. "On Literature as Ideological Form." In *Untying the Text*, ed. Robert Young. New York: Routledge and Kegan Paul, 1981.

Berger, John. *And Our Faces, My Heart, Brief as Photos*. New York: Pantheon, 1984.

Bock, Deborah, ed. *Pearls*. Springfield, Va.: Educational Film Center, 1979.

Bruchac, Joseph, ed. *Breaking Silence: An Anthology of Contemporary Asian American Poets*. Greenfield Center, N.Y.: Greenfield Review Press, 1983.

Buaken, Manuel. *I Have Lived with the American People*. Caldwell, Idaho: Caxton Printers, 1948.

Bulosan, Carlos. *America Is in the Heart*. 1946. Seattle: University of Washington Press, 1973.

———. *If You Want to Know What We Are*. Minneapolis: West End Press, 1983.

———. *The Laughter of My Father*. New York: Harcourt, 1944.

———. *The Power of the People*. 1977. Manila: National Book Store, 1986.

———. "Writings of Carlos Bulosan." *Amerasia Journal* (special issue) 6.1 (May 1979).

Cabezas, Amado, and Gary Kawaguchi. "Race, Gender and Class for Filipino Americans." In

*A Look Beyond the Model Minority Image*, ed. Grace Yun. New York: Minority Rights Group, 1989.

Campomanes, Oscar. "Filipinos in the U.S.A. and Their Literature of Exile." In *Reading the Literatures of Asian America*, ed. S. Lim and A. Ling. Philadelphia: Temple University Press, 1992.

Casper, Leonard. "Introduction." In Bienvenido Santos, *Scent of Apples*. Seattle: University of Washington Press, 1979.

Catholic Institute for International Relations. *The Labor Trade*. London: CIIR, 1987.

Chan, Sucheng. *Asian Americans*. Boston: Twayne, 1991.

Cheung, King-kok, and Stan Yogi, eds. *Asian American Literature*. New York: Modern Language Association, 1988.

Constantino, Renato. "The Miseducation of the Filipino." In *The Filipinos in the Philippines and Other Essays*. Quezon City: Malaya Books, 1966. Also in *The Philippines Reader*, ed. D. B. Schirmer and Stephen Shalom. Boston: South End Press, 1987.

Cordova, Fred. *Filipinos: Forgotten Asian Americans*. Dubuque, Iowa: Kendall Hunt, 1983.

Cruz, Emeterio. "Filipino Life in the Alaskan Fish Canneries." *Philippine Magazine* 30 (June 1933): 25, 34–36.

Deleuze, Gilles, and Félix Guattari. *Kafka: Toward a Minor Literature*. Minneapolis: University of Minnesota Press, 1986.

———. *A Thousand Plateaus: Capitalism and Schizophrenia*. Minneapolis: University of Minnesota Press, 1987.

Deutsch, Babette. "Critical Essay." In *Poems 55* by Jose Garcia Villa. Manila: Alberto Florentino, 1962.

Dionisio, J. C. "Cannery Episode." *Philippine Magazine*, August 1936: 397, 412–13.

Feleo-Gonzalez, Marina. *A Song For Manong*. Daly City, Calif.: Likha Promotions, 1988.

Fuchs, Lawrence H. *The American Kaleidoscope*. Hanover and London: University Press of New England, 1991.

Gonzalez, N. V. M. "The Long Harvest." *Midweek*, May 23, 1990: 25–26, 28.

Guillory, John. "Canon." In *Critical Terms for Literary Study*, ed. Frank Lentricchia and Thomas McLaughlin. Chicago: University of Chicago Press, 1990.

Hagedorn, Jessica. *Dogeaters*. New York: Pantheon, 1989.

Hebdige, Dick. *Subculture: The Meaning of Style*. London: Methuen, 1979.

Kim, Elaine. *Asian American Literature*. Philadelphia: Temple University Press, 1982.

Kolko, Gabriel. *Main Currents in Modern American History*. New York: Pantheon, 1976.

Kristeva, Julia. *Strangers to Ourselves*. New York: Columbia University Press, 1991.

Kunitz, Stanley, ed. *Twentieth Century Authors*. New York: H. W. Wilson, 1955. 144–45.

Lauter, Paul, et al., eds. *The Heath Anthology of American Literature*. Boston: D. C. Heath, 1990.

McWilliams, Carey. *Brothers under the Skin*. Boston: Little, Brown, 1964.

———. "Introduction." In Carlos Bulosan, *America Is in the Heart*. Seattle: University of Washington Press, 1973. vii–xxiv.

Melendy, H. Brett. *Asians in America*. 1977. New York: Hippocrene Books, 1981.

———. "Filipinos." In *Harvard Encyclopedia of American Ethnic Groups*. Cambridge, Mass.: Harvard University Press, 1980: 354–62.

Navarro, Jovina, ed. *Diwang Pilipino*. Davis, Calif.: Asian American Studies, 1974.

Nee, Victor, and Jimy Sanders. "The Road to Parity: Determinants of the Socioeconomic Achievements of Asian Americans." *Ethnic and Racial Studies* 8.1 (January 1985): 75–93.

O'Brien, Edward J. "Introduction." In Jose Garcia Villa, *Footnote to Youth*. New York: Scribner's, 1933.

Occeña, Bruce. "The Filipino Nationality in the U.S.: An Overview." *Line of March*, fall 1958: 29–41.

O'Hare, William P., and Judy C. Felt. *Asian Americans: America's Fastest Growing Minority Group*. Washington, D.C.: Population Reference Bureau, 1991.

Palumbo-Liu, David. "Model Minority Discourse and the Course of Healing." Forthcoming in *Minority Discourse: Ideological Containment and Utopian/Heterotopian Potential*, ed. Abdul JanMohamed.

Penaranda, Oscar, Serafin Syquia, and Sam Tagatac. "An Introduction to Filipino-American Literature." In *Aiiieeeee! An Anthology of Asian-American Writers*, ed. Frank Chin, Jeffery Paul Chan, Lawson Fusao Inada, and Shawn Wong. Washington, D.C.: Howard University Press, 1983.

Philippine Center for Immigrant Rights. *Filipinos in the USA*. New York: Philcir, 1985.

Pido, Antonio. *The Pilipinos in America*. New York: Center for Migration Studies, 1986.

Quinsaat, Jesse, ed. *Letters in Exile*. Los Angeles: UCLA Asian American Studies Center, 1976.

Ruoff, A. LaVonne Brown, and Jerry Ward Jr., eds. *Redefining American Literary History*. New York: Modern Language Association, 1990.

Said, Edward. "Reflections on Exile." In *Out There: Marginalization and Contemporary Culture*, ed. Russell Ferguson et al. New York: New Museum of Contemporary Art, 1990.

San Juan, E. "Beyond Identity Politics: The Predicament of the Asian American Writer in Late Capitalism." *American Literary History* 3.3 (fall 1991): 542–65.

———. *Bulosan: An Introduction with Selections*. Manila: National Book Store, 1983.

———. *Carlos Bulosan and the Imagination of the Class Struggle*. New York: Oriole Editions, 1972.

———. *Crisis in the Philippines*. South Hadley, Mass.: Bergin & Garvey, 1986.

———. "Mapping the Boundaries: The Filipino Writer in the U.S.A." *Journal of Ethnic Studies* 19.1 (spring 1991): 117–31.

———. *Racial Formations/Critical Transformations*. Atlantic Highlands, N.J.: Humanities Press, 1992.

———. *Reading the West/Writing the East*. New York: Peter Lang, 1992.

———. *Toward a People's Literature*. Quezon City: University of the Philippines Press, 1984.

Santos, Bienvenido. *Scent of Apples*. Seattle: University of Washington Press, 1979.

Scharlin, Craig, and Lilia Villanueva. *Philip Vera Cruz: A Personal History of Filipino Immigrants and the Farmworkers Movement*. Los Angeles: UCLA Asian American Center, 1992.

Scholes, Robert. "Canonicity and Textuality." In *Introduction to Scholarship in Modern Languages and Literatures*, ed. Joseph Gibaldi. New York: Modern Language Association, 1992.

Skinner, Michelle Cruz. *Balikbayan: A Filipino Homecoming*. Honolulu: Bess Press, 1988.

Solberg, S. E. "An Introduction to Filipino American Literature." In *Aiiieeeee! An Anthology of Asian-American Writers*, ed. Frank Chin, Jeffery Paul Chan, Lawson Fusao Inada, and Shawn Wong. Washington, D.C.: Howard University Press, 1983.

Sollors, Werner. *Beyond Ethnicity*. New York: Oxford University Press, 1986.

Somera, Rene. "Between Two Worlds: The Hawaii Ilocano Immigrant Experience." *Diliman Review*, January–February 1982: 54–59.

Stanley, Peter. "The *Manongs* of California." *Philippine U.S. Free Press*, November 1985: 4, 7–8, 45.

Stegner, Wallace. *One Nation*. Boston: Houghton Mifflin, 1945.

Takaki, Ronald, ed. *From Different Shores*. New York: Oxford University Press, 1987.

———. *Strangers from a Different Shore*. Boston: Little, Brown, 1989.

Villa, Jose Garcia. *Footnote to Youth*. New York: Scribner's, 1933.

Villanueva, Marianne. *Ginseng and Other Tales from Manila*. Corvallis, Ore.: Calyx Books, 1991.

Wand, David Hsin-Fu, ed. *Asian American Heritage*. New York: Washington Square Press, 1974.

Weimann, Robert. *Structure and Society in Literary History*. Baltimore: Johns Hopkins University Press, 1984.

# A Rough Terrain

## The Case of Shaping an Anthology of Caribbean Women Writers

BARBARA CHRISTIAN

At present I am engaged along with one of my sisters, Opal Palmer Adisa, in constructing an anthology of English-speaking Caribbean women's creative and critical writings especially for use in college classrooms. Opal and I have for many years bemoaned the fact that such a text does not exist, particularly since Caribbean Women's writing in the Islands as well as in the United States, the United Kingdom, and Canada is flourishing. If "merit" were the measure, if the appearance of new forms and concerns and different approaches to language were criteria, these writers would, we thought, be at the top of reading lists in English, comparative literature, and other literature courses.

In one sense, the constructing of such an anthology might seem to be a focused endeavor. Yet I have found in my attempt to frame it as accurately and as fully as possible that conceptualizing this collection is fraught with both possibilities and contradictions, and brings up issues not only about the politics of articulating a Caribbean identity but also about the politics of a literature defined by racial or gendered identity in general. Especially when confronted, on the one hand, with this postmodernist critical moment and, on the other, the movement toward diversity, shaping a field (which is what anthologies tend to do) is at bottom a sociopolitical as well as an educational act.

This exploratory essay is more a meditation of thoughts generated by this project than a presentation on Caribbean women writers. I found that much of my thinking about anthologizing this particular body of writing has been affected by my own personal assessment of present "multicultural" educational movements in this country, as well as my own belief that very few of us know or recall the *history* of these movements.

As a result of many decades of activism on the part of U.S. intellectuals of color, and the political factor of changing demographics, some U.S. institutions of higher learning have begun to accept the premise that their curricula have been largely Eurocentric and that possibly there may be non-European intellectual traditions that students need to know. From my experience as a speaker and workshop leader, teachers all over the country are trying to diversify their courses, particularly in the areas of history and literature. But most of these teachers have themselves not been educated in the literatures of racial minorities in the United States, much less of other peoples, such as those of the Caribbean. Even scholars of one of these groups, let us say, African Americans, are not necessarily knowledgeable about Chicano or Asian American literatures. That realization has been most forcefully felt at the University of California, Berkeley, with the passage of an American Cultures requirement, which is predicated on the idea that there are many intersecting American cultures. How does one begin to teach about those groups with whose *intellectual* tradition one has had little contact?

Even when there is a clearly defined Ethnic Studies department that focuses on American ethnic racial minorities, as there is at my university, there are major concerns as to what and whom we should study; for the "Four Food Groups," as my students sometimes call our simplistic categorization of American minorities, are not as discrete as they seem to be. For example, there are distinct groups of people with distinct histories, cultures, and concerns whom we label "Latinos." Puerto Ricans come from a Caribbean island colonized by Spain and most recently by the United States. They are racially Black, Indian, or white, but most likely a combination of these three racial groups, and have had a long history of migration to the East Coast, where racial differentiation is a critical issue. Some Chicanos have resided in the Southwest even before it was wrested from Mexico by the United States, whereas others have just recently migrated from Mexico. Moreover, the identities of many groups labeled Latinos, Hispanics, African Americans, or Asians are not fixed. The migrations of the sixties and seventies have resulted in the mingling and mixing of many groups—

those who have migrated from Central and Latin American, African Americans and recently arrived Jamaicans and Africans, Vietnamese and Southeast Asian Americans. What we often forget is that even though these groups are all peoples of color and have experienced racism in the United States, race and another social construct, gender, have not meant the same thing for each of them, either in the "old country" or here in the United States. Issues of fluctuating identities, then, must be understood as central to the achievement of multicultural education in the United States, lest we misrepresent peoples of color as static and unchanging. In this complex construct of cultures, anthologies become extremely important, for it is often to an anthology that one turns, at least as a guide, when one knows little about an intellectual area.

If American teachers are not generally knowledgeable about the "Four Food Groups" of the United States, consider how scanty might be their knowledge of a region as complex as that of the Caribbean, which consists of many islands, first populated by Indians, colonized by various European powers who imported large numbers of African slaves, and in some cases indentured East Indians, and to which other peoples such as the Chinese and various Arab peoples have migrated. For at least a century, this region has been a fulcrum of different races and cultures, anticipatory of the present condition of the United States. The Caribbean is also a region that, because of its proximity to the United States (even before it was part of the United States), has both had much impact on and been gravely affected by its large, sometimes superpower neighbor.

I suppose some people would consider me a Caribbean woman writer, although I have studied and written primarily on African American women. My formative years were spent in the Caribbean, which affected my sense of the oral and written language of cultural forms and referents. Still, I have spent most of my adult life in the United States as an African American of Caribbean descent. It is interesting that many notable African American critics—for example, Arnold Rampersad, the distinguished biographer of Langston Hughes—are also originally from the Caribbean and have, like me, lived much of their adult life in the United States. As such, we bridge two cultures—or is it three or four? Rampersad, for instance, is partially East Indian in origin, as are many Afro-Caribbean peoples. If we extend the articulation of a Caribbean identity to the many linguistic domains of the region—English, Spanish, French, Dutch, not to mention Creoles—the quest of identity is even more complex, although those residing in the region would insist that there are certain similarities that transcend language.

Recent collections that include the works of Caribbean women are indications of the myriad ways in which the writing of a Caribbean American woman writer like myself might be framed. Responding to the fact that collections on Caribbean writers are rare, and that generally speaking, because of the marginalization of the region, even those rare collections are primarily male-oriented,[1] Caribbean women writers have included themselves in United States-based anthologies such as

Diasporic Black Women's Writing
African American Women's Writing
Third World Women's Writing
Women of Color Writing
Women Writers of the Americas.

These categories are not arbitrary and are in fact engendered within political strategies that are engaged in the question of how a body of thought might be studied within the academy. Anthologies are often the mode by which categories such as racial, ethnic, regional, linguistic, gendered, and political affiliations take on visibility. It is important, particularly now, to think about what these differentiated constructs signify in this age of official multiculturalism.

Of course I find it exhilarating and important that Caribbean women can be so variously characterized. Such a multiplicity of selves, at least in relation to linguistic labeling, speaks to the complexity of my experience historically and presently, and is certainly an advance over the long centuries of repression and of coerced silence or narrowly constricted language within which those like myself have had to maneuver. Still, I am concerned about what each of these categories really signifies in terms of who I was, am, have meant, and, even more important, might be or mean. To what extent does each of these categories liberate the voices of Caribbean women and authentically communicate their experiences and history? To state my concern in a broader way: Is there a false unity camouflaging dominance and subordination for various groups of women writers depending on the category within which they are studied? To what extent do anthologies reproduce modes of exclusion or dominance? How does the use of one category or another affect curriculum, institution building, configurations of study within academic institutions as to what is significant enough to be studied about these various groups? Who are the users and the used, the communicators, the consumers, the audience?

In foraging out the meanings—or, to be more accurate, the *changing* meanings—of these categories, I have found myself turning to the history of the terms themselves, at least as I have experienced them within the American university system. For me and for many women literary activists in the United States, the point at which we could be studied in the academy was first sharply articulated within the cultural nationalist movements of the 1960s. It is to that period that I will go for some clarification as to political strategies embodied in different academic configurations of study. I will then focus on some recent anthologies and the way in which they have tried to resolve some of these issues.

Not often mentioned about the cultural nationalist movements of the 1960s is the degree to which they were influenced by liberation movements in the Third World. This fact is *crucial* for the evolution of the academic nomenclature of the time. The Mau Maus in Kenya, the Cuban Revolution, the Independence Movement in India and Ghana, the Vietnam War, to name a few such liberation struggles, influenced major thinkers such as LeRoi Jones (later Imamu Baraka), as well as ordinary people like myself, in terms of how we saw the world. Jones would document the effects of the Cuban Revolution on his art and politics in his essay, "Cuba Libre," explaining how his visit to that country made him see the relationship between art and politics.[2] And in 1962, Harold Cruse, one of the major intellectual critics of that period, was already seeing "Negroes as a potential revolutionary force aligned to that of the Third World."[3] The term "the Third World", which had been used at the 1955 Bandung Conference of African and Asian nations to characterize those countries colonized by the West and/or held under control by the struggle between the West and the Communist East, began to replace, in many progressive groups, the pejorative term, "underdeveloped countries."

What was significant about the many and various societies of the Third World was that most of these countries had experienced colonialism (the unacknowledged cause of their supposed underdevelopment), and that these peoples were darker peoples while the colonizers were usually whites. Racism and colonialism were intertwined, a phenomenon that Richard Wright astutely analyzed in his collection of essays, *White Man, Listen* (1951). Given that analysis, one could posit that African Americans, although they lived within the United States, were, because of their historical experience of slavery and contemporary experience of racism, an internally colonized group just as the colored folk in the majority of the world were oppressed under the yoke of colonialism.[4] The making of that link between colored folk in the United States and those in the Third World would be crucial to the cultural nationalist movements of African Americans and to Puerto Ricans, Native Americans, Chicanos, and Asian Americans who followed the lead of African Americans.

Frantz Fanon's *Wretched of the Earth* (1961/1966) did much to underline not only the material exploitation of colored folk by the West that even Marx had not pinpointed, but also the ways that material exploitation was made possible by strategies of psychological oppression, that is, by the colonizers' attempt to eliminate every culture as useless unless it emanated from the white West. Cultural exploitation was integral to political and economic exploitation, a point that many politicos of color in the West have yet to understand. That Fanon was from Martinique in the Caribbean was certainly a factor in his growing awareness of the use of hegemonic, neocolonial strategies as well as his studies of the overtly, psychically abusive oppression of the Algerians.

When I took part in the City College of New York (CCNY) student strike of 1968–69, some of us were really concerned as to whether our focal demand for Black Studies was enough—should it not be for Third World Studies? We had been influenced by Third World struggles and by the folk in our movement—Caribbeans, Puerto Ricans, Africans, East Indians, and Chinese—who embodied these struggles. The Vietnam War was also raging, a galvanizing force in our thinking about ourselves. Still, there were those of us who warned that an international focus was so much more glamorous than a local one and might deflect from the difficult job of dismantling racism in the United States, of giving worth to our cultural contributions and dilemmas in the United States. So often progressive peoples like to focus on broad abstract issues of economic exploitation and racism but are not interested in the lives of people of color who are living but a few miles from them. That tension was dramatically acted out at Six PAC, the Sixth Pan African Congress (1974), over the debate as to whether Cubans should be allowed to participate, since it was not clear that these Caribbean people were Black. For some, the tension resolved itself in Malcolm X's visit to Mecca, where he declared the revolutionary possibility of the equality of races under Islam.

On the academic and literary front, the cultural nationalist impetus of the sixties resulted in anthologies like *Black Fire* (1968), and generic ones on Chicano literature, Third World writers, and so on, and in the demand for not only Black but also Chicano and Ethnic Studies programs and depart-

ments within the university as other groups of color in the United States began to articulate their own exclusion. If there was anything we activists in
the sixties learned, it was that we did not know our official history and that
to know it and to keep it alive for generations, we had to institutionalize it.
At the same time, outside the United States in my natal world, the Caribbean, where there had also been liberation and independence movements,
the realization that cultural Western hegemony was rampant resulted in
Afro-Caribbean movements that brought to the fore the African influences
on cultures within which we all lived, cultures that had been declared by
our Western Masters (and too often by ourselves) to be nonexistent. Many
of these movements underscored the dominance of European culture over
African cultures, which were usually depicted by Western culture as patho-
logical.

As Black Studies and Ethnic Studies departments were being precari-
ously institutionalized in but a few places, another nomenclature began to
surface in the United States. Ethnic peoples of color were increasingly being
lumped together by officials and policymakers under the label "minority," a
term that implicitly dissociated these groups from the majority of the world
who were people of color. The term "minority" undercut the connotation
of that multiuniverse and of the possibility of the strength in numbers that
the phrase "Third World people" had suggested.

As the Vietnam War and the War on Poverty ended, it seems to me that
there was a new attempt on the part of the dominant culture to undercut
the possibilities of the sixties. Perhaps the most devastating blow to the discourse on racism that developed at that point were the many Euro-
American appropriations of the term "ethnic." That word had, in the sixties,
meant those peoples in America who were not considered by the general
populace to be "real" Americans because of their race and non-European
cultural base. European Americans began challenging that concept by declaring that they too belonged to specific ethnic groups. Why, then, should
Ethnic Studies not include the study of Italian or German Americans? In refusing to accept how the experience of racism against a group was the ker-
nel of the definition of the word "ethnic" as it had been used in the sixties,
whites could camouflage the primary thrust of the just-emerging Ethnic
Studies movement as well as the new scholarship just beginning to be produced on the histories, literatures, and cultures of the United States peoples
of color.

Coalitions of peoples of color were experiencing conflict within their
own ranks, for we found that we often did not know each other and that

there were critical historical and cultural differences among the groups. Those differences were also exacerbated by the official favoring of some groups over others, for instance, the labeling of Asians and West Indians as "model minorities." Coalitions based on the idea of racism as a common group experience were confronting difficulties because of the claim to a unity that was often a false one, especially in the context of the power dynamics of American society.

One effect of that uncoalitioning, I believe, is the fact that few men of color writers and scholars seemed to be collaborating with each other across ethnic-color lines to produce new concepts or anthologies of writing. Much of the discourse on race in anthologies was, in fact, just that—academic discourse (one exception was Ishmael Reed's *Yard Bird Lives!* [1975] and his organization, Before Columbus). Thus, collections of creative writing began to give way to collections of critical writing or of major writers of the past. For example, I recall the publication of only one major anthology of contemporary Afro-American literature in the 1980s: *Breaking Ice* (1990), edited by Terry MacMillan, who is of course labeled a writer rather than a scholar.

The major exception to this trend of fragmentation in the Black and Ethnic Studies literary movement of the 1970s and 1980s was the coalescing of women in the African American, Chicano, Native American, and Asian groups. As the term "Third World" gave way to the more limited term "minority" (in the official discourse), women, colored and white, were beginning to articulate themselves as women. Contrary to what some of our major scholars are saying today, the second wave of American feminism and the call for Women's Studies followed Black and ethnic movements and, in pivotal ways, resulted from women's objections to being largely excluded from their nationalist groups' definitions and concerns. White women learned from their experiences in the civil rights movement how restricted they were as women, as Sara Evans documents in her book *Personal Politics* (1979). And women of color in their respective cultural nationalist groups discovered that not only were they not perceived as central, they were in fact subordinated to men. One can see the beginnings of that realization, for example, in Toni Cade Bambara's anthology, *The Black Woman*, which was published in 1970. But because of the access white women had to the American media, the United States women's movement was often characterized as an exclusively white women's movement.

As a result of the sexism women were experiencing in their own political nationalist groups and their exclusion from the white women's movement,

Chicanas, African, Asian, and Native American women formed their own organizations and, particularly on the West Coast, came together in women of color organizations. One result of this coalescing was the explosion in publishing in the 1970s by African American women writers, who published more than they ever had before, and beyond that an explosion of Chicana, Native American, and Asian American writing in the 1980s.

Pivotal anthologies in the late seventies and eighties pointed to new frames for the study of women's writing. The anthology, *All the Women Are White, All the Blacks Are Men, But Some of Us Are Brave: Black Women's Studies* (1982), articulated the unique space within which African American women writers, scholars, and activists moved since Black women were not perceived as central to their own ethnic, racial, and sociopolitical organizations or to the white Women's Studies movement. The anthology *The Black Woman Cross-Culturally* (1981), edited by Philomena Steady, and *Sturdy Black Bridges* (1979) took, respectively, diasporic social-scientific and humanistic approaches to the study of Black women. The anthology *This Bridge Called My Back* (1981), which focused on similarities and differences among United States women of color, signaled growing alliances among writers in the different colored ethnic groups. On an international level, women from the previously colonized countries of the world challenged, at international conferences, American women's right to define feminism. Many United States women of color activists agreed with the concerns of Third World women outside the United States. One result was anthologies on the writings of postcolonial women such as the special edition of *Inscriptions*, "Travelling Theories, Travelling Theorists," brought out by the group for the Critical Study of Colonial Discourse at the University of California at Santa Cruz. Another development was the production of anthologies by "local" women such as *Jamaica Woman* (1980) and *Savacou* (1977). Such anthologies, however, were hampered by their lack of access to the publishing and distributing muscle of the metropolis and are therefore not very well known or accessible to many people or to the academic institutions that are often the lifeline for anthologies.

One reason anthologies on Caribbean women published in the United States are so important is precisely because of the issue of access, even as that access signals the dominant role that American publishing companies play in the literary world. Scholars and writers who publish in the United States and include Caribbean women writers in their anthologies have considerable effect on the ways these writers are perceived in the academy. In the last decade, these scholars and writers have used different strategies to shape the ways in which Caribbean women's texts might be read. By calling attention to the following anthologies, I do not intend to privilege them over other anthologies on this subject or to insist that any one of them is superior to another. Rather, I am concerned with what each of them tells us about its ideological literary position. I am also interested in the purposes to which they might be put to use in different kinds of classroom settings.

I have selected two different groups of anthologies featuring Caribbean women writers in order to discuss the complexities of anthologizing in this movement of institutionalized "multiculturalism." The first group I am calling the "Metropolis Frame"—that is, those editions by non-Caribbean scholars who include these writers in a frame that is wider than that of a specific Caribbean "identity." The second group I am calling "Placed and Displaced Caribbean Frames"—anthologies generated by varying concepts of what it means to be a Caribbean woman.

In the first group, I will discuss *Reading Black, Reading Feminist* (1990), edited by Henry Louis Gates Jr., a scholar in the African American tradition; *Wild Women in the WhirlWind* (1990), edited by Joanne Braxton and Andree McLaughlin, African American women scholars; and *Making Face, Making Soul* (1990), edited by Gloria Anzaldúa, a Chicana poet and woman of color activist.

*Reading Black, Reading Feminist* is comprised primarily of essays on African American women's writing by critics noted for their work in African American literature. As is true of Gates's orientation, critics featured here are Africans, African Americans, and Euro-Americans. There is a focus in this volume on what might be considered "major writers" in the tradition. It is interesting that the recent tendency to canonize *Black* female writers results in a plurality of essays on *African American* writers, and that the only Caribbean writer featured in *Reading Black, Reading Feminist* is Jamaica Kincaid. Her singular presence seems somewhat tokenistic, for her inclusion in the volume seems to signal that she belongs to the African American canon ("Black" in this anthology). Kincaid has lived in the United States for many years and could, I suppose, be considered an African American writer. I wonder whether her being chosen for this volume has as much to do with her cultural origins as a Caribbean woman as it does with her popularity among critics. Although Kincaid's work is certainly about the Caribbean, and about Caribbean peoples who have migrated to the United States, hers is but one view of the region and of the process of migration. Readers who know little about the history and politics of the region may accept her perspective as if it were the only view—the danger, of course, in including only one writer from the region. In a real sense, Kincaid's writing is culturally displaced in this volume by a frame that privileges the metropole and marginalizes those outside it. Gates's collection is useful, however, particularly for those classrooms in which knowledge of the latest critical writing on African American literature is the goal—classes on African American literature and literary theory, even Black feminist theory.

While *Reading Black, Reading Feminist* consists almost entirely of critical writing by or about well-known authors, Gloria Anzaldúa's *Making Face, Making Soul* is a compilation of personal narratives, poetry, and critical essays by U.S. women of color writers, many of them not well known, a kind of sequel to *This Bridge Called My Back*, the first anthology that framed women writers as women of color and one that Anzaldúa also helped to edit. *Making Face* includes more Caribbean writers: two creative writers from Jamaica and Puerto Rico, and even a few critics, as well as the writings of two well-known women of Caribbean descent, June Jordan and Audre Lorde. However, none of the works selected for the volume by these writers has to do with a Caribbean context. Rather, the writings by Caribbean women are primarily related to positions they share as women of color with other women of color in the United States.

Anzaldúa's collection is fresh, filled with creative writing and innovative critical works, and would be a fine text for inspiring especially women students of color, informing and challenging them about issues of the interrelatedness of race and gender and sexual preferences. But in order to do that, this anthology tends to flatten out the contextual differences of the various women of color groups in the United States as an argument for coalitions for struggle. Given the history of the last decade, the naive reader might assume more homogeneity among these groups than there really is. Finally, because the writings of women of color who share Spanish as part of their linguistic heritage has been neglected in the past, the volume tends to foreground that literature. Perhaps because of that focus, two of the four women writers featured in *Making Face* are Puerto Ricans, a reminder that the Caribbean is also a part of that linguistic construct.

An important difference between Gates's anthology and Anzaldúa's that might have much to do with their respective approaches is that while *Reading Black, Reading Feminist* is published by a New York mainstream publishing company, Meridian, Anzaldúa's is published by a small press on the West Coast, Aunt Lute Foundation. Gates's selections tend to privilege an East Coast mainstream view, while Anzaldúa's choices indicate a literary landscape beyond that of the mainstream publishing East, as far south as Texas, as far west as Seattle. Her volume suggests the variety of places in the United States to which Caribbean women have migrated and begins to refute the much-believed idea that Caribbean peoples reside only on the East Coast.

While Anzaldúa focuses on color and gender in the United States, Joanne Braxton and Andree McLaughlin's *Wild Women in the WhirlWind* uses a different frame—that of women writers writing in the African Diaspora (Africa, the United States, the Caribbean, Great Britain). In her introduction, Braxton proclaims the existence of a literary and activist Black Women's Renaissance. This volume is unique in that it relates Black women's activism to Black women's folklore and literature, to the oral as well as to the literary traditions, a frame that might do much to illuminate Caribbean women's writings. Yet even as the introduction expresses a belief in the African Diaspora, most of the essays are on African American women writers and activists and are written by African American women critics. What Braxton and McLaughlin's collection indicates is the difficulty, at least at present, of compiling an African diasporic collection when Black women writers from Africa and the Caribbean, Great Britain, and Canada as well as from the United States are in themselves quite varied in their historical and cultural contexts. The volume is significant *because* it announces the possibility that there are common themes, issues, and forms in the African *female* Diaspora, but the volume does not fulfill its promise perhaps because those who attempt to discover women writers in the Diaspora and outside of the United States find that that task is difficult. The scarcity of publishing outlets makes it difficult for many Black women writers outside the United States to be heard. This volume at least lets us know they are there. *Wild Women* suggests the possibility of multiple Black women's writings beyond the United States and may well pave the way for more focused anthologies that more fully explore their histories, cultures, literary forms.

Anthologies of Black feminist, diasporic, and women of color writings have not included many Caribbean women authors, whose racial, cultural, and ethnic identities are varied, sometimes fluid, and for whom the issue of the relationship between orality and literacy is a complex one. However, collections specifically focused on these women are now beginning to be published. In this second group, what I call "Placed and Displaced Caribbeans," I am going to discuss three anthologies: *Out of the Kumbla* (1990), edited by Carole Boyce Davies and Elaine Savory Fido, scholars of Caribbean and African literature; *Caribbean Women Writers* (1990), edited by Selwyn Cudjoe, a scholar of Caribbean literature and politics; and *Green Cane and Juicy Flotsam* (1991), edited by Carmen C. Estevez and Lizabeth Paravisini-Gebert, scholars of Caribbean literature.

As if responding to the absence of historical context so often a characteristic of anthologies, Carole Boyce Davies introduces *Out of the Kumbla* with a searching essay on the history of the Caribbean and how women occupy specific roles in this history. Davies articulates as well differences among Caribbean women according to which island they came from, their class, nationality, and language. She asks a pivotal question—whether writers who were born in the Caribbean but migrated to Great Britain, Canada, or the United States should be called Caribbean writers. The economic necessity to migrate is a characteristic of Caribbean societies themselves, but when does one stop being a Caribbean and become African American or British Black?

Davies also questions the tendency of scholars to avoid the obvious multiplicity of ethnicities in the Caribbean—not only African and European Caribbeans exist and write, but also East Indians, Chinese, and Arabs. However, even as her introduction signals these issues as significant to our understanding of the Caribbean context, the critical essays in *Out of the Kumbla* focus on well-known writers, most of whom have left the Caribbean and come from relatively privileged backgrounds. As Davies notes, one reason for this might be that many Caribbean women who are writing in the Caribbean operate in the oral tradition, in poetry and theater, arts that are communal and are not necessarily written down for the reading public of the metropolis. Sistren, a theater group in Jamaica, is an example of the tremendous creativity of women; yet much of Sistren's work is not available to a reading public.

One other important characteristic of *Out of the Kumbla* is that it is comprised entirely of critical essays. Many of the creative writings on which the essays are based are not readily accessible to the audience to which they are addressed. Perhaps Davies thought that the existence of criticism would lead to an increased awareness that these writers are there, and to the publication of more anthologies that might feature the writers themselves. That she chose to emphasize critical works might also indicate the great influence the academy has on what is considered "literature" (and what is not).

As such, *Out of the Kumbla* is an excellent anthology for classes in critical theory as well as in literature and Women's Studies classes. Yet in this volume the voices of the writers themselves are not heard.

Davies's anthology is an example of the cultural force that anthologies can have, for it helped to galvanize the first Conference of Caribbean Women Writers in the United States (1989), the conference upon which Selwyn Cudjoe's anthology *Caribbean Women Writers* is based. Like Davies's anthology, Cudjoe's collection is primarily a collection of criticism. What distinguishes his collection, however, is that it includes a significant number of essays by the writers themselves concerning what they think they are doing and why. A Caribbeanist, Cudjoe has written on the politics of resistance in the Afro-Caribbean region. Heretofore, when he wrote on literature, he focused primarily on male writers who seemed to be emblematic of that resistance. This new anthology also charts overtly political territory, now including feminist or at least women's writing as part of that terrain, an important advance. Perhaps because his view of literature is that of opposition to injustice, and because historically it is clear that opposition has occurred throughout the Caribbean, Cudjoe does present an overview of the Spanish and French Caribbean. Still, most of the essays in this collection are from the English Caribbean.

A recently published anthology on Caribbean women's writing called *Green Cane and Juicy Flotsam,* edited by Carmen C. Estevez and Lizabeth Paravisini-Gebert, is a sign that some scholars are attempting to correct the American academic view of the region as only that of the English-speaking islands. Importantly, this volume is published by a well-known academic press (Rutgers University Press), an indication that the academy is beginning to pay more attention to the writings of Caribbean women. The editors, two scholars of Caribbean literature, assume that the "Caribbean" means an integral geographical region regardless of the differences in history, language, and, to some extent, culture. A collection of short stories by women writers, this anthology shapes the field in a particular way— Caribbean women, regardless of whether they come from Cuba, Guadeloupe, or Jamaica, or are of African, Indian, or Chinese descent, share a history of slavery, servitude, colonialism, literary voicelessness, and patriarchal oppression. The collection privileges similarities that the editors perceive among different groups residing in these islands. One gets a sense of the integrity of the region in terms of women writers' concerns, themes, forms, so that the narratives create in themselves a larger story—one of community, coalition, and possibility. The editors demonstrate, through their juxtapositions, what the themes, forms, customs, concerns of Maryse Conde from Guadeloupe have in common with those of Opal Palmer Adisa from Jamaica or Rosario Ferre from Puerto Rico.

Yet, in order to forge such a unity, the editors had to sacrifice certain important elements in their construction of Caribbean women's writings. Most obvious is the fact that there are differences in the colonial histories of these many islands. Differences between the histories and representations of Spanish, French, Dutch, and British slavery and colonialism tend to be minimized in this volume. Of course, the islands have not remained static since they became "independent." Cuba has pursued a socialist path. Guadeloupe has remained very close to its mother country, France. Jamaica has had movements toward and away from socialism and has been greatly influenced by its giant neighbor, the United States. To what extent and in what ways have the islands' "modern" histories effected different views of race and gender, sexuality and ethnicity? For example, do Dominican women writers of African descent use the same forms, have the same concerns, as their white Dominican sisters?

Unlike many anthologies on the Caribbean, *Green Cane* presents writings by Caribbean women from all over the region rather than critical essays or historical analyses. The anthology foregrounds Caribbean women's voices. It is an excellent introduction to those voices—except that the exclusive genre represented in the anthology is narrative fiction. This is an important point since in the Caribbean the prevalent literary/oral arts of women tend to be those of poetry and theater. The question that the construction of this anthology poses for me is whose voices are being heard, who writes fiction as opposed to other forms—class concerns that one cannot ignore if one is to accurately represent Caribbean women's voices. Because the authors do not provide us with historical distinctiveness about class as well as regional and ethnic differences, the unknowing reader or teacher might assume that the emphasis on sexual repression is the same in an English-speaking island like Jamaica and a Spanish-speaking island like the Dominican Republic and that women who till the soil or work in factories or go to school or become housewives are concerned with the same issues. In effect, this anthology might suggest that one is voiceless if one does not publish fiction. *Green Cane* leaves me with the difficult issue that many women in the Caribbean do not operate in the sphere of literacy even as that sphere is the primary one that is privileged in the West. Still, because this anthology does present the voices of Caribbean women as represented by writers, rather than criticism or history, it does open up spaces for more varied, experimental manifestations of Caribbean women's linguistic activities.

As I reflect upon this case study, my attempt to shape an anthology on Caribbean women's writings, I want to return to the questions I posed at the beginning of this essay. The first was, To what extent do the different types of anthologies liberate the voices of the women in the categories within which I, as an African American Caribbean woman, might be included?

I am impressed, first of all, by what anthologies can do. Anthologies do chart a field, as the cultural nationalist anthologies of the sixties and the women's anthologies of the seventies demonstrate. They can be a significant cultural force in creating interest in a field, as in the case of Carole Boyce Davies's *Out of the Kumbla*. They are not fixed in stone, as revisionist women of color anthologies exemplify. Anthologies as an intersection of many identities do develop, change, revise themselves. Obviously, the process of anthologizing is worth it for those of us in "new fields." And yet I am also struck by the limitations of anthologies, limitations that recall another of my initial questions: Is there a false unity camouflaging dominance and subordination? Do anthologies reproduce exclusion or dominance? Anthologies can appear to be comprehensive when they are not, since specific historical moments affect their shaping. Thus it is important for the anthologist to indicate her/his frame, limits, purposes, so as not to mislead the teacher or the reader. For example, an anthology that emphasizes the subject of immigration, a particularly hot topic today in the multicultural marketplace, might give the impression that this topic is the only one about which Chicano or Asian Americans write.

Creating overarching paradigms is a tendency among academic scholars. If paradigms such as Diaspora, Women of Color, Oppositional or Postcolonial Literature become the frame, the gain for a literature such as that of Caribbean Women's Writings is that links between racism, sexism, and class exploitation can be perceived and studied so that one can see commonalities in the workings of these phenomena. Yet such linkages, unless carefully analyzed, camouflage the ways in which some categories, depending upon the particular historical moment, are more privileged than others. As important, the difference of historical process among various configurations of groups, as well as their specific cultural mores, are hidden under abstract declarations of unity. For example, often African American women become the spokeswomen for women of color, as if we were all the same, or Caribbean women become subordinated to women of color categories without an acknowledgement of their quite different definitions of race and gender. Such a process is itself the epitome of racism, for we become homogenized, dehumanized under terms that are primarily oppositional to whites. As such, "white definitions" remain the norm.

I am also intrigued by anthologies' effects on the publishing trends of the literatures they present, effects that recall my question about configurations of study within academic institutions, the purposes in fact of literatures becoming part of the academy. For one, I find that as a group's literature becomes more institutionalized in the academy, its contemporary literature, that is, the literature coming into being in the present, is less and less discussed and analyzed in academic publications. In the beginnings of each of the socio/political/literary movements I have mentioned, the writers emphasized these connections with their own communities, a recommendation for doing anthologies on specific groups. As these literatures begin to be legitimized by the academy, more and more critics contribute historical and literary stances. Thus a critical language and a tradition of critical studies develops, an important aspect of any community's literary and scholarly tradition. What is sometimes lost, however, is that as the literature, let us say of African Americans, becomes more acceptable to the academic world of the metropolis, the past literature of that group becomes the norm for study, and few examples of that group's contemporary literature, its contemporary utterances, appear in anthologies. Fewer and fewer anthologies featuring specifically contemporary literature are published. At the present time, for example, few anthologies of contemporary African American poetry are being published, in contrast to the many anthologies that were published in the late sixties and early seventies. At times, one result of this tendency is the split between critical approaches and contemporary stances of the writers themselves, or even more important, the decline of a dialogue between contemporary critics and writers. Anthologists might do well to consider the ease with which they can chart the past without engaging the pressing debates, expressions of the present.

Anthologies also confront us with the issue as to whether a community of women writers (or any writers, for that matter) actually represent their community, a critical issue about which I am constantly thinking—since so often cultures are represented in the classroom by writings, either by critical studies of a particular group or of writings by that group. In contrast, many cultures invest much in oral traditions and increasingly in visual media. This issue also reminds us that we often think of the users, the consumers of literature, as limited to those in the classroom, or to the "intellectual marketplace." Caribbean women writers, after all, do not write primarily for the purpose of being taught in the classrooms of the metropolis. They write for many reasons, not the least of which is speaking to those who do not necessarily now have the means of reading their books. In other words, they write to those who may not yet read and cannot now buy their books. They write to the future as well as to the present. To create an anthology of their writings brings to mind Gayatri Spivak's statement that "to confront them [those who do not write] is not to represent them but to learn to represent ourselves."[5]

As teachers, many of us tend to equate writing with the reality of a folk, and in fact writers do express *their* view of being in a particular construct, history. Yet, as I reflect on this process, I think it is important for scholars, anthologists, and teachers to realize the limits, as well as the possibilities, of "literature" and of "writings" and to discuss these issues with students. If not, the multicultural curriculum we are trying to create may generate new, though different, stereotypes, the continuation of that academic stereotype called "others." Even as I know that creating an anthology of Caribbean women's writings of the English-speaking Caribbean is a worthwhile intellectual and political endeavor, I am increasingly aware of that endeavor's limitations and of the importance of signaling to the reader those limitations.

It is remarkable to me how fields grow, and change. Ethnic Studies, African American Studies, the intellectual terrain that I have been treading for some twenty-five years, has grown to such an extent that it is now questioning its own premises as to the meaning of racial identity. Because of the depth and extent of our scholarship, our identity from the perspective of ethnicity, race, gender, class affiliations can no longer be asserted as singular; rather, it is—or rather, they are—a multiplicity of selves. What that new configuration will mean for our present institutional labels, coalitions, and concerns is one challenge for the future. Anthologies can help us to assess our institutional stances, so that our sites in the academy keep pace with our intellectual questionings, our political developments.

Ethnic and African American Studies in the United States are, in a sense, just beginning to catch up with the complexities of the very concept of identity, complexities acknowledged by Caribbean peoples, for in that region identity is seldom characterized by a simple or single label. So, although the constructing of an anthology on Caribbean women's writings presents the anthologist with a rough, not yet leveled terrain (in other words, one that refuses to be simply and easily traveled), for that very reason, it challenges our assumptions that other terrains are as even as they seem. In testing the assumptions of a terrain as varied as that of the Caribbean, we also confront the shape of those fields that figure racial/gendered/ethnic intellectual institutions in the United States.

## Notes

I want to acknowledge my gratitude to Dr. Guila Fabi, now of the University of Bologna, Italy, and also a Ph.D. graduate of the Ethnic Studies Program at Berkeley, for her illuminating comments on this essay. I also want to thank Alberto Perez, a Ph.D. student in ethnic studies at Berkeley, for critiquing this essay.

1. Major collections of Caribbean literatures include Andrew Salkey, ed., *West Indian Stories* (London: Faber and Faber, 1971); O. R. Dathorne, ed., *Caribbean Narrative* (London: Heinemann Educational Books, 1973); Stewart Brown and Mervyn Morris, eds., *Caribbean Poetry Now* (London: Hodder and Stonghton, 1984); Stewart Brown, Mervyn Morris and Gordon Rohlehr, eds., *Voice Print* (London: Longman, 1989).

2. LeRoi Jones, "Cuba Libre," in *Home: Social Essays* (New York: William Morrow, 1966).

3. Harold Cruse, "Revolutionary Nationalism and the Afro-American," *Studies on the Left* 2, no. 3 (1962): 12–28.

4. African American writers such as LeRoi Jones, and political activists such as Stokely Carmichael, were, as early as 1964, articulating the concept of internal colonialism, long before it became an operative theory in the academy.

5. Gayatri Spivak, "Can the Subaltern Speak?" in *Marxism and the Interpretation of Culture*, ed. Cary Nelson and Lawrence Grossberg (Urbana: University of Illinois Press, 1988).

~

# *M. Butterfly* and the Rhetoric of Antiessentialism

## Minority Discourse in an International Frame

COLLEEN LYE

Few works by Asian American artists have captured as much attention as David Henry Hwang's dramatic adaptation of a newspaper account of a French diplomat's affair with a Peking Opera diva later revealed to be a man and a spy for the People's Republic of China. Winning mainstream accolades such as the Tony Award for Best Play of the Year in 1988, *M. Butterfly* has also been taken up by many Asian American and feminist critics as an example of politically subversive theater.[1] Chalsa Loo praises the play as a work of "complexity and brilliance," in the way that it "deconstructs Giacomo Puccini's famous opera *Madame Butterfly*" (16), and Dorinne Kondo writes that "perhaps the most creative subversiveness of Hwang's play best emerges most clearly in contrast with the conventions of the opera *Madame Butterfly*, to which it provides ironic counterpoint. . . . Hwang reappropriates the conventional narrative of the pitiful Butterfly and the trope of the exotic, submissive 'Oriental' woman" (7). Robert Skloot concurs in claiming *M. Butterfly* to be "thoroughly subversive" by "confronting [audiences] with challenges to cultural and gender assumptions" (59). For Marjorie Garber, "The (de)construction or (de)composition of the fantasy of 'character' is precisely what is at work and on display in *M. Butterfly*" (143).

These responses mark the critical modality shared by wide-ranging commentators and the playwright, who himself calls his work a "deconstructivist *Madame Butterfly*."² Through its self-conscious use of the "rue story" of Boursicot as the occasion for exploring and dismantling Western perceptions of Asians, the play has been presented and widely received as a "subversive" project that "deconstructs" dominant Orientalist discourses of which the Puccini classic is treated as paradigmatic.³ As such, *M. Butterfly* can be said to position itself, and to be commonly positioned by critics, within the field known as minority discourse.⁴ The widespread characterization of the play as "deconstructive" to mean "undermine" and "expose as a (social) construction" marks a convergence between a rhetoric of political oppositionality and the modality of celebratory postmodernism. However, we may want to pay closer attention to what particular dominant representation the play seeks to "subvert."

A struggle between two readings of the canonical Western text to which *M. Butterfly* constitutes a response is the substance of the very first encounter between the two protagonists in the play. After viewing Song Liling's rendition of the Italian opera, the diplomat Gallimard's expression of admiration meets with the following response from the Asian performer:

> It's one of your favorite fantasies, isn't it? The submissive Oriental woman and the cruel white man. . . . Consider it this way: what would you say if a blonde homecoming queen fell in love with a short Japanese businessman? He treats her cruelly, then goes home for three years, during which time she prays to his picture and turns down marriage from a young Kennedy. Then, when she learns he has remarried, she kills herself. Now, I believe you would consider this girl to be a deranged idiot, correct? But because it's an Oriental who kills herself for a Westerner—ah! you find it beautiful. (Act 1, scene 6, p. 17)

Song criticizes Puccini's opera for perpetuating the image of the "submissive Oriental woman" whose counterpart is the emasculated Asian man, as exemplified by the hypothetical "short Japanese businessman" proposed as the preposterous object of desire. But if *M. Butterfly* seems to engage the problem of the feminine gendering of Asian ethnicity with which so many Asian American texts are concerned, critics may be overhasty in assuming that objections to the "submissive Oriental woman" proceed from politically noncontradictory standpoints.⁵ Nationalist discourses, for instance, often articulate resistance to colonial modernity through figurations of gender that construct women as the site of "tradition," while colonial discourses may generate the idea of "white men saving brown women from brown men."⁶ Gender, in other words, often serves as the site of contestation between groups that are not particularly feminist.

The particular image of "brown women" submissive to "white men" may not stem from the desire to liberate "brown women" but in fact register, in deeply misogynist ways, the colonial anxieties of "brown men." Hwang's own account of the genesis of the idea of *M. Butterfly* is particularly revealing when he says, "I didn't even know the plot of the opera! I knew Butterfly only as a cultural stereotype; speaking of an Asian woman, we would sometimes say, 'she's pulling a Butterfly,' which meant playing the submissive Oriental number" ("Afterword," 95). In Hwang's usage, in the implied status of the "we" who invoke the Butterfly metaphor, the metaphor clearly emerges as a term of reproach used by Asian American men against Asian American women. Hwang's conceptualization of the problem of "Butterfly," furthermore, reflects an engagement with representation as false stereotype or myth, rather than as a discourse of power.

Yet the play's effort to allegorize the sexual drama between a white man and an Asian (wo)man as a story of geopolitical relations between East and West has led critics to discuss the play's contention with "Orientalism" in terms of power relations at the simultaneous registers of minority identity and of the nation. I will argue that it is precisely the difference between minority politics and geopolitics, as well as the difference between a refusal of cultural stereotype and an analysis of power or domination, that critical discussion around the play has tended to blur—by use of the concept-metaphor of gender. For this reason, it is important that we briefly review the terms in which *M. Butterfly*'s gender politics are appraised.

Dorinne Kondo's account of a 1989 Asian American Studies Association panel discussion on *M. Butterfly* describes a critical debate that breaks down between supportive feminist critics on the one hand and hostile male critics on the other. Her account posits a consistent separation between feminist and male critics on the basis of their response to the figure of the Asian transvestite—a figure whose subversive interrogation of fixed, stable identity, she implies, is measured in its profound disturbance of male critics' sense of masculinity (25–27). Chalsa Loo, who presented a paper at this panel that was later published in *Asian Week*, ascribes a feminist perspective to the play for affording "the Asian American woman (who is acutely aware of racism, sexism and imperialism) vicarious satisfaction in telling off the chauvinist, colonialist male" (16). Although Loo embraces the play from a humanistic standpoint with which Kondo's critique of "substance-metaphysics" would appear to be at odds, her assertion that "it matters not to many feminists that Song Liling is a woman played by a man" (16) permits us to place her in line with antiessentialist feminist perspectives that have found reason to celebrate the play. Finally, that a significant feminist critic outside the field of Asian American studies altogether has alighted upon *M. Butterfly* for material for her work on transvestism, arguing that the play's transvestite scandal tells the "truth" about the constructedness of gender, further reflects the insertion of *M. Butterfly* into broad antiessentialist trends in feminism (Garber, 143).

The few existing attacks on the play for being antifeminist, on the other hand, seem only to fortify an antiessentialist celebration of the play by basing their arguments on a notion of femininity violated by the transvestite. Gabrielle Cody's complaint, for example, that Hwang "take[s] the female gender out of Butterfly by overfeminizing her" and that her "grotesque idealized femaleness" suggests a presence that, "in short, is not female" itself seems to operate from a feminist position scandalized by gender parody (26). Hence, although Marjorie Garber's reading also acknowledges the presence of a certain misogynist humor and concludes that by "focusing on male pathos and male self-pity, *M. Butterfly* is intermittently anti-feminist and homophobic" (141), these misogynistic traces are ultimately reconciled in her reading of the play as an example of antiessentialist gender performance. Rather than permitting the misogyny to present a contradiction to her assessment of the play's subversive gender politics, Garber integrates misogyny as an effect of male transvestite theater, which often implies that "a man may be (or rather, make) a more successful 'woman' than a woman can" (141). Furthermore, the antibutch humor of Song's put-down of Comrade Chin as "passing for a woman" seems to betray a fear of women and women's difference but, according to Garber, this fear actually reflects the "subconscious recognition" of the "artificial" nature of "woman" in patriarchal society and, concomitantly, the artificiality of "man" (142).

It is precisely the reading of the play in terms of gender performativity that enables critics, in different ways, to link gender and national politics in a double subversion of the binarisms understood to be constitutive of Orientalism. Garber focuses on the Asian transvestite as the scandal that stands at the "crossroads of nationalism and sexuality." The single figure of the transvestite, in other words, serves as the vehicle for category crisis; one category crisis leads metonymically to another, and "as the figure of the transvestite deconstructs the binary of male and female, so all national binaries and power relations are put into question" (Garber, 130). Kondo likewise argues that "through its use of gender ambiguity present in its very title . . . through power reversals, through constituting these identities within the vicissitudes of global politics, Hwang conceals, reveals and then

calls into question so-called 'true' identity, pointing us toward a reconceptualization of the topography of 'the self'"(Kondo, 7). Readings of the play
as gender performance thus form the basis of arguments on behalf of the
play's political subversiveness at various levels of identity. Of these, Kondo's
and Garber's are exemplary. My essay will take issue with their arguments,
not out of a particular interest in asserting just a different reading of the
play, but in order ultimately to signal wider problems within contemporary
feminist and minority discourse theory revealed by *M. Butterfly* and its reception. A much more problematic view of the play gradually becomes
more visible when we observe its staging in a different site and read it
alongside the textual antecedents it is thought to subvert.

## *M. Butterfly* in Singapore

In the summer of 1990, *M. Butterfly* opened for a brief one-week run in Singapore as the showpiece of the state-sponsored festival of arts. Much discussion around the arts festival had been filling newspaper pages in the preceding weeks, in which readers were treated to lectures by the Ministry of
Culture on the barrenness of a technocratic society to which the festival was
to offer antidote and relief. The festival featured cultural events that ranged
conspicuously from high to low, a demarcation that neatly coincided with
"Western" and "local." Playing in the most prestigious and formal concert
halls, performances by Alvin Ailey and the Houston Symphony constituted
the major events in the festival's calendar; around these foreign imports
were scheduled a variety of performances by local artists dubbed "Festival
Fringe" and available for free consumption in informal venues such as
shopping malls and hotel lobbies. *M. Butterfly,* which closed, and in some
sense represented the finale of, the festival, straddled perfectly this divide.

A production of Theatreworks, the only professional theater company in
Singapore, *M. Butterfly* also received highly publicized consultation from
the playwright himself, who was personally flown in during the rehearsal
and planning stages of the production. A local production of a foreign
script, *M. Butterfly* thus represented a collaboration and crossover between
the foreign and the local—the Western and the Asian?—a fusion the festival overtly celebrated by according it pride of place, scheduling its performance for the Victoria Theater, the nation's most prestigious of institutional spaces of culture.

How are we to understand the selection of an Asian American play for
the promotion of culture in Singapore, a place distinguished by extensive

state vigilance over all forms of expression? Although its Economic Development Board expressly seeks the investment of information technologies and markets the country as the communications hub of southern Asia, the Singapore government subjects all books, magazines, music, and movies to political and moral censorship.[7] In a context where "consent" is "manufactured" by the state, what gets seen, heard, or read therefore bears a direct relationship to what the state apparatus decides is ideologically appropriate. Publicity given Hwang, along with other popular Asian American artists such as Amy Tan, by the state-controlled *Straits Times* reflects a certain overt interest taken by the Singapore state apparatus in Asian American cultural icons.[8] The constant media appearance of Asian Americans in the form of "success narratives in the West" indicates their potential serviceability for helping articulate an official nationalism.

The play's directors, Krishen Jit and Christine Lim, seem particularly attracted to the play's concern with questions of multiculturalism precisely insofar as it echoes the rhetoric of Singapore's particular national self-representation. Their message, inscribed within the playbill, extols:

> How we perceive others is the reflection of our own prejudices, stereotypes, obsessions and fantasies. When we diminish others, we diminish ourselves. . . . David Hwang is telling us that is what happens when East meets West and when men meet women. He is also telling us that we can purge our distortions if at first we can expose them to ourselves. . . . We find his appeal for this kind of truth to be vivid and poignant in a multi-racial and post-colonial Singapore. In a small and less dramatic way, we too have struggled to reconcile problems that inevitably arise between people of various cultures.[9]

Official narratives of the nation construct Singapore as the site of East-West crossing, literalized through its historical basis as an entrepôt economy dependent upon a strategic location at the intersection of international trade routes. These narratives construct Singapore as a nation of diverse racial identities, the harmonious assemblage of which has been made possible only through the activity of the state. It is perhaps no accident, then, that Hwang's play, an allegory of an encounter between East and West, exercises particular resonance in a place where an official nationalist discourse of East-West crossing and multiracial identity has long been foundational.

The appearance of *M. Butterfly* in Singapore may seem at first to constitute mere testimony to our "postmodern" age of information, whose uninterrupted circuits allow for such continuity between Asian cultural nationalism and Asian American minority discourse. Yet the uncanny facility with which an ostensibly oppositional project from within one context travels into another, exercising altogether different and untold discursive effects, should perhaps give us at least a moment's pause. It is important to know that official nationalism in Singapore takes a particular form and emerges in a particular historical context. After an initial and highly successful drive toward Western development in the first fifteen years after independence, the government, in a turn toward touting "Asian values," began by the mid-1980s to construct Western liberalism as the nation's most dangerous enemy. Drawing upon and contributing to growing Western public interest in the "economic miracle" of the so-called four tigers (South Korea, Taiwan, Hong Kong, and Singapore), the Singapore government, led by its former prime minister, Lee Kuan Yew, represents one of the loudest advocates of authoritarian capitalism—presented as an attractive, more efficient alternative to the path of Western modernity, an alternative combining "Western economics" with "Eastern culture." As a key cultural commodity deemed appropriate for the cultural education of deracinated Singaporeans, *M. Butterfly* appeared on stage in the context of Singapore's more recent double drive to draw in Western capital and to filter out "Western values."

The interest the Singapore government might take during the late 1980s in a play that critiques the "West" from an "Asian" point of view could simply be read as an act of appropriation—that of an oppositional minority discourse by a cultural nationalist project forced to ignore the contradictions of its own position. Whether promoting its major airline in international markets through slogans like "Singapore Girl: you're a great way to fly" or attempting to articulate hegemonic forms of Chineseness most suited to internal political quiescence, the Singapore government is, after all, notorious for having discovered the economic and political dividends of promoting certain essentialist notions of ethnic identity. Discussing the tactics of an "invention of tradition" that manages to insert the nation-state into a narrative of Chinese racial history through a definition of idealized Chineseness that is simultaneously consonant with the requirements of a fully market economy, Geraldine Heng and Janadas Devan have called Singapore's promulgation of Confucian tenets an "internalized Orientalism."[10] Given the political complexity of its discursive effects once displaced beyond the U.S. context, what might *M. Butterfly*'s Singapore appearance disclose about the particular terms of its Orientalist critique?

Since the play is conventionally viewed as an Asian American "response" to the "West," of which Puccini serves as the canonical representative, its performance in Asia is particularly interesting. Staged outside Euro-

America, the play's assumption of a Western performance context becomes more noticeable. Despite claims that the play "gives voice" to the Asian subject, its general strategy of defamiliarizing Orientalism from within depends upon structurally placing Gallimard at the center and Song at the margin.[11] The French diplomat Gallimard, for instance, directly addresses the audience in brief asides that give the viewers direct access to his point of view and that invite them to share in his desires for an Oriental butterfly; the Asian transvestite lover Song Liling, by contrast, neither communicates directly with the audience nor offers explanations for his own actions. In an interview, Hwang implies the kind of audience he has in mind when he says, "I assumed that many in the audience would be coming to the theater because they hoped to see something exotic and mysterious, but what exactly is behind the desire to see the 'exotic East'?"[12]

Directorial changes to the Singapore production, however, appeared to respond to the question of what it means to stage a cultural event outside the majority frame from within which it was conceptualized. The stage set itself appeared far less lavish in its display of Oriental design motifs than in the New York and London productions, onstage Chinese viewers were added to the Peking Opera scene and provided noisy comic relief, and the length of the Peking Opera performance was significantly condensed. According to director Krishen Jit, such adjustments were made because "You can't fool an Asian audience with the Peking Opera. There are people out there who really know it. So we decided to cut down on that scene and use the Chinese audience as a distraction."[13] In other words, the Singapore production seemed to be registering signs of discomfort with the play's implication in certain techniques of Orientalist seduction.

Not all Orientalist aesthetic strategies were modified, however. In the manner of the New York and London productions, the Singapore production made use of certain visual icons and aural devices to symbolize the eruption of the historical events of the Cultural Revolution. Giant red banners, uniform human bodies mechanically marching to the sound of slow, ominous drumbeats—all provided aesthetic reinforcement for the dramatic representation of the Cultural Revolution's Oriental despotic character.[14] Since the Singapore staging intervened against the play's Orientalist aesthetics on the subject of *cultural* "Asia" (the Peking Opera), its uncritical adoption of Orientalist tropes deployed against *political* "Asia" is worth remarking. It is not surprising that a play that demonizes the People's Republic of China should find its way onto the stage in a virulently anticommunist state.

Throughout the fifties and sixties during the Malayan struggle for independence, before the destruction of a powerful communist and trade-union movement with ties to China, the colonial powers particularly feared that a domino effect sweeping down from the north would turn Singapore into the "Cuba" of Southeast Asia. A partnership between the British government and the People's Action Party (PAP), which rules to this day, managed, through a combination of legislative sleights and police repression, to exclude the communists from power. From that period of internal struggle, to the immediate "postcolonial" period of dependency upon the British military base for employment, to the present one in which Singapore has proposed itself as the alternative to Subic Bay in the insurgency-racked Philippines, Singapore not only constitutes a prominent economic counterexample to Western underdevelopment of the "Third World"—it also has a place of importance on the geopolitical map, as the island fortress that helped stem the red tide that once threatened to engulf all of Asia.

The triangulation between the United States, Singapore, and China enacted by the Singapore staging of *M. Butterfly* thus bears particular pertinence to the geopolitical imaginary to which Singapore belongs and which is deeply constitutive of its national identity. Historically, the political struggle between communists and the PAP was figured as the alternative between pro-Chinese and pro-Western positions, with the period of postindependence political repression entailing the massive shutdown of Chinese-language schools, newspapers, and clan associations. Only after the complete elimination of internal resistance, only in the late 1970s and early 1980s did the government begin to reverse its pro-Western rhetoric, and to temper its advocacy of pro-Western development strategies with the call for a return to "Asian"—in particular, "Confucian"—values, and to Chinese-language learning. The disjunction between where Orientalist representation is refused and where it is reproduced in the Singapore staging of the Western text may be more than a mere acknowledgment of a formal gap between the cultural and the political. Here, it may be specifically indicative of the space for a politically conservative identity to adopt a cultural nationalist position.

A reading of the play only from within the critical frame of minority discourse precludes an understanding of how the Orientalist tropes of an American play can be used by one Asian nation-state to say something about another. At the same time that this Asian nation-state seems to be establishing identity with an Asian American subject position in a critique of the "West," it is also establishing identity with the "West" in a critique of

"Asia." In my discussion of the narratological transformations of the *Madame Butterfly* convention that follows, I will argue for a reading of Hwang's text that allows us to see how *M. Butterfly's* transformation of Puccini inherently enables this culturally contradictory ambivalence. I would say that the very unaccidental appearance of *M. Butterfly* in Singapore's state-sponsored Arts Festival has something to do with the way in which the play fundamentally constructs the Orientalism it sets out to subvert. The liabilities of *M. Butterfly's* construction of the problem of Orientalism become even more visible when read alongside the "Western" texts to which it constitutes a response.

## Loti, Long, and Puccini

First performed in 1904 at La Scala, *Madame Butterfly* the opera derives from an 1898 American magazine short story of the same name by John Luther Long and from its one-act stage adaptation by David Belasco in 1900; Long's text, in turn, draws from the 1887 French novel *Madame Chrysanthemum* by Pierre Loti.[15] A prolific writer whose many novels and stories are set in exotic Eastern locations from Turkey to Tahiti, Loti is often credited with popularizing Orientalist narrative conventions of intercultural romance within the Western literary imagination. In virtually all of Loti's stories, a Western traveler engages in a sexual adventure with a worshipful Oriental woman who elicits sensuous desire but not love. Ironically enough, it is precisely Loti's "Japanese" novel that runs counter to these Orientalist conventions.[16]

 *Madame Chrysanthemum* narrates the tale of a French sailor who arrives in Japan with the intention of purchasing a wife for the duration of his ship's call to port. The arbitrary and almost accidental origin of his match with Chrysanthemum—she is noticed by his friend from among a group of women observing the intended, but failed, match with Jasmin—marks the lack of sentimental attachment within the relationship from its very initiation. While the narrator fluctuates between humorous indifference and physical loathing toward his bride, Chrysanthemum is herself shown to be impersonally deferential. Dramatic passion temporarily threatens to overcome indifference only when the hero suspects his best friend and wife of an incipient adulterous affair that ultimately proves fictitious. The dispersal of the narrator's jealous doubts leads him to project in Chrysanthemum hidden passionate attachment for himself and grief at his imminent departure. But when he revisits his house unexpectedly at the end, expecting to witness sorrow, he discovers her cheerfully counting out the money earned from the "marriage." In a revelation that takes place at the French protagonist's comic expense, Loti's far from tragic narrative actually exposes the conscious economic relationship upon which this interracial "marriage" is based.

John Luther Long's American magazine story, "Madame Butterfly," makes certain critical adjustments to Loti's narrative, including rewriting the French sailor as an American naval officer and renaming Madame Chrysanthemum. The sailor buddy who shows greater affection for the Japanese woman than does the protagonist is replaced by the compassionate American consul who functions as the conscience of his heartless compatriot. In Long's text, instead of being an inscrutable secondary character, the Japanese woman becomes the main character and the victim of tragic, unrequited love. While Loti's text ends with the sailor's departure, Long's story centers on the Japanese woman's lonely wait for her beloved's return, and introduces the significant plot feature of the birth of her interracial child. The story ends with Butterfly's suicide attempt when she learns of her husband's marriage to an American woman.

A collaboration between composer Puccini, librettist Luigi Illica, and dramatist Giuseppe Giacosa, the opera largely adopts the narrative of Long's short story, while following Belasco's play in ending with Butterfly's actual suicide. Perhaps the most striking feature of Puccini's *Madame Butterfly* lies in the significant alterations made to the original libretto as a result of the flop opening at La Scala, Milan, in 1904. The successful Paris performance of 1906, whose version of the libretto is established as the conventional one, reflects key changes made by the composers in response to what they considered awkward about the original. Critics have noted that almost all of these changes concerned the representation of the operatic "hero" Pinkerton, whose lines convey a character cruel in his treatment of Butterfly and weak in his inability to face her truthfully.[17]

Pinkerton deliberately avoids telling Butterfly that he can give up the lease on the house on a month's notice, and leads her to believe that the house will be paid for for nine hundred and ninety-nine years. He finds Butterfly's relations an "appalling horde," bans them from the house, and then encourages her to adopt Christianity, which ensures her ostracization. Later in the story, the consul reflects that it was entirely like Pinkerton to take the "dainty, vivid, eager, formless material, and mould it to his most wantonly whimsical wish," and having left her, "he had probably not thought of her again, except as the wife of another man" (Smith, 18). The Paris version's

elimination of some of Pinkerton's most racially derogatory lines and behavior, as well as those of his American wife Kate, reflects the centrality of the
representation of racial attitude to the problem of *Madame Butterfly's*
"weak" operatic hero. The need to soften Pinkerton's character and to senti-
mentalize the interracial liaison signals the transgressive potential of this
paradigmatic Orientalist narrative.

I want to argue that the narrative convention of an Oriental woman who
commits suicide because of brutal treatment by a white man can incorporate a political critique. In the case of John Long's short story and the original Italian opera that followed it, the use of this convention for the stuff of
high tragedy carried political implications whose discomfiting effects on
European audiences of the time were measured by the libretto's continual,
uneasy revision. The same narrative that proceeds according to an Orientalist ascription of Japanese female devotion to an American adventurer also
hinges its tragic structure upon the dashing of that devotion. More than just
meeting with betrayal, her devotion to Pinkerton is shown from the beginning to be *always already* founded upon a lie. This unfounded faith extends
from Pinkerton the individual to a set of ideals represented by the United
States in general. Her confidence in the strength of his marriage vows, for
instance, is connected to her claiming of the United States as her country,
which she believes, for reasons of gender politics, to be superior to Japan:

GORO and YAMADORI: She still thinks she is married.

BUTTERFLY: I don't think it, for I know it . . .

GORO: But the law says:

BUTTERFLY: What's that to me?

GORO: . . . that the wife who is deserted/Has the right to seek divorce.

BUTTERFLY: That may be Japanese law . . . /But not in my country.

GORO: Which one?

BUTTERFLY: The United States.

SHARPLESS: (Poor little creature!)

BUTTERFLY: I know, of course, to open the door/And to turn out your wife at
any moment,/Here, is called divorce. But in America that is not allowed. (103)

Her enthusiasm for "America," also symbolized in the moment when she
instructs her child to wave the American flag, underscores the significance
of the Americanization of the original French tale. The transformation of
the French sailor into Lieutenant Benjamin Franklin Pinkerton signals a
larger and important shift in the nature of the colonial relation that the

"East-West" romance allegorically represents. Loti's is a travel narrative in which the Occidental visitor's relation to the foreign locale consists of the (sexualized) anthropological activities of observation, acquisition, and experimentation. The Italian opera, set in Japan, can still, of course, be read as an exotic tale. Assigning the role of protagonist to the Japanese woman, however, has the crucial effect of focusing the text away from representing Western experience of the exotic to representing Eastern desire or longing for the West. In the specific case of Puccini, Occidentalist desire takes the form of an emigration fantasy, one that is clearly peculiar to the ideological structure of American—as opposed to French—global power. Given Puccini's textual source, which is the site of the crucial transformation of Loti, the Italian opera can be read as a profoundly American text, and as such, the Japanese fantasy of emigration it articulates belongs in fact to an American discourse of immigration.

Reading the opera as a text that participates in an American discourse of immigration makes sense of the decision to turn what was originally a careless liaison in Loti into a reproductive union. The liaison's reproductive logic functions to enable the partial fulfillment of Butterfly's impossible desire through generational displacement. Ultimately, the biracial child is to be adopted by "America," but only upon the necessary exclusion of "Japan"—doubly represented by Butterfly's death and the child's remarkable blondness. The historical context of late nineteenth- and early twentieth-century America witnessed a peak in anti-Asian racism, with white anxieties about the inflow of Asian immigrants expressed in the slogan of the "Yellow Peril" helping to enact policies such as the Chinese Exclusion Act of 1882 and the 1908 Gentleman's Agreement restricting the numbers of incoming Japanese laborers. As an expression of white American anxiety about Asian immigration, *Madame Butterfly* achieves a resolution that simultaneously closes and opens the door. The exclusion of Butterfly is ameliorated by the inclusion of a biracial child whose blondness erases the signs of racial difference and seems to preempt the process of assimilation. If the child's inclusion marks the moment of redemption, however, the mother's exclusion inescapably constitutes the moment of tragedy. Her sacrifice is necessary for the preservation of white America, but the dramatic power of her sacrifice stems precisely from its injustice. Her desire for America elicited only by American arrival in Japan, Butterfly is the victim of imperial deception. Blind to Pinkerton's evident attitude of racial superiority, Butterfly's tragedy consists of misconstruing relations of domination as those of openness and equality. Hence, the very same text that enacts the exclusion of "Asia" does so by exposing American principles of openness as a myth. As such, it is possible to see how the operatic text offers a stringent critique of American domination in the Pacific.

## Hwang's "Subversion"

*M. Butterfly* plays upon the Puccini narrative by turning the tables on the Western man who thinks he has conquered an "Oriental butterfly." Whereas the interracial affair in Puccini ends with the Oriental woman's death, in Hwang the interracial liaison takes place at the Westerner's expense. In this sense, the two texts are perfectly symmetrical: in Puccini an Asian woman's Occidentalist illusions lead to her suicide; in Hwang a Western man's Orientalist fantasy leads to his. By reversing the consequences of interracial sexual desire, *M. Butterfly* serves as a cautionary tale, a lesson in the potential pitfalls of Orientalist desire. Not only do Song and Gallimard switch fates, they also switch genders, and this gender-crossing, simultaneously a culture-crossing, is sartorially represented in Song's final assumption of an Armani suit and Gallimard's donning of a Japanese kimono. Although Song and Gallimard symbolically switch genders, however, they do not do so on the same register. For Song, the switch transpires on the level of "real" gender identity, an identity exposed, as it were, by the deliberate, slow process of unveiling that takes place between acts on stage. Gallimard's process of feminization, culminating in his assumption of the role and costume of *Madame Butterfly,* is metaphoric. His gender-crossing derives from a sexuality put into question by Song's gender disclosure. Ambiguity, I would argue, resides not in Song, whom we all "know" to be a "man," but in Gallimard, and it involves not his gender, but his sexuality. Gallimard's symbolic regendering is an effect of his ambiguous sexuality.

Thus, in each of the two characters, homosexuality and transvestism intersect in different, but equally problematic, ways. In Gallimard, we are presented with a treatment of (homo)sexual desire that ends in the act of cross-dressing; in the case of Song we find the practice of cross-dressing in which the subject of desire is entirely suspended. Song's character seems to function as the dramatic device through which numerous other forces achieve expression—Gallimard, the Chinese state apparatus, and finally the author, who offers through Song's voice a metacommentary on the preceding events of sexual play. In the instance of Gallimard, (homo)sexual desire is reduced to an imperialist will to power; in the instance of Song, (homo)sexual desire is erased. In the way that it attaches the signs of effeminacy to (homo)sexual identity, *M. Butterfly* reflects a deeply problematic gender and sexual politics. The intermittent "homophobia" and "antifeminism" that Garber cannot help noticing is hardly a side effect of an otherwise politically subversive male transvestite theater, but the product of a play whose ironic twists actually depend upon enforcing the congruence of gender and sexual identity in which "male" remains associated with power, and "female" and "homosexual" with weakness and defeat. Precisely because cross-dressing is the critical vehicle that enables the reversal of power between the two characters, that reversal of power mobilizes significations of masculinity and femininity that reproduce the way in which power relations are conventionally gendered.

At the level of geopolitics, the play's strategy of reversal with regard to the two terms "East" and "West" also reflects a conceptualization of power that requires serious interrogation. It suggests to us in the first place that what Hwang particularly deplores in the Puccini opera is that, in Kondo's words, "West wins over East, Man over Woman, White Man over Asian Woman" (Kondo, 10). The trial scene in France at the end serves as a kind of reckoning and offers the play's interpretation of the conditions of possibility for Gallimard's mistaking of Song's gender identity:

> SONG: You expect Oriental countries to submit to your guns and you expect Oriental women to be submissive to your men. That's why you say they make the best wives.
>
> JUDGE: But why would that make it possible for you to fool Monsieur Gallimard? Please—get to the point.
>
> SONG: One, because when he finally met his fantasy woman, he wanted more than anything to believe that she was, in fact, a woman. And second, I am an Oriental. And being an Oriental, I could never be completely a man.
>
> JUDGE: Your armchair political theory is tenuous, Monsieur Song.
>
> SONG: You think so? That's why you'll lose in all your dealings with the East. (Act 3, scene 1)

The representation of geopolitical relations of power by the sporting or military metaphor of winners and losers provides some insight into the terms in which the play addresses the problem of Orientalism. If what Hwang objects to in Puccini is that the West "wins," then it is not surprising that the response should present a scenario in which the East "wins" instead. This structure of winning and losing expresses itself, as we have already seen, in problematically conventional ways, through gender and sexual signification. The feminizing effect of Song's gender disclosure upon Gallimard follows from *M. Butterfly*'s proposal that Orientalism functions to secure Western masculinity. Just as his affair with Butterfly marks a rise in Gallimard's masculine confidence as lover and as diplomat, the exposure of his conquest as pure fantasy once again throws his masculinity into jeopardy. The problem, however, is that *M. Butterfly* attempts not just to dramatize the effects of Orientalist desire, but to naturalize its origins. Orientalist fantasy in *M. Butterfly* serves to secure Western masculinity *because* the West is shown as "actually" emasculated.

The play begins with scenes of Gallimard's adolescent experiences of (hetero)sexual failure, and insinuates that Gallimard's Orientalist desires derive from an original condition of sexual inadequacy—to which his final emasculation therefore only symbolically enacts a return. This story transpires at the parallel levels of sexual and political drama: just as Gallimard was always already emasculated, his foreign policy predictions on Vietnam are also proved to be woefully "wrong." Hwang's response to Orientalism consists of a double assertion of intrinsic Asian masculinity that takes its revenge against the feminizing imperative of Western discourses at the level of love and of politics. The play's linking of the levels of sexuality and politics has the effect not of complicating each by implicating it in the other, but of reducing each to the other—(homo)sexual desire is reduced to a greater reality of political power and political power as a reaction to sexual inadequacy.

What are the consequences of representing the Western state as intrinsically weak? The historical instances of Vietnamese victory against the United States and the resurgence of Chinese anti-Western nationalism during the period of the Cultural Revolution serve as a backdrop to a parable about a Westerner's reversal of fortune. Especially troubling about the play's representation of anti-imperialist Asian nationalism is that, on the one hand, it seems overly sanguine in imagining that certain instances of militarily successful Asian anticolonial resistance have mounted enough historical weight to tip the scales of Western imperialism. On the other hand, the play is also politically derisive of such anticolonial movements. It caricatures the Cultural Revolution and its representatives in the construction of the character of Comrade Chin, whose androgyny is also the target of antifeminist humor. Song's miming of a traditional Oriental butterfly is juxtaposed to the sartorially and gesturally unfeminine Comrade Chin, who is now "what passes for a woman in modern China" (act 2, scene 4). In fact, whether by ridiculing contemporary Chinese women's struggles against traditional standards of femininity, or through remarks such as Gallimard's about finding "better Chinese food" in Paris than in China, the play seeks humorous mileage from establishing a connection between political movements in Asia and a fall from cultural "authenticity."

In this sense, the play's assertion of Asian masculinity can hardly be read as an avowal of nationalist resistance to Western—or feminist resistance to patriarchal—domination. On the contrary, its assertion of "actual" Asian masculinity actually seeks to expose Asian submissiveness as a myth, and to demystify Western power as a fantasy. According to the logic of "actual" Western emasculation, Asian nationalist resistance carries no political purchase, and any direct representation of Asian politics in the play thus assumes a reductive and absurdist form. In fact, the places in which the play portrays Asian politics are precisely those of extreme farce. Among the three secondary female characters, who are all in some sense caricatures, Comrade Chin alone cannot be read against the grain of her comic reduction. Gallimard's wife Helga is the caricature of a shallow and racist white woman, but her final abandonment generates pathos and a reproach of Gallimard's position. Renée, the Swedish exchange student with whom Gallimard has a brief fling, functions to convey the absurdity of the sexually liberated woman, but she ceases to be attractive precisely because she exposes Gallimard's phallic inadequacy by deflationarily referring to his penis as a "weenie." The single Chinese woman in the play, who also happens to represent the Asian political subject, is the only character who presents no implicit critique of Gallimard, and against whose homophobia, unpleasant stupidity, and political repressiveness the Western male subject position and the Western state achieve relative validity.

As some readers have uncritically observed, *M. Butterfly* is indeed a revenge fantasy.[18] By fulfilling "the desire of Asian American women to be able to 'stick it to 'em'" (Loo, 16), *M. Butterfly* enacts a reversal that keeps the binary terms of East/West and female/male in place, and that actually renders invisible the structure of power that constitutes them. By reversing the gendering of ethnicity, the play reflects a concern with Orientalism as a problem of cultural stereotyping or myth and therefore as a problem whose rectification involves restituting the masculine as the sign of the "human truth" of Asian identity. Hwang's afterword clarifies that his critique of Orientalism has very little to do with "East" and "West" as markers of materially differential locations:

> *M. Butterfly* has sometimes been regarded as an anti-American play, a diatribe against the stereotyping of the East by the West, of women by men. Quite to the contrary, I consider it a plea to all sides to cut through our respective layers of cultural and sexual misperception, to deal with one an-

other truthfully for our mutual good, from the common and equal ground we share as human beings. . . . For the myths of the East, the myths of the West, the myths of men, and the myths of women—these have so saturated our consciousness that truthful contact between nations and lovers can only be the result of heroic effort. (100)

There are obvious limitations to assigning authority to authorial intention. Hwang's reading of his own play, a reading that subordinates a political critique to a universal humanist reflection, is worth considering only in its resemblance to other readings. In particular, we are reminded of the Singapore directors' message: "If we have done our job well, you will find no heroes or villains in this play. No one character in David Hwang's drama can be singled out for praise or for blame. . . . When we diminish others, we diminish ourselves."[19]

## Antiessentialist Feminism and Minority Discourse

Readings that celebrate the play's subversiveness do so on the basis that it exposes the constructedness of gender identity, and therefore other kinds of identity. My own reading has argued that if we conceptualize the problematic of Orientalism in terms of power, rather than in terms of identity, we find the play reinscribing the binarisms it ostensibly sets out to undo. The current feminist preoccupation with the problem of essentialism, converging with "post-Marxist" theoretical developments in general, should be understood as the outgrowth of the need to challenge earlier theoretical formulations for their racial, sexual, geographic, and class omissions.[20] However, the radical critique of what was the starting point of the feminist project—the attempt to define "woman"—appears to have altogether displaced its end point: the emancipation of women. Although antiessentialist feminist theorizing emerged out of the need to broaden and complicate a political agenda founded on naturalized assumptions about identity, the concern with identity categories, *identity as category,* seems to have hegemonized the content of the feminist political agenda itself. Thus, I would hold that although this form of feminist theory is rightly critical of identity politics, it has actually failed to move us beyond the frame of *identity-based politics.*[21]

The isolated act of demonstrating the discursive constitution of identities can be construed as adequately "political" only if we homogenize the dispositions of, and differences in power between, various kinds of discursive formations. To reintegrate the question of conditions into a discourse analysis requires acknowledging the priorities necessary to building what looks like an external (though not necessarily temporarily prior) frame of reference within which to place discourses, but "post-Marxist" theorists have been reluctant to run the risk of being accused of reductionism or exclusionism that attends committing to a set of political or conceptual priorities. The incoherence into which Ernesto Laclau and Chantal Mouffe's influential model of open-ended articulations descends exemplifies the costs that accompany the refusal to accept the burden of staking priorities. In the first place, their model of multiple articulations presents so vague a geometric figure for relating oppressions that it lends itself to category confusions and slippery parallelisms of all kinds, as we will see in Garber and Kondo. In the second place, the logic of their argument for a "radical democracy" that establishes a theoretical, and by implication a developmental, partition between authoritarian societies and advanced capitalist ones, only to which the "democratic subject position" is appropriate, reflects the foreclosure of an internationalist praxis.[22]

The textual readings performed by Marjorie Garber and Dorinne Kondo on M. Butterfly indicate the limitations of identity-based approaches when placed within an international frame. Garber's treatment of the transvestite as a figure of gender and sexual subversion leads her to posit a conceptually parallel argument with regard to national binaries. The levels of nationalism and sexuality are linked through establishing the activities of transvestism and espionage as structurally cognate: both involve border crossings. "These border crossings," she writes, " . . . present binarisms in order to deconstruct them. As the figure of the transvestite deconstructs the binary of male and female, so all national binaries and power relations are put in question" (131). The first instance of national border crossing lies in Gallimard's conflation of China and Japan, but this is read by Garber, quite rightly, as a reflection of Gallimard's Orientalist perception. Garber then proceeds to point out a second instance of the conflation of national qualities, this time between China and France. Gallimard's discovery of "better Chinese food" in France and the eruption of French Maoist demonstrations are read by Garber as examples of the circulation of signs in a "global cultural economy" whereby "all constructions are exportable and importable" (130). While the instance of Gallimard's conflation of Japan and China is a "bad" example of border crossing—indeed, an instance of Orientalism in operation—this conflation of Chinese and French national qualities is presumably "good." Presumably, it constitutes a transgression by putting "all national binaries and power relations in question."

What does it mean to propose national crossing between France and China as a transgressive scandal? Following the work of the subaltern historians, cultural critics everywhere are trying to counter hegemonic nationalist discourses by undertaking critiques that expose the nation as an "imagined community."[23] Garber repeatedly refers to the "crisis of nationalism and sexuality troped on the transvestite figure" (125) and to the "crossroads of nationalism and sexuality" (127). Yet at stake here is in fact not the subject of the nation, much less nationalism, but the inter-national relationship between two countries of unequal and uneven development. The uncritical reference to the "global cultural economy" of which Garber suggests French-Chinese national crossing is a function reflects the way in which the attempt to model global relations upon the binary relations of—in this case, gender—identity entirely occludes the questions of imperialist power and global capitalism. In fact, it sanctions them. In her reading, the global cultural economy of late capitalism actually enables national crossing, and to that extent, we might read the slip as symptomatic of how contemporary identity-based theories are themselves a part of the culture and practices of late capitalism they are unable to critically address.[24]

Dorinne Kondo's celebration of *M. Butterfly*'s both sexually and globally transgressive politics also depends upon assuming the possibility of simply homologizing categories of "gender," "race," and "nation." Kondo, for instance, writes:

> Hwang de-essentializes the categories, exploding conventional notions of gender and race as universal, ahistorical essences or as incidental features of a more encompassing, abstract "concept of the self." By linking so-called "individual" identity to global politics, nationalism, and imperialism, Hwang makes us see the cross-cutting and mutually constitutive interplay of these forces on all levels. *M. Butterfly* reconstitutes selves in the plural and shifting positions in moving, discursive fields, played out on levels of so-called individual identities, in love relationships, in academic and theatrical narratives, and on the stage of global power relations. (26–27)

As this quote shows, Kondo actually believes herself to be engaging with the question of Orientalism in a social and political sense. Yet her argument is disturbingly not so different from Garber's in the way it invokes an unelaborated "linking" of individual, national, and global entities, whose relationship to each other ultimately depends upon a conceptual parallelism. Kondo expressly questions the adequacy of "a simple calling into question of fixed gender identity," but on the reductive basis that "deconstructive analyses of identity" result in "a fixed meaning . . . always [being] deferred in a postmodern free play of signifiers" (25). Her celebration of Hwang for offering a "power-sensitive analysis" (26) seems to be based on the idea that this devolves from embracing "selves in the plural." Hwang is to be praised because he "de-essentializes the categories, exploding conventional notions of gender and race as universal, ahistorical essences." As against "refigurations of identity as an empty sign" (25), Kondo presents us with the alternative of "complex, shifting 'selves' in the plural" (26); as against the "postmodern" emptying of meaning, we are offered an overabundance of meaning. The claim that this resulting multiplicity is somehow contestatory conceives power relations as binary relations whose "deconstruction" is to be effected by de-essentializing the individual terms of which they are composed.[25]

It is only Kondo's concluding comments that fully expose the extent to which the capacity to homologize the global and the individual derives from a theoretical position blind to its own national frame. "Hwang's distinctively Asian-American voice," Kondo writes, "reverberates with the voices of others who have spoken from the borderlands, those whose stories cannot be fully recognized or subsumed by dominant narrative conventions, when he speaks eloquently of the failure to understand the multiplicity of Asia and of women" (28). This plea for the recognition of identity's heterogeneity, the plea familiarly articulated from the standpoint of a postmodern minority politics, must fundamentally be understood as conditioned by its location. Its subsequent transposition out of that location into the international arena—the extension of the deconstruction of a topography of closure onto geopolitical terrain—threatens to be depoliticizing when the logic of Kondo's argument leads her to uphold Hwang for suggesting that East and West should not "form closed, mutually, exclusive spaces where one term inevitably dominates the other" (29). Set within the space of geopolitics, Kondo's antiessentialist argument appears little removed from Hwang's liberal humanist avowal. The linkage between the different registers of relations, instead of effecting the politicization of the personal, ends up abolishing a notion of power in any register. If the problems in the love relations between a white man and an Asian (wo)man reflect the larger problems of East-West relations, we are told that East-West power relations can be, in Hwang's terms, reconciled, or in Kondo's, "deconstructed." In the end, it would seem, the antiessentialist political project, despite its ostensible antihumanism, lands us not so far afield from a liberal multicultural identity politics. Both propel us toward demanding the recognition of "our" heterogeneity, which often *homogenizes* the differential locations, the conditions of possibility, or the usefulness of that demand.

## Orientalism and Contemporary Asian Cultural Studies

Setting *M. Butterfly* within a genealogy of Orientalist romantic conventions allows us to perceive Orientalist form historically, to allow for different kinds of Orientalist tropes and for historically shifting kinds of power relations between East and West. All too often, Edward Said's theorization of European colonial relations with the Middle East has been unimaginatively hypostasized and at the same time loosely extended to a heterogeneity of Oriental sites.[26] The Orientalist romantic convention to which *M. Butterfly* responds is in fact not singular, but plural and ambivalent. It may be important to note, for instance, the ways in which Loti's Japanese novel resists the Orientalist romantic conventions Loti was instrumental in popularizing. Not only does it expose the economic relation on which cross-cultural marriage is based, refusing the possibility of "love," but *Madame Chrysanthemum* also refuses to take bodily desire for granted. In observing three geisha girls performing for Japanese customers in a neighboring room, Loti's protagonist remarks upon the unnatural allure of "Japanese woman" to Western eyes. Viewing the performing geishas from behind, the narrator expresses the fear that they may turn around and reveal "faces which might destroy the enchantment."[27] Existing only in performance (gesture and ritual behavior) and in outward signs (costume and headgear), Japanese femininity can be read as the sign, in Loti's text, for artifice itself.

We may choose to read Loti's text as telling us the "truth" about gender as (always and everywhere) a construction, or explore the particular historical dispensations of a given Orientalist construction. The former approach would make the same discoveries in Loti's text as it does in Hwang's. The latter approach might use the reading of the artificiality of Loti's "Japanese woman" in order to argue how the site of gender registers fin de siècle Western discomfort with Japanese modernity, a modernity of which the impossiblity of Western power/knowledge/desire in Japan is the sign.[28] Ironically, despite the many aspects of *Madame Chrysanthemum*'s nonconformity to Orientalist convention, its diminutive representation of Japan is said to have informed the imagination of the Russian court, which disastrously underestimated Japan's military strength.[29] The operatic staging of an aestheticized and tragic version of the original French text just nine days after the outbreak of the Russo-Japanese War could therefore also be read as a fantasy of Japanese submissiveness at perhaps the most famous early moment of East-West military reversal.

For Dorinne Kondo to suggest, therefore, that Hwang's 1988 play reflects the disjunctures of a moment when power relations have shifted but the

"West" continues to perceive the "East" as essentially weak (29) overlooks the way in which the constantly evolving figure of Madame Butterfly has long embodied Western perception of Japanese power. Indeed, the discursive impossibility of assimilating Japan to the image of a submissive and weak Orient, the construction of Japan's Oriental exceptionalism, seems to underlie the figure of Madame Butterfly.[30] The failure to recognize the heterogeneity of Orientalist discourses—the heterogeneity of the construct "the Orient"—may very well lead us to think that valorizing the late twentieth-century "rise of Japan" disrupts Western hegemony rather than participates in a discursive formation that may well be a decisive and longstanding component of that hegemony.

In another sense, Hwang's version of Madame Butterfly, performed against the backdrop of Vietnamese and Chinese anticolonial nationalisms, represents more than just a repetition of Western perceptions of the "Asian challenge" since the Russo-Japanese War. As my essay has argued, the historical occasion of M. Butterfly also marks the limitation of a prevailing critical discourse whose preoccupation with essentialism reflects a politics profoundly circumscribed by a national frame. The difficulties of extending postmodern minority discourse onto international terrain, however, may only make visible its inherent liabilities for minority oppositionality itself. We must question what is at stake in a politics currently grounded upon demonstrating the constructedness of identity, whether with regard to ethnic minorities or women. The ostensibly paradoxical humanism disclosed by certain types of antiessentialist projects' demand for recognition of "our" heterogeneity reflects the profoundly liberal sentiment that often underwrites multiculturalist politics—especially when, in the instance of an author's apologia and a state-sanctioned message, we notice that the reading that posits this demand functions as the *alternative* to a political reading. Madhava Prasad's critique of the way in which the subalternist intervention has "led to its appropriation by a kind of politics that . . . regards celebration of the other as the only possible source of a new politics" can perhaps be extended to certain trends within the minority discourse project here.[31] "The current tendency," Prasad writes of subalternist-inspired approaches, "is to find new and multiple subjects of fragmented histories, so that history itself is divided into any number of independent, self-propelled trajectories, each with its own share of the 'homogeneous, empty time' of capitalism" (67). In their introductory notes "Toward a Theory of Minority Discourse," JanMohamed and Lloyd do insist upon the "class basis of discrimination and the systematic economic exploitation of minorities that underlie postmodern culture" (10), but their critique of pluralism insofar as it may be "mendacious" and "disguises the perpetuation of exclusion" leaves room for subsequent critics to recuperate "genuine" pluralism as the final, limited objective of a minority politics.

M. Butterfly's response to Orientalism as fundamentally a problem of the false representation of Asian identity seems to structurally require that it erase the critique of imperialism present in Puccini. Kondo's argument exemplifies the way in which the antihumanist critique of totality and of essence can simply result in a pluralist claim that is often interchangeable with the desire to overturn stereotypes. The belief in the political subversiveness of questioning binary identities alone actually rests upon conceptualizing power in reductively binary terms. A minority discourse project that proceeds along these presuppositions will have difficulty theorizing Orientalism beyond a problem of East-West relations at a moment when the practitioners of Orientalism are getting even more heterogeneous, its form more varied, and its location and movement more dispersed. Orientalism constitutes a discourse of power about the "East," implicated in the globalizing logic of capital. If, however, nineteenth-century capital expansion took the form of Western imperial domination, which turned various parts of Asia into the administered colonies and semicolonies of the West, the uneven and unequal development of Asia that now includes such disparate economies as Japan, China, and Vietnam makes it ever more impossible to assume that Asian countries exist in the same relationship to the "West" or, for that matter, to each other.

One of the consequences of the uneven and unequal development of capitalism in Asia is that we must avoid positing any homogeneous relationship between Orientalist discourse and the geographical location of its articulation. Orientalist fantasies are deployed by and pitched to a variety of subjects in different sites, many of which are themselves "Asian." The way Thai agencies sell sex tours to Japanese customers or the way the Malaysian development board markets the country's female labor to Japanese multinationals, for example, are prime examples of the use of Orientalist discourses by, and their direction toward, Asian subjects. This does not mean that Westerners still do not constitute the major audience/market for Orientalist representations of Asia, but the extent to which Asian governments or comprador elites themselves profit from constructing various kinds of essential representations of Asian identity requires that we detach our comprehension of Orientalism from the binding constraints of East-West terms. The bipolar conceptualization of Orientalism is as inadequate as the unidirectionality of the relationship between the two terms. That an authoritarian capitalist state like Singapore does not find *M. Butterfly* subversive suggests how the play articulates a kind of Asian rejoinder to the "West" in a register that does not in the least threaten Western capital. At a time when capital is no longer strictly "Western"—and, in the context of Southeast Asia, largely Japanese—an Asian rejoinder to the "West" may in fact be altogether beside the point.

A historical-materialist approach to Orientalism *presumes* the recognition that identities are constructed and in heterogeneous ways, but does not make that recognition a political end in itself. Only by investigating the various, and often contradictory, interests invested in the construction of different identities can we hold out a challenge to hegemonic formations. To insist that we attend to the material conditions that form all kinds of identity does not preclude the need to think through the mutually constitutive nature of identities.[32] Indeed, it requires it, because a historical-materialist approach proceeds from an antiessentialist view of identity—refusing any unchanging gendered form of race or raced form of class—while retaining a notion of the political still measured by social change. In this sense, the liminality of Asian Americans as a minority identity within a contemporary discursive formation that includes the production of "the model minority" and "the Asian economic miracle" can, instead of being disabling for constructing our oppositionality, actually serve as the lever for a critique of minority discourse as a whole.[33] Insofar as that which makes Asians signify obtrusive danger from beyond U.S. borders also makes them invisible as minorities within, the particularly visible porousness of the relationship between Asians and Asian Americans should be used to help us think beyond the national frame. Indeed, it is precisely the national conditioning of identity-based approaches that is responsible for generating oppositional projects that can prove dangerously reactionary in different contexts.

If Asian American and Asian Studies work toward eliminating their own disciplinary borders,[34] and given a persistent politicization of the shared object of study, critics within this field may find themselves particularly well placed to contribute to discussions of the global economies of race and gender, as well as the contradictory and always shifting identitarian features of capital. After all, that post-Fordism should exercise a particular preference for the labor of Asian women has not yet been satisfactorily theorized as an integral component of capital logic, while the implications of this development for theories of gender oppression have barely made an impact on the current direction of feminist theory.[35] It is the "nimble fingers" attached to these women's bodies that we must keep in view in any attempt to rethink the contemporary political significance of *Madame Butterfly*.

## Notes

An early version of this essay was delivered at the Modern Language Associaton in 1991. Many thanks to King Kok Cheung for supporting the initial project and to Geraldine Heng for taking me to see *M. Butterfly* in Singapore. I am indebted to Joseph Cleary, David Pickell, and Alys Eve Weinbaum for their rigorous criticisms and suggestions. I also wish to thank Jean Howard, Qadri Ismail, Nikhil Pal Singh, and Sau-ling Wong for commenting on drafts of this essay.

1. Major press coverage of Hwang includes: "David Hwang: Riding the Hyphen," *New York Times Magazine*, March 13, 1988, and "Seductive 'M. Butterfly,'" *Los Angeles Times Calendar*, July 5, 1991. For critical praise for *M. Butterfly*, see Chalsa Loo, "*M. Butterfly*: A Feminist Perspective," *Asian Week*, July 14, 1989; Robert Skloot, "Breaking the Butterfly: The Politics of David Henry Hwang," *Modern Drama* 33:1 (March 1990): 59–66; Dorinne Kondo, "*M. Butterfly*: Orientalism, Gender and a Critique of Essentialist Identity," *Cultural Critique* 16 (fall 1990): 5–29; Marjorie Garber, "The Occidental Tourist: *M. Butterfly* and the Scandal of Transvestism," in Andrew Parker, Mary Russo, Doris Sommer, and Patricia Yaeger, eds., *Nationalisms and Sexualities* (New York and London: Routledge, 1992). One of the few negative responses to the play I have come across is Gabrielle Cody's "David Hwang's *M. Butterfly*: Perpetuating the Misogynist Myth," *Theater* 20:2 (spring/summer 1989): 24–27.

2. David Henry Hwang, "Afterword," in *M. Butterfly* (New York: Plume, 1986), 95.

3. Nowhere does the specific term "Orientalism" itself get used in the play to describe the issues at stake in the interracial sexual drama, nor does Hwang's anecdotal account of the genesis of the idea for *M. Butterfly* include reading Edward Said's *Orientalism*. However, extratextual evidence that supports reading the play in terms of Said's critique of Western representation of the East can be found in Hwang's 1989 Introduction to *FOB and Other Plays*. Hwang writes: "While in London recently preparing the West End production of *M. Butterfly*, I wrote an article for *The Guardian* about Orientalism, defined by the scholar Edward Seyd [*sic*] as a view of the East as mysterious, inscrutable, and ultimately inferior" (Introduction, *FOB and Other Plays* [New York: Plume, 1990]). In her essay on *M. Butterfly*, Dorinne Kondo writes: "Hwang—in a move suggestive of Edward Said's *Orientalism*—explicitly links the construction of gendered imagery to the construction of race and the imperialist mission to colonize and dominate" (24–25).

4. The term "minority discourse" is given articulation by Abdul JanMohamed and David Lloyd, who write: "An emergent theory of minority discourse must not be merely negative in its implications. Rather the critique of the apparatus of universal humanism entails a second theoretical task which the recovery of excluded or marginalized practices permits" ("Toward a Theory of Minority Discourse," which introduces two special issues on the theme "The Nature and Context of Minority Discourse" in *Cultural Critique* 6 and 7 [spring–fall 1987]).

5. In a study of literature by Chinese immigrant and American-born writers, Wong makes the point that the concern with the gendering of ethnicity is specific to works by American-born Chinese writers, while first-generation writing tends to focus on the ethnicizing of gender. See Sau-Ling Wong, "Ethnicizing Gender: An Exploration of Sexuality as Sign in Chinese Immigrant Literature," in *Reading the Literatures of Asian America*, ed. Shirley Geok-Lin Lim and Amy Ling (Philadelphia: Temple University Press, 1992).

6. The phrase comes from Gayatri Chakravorty Spivak, "Can the Subaltern Speak?" in *Marxism and the Interpretation of Culture*, ed. Cary Nelson and Lawrence Grossberg (Urbana and Chicago: University of Illinois Press, 1988), 297.

7. Banned materials include old Beatles favorites such as "Yellow Submarine" and some albums by the Rolling Stones, Eric Clapton, and Elton John, often because song lyrics contain references to drugs. Magazines banned on account of sexual immorality include not just *Playboy*, but *Cosmopolitan*. Unable to prevent foreign transmissions from penetrating the nation's airwaves, the government has banned satellite-reception dishes so that the only news programs available are those the Singapore Broadcast Corporation (SBC) chooses to broadcast. See Stan Sesser, "A Reporter At Large: A Nation of Contradictions," *New Yorker*, January 13, 1992.

8. As an example of the big press accorded Hwang in Singapore even before the local arrival of *M. Butterfly*, see Alan Hubbard's "Mr. Butterfly Takes Flight," *Sunday Times*, June 11, 1989. The casting of Singaporean actor Glen Goei in the London West End production helped trigger early interest in a play that could not (yet) be seen in Singapore.

9. From playbill for Singapore Theatreworks production of *M. Butterfly*, 1990.

10. The term is particularly appropriate because state efforts to promote Confucian ideology as the "authentic" content of the citizen-subject have derived from the knowledge base of American academic institutions. Work by scholars from the East Asian Languages and Literatures departments of universities like Harvard and Columbia is used to authorize the government's case; they are invited to design educational textbooks and to participate in the Institute of East Asian Philosophy, founded specifically for the purpose of promoting Confucian scholarship. See Geraldine Heng and Janadas Devan, "State Fatherhood: The Politics of Nationalism, Sexuality and Race in Singapore," in *Nationalisms and Sexualities*, ed. Parker et al.

11. Skloot makes a similar point when he writes that the play operates by forcing audiences into complicity with "the discovery, dismantling, and re-establishment of theatrical illusion" (59).

12. From John Louis DiGaetani, "*M. Butterfly*: An Interview with David Henry Hwang," *Drama Review* 33:3 (fall 1989): 141–53.

13. Author's interview with director after the performance.

14. The term "Oriental despotism" can be traced to eighteenth-century European texts of political economy to characterize India, and particularly, China. Karl Wittfogel's influential *Oriental Despotism* is an exemplary contemporary text that attributes an inherent despotic tendency to China as a "hydraulic society"; see Wittfogel, *Oriental Despotism: A Comparative Study of Total Power* (New Haven: Yale University Press, 1957). The aesthetic strategies used by *M. Butterfly* to represent the Chinese communist state bear a striking similarity to those used by *Miss Saigon* to represent the demonic rise of Ho Chi Minh in Vietnam. The similarity is particularly ironic given the widespread recognition that *Miss Saigon*, a musical produced after *M. Butterfly*, is an updated version of the very Madame Butterfly convention Hwang's play critiques. In *Miss Saigon*, an American GI in Vietnam gets involved with a local prostitute with a heart of gold, whom he is forced to leave behind in the panic of American withdrawal. She bears his child, longs for his return so that he can take her to America, and refuses an important offer of marriage. In the meantime, the American has married a white American woman, with whom he travels to Thailand, where his former Vietnamese lover lives in a refugee camp. When she discovers that he has remarried, she commits suicide so that her child may be adopted by the American couple. The hidden similarity between this modern version of *Madame Butterfly* and its Asian American parody could be productively examined by also taking into account Hwang's stance on *Miss Saigon*. Although the musical was later criticized by Asian American groups for its content, the initial protests—led by Hwang and actor B. D. Wong, who played Song Liling in the Broadway production of *M. Butterfly*—revolved around the demand for greater inclusion of Asian American actors.

15. Critics differ over whether or not to treat Belasco's play as distinct enough from the Long short story to constitute a separate textual influence on the opera. Compare Arthur

Groos, "Lieutenant F. B. Pinkerton: Problems in the Genesis of an Operatic Hero," *Italica* 64:4 (winter 1987): 654–75, and Julian Smith, "Tribulations of a Score," in the English National Opera Series edition of *Madame Butterfly* (London: John Calder, 1984). For the purposes of my argument, Long's remains the more important of the opera's two sources, as it is the text that critically transforms the French novel into an American narrative.

16. *Aziyade*, the novel set in Turkey, is exceptional in almost an opposite sense. While his novel about Japan represents the most indifferent extreme of exotic love, the novel about Turkey represents the most deeply invested. For a discussion of Loti's special attachment to the subject of Turkish women, see Irene Szyliowicz, *Pierre Loti and the Oriental Woman* (London: Macmillan, 1988).

17. Both Groos and Smith agree that the weakness of the unconventional hero in this opera accounts for its initial failure.

18. Chalsa Loo praises *M. Butterfly* for allowing "women who have felt the sting of male abandonment and betrayal [to] silently rise in applause as Butterfly's death is avenged" (16). The inconsistent reading, however, is the one by Kondo, who celebrates Hwang for, on the one hand, subverting or displacing essential dualisms, and, on the other hand, for reversing them. Her critique of Puccini for representing the victory of West over East, and for the "tragic—but oh so satisfying—denouement: Butterfly, the little Asian woman, crumpled on the floor" (10), suggests that, despite her poststructuralist critique of humanism and her political critique of imperialism, Kondo, like Loo, basically objects to the stereotype of Asian/female weakness.

19. Playbill, Theatreworks production of *M. Butterfly,* Singapore.

20. By essentialism-preoccupied theory, I refer to the influential work of Diana Fuss, Judith Butler, and Chantal Mouffe. Michele Barrett's work—as seen in the trajectory from *Women's Oppression Today* to its apologetic new Introduction in the revised edition, and finally to *The Politics of Truth*—exemplifies the shift from Marxist feminism to discourse theory. Barrett is responding to Hazel Carby's accusations against her for racial occlusions in her treatment of the family. Within Marxism, it is worth noting that the critique of totality on the basis of its essentialism authorizes itself by pointing to, among other things, discussions on the "subject" of feminism. In the key text that makes the argument for a post-Marxism, Ernesto Laclau and Chantal Mouffe point to theoretical developments within feminism that have problematized the idea of a single mechanism of women's oppression, which "opens up" an "immense field of action . . . for feminist politics" (*Hegemony and Socialist Strategy* [London: Verso, 1985], 116–18).

21. Teresa Ebert refers to this trend as a ludic postmodern feminism, against which she proposes a resistance postmodern feminism. See Teresa Ebert, "Ludic Feminism, the Body, Performance and Labor: Bringing Materialism Back into Feminist Cultural Studies," *Cultural Critique* 23 (winter 1993): 5–50.

22. Laclau and Mouffe, *Hegemony and Socialist Strategy,* 131. It is no accident that Mouffe's later work—on citizenship—should follow increasingly nation-state-centered directions. For example, see Chantal Mouffe, "Feminism, Citizenship and Radical Democratic Politics," in *Feminists Theorize the Political,* ed. Judith Butler and Joan Scott (New York: Routledge, 1992). For a critique of the looseness of their theoretical model, see Norman Geras, *Discourses of Extremity: Radical Ethics and Post-Marxist Extravagances* (London: Verso, 1990).

23. The term comes from Benedict Anderson, *Imagined Communities* (London: Verso, 1983).

24. Efforts to link questions of sexuality and gender with questions of the nation bear great potential for breaking down artificially enforced distinctions between the public—the realm of work and the state—and private, to which issues concerning women have been thought to be restricted. How nationalist discourses articulate the nation through figurations of gender, and how on the other hand, the most apparently "private" domains of sexual or re-

productive choice are ideologically interpellated, are crucial in the way they help extend our understanding of the constitutive relation between individual and collective identities, and power. But this is not what Garber does. Her linkage of nationalism and sexuality consists of a conceptual parallelism, not even an "intersection," itself a popular and overused concept; her argument also has nothing to do with questions of power.

25. In her critique of Michel de Certeau's reification of the opposition between the World Trade Center and the street, Meaghan Morris is making a similar argument when she writes: "'The Tower' here serves as an allegory of the structural necessity for a politics of resistance based on a bipolar model of power to maintain the imaginary position of mastery it must endlessly disclaim" (Meaghan Morris, "Great Moments in Social Climbing: King Kong and the Human Fly," in *Sexuality and Space,* ed. Jennifer Bloomer and Beatriz Colomina [New York: Princeton Architectural Press, 1992], 13).

26. An example of the simple application of Said's definition of Orientalism to another set of discourses about another site is Rolf Goebel's "Constructing Chinese History: Kafka's and Dittmar's Orientalist Discourse," *PMLA* 108:1 (January 1993): 59–71.

27. Pierre Loti, *Madame Chrysanthemum* (London: KPI Limited, 1985), 41. To the extent that the representation of "Japanese woman" receives any embodiment, she is represented as a "darling little fairy" (42), whose appeal rests not upon sexual fullness but a prepubescent asexuality.

28. Szyliowicz notes Loti's particular dislike for Japan (*Pierre Loti and the Oriental Woman,* 33).

29. See William Schwartz, *The Imaginative Interpretation of the Far East in Modern French Literature* (Paris: H. Champion, 1927).

30. In his examination of Japanese and American representations of each other recorded during the first Japanese embassy to the United States in 1860, Masao Miyoshi notes American rhetorical approval of the Japanese that depends upon establishing their difference from Chinese coolies. The San Francisco *Daily Alta California* declares, "The countenance of these people wore a far more intelligent look than any Chinese that we have seen." Marking Japanese difference from other Asian races, moreover, often converged with postulating Japanese identity with the "West": for example, the *Daily Evening Bulletin* writes, "Their dress bears some resemblance to that of richer Chinese, but exhibits a taste more in harmony with our own" (Masao Miyoshi, *As We Saw Them* [Berkeley: University of California Press, 1979], 67).

31. Madhava Prasad, "On the Question of a Theory of (Third World) Literature," *Social Text* 31/32 (1992): 64.

32. Sau-ling Wong's analysis of Chinese immigrant literature is an excellent example of work that moves beyond positing the simultaneous and mutually determining relation between all categories by seeking to make careful and precise distinctions in the way ethnicity and gender constitute each other. In an argument that does not shy away from distinguishing the conditions under which different categories may assume analytical priority, Wong hypothesizes that first-generation writing focuses on the ethnicizing of gender, whereas works by American-born writers reflect the concern with the gendering of ethnicity (Wong, "Ethnicizing Gender," 124).

33. In the double issue of *Cultural Critique* devoted to the study of minority discourse, Sylvia Wynters's article on the "disenchanting" dimensions of minority discourse, without explanation or further discussion, positions "Asian" on the side of the "Caucasian." "Asian" and "Caucasian," as owners of "capital-as-moveable wealth," together form the hyphenated majority term against which "negroid peoples" are defined (Sylvia Wynters, "On Disenchanting Discourse: 'Minority' Literary Criticism and Beyond," *Cultural Critique* 7 [fall 1987]: 233). Whether we read Wynters as critically or uncritically placing "Asian" within the majority term, this grouping must be taken seriously as symptomatic of a larger discursive formation that considers Asian Americans a dubious minority. The most significant policy reflection of this lies in

the way Asian Americans were positioned in the affirmative action debates of the 1980s, and their continuing disqualification from major national and local minority fellowships. For a discussion of the problematic marginality of Asian Americans and a critique of the pursuit by Asian American writers of "molecular micropolitics," see E. San Juan, "Beyond Identity Politics: The Predicament of the Asian American Writer in Late Capitalism," *American Literary History* 3:3 (fall 1991): 542–65. Interestingly, San Juan ends his critique of identity politics by invoking *M. Butterfly* as a "provisional example of the 'and/or' strategy of disruption."

34. My thoughts on many of these questions owe much to stimulating discussions with Nikhil Pal Singh. For an excellent analysis of the need to connect Asian American and Asian Studies, see Sucheta Mazumdar, "Asian American Studies and Asian Studies," in *Asians and Asian Americans: Comparative and Global Perspectives*, ed. Shirley Hune et al. (Pullman: Washington State University Press, 1991), 29–44.

35. It has been more than a decade since the publication of Annette Fuentes and Barbara Ehrenreich's *Women in the Global Factory* (1983), which made famous the Malaysian government investment brochure touting the "manual dexterity of the Oriental female." Work that has brought together gender and political economy has developed largely within the social sciences. See, for instance, Swasti Mitter, *Common Fate, Common Bond* (London: Pluto Press, 1986). With a few exceptions, such as the work of Gayatri Chakravorty Spivak, however, feminist theory seems to have moved farther and farther away from theorizing gender in connection with global inequalities.

# Contributors

Norma Alarcón is associate professor of Chicano/Ethnic Studies at the University of California, Berkeley. She has published a book on the Mexican writer Rosario Castellanos, *La poética feminista de Rosario Castellanos: El discurso de la diferencia*, as well as numerous essays on the literature of Chicanas and Latinas.

Paula Gunn Allen is a prominent poet, novelist, essayist, and cultural critic, and is professor of English at the University of California, Los Angeles. In 1990 she was awarded the Native American Prize for Literature, and that same year her anthology of short stories, *Spider Woman's Granddaughters*, was awarded the American Book Award sponsored by the Before Columbus Foundation. She has published seven volumes of poetry, a novel, a collection of essays, and two anthologies. Her most recent project is a two-volume set, *Voice of the Turtle: An Anthology of Twentieth-Century American Indian Fiction*.

Elliott Butler-Evans is associate professor of English and former director of the Black Studies Center at the University of California, Santa Barbara. He teaches courses in modern American literature, including African American and other "ethnic" literatures, as well as courses in literary and cultural theory. Among his most recent publications are *Race, Gender and Desire: Narrative Strategies in the Fiction of Toni Cade Bambara, Toni Morrison, and*

Alice Walker, and journal articles focused on the application of semiotic and narrative theory to American ethnic texts.

Barbara Christian is professor of Afro-American Studies at the University of California, Berkeley. Her books include *Black Women Novelists: The Development of a Tradition, In Search of Our Past*, and *Teaching Guide to Black Foremothers*.

Lisa Lowe is associate professor of comparative literature at the University of California, San Diego. Her writings include *Critical Terrains: French and British Orientalisms* and essays on ethnic and postcolonial literatures in *Diaspora* and *Yale French Studies*.

Colleen Lye is a Ph.D. candidate in the Department of English and Comparative Literature at Columbia University. She is writing a dissertation on Orientalism and twentieth-century geopolitical discourses.

David Palumbo-*Liu* is associate professor of comparative literature at Stanford University. His essays have appeared in *American Literary History, Amerasia Journal, Cultural Critique, Public Culture*, and in various critical collections. He is a contributing editor for the *Review of Education, Pedagogy, and Cultural Studies*, a member of the editorial collective of *Positions: East Asia Culture Critique*, and a coeditor of the series on Asian American studies published by Temple University Press. His book *The Poetics of Appropriation* appeared in 1993.

Ramón Saldívar is professor of English and comparative literature at Stanford University and author of *Figural Language in the Novel: The Flowers of Speech from Cervantes to Joyce* and *Chicano Narrative: The Dialectics of Difference*.

E. San Juan Jr., professor of English and comparative literature at the University of Connecticut, Storrs, was 1987–88 Fulbright Lecturer at the University of the Philippines, and 1993 Fellow at the Institute for the Advanced Study of the Humanities, University of Edinburgh, Scotland. His recent books are *Writing and National Liberation, Reading the West/Writing the East*, and *Racial Formations/Critical Transformations* (which received the 1993 National Book Award from the Association for Asian American Studies). He also won an award from the Gustavus Myers Center for Human Rights. He teaches ethnic studies and American culture studies at Bowling Green State University.

**Rosaura Sánchez** is professor of literature at the University of California at San Diego and author of *Chicano Discourse* and *Telling Identities* (Minnesota, 1995).

**Jana Sequoya-Magdaleno** is a doctoral candidate in the Program in Modern Thought and Literature at Stanford University. She has published essays in the *American Indian Quarterly, New Voices in Native American Criticism,* and *Global Literacy.*

**Sau-ling Cynthia** *Wong* is associate professor of Asian American studies at the University of California, Berkeley. She has published *Reading Asian American Literature: From Necessity to Extravagance* as well as a number of essays on Asian American literature.

# Index

COMPILED BY EILEEN QUAM
AND THERESA WOLNER